AMERICAN

NEGRO

FOLKLORE

Books by J. Mason Brewer

Humorous Folktales of the South Carolina Negro
The Word on the Brazos
"Aunt Dicy" Tales
Dog Ghosts and Other Texas Negro Folk Tales
Worser Days and Better Times

AMERICAN NEGRO FOLKLORE

By

J. MASON BREWER

Quadrangle / The New York Times Book Co.

Library of Congress Catalog Card Number: 68-10833   ISBN: 0-8129-0452-4

Typography by Vincent Torre
First paperback edition

GRATEFUL ACKNOWLEDGMENT is made to the following publishers and individuals for permission to reprint selections in this book:

Roger D. Abrahams, for "Brand Name Stories," "The Big Watermelon," and "The Coon in the Box" from *Deep Down in the Jungle* (Folklore Associates, 1964).

George C. S. Adams and Stephen B. Adams, for "A Yellow Bastard" from *Nigger to Nigger* by E. C. L. Adams (Charles Scribner's Sons, 1928).

American Folklore Society, for "John Green Peas" from *Louisiana Folk-Tales* by Alcée Fortier, and "Riddles" from *Folklore of the Sea Islands, South Carolina* by Elsie Clews Parsons.

Appleton-Century-Crofts, for "The Wonderful Tar-Baby Story," "How Mr. Rabbit Was Too Sharp for Mr. Fox," "Mr. Rabbit and Mr. Bear," "Mr. Fox Goes a-Hunting, but Mr. Rabbit Bags the Game," "Why the Negro Is Black," and "Plantation Proverbs" from *Uncle Remus: His Songs and His Sayings* by Joel Chandler Harris. Copyright © 1921 by Esther LaRose Harris.

Hamilton Brown, for "Jim Beckwourth, Frontiersman" from *Jim Beckwourth—Great Negro Frontiersman, the West* (Maverick Publications, Inc., 1967).

Mrs. David L. Cohn, for "The Green Runner" from *God Shakes Creation* by David L. Cohn.

Mrs. Portia N. Crawford, for "Honey Bee," "Dis Ole Rock Mine," and "Sweet Mamie Chadman," from her master's thesis, "A Study of Negro Folk Songs from Greensboro, North Carolina, and Surrounding Towns" (University of North Carolina, 1965).

Fawcett World Library, for "The Talking Mule," "The White Quail," "Why the Jews Don't Eat Hog," and "Twelve Days after Christmas," reprinted from *American Negro Folktales*, collected, and with introduction and notes, by Richard M. Dorson. This material first appeared in *Negro Folktales in Michigan*, by Richard M. Dorson.

Folkways Music Publishers, Inc., for "Careless Love," "De Ballit of de Boll Weevil," "Ella Speed," and "Good Mornin' Blues"; words and music by Huddie Ledbetter, collected and adapted by John A. Lomax and Alan Lomax.

Lawrence Gellert, for "I Went to Atlanta" and "Workin' on de Railroad" from Negro *Songs of Protest* (Carl Fisher Music Company).

Harcourt, Brace and World, Inc., for "John Henry" and "Frankie Blues" from *The American Songbag* by Carl Sandburg, copyright © 1927 by Harcourt, Brace and World, Inc.; copyright © 1955 by Carl Sandburg.

Harvard University Press, for "Aurore Pradère" and "Bob-ree Allin," from Dorothy Scarborough, *On the Trail of Negro Folk Songs*, copyright © 1925, 1953.

Houghton Mifflin Company, for "Treasure Hunting Story," "The Sprinkle Man," "A Ghost Voodoo Story," "Omens," "Play and Nursery Songs," "Street Cries," "Superstitions," "New Orleans' First 'Baby Doll,'" "Experiences of a Chimney Sweeper" from *Gumbo Ya-Ya* by Lyle Saxon.

Arthur Palmer Hudson, for "Brother Johnson's Toast," "The Kosciusko Bootlegger's Gripe" (from his folklore collection), and "Some Curious Negro Names" (from *Southern Folklore Quarterly*, December 1938).

For my Grandson, J. Mason Brewer III (Butch)
and all his little playmates
in Compton, California

FOREWORD

The folk literature of the American Negro has a rich inheritance from its African background. Without this major cultural ingredient there would be no Negro folklore as distinct from that of other regional folk literatures of the New World. Probably no people have been so completely the bearers of tradition as the African slave-immigrants. They brought with them no material possessions to aid in preserving the arts and customs of their homeland. Yet though empty handed perforce, they carried in their minds and hearts a treasure of complex musical forms, dramatic speech, and imaginative stories, which they perpetuated through the vital art of self-expression. Wherever the slaves were ultimately placed, they established an enclave of African culture that flourished in spite of environmental disadvantages. As a result, the original treasure has diffused and grown, for the enrichment of themselves and of others.

Because of the diversified nationalities of the American colonists with whom the Negro slaves were forced to live—English, French, Spanish, German—and the later association of their descendants with American Indians and Mexicans, the Negro's culture in this section of the New World became localized and varied, rather than national and unified. The common culture of the Afro-Americans who dwelt along the eastern and southern seaboards of the United States, on sea islands off the Atlantic coastline, and in the swamplands and river bottoms of the South and Southwest became infused with local characteristics. These regional variations, however, may be regarded as aspects of a historical whole. The many local patterns of song, story, belief, and speech all manifest a common cultural background.

In this anthology I have tried to avoid the inclusion of literary productions by authors who have utilized folklore as source material for their writings. My purpose has been to include only those items that can be logically classed as authentic in the Negro folklore tradition. They are from and about the folk Negro—his customs, habits, beliefs, philosophy, way of life, and reactions to the incidents and pressures in his environment. Many are from his own lips, in his own words, or both.

Negro folklore is definitely in the mainstream of American tradition, but rich strata of Negro folk phenomena still remain undiscovered. When these are unearthed and brought to light, they will constitute a meaningful and worthy supplement to the great mass of Negro folk material that already exists.

J.M.B.

Salisbury, North Carolina
August 1968

ACKNOWLEDGMENTS

In any work of this nature, which requires extensive research, it is necessary that financial assistance be made available to the investigator. The funds needed for investigations leading to the acquisition of the materials in this volume were provided by a grant-in-aid from the American Philosophical Society, to which I offer special thanks and deep gratitude. I also wish to express my appreciation to B. A. Botkin, who made me aware of the Society's interest in projects similar to mine and who rendered invaluable service in pointing out to me important sources in the Library of Congress. I am equally obligated to the late Charles S. Johnson, president of Fisk University and former chairman of its Division of Social Sciences, for giving me unlimited access to the slave narratives housed in the university library. To Daniel W. Patterson, professor of English at the University of North Carolina, and to my niece, Minnie Marianne Miles, art instructor at Fisk University, I am deeply indebted for their aid in securing rare materials vital to the completion of the anthology. Many thanks also to Arthur Palmer Hudson, former Keenan professor of English at the University of North Carolina, for his contributions, guidance, and advice in the preparation of the manuscript.

Finally, I would like to extend thanks to my wife, Ruth Helen Brewer, whose sympathetic interest in the project proved constantly stimulating and encouraging.

CONTENTS

PART I. *Tales*

Contents

Contents

PART II. *The Negro's Religion*

PART III. *Songs*

Contents

PART IV. *Personal Experiences*

Contents

PART V. *Superstitions*

PART VI. *Proverbs*

PART VII. *Rhymes*

Contents

AMERICAN
NEGRO
FOLKLORE

PART I

Tales

Animal Tales

Although the Negro slave had long created songs, tales, and rhymes, it was not until after the Civil War period that collectors and writers decided to capture some of these folk gems and put them into print. The first, and still the most significant and authentic, volume of Negro animal tales is Joel Chandler Harris' Uncle Remus: His Songs and His Sayings, published in 1880. Harris lived on a Georgia plantation where he heard elderly Negroes tell about Brer Rabbit and his antics. He jotted them down and eventually put them into print. Another early collector of animal tales was Charles C. Jones, Jr., whose Negro Myths from the Georgia Coast, told in the Gullah dialect, was published in 1888. A considerable number of animal tales are also included in a volume of folklore by Elsie Clews Parsons, Folk-Lore from the Sea-Islands, South Carolina, published as a memoir of the American Folklore Society in 1923. Another big collection of animal tales is Mary Alicia Owen's Old Rabbit, the Voodoo, and Other Sorcerers (1893). Smaller collections like A. W. Eddins' animal tales in From the Brazos Bottoms (Texas Folklore Publications, 1931) have made their appearance from time to time, but no comprehensive compilation has been published recently.

The role of the rabbit in the tales of the American Negro is similar to that of the hare in African folk narratives—that of the trickster who shrewdly outwits and gains a victory over some physically stronger or more powerful adversary. The animal tales told by Negro slaves with Brer Rabbit as the hero had a meaning far deeper than mere entertainment. The rabbit actu-

3

ally symbolized the slave himself. Whenever the rabbit succeeded in proving himself smarter than another animal the slave rejoiced secretly, imagining himself smarter than his master.

(The Wonderful Tar-Baby Story

"Didn't the fox *never* catch the rabbit, Uncle Remus?" asked the little boy the next evening.

"He come mighty nigh it, honey, sho's you born—Brer Fox did. One day atter Brer Rabbit fool 'im wid dat calamus root, Brer Fox went ter wuk en got 'im some tar, en mix it wid some turkentime, en fix up a contrapshun w'at he call a Tar-Baby, en he tuck dish yer Tar-Baby en he sot 'er in de big road, en den he lay off in de bushes fer to see what de news wuz gwine ter be. En he didn't hatter wait long, needer, kaze bimeby here come Brer Rabbit pacin' down de road—lippity-clippity, clippity-lippity—dez ez sassy ez a jay-bird. Brer Fox, he lay low. Brer Rabbit come prancin' 'long twel he spy de Tar-Baby, en den he fotch up on his behime legs like he wuz 'stonished. De Tar-Baby, she sot dar, she did, en Brer Fox, he lay low.

" 'Mawnin'!' sez Brer Rabbit, sezee—'nice wedder dis mawnin',' sezee.

"Tar-Baby ain't sayin' nothin', en Brer Fox, he lay low.

" 'How duz yo' sym'tums seem ter segashuate?' sez Brer Rabbit, sezee.

"Brer Fox, he wink his eye slow, en lay low, en de Tar-Baby, she ain't sayin' nothin'.

" 'How you come on, den? Is you deaf?' sez Brer Rabbit, sezee. 'Kaze if you is, I kin holler louder,' sezee.

"Tar-Baby stay still, en Brer Fox, he lay low.

" 'You er stuck up, dat's w'at you is,' says Brer Rabbit, sezee, 'en I'm gwine ter kyore you, dat's w'at I'm a gwine ter do,' sezee.

"Brer Fox, he sorter chuckle in his stummick, he did, but Tar-Baby ain't sayin' nothin'.

" 'I'm gwine ter larn you how ter talk ter 'spectubble folks ef hit's de las' ack,' sez Brer Rabbit, sezee. 'Ef you don't take off dat hat en tell me howdy I'm gwine ter bus' you wide open,' sezee.

"Tar-Baby stay still, en Brer Fox, he lay low.

"Brer Rabbit keep on axin' 'im, en de Tar-Baby, she keep on sayin' nothin', twel present'y Brer Rabbit draw back wid his fis', he did, en blip he tuck 'er side er de head. Right dar's whar he broke his merlasses jug. His fis' stuck, en he can't pull loose. De tar hilt 'im. But Tar-Baby, she stay still, en Brer Fox, he lay low.

" 'Ef you don't lemme loose, I'll knock you agin,' sez Brer Rabbit, sezee, en wid dat he fotch 'er a swipe wid de udder han', en dat stuck. Tar-Baby, she ain't sayin' nothin', en Brer Fox, he lay low.

" 'Tu'n me loose, 'fo' I kick de natchul stuffin' outen you,' sez Brer Rabbit, sezee, but de Tar-Baby, she ain't sayin' nothin.' She des hilt on, en den Brer Rabbit lose de use er his feet in de same way. Brer Fox, he lay low. Den Brer Rabbit squall out dat ef de Tar-Baby don't tu'n 'im loose he butt 'er cranksided. En den he butted, en his head got stuck. Den Brer Fox, he sa'ntered fort', lookin' des ez innercent ez one er yo' mammy's mockin'-birds.

" 'Howdy, Brer Rabbit,' sez Brer Fox, sezee. 'You look sorter stuck up dis mawnin',' sezee, en den he rolled on de groun', en laughed en laughed twel he couldn't laugh no mo'. 'I speck you'll take dinner wid me dis time, Brer Rabbit. I done laid in some calamus root, en I ain't gwine ter take no skuse,' sez Brer Fox, sezee."

Here Uncle Remus paused, and drew a two-pound yam out of the ashes.

"Did the Fox eat the Rabbit?" asked the little boy to whom the story had been told.

"Dat's all de fur de tale goes," replied the old man. "He mought, en den again he moughtent. Some say Jedge B'ar come long en loosed 'im—some say he didn't. I hear Miss Sally callin'. You better run 'long."

⟮ How Mr. Rabbit Was Too Sharp for Mr. Fox

"Uncle Remus," said the little boy one evening, when he had found the old man with little or nothing to do, "did the Fox kill and eat the Rabbit when he caught him with the Tar-Baby?"

"Law, honey, ain't I tell you 'bout dat?" replied the old darkey, chuckling slyly. "I 'clar ter gracious I ought er tole you dat, but old man Nod wuz ridin on my eyeleds twel a leetle mo'n I'd a dis'member'd my own name, en den on to dat here come yo' mammy hollerin' atter you.

"W'at I tell you w'en I fus' begin? I tole you Brer Rabbit wuz a monstus soon creetur; leas'ways dat's w'at I laid out fer ter tell you. Well, den, honey, don't you go en make no udder calkalashuns, kaze in dem days Brer Rabbit en his fambly wuz at de head er de gang w'en enny racket wuz on han', en dar dey stayed. 'Fo' you begins fer ter wipe yo' eyes 'bout Brer Rabbit, you wait en see whar'bouts Brer Rabbit gwine ter fetch up at. But dat's needer yer ner dar.

"W'en Brer Fox fin' Brer Rabbit mixt up wid de Tar-Baby, he feel mighty good, en he roll on de groun' en laff. Bimeby he up'n say, sezee:

" 'Well, I speck I got you dis time, Brer Rabbit,' sezee; 'maybe I ain't, but I speck I is. You been runnin' roun' here sassin' atter me a mighty long time, but I speck you done come ter de een' er de row. You bin cuttin' up yo' capers en bouncin' roun' in dis neighborhood ontwel you come ter b'leeve yo'se'f de boss er de whole gang. En den you er allers somers whar you got no bizness,' sez Brer Fox, sezee. 'Who ax you fer ter come en strike up a 'quaintance wid dish yer Tar-Baby? En who stuck you up dar whar you iz? Nobody in de roun' worl'. You des tuck en jam yo'se'f on dat Tar-Baby widout waitin' fer enny invite,' sez Brer Fox, sezee, 'en dar you is, en dar you'll stay twel I fixes up a bresh-pile and fires her up, kaze I'm gwine ter bobbycue you dis day, sho,' sez Breer Fox, sezee.

"Den Brer Rabbit talk mighty 'umble.

" 'I don't keer w'at you do wid me, Brer Fox,' sezee, 'so you don't fling me in dat brier-patch. Roas' me, Brer Fox,' sezee, 'but don't fling me in dat brier-patch,' sezee.

" 'Hit's so much trouble fer ter kindle a fire,' sez Brer Fox, sezee, 'dat I speck I'll hatter hang you,' sezee.

" 'Hang me des ez high as you please, Brer Fox,' sez Brer Rabbit, sezee, 'but do fer de Lord's sake don't fling me in dat brier-patch,' sezee.

" 'I ain't got no string,' sez Brer Fox, sezee, 'en now I speck I'll hatter drown you,' sezee.

" 'Drown me des ez deep ez you please, Brer Fox,' sez Brer Rabbit, sezee, 'but don't fling me in dat brier-patch,' sezee.

" 'Dey ain't no water nigh,' sez Brer Fox, sezee, 'en now I speck I'll hatter skin you,' sezee.

" 'Skin me, Brer Fox,' sez Brer Rabbit, sezee, 'snatch out my eyeballs, t'ar out my years by de roots, en cut off my legs,' sezee, 'but do please, Brer Fox, don't fling me in dat brier-patch,' sezee.

"Co'se Brer Fox wanter hurt Brer Rabbit bad ez he kin, so he cotch 'im by de behime legs en slung 'im right in de middle er de brier-patch. Dar wuz a considerabul flutter whar Brer Rabbit struck de bushes, en Brer Fox sorter hang 'roun' fer ter see w'at wus gwine ter happen. Bimeby he hear somebody call 'im, en way up de hill he see Brer Rabbit settin' cross-legged on a chinka-pin log koamin' de pitch out'n his ha'r wid a chip. Den Brer Fox know dat he bin swop off mighty bad. Brer Rabbit wuz bleedzd fer ter fling back some er his sass, en he holler out:

" 'Bred en bawn in a brier-patch, Brer Fox—bred en bawn in a brier-patch!' en wid dat he skip out des ez lively ez a cricket in de embers."

([De Wolf, de Rabbit, and de Tar Baby*

Now de wolf 'e berry wise man, but 'e not so wise as de rabbit. De rabbit, 'e mos' cunnin' man dat go on fo' legs. 'E lib in de brier bush.

Now de wolf 'e done plant corn one 'ear, but rabbit, 'e ain't plant nuthin' 'tall; 'e lib on wolf corn all winter. Nex' 'ear, wolf ain't plant corn; 'e tink corn crop too poo'; 'e plant groun'nut. (That is, peanuts.) Rabbit 'e do jes' de same as befo'.

Well, wolf 'e biggin' to tink someting wrong. 'E gone in de mawnin', look at 'e groun'nut patch, look berry hard at rabbit track, say, "I 'spicion somebody ben a tief my groun'nut." Nex' mawnin' 'e 'gain meet mo' groun'nut gone, say same ting. Den 'e say, "I gwine mek one skeercrow for set up in dis yere groun'nut patch for skeer de tief." So 'e mek one ole skeercrow an' set um in de middle ob de groun'nut patch.

Dat night, when rabbit come wid' 'e bag for get groun'nut, 'e see de skeercrow stan' berry white in de moonshine, an' 'e say, "Wha' dat?" Nobody ain't say nuthin'. "Wha' dat?" 'e say 'gain. Den nobody ain't say nuthin' an' 'e ain't see nuthin' moobe, so 'e gone leetle closer an' leetle closer, till 'e git close ter um. Den 'e put 'e paw an' touch de skeercrow. Den 'e say, "You ain't nuthin' but one ole bundle o' rag. Wolf tink I gwine 'fraid you? Mus' be fool." So 'e kick ober de skeercrow an' fill 'e bag wid groun'nut an' gone back home to de brier bush.

Nex' mawnin', wolf gone out for look at 'e groun'nut patch, an' when 'e meet mo' groun'nut gone an' de skeercrow knock down, 'e berry mad. 'E say, "Nebber you min', I fix ole rabbit dat done tief all my groun'nut; jus' let me show you." So 'e mek one baby out o' tar an' set up in 'e groun'nut patch, an' say, "Jus' let ole rabbit try for knock over dis yere tar baby, an' 'e'll see! I jus' want um for try."

Dat night when rabbit come 'gain wid 'e bag for get groun'nut an' see de tar baby stan' berry black in de moonshine, 'e say, "Wha' dat? Ole wolf done gone set up nodder skeercrow, mus' be." So 'e moobe leetle nearer, an' leetle nearer. Den 'e stop an' say, "Dis yere enty no skeercrow; dis yere mus' be one gal! I mus' study 'pon dis."

So 'e tun roun' an' spread out 'e bag an' sit down in de middle ob de groun'nut patch an' look hard at tar baby. Bimeby 'e say, "Gal, what you name?" Gal ain't say nuthin'. "Gal, why don't you speak me? What you do dere?" Den 'e listen long time, ain't hear nuthin' 'cep' whippoorwill in de swamp.

---

* Published as "A Familiar Legend" in *The Hillsborough Recorder*, Hillsborough, North Carolina, on August 5, 1874, six years earlier than the two preceding Uncle Remus stories.

So 'e gone close up ter um an' say, "Gal, you speak me, you min'! Gal, if you ain't speak me I knock you. I knock you wid my right paw; den you tink it tunder!" Tar baby ain't say nuthin', so 'e knock um wid 'e right paw, an' 'e paw stick!

Den 'e biggin for holler. "Gal, le' go me, I tell you, le' go me. Wha' for you hole me? If you don't le' go me I knock you wid my lef' paw; den you tink it tunder an' lighten too!" So 'e knock um 'gain wid 'e lef' paw, an' 'e lef' paw stick!

Den 'e say, "Gal, lef' me loose, lef' me loose, I tell you. If you don't I kick you wid my right foot; den you tink colt kick you!" So 'e kick um wid 'e right foot, an' 'e foot stick!

Den 'e say, "Now, gal, if you ain't lef' me loose mighty quick I kick you wid my lef' foot; den you tink hoss kick you." So 'e kick um wid' 'e lef' foot, an' 'e lef' foot stick!

Den 'e say, "Min' now, gal. I ain't do nuthin' to you. Wha' for you hole me? Mebbe you tink I can't do nuthin' to you. Ain't you know I can bite you, dough? If you ain't lef' me loose I gwine bite you. Ain't you know my bite worse dan snake bite?" So 'e bite um an' 'e nose stick!

Nex' mawnin', 'fore sun-up, wolf gone out to 'e groun'nut patch for see what 'e kin fin' an' 'e meet poo' rabbit wid 'e paw an' 'e feet an' 'e nose all farsten on tar baby, an' 'e say, "Enty I tole you so? Look a-yawnder! I reckon tar baby done cotch ole rabbit dis time." So 'e tuk rabbit off an' say, "You done tief half my groun'nut. Now what I gwine do wid you?"

Den rabbit biggin for beg. "Oh, maussa wolf, do le' me go an' I nebber tief groun'nut no mo'." Wolf say, "No, brudder rabbit, you ben a tief my corn las' 'ear, an' you ben a tief my groun'nut dis 'ear, an' now I gwine eat you up."

Den rabbit say, "Oh, maussa wolf, le' me beg you. You ma' roas' me, you ma' toas' me, you ma' cut me up, you ma' eat me, but, maussa wolf, whatebber you do, don't trow me in de brier bush. Ef you trow me in de brier bush I gwine dead."

So wolf say, "You ain't want me for trow you in de brier bush, enty? Das jes' what I gwine do wid you." So 'e fling um in de bramble bush, an' den rabbit laugh an' say, "Hi! maussa wolf. Ain't you know I lib in de brier bush? Ain't you know all my fambly born an' bred in de brier bush? Dis jes' whar I want you for put me. How is you gwine get me 'gain?"

Den wolf berry mad 'cause 'e see rabbit too wise man for him. 'E home an' tell 'e wife, "No rabbit soup for dinner today." An' dey biggin for contribe, an' dey mek plan for get rabbit for come to deir house. So one day wolf wife call neighbor dog an' tell um, "Neighbor dog, I want you for do one erran' for me. I want you for git on you hoss an' ride fars' as you kin to rabbit doo' an' tell brudder rabbit wolf dead, an' 'fo' 'e die 'e leabe solemn word 'e don't want nobody else for lay um out but brudder rabbit. An' do, neighbor dog, beg um for come ober quick as 'e kin so we all kin hab de funeral, for wolf say 'e won't hab nobody for lay um out but brudder rabbit."

So neighbor dog 'e git on 'e hoss an' ride fars' as 'e kin to rabbit doo'. Den 'e knock an' say, "Brudder rabbit, brudder wolf dead an' 'e leabe solemn word 'e won't have nobody for lay um out but brudder rabbit."

Rabbit say, "How, brudder wolf dead?" "Yes, 'e die las' night, an' 'e ain't want nobody else for lay um out, an' sister wolf beg you for come ober an' lay um out quick as you kin so dey all kin have de settin' up."

So rabbit git on 'e hoss an' ride to wolf doo'. Den 'e knock an' say, "How! I yeardy brudder wolf dead." Wolf wife say, "Yes, 'e dead for true, an' 'fo' 'e dies 'e leabe solemn word 'e ain't want nobody else for lay um out but brudder rabbit."

Den rabbit say, "Kin I shum (see him)?" So wolf wife tuk um in de bedroom an' show um wolf lie on de bed cober up wid a sheet. Rabbit lif' up de corner ob de sheet an' peep at wolf. Wolf nebber wink! So rabbit tuk out 'e snuffbox an' drop one leetle grain ob snuff on wolf nose, an' wolf sneeze!

Den rabbit say, "Hi! How can dead man sneeze?" So 'e got on 'e hoss an' ride home fars' as 'e kin. An' wolf see rabbit too wise man for him, an' nebber try to cotch um no mo'.

(Eyeball Candy

This tale was part of the repertoire of Mose Miles, a Negro believed to be in his eighties although no one knew his birthday, who lived on the plantation of Mrs. William Roberts about nine miles north of Tallahassee, Florida. Mose could neither read nor write and never traveled more than a hundred miles from Tallahassee. His longest trip was to White Springs, Florida, where he told his tales at the second annual Florida Folk Festival in May 1954. He firmly believed that he had created all the animal tales he knew. He had never heard of Joel Chandler Harris. The tale of "Eyeball Candy" is the most unusual one he knew. Perhaps it was his own invention. It has no analogue in the Aarne-Thompson Types of the Folktale but resembles in part Type 135B ("Fleeing Fox Loses an Eye in the Briars. . . ." Returns the next day and eats it, thinking that it tastes like chicken). It also echoes Type 21 ("Eating His Own Entrails") and Type 21 ("The She-Fox Declares She Is Eating Her Own Brains").

Buh Fox come along one day. Buh Rabbit had some just little round ball candy. He called it eyeball candy. He come on up dere where Buh Fox was.

Buh Fox, he said, "Buh Rabbit!"

9

He said, "Uh huh."

"What dat you eatin'?"

"Oh, man, dis somp'un good. You wanna taste it?"

"Yeah! I wanna taste it."

So he let him taste a piece of the candy. And Buh Fox taste it.

He say, "What you call it?"

"Eyeball candy."

He said, "Reckon if I pull out one of my eyes, it'd eat like dis?"

He said, "Oh, man, yeah! yeah! It'd eat like dat, sho!"

So he let Buh Rabbit pull one of his eyeballs out. Buh Rabbit took some of the candy and just smeared it all over the eyeball to make it taste sweet, ya know.

So when he got it, well, dat taste all right to Buh Fox.

Buh Fox said, "Pull out de other one!"

When he pulled out de other one, den he called da hounds, said, "Hyeah, hyeah, hyeah!"

And Buh Fox just tore out of there and just butt his fat head on 'gainst the tree.

Buh Rabbit just slick to death!

—J. Russell Reaver
Florida State University

⟨ # Mr. Rabbit and Mr. Bear

"Dar wuz one season," said Uncle Remus, pulling thoughtfully at his whiskers, "w'en Brer Fox say to hisse'f dat he speck he better whirl in en plant a goober-patch, en in dem days, mon, hit wuz tech en go. De wud weren't mo'n out'n his mouf 'fo' de groun' 'uz brok'd up en de goobers 'uz planted. Ole Brer Rabbit, he sot off en watch de motions, he did, en he sorter shet one eye en sing to his chilluns:

> " '*Ti-yi! Tungalee!*
> *I eat um pea, I pick um pea.*
> *Hit grow in de groun', hit grow so free;*
> *Ti-yi! dem goober pea.'*

"Sho nuff w'en de goobers 'gun ter ripen up, eve'y time Brer Fox go down ter his patch, he fin' whar somebody bin grabblin' 'mongst de vines, en he git mighty mad. He sorter speck who de somebody is, but ole Brer Rabbit he cover his tracks so cute dat Brer Fox dunner how ter ketch 'im. Bimeby, one day Brer Fox take a walk all roun' de groun'-pea patch, en 'twa'n't long 'fo' he fin' a crack in de fence whar de rail done bin rub right smoove, en right dar he sot 'im a trap. He tuck'n ben' down a hick'ry saplin', growin' in de fence-cornder, en tie one een' un a plow-line on de top, en in de udder een' he fix a loop-knot, en dat he fasten wid a trigger right in de crack. Nex' mawnin' w'en ole Brer Rabbit come slippin 'long en crope thoo de crack, de loop-knot cotch 'im behime de fo'legs, en de saplin' flew'd up, en dar he wuz 'twix' de heavens en de yeth. Dar he swung, en he fear'd he gwine ter fall, en he fear'd he weren't gwine ter fall. W'ile he wuz a fixin' up a tale fer Brer Fox, he hear a lumberin' down de road, en present'y yer cum ole Brer B'ar amblin' 'long fum whar he bin takin' a bee-tree. Brer Rabbit, he hail 'im:

" 'Howdy, Brer B'ar!'

"Brer Ba'r, he look 'roun en bimeby he see Brer Rabbit swingin' fum de saplin', en he holler out:

" 'Heyo, Brer Rabbit! How you come on dis mawnin'?'

" 'Much oblije, I'm middlin', Brer B'ar,' sez Brer Rabbit, sezee.

"Den Brer B'ar, he ax Brer Rabbit w'at he doin' up dar in de elements, en Brer Rabbit, he up'n say he makin' dollar minnit. Brer B'ar, he say how. Brer Rabbit say he keepin' crows out'n Brer Fox's groun'-pea patch, en den he ax Brer B'ar ef he don't wanter make dollar minnit, kaze he got big fambly er chilluns fer to take keer un, en den he make sech nice skeercrow. Brer B'ar 'low dat he take de job, en den Brer Rabbit show 'im how ter bend down de saplin', en 'twan't long 'fo' Brer B'ar wuz swingin' up dar in Brer Rabbit place. Den Brer Rabbit, he put out fer Brer Fox house, en w'en he got dar he sing out:

" 'Brer Fox! Oh, Brer Fox! Come out yer, Brer Fox, en I'll show you de man w'at bin stealin' yo' goobers.'

"Brer Fox, he grab up his walkin'-stick, en bofe un um went runnin' back down ter der goober-patch, en w'en dey got dar, sho nuff, dar wuz ole Brer B'ar.

" 'Oh, yes! you er cotch, is you?' sez Brer Fox, en 'fo' Brer B'ar could 'splain, Brer Rabbit he jump up en down, en holler out:

" 'Hit 'im on de mouf, Brer Fox; hit 'im on de mouf'; en Brer Fox, he draw back wid de walkin'-cane, en blip he tuck 'im, en eve'y time Brer B'ar'd try ter 'splain, Brer Fox'd shower down on him.

"W'iles all dis 'uz gwine on, Brer Rabbit, he slip off en git in a mud-hole en des lef' his eyes stickin' out, kaze he know'd dat Brer B'ar'd be a comin' atter 'im. Sho nuff, bimeby here come Brer B'ar down de road, en w'en he git ter de mud-hole, he say:

" 'Howdy, Brer Frog; is you seed Brer Rabbit go by yer?'

" 'He des gone by,' sez Brer Rabbit, en ole man B'ar tuck off down de road like a skeer'd mule, en go home ter his fambly same ez enny udder man."

"The Bear didn't catch the Rabbit, then?" inquired the little boy, sleepily.

"Jump up fum dar, honey!" exclaimed Uncle Remus, by way of reply. "I ain't got no time fer ter be settin' yer proppin' yo' eyelids open."

❨ Mr. Fox Goes a-Hunting, but Mr. Rabbit Bags the Game

"Atter Brer Fox hear 'bout how Brer Rabbit done Brer Wolf," said Uncle Remus, scratching his head with the point of his awl, "he 'low, he did, dat he better not be so brash, en he sorter let Brer Rabbit 'lone. Dey wuz all time seein' one nudder, en 'bunnunce er times Brer Fox could er nab Brer Rabbit, but eve'y time he got de chance, his min' 'ud sorter rezume 'bout Brer Wolf, en he let Brer Rabbit 'lone. Bimeby dey 'gun ter git kinder familious wid wunner nudder like dey useter, en it got so Brer Fox'd call on Brer Rabbit, en dey'd set up en smoke der pipes, dey would, like no ha'sh feelin's 'd ever rested 'twixt um.

"Las', one day Brer Fox come 'long all rig out, en ax Brer Rabbit fer ter go huntin' wid 'im, but Brer Rabbit, he sorter feel lazy, en he tell Brer Fox dat he got some udder fish fer ter fry. Brer Fox feel mighty sorry, he did, but he say he b'lieve he try his han' enny how, en off he put. He wuz gone all day, en he had a monstus streak er luck, Brer Fox did, en he bagged a sight er game. Bimeby, to'rds de shank er de evenin', Brer Rabbit sorter stretch hisse'f, he did, en 'low hit's mos' time fer Brer Fox fer ter git 'long home. Den Brer Rabbit, he went'n mounted a stump fer ter see ef he could year Brer Fox comin'. He ain't bin dar long, twel sho nuff, yer come Brer Fox thoo de woods, singin' like a nigger at a frolic. Brer Rabbit, he lipt down off'n de stump, he did, en lay down in de road en make like he dead. Brer Fox he come 'long, he did, en see Brer Rabbit layin' dar. He tu'n 'im over, he did, en 'zamine 'im, en say, sezee:

"'Dish yer rabbit dead. He look like he bin dead long time. He dead, but he mighty fat. He de fattes' rabbit w'at I ever see, but he bin dead too long. I feard ter take 'im home,' sezee.

"Brer Rabbit ain't sayin' nothin'. Brer Fox, he sorter lick his chops, but he went on en lef' Brer Rabbit layin' in de road. Dreckly he wuz outer sight, Brer Rabbit, he jump up, he did, en run 'roun' thoo de woods en git befo' Brer Fox agin. Brer Fox, he come up, en dar lay Brer Rabbit, periently col' en stiff. Brer Fox, he look at Brer Rabbit, en he sorter study. Atter study while he onslung his game-bag, en say ter hisse'f, sezee:

" 'Deze yer rabbits gwine ter was'e. I'll des 'bout leave my game yer, en I'll go back'n get dat udder rabbit, en I'll make folks b'lieve dat I'm ole man Hunter fum Huntsville,' sezee.

"En wid dat he drapt his game en loped back up de road atter de udder rabbit, en w'en he got outer sight, ole Brer Rabbit, he snatch up Brer Fox game en put out fer home. Nex' time he see Brer Fox he holler out:

" 'What you kill de udder day, Brer Fox?' sezee.

"Den Brer Fox, he sorter koam his flank wid his tongue, en holler back:

" 'I cotch a han'ful er hard sense, Brer Rabbit,' sezee.

"Den ole Brer Rabbit, he laugh, he did, en up en 'spon', sezee:

" 'Ef I'd a know'd you wuz atter dat, Brer Fox, I'd a loant you some er mine,' sezee."

(Granny's Version of the Owl

"De way I hyeah dat tale o' Owl wuz diffunt," she said. "De way I hyeah hit, Owl, she do hab heap o' young hubsums (husbands) an' w'en she git out-done wid um, she kilt um in dey sleep and tuck out dey hahts and sucked up de strenk ob um. Dat kip up too, twell she kill Rain Crow, w'ich wuz de kinfolks o' de big T'undeh-Buhd dat lib in de mountains way out yondeh at de end o' de perarer. De willer tree see Rain Crow kilt, an' seen 'im flung de crik mungs de big flags too, arter he haht wuz out. De flags wuz w'ite, but dat cole kyarkiss mek um so cole dey tuhn blue and dey tell hit ter de willer tree dat see de trouble. De willer tree tell de maple dat hit sholy wuz a buhnin' shame dat de flag sarve dataway, an' de maple tell de cotton-wood, an' de cotton-wood tell de plum tree, an' de plum tree tell de warnut, an' de warnut tell de hick'ry. De hick'ry ain't 'feard o' nuttin', an' 'buse dat witch out an' out an' holler 'crost de woods ter de ellums ter tell de oaks ter tell de pines ter tell de whole meanness ter Ole T'undeh-Buhd (Thunder Bird) hisse'f. Dataway de trees all tek up foh Rain Crow. My! T'undeh-Buhd (Thunder-Bird Eagle) wuz mad an' up an' a-gettin', but he ain't git up fas' nuff. Er lil traipsin', wuthless puff-ball, a-rollin' hyeah and dar, hyeah all de ruckshin an' tole Miss Owl an' she putt foh huh grandaddy, Ole Rattlesnake."

(Sheer Crops

Br'er Bear en Br'er Rabbit dey wuz farmers. Br'er Bear he has acres en acres uf good bottom land, en Br'er Rabbit has des' er small sandy-land farm. Br'er Bear wuz allus er "raisin' Cain" wid his neighbors, but Br'er Rabbit was er most engenerally raisin' chillun.

Arter while Br'er Rabbit's boys 'gun to git grown, en Br'er Rabbit 'lows he's gwine to have to git more land if he makes buckle en tongue meet.

So he goes ober to Br'er Bear's house, he did, en he say, sez he, "Mo'nin', Br'er Bear. I craves ter rent yer bottom field nex' year."

Br'er Bear he hum en he haw, en den he sez, "I don't spec I kin 'commodate yer, Br'er Rabbit, but I moughten consider hit, bein's hit's yer."

"How does you rent yer land, Br'er Bear?"

"I kin onliest rent by der sheers."

"What is yer sheer, Br'er Bear?"

"Well," said Br'er Bear, "I takes der top of de crop fer my sheer, en yer takes de rest fer yer sheer."

Br'er Rabbit thinks erbout it rale hard, en he sez, "All right, Br'er Bear, I took it; we goes ter plowin' ober dare nex' week."

Den Br'er Bear goes back in der house des' er-laughin'. He sho is tickled ez to how he hez done put one by ole Br'er Rabbit dat time.

Well, 'long in May Br'er Rabbit done sont his oldest son to tell Br'er Bear to come down to the field to see erbout dat are sheer crop. Br'er Bear he comes er-pacin' down to de field en Br'er Rabbit wuz er-leanin' on de fence.

"Mo'nin', Br'er Bear. See what er fine crop we hez got. You is to hab de tops fer yer sheer. Whare is you gwine to put 'em? I wants ter git 'em off so I kin dig my 'taters."

Br'er Bear wuz sho hot. But he done made dat trade wid Br'er Rabbit, en he had to stick to hit. So he went off all huffed up, en didn't even tell Br'er Rabbit what to do wid de vines. But Br'er Rabbit perceeded to dig his 'taters.

'Long in de fall Br'er Rabbit 'lows he's gwine to see Br'er Bear ergin en try to rent der bottom field. So he goes down to Br'er Bear's house en after passin' de time of day en other pleasant sociabilities, he sez, sez he, "Br'er Bear, how erbout rentin' der bottom field nex' year? Is yer gwine ter rent hit to me ergin?"

Br'er Bear say, he did, "You cheat me out uf my eyes las' year, Br'er Rabbit. I don't think I kin let yer hab it dis year."

Den Br'er Rabbit scratch his head er long time, en he say, "Oh, now, Br'er Bear, yer know I ain't cheated yer. Yer jes' cheat yerself. Yer made de trade yerself en I done tuck yer at yer word. Yer sed yer wanted de tops fer yer sheer, en I gib um ter yer, didn't I? Now yer jes' think hit all ober ergin and see if yer can't make er new deal fer yerself."

Den Br'er Bear said, "Well, I rents to yer only on dese perditions: dat yer hab all de tops fer yer sheer en I hab all de rest fer my sheer."

Br'er Rabbit he twis' en he turn en he sez, "All right, Br'er Bear, I'se got ter hab more land fer my boys. I'll tuck hit. We go to plowin' in dare right erway."

Den Br'er Bear he amble back into de house. He wuz shore he'd made er good trade dat time.

Way 'long in nex' June Br'er Rabbit done sont his boy down to Br'er Bear's house ergin, to tell him to come down ter de field ter see erbout his rent. When he got dare, Br'er Rabbit say, he did:

"Mo'nin', Br'er Bear. See what er fine crop we hez got? I specks hit will make forty bushels to der acre. I'se gwine ter put my oats on der market. What duz yer want me ter do wid yer straw?"

Br'er Bear sho wuz mad, but hit wa'n't no use. He done saw whar Br'er Rabbit had 'im. So he lies low en 'lows to hisself how he's gwine to git eben wid Br'er Rabbit yit. So he smile en say, "Oh, der crop is all right, Br'er Rabbit. Jes' stack my straw anywheres eround dare. Dat's all right."

Den Br'er Bear smile en he say, "What erbout nex' year, Br'er Rabbit? Is yer cravin' ter rent dis field ergin?"

"I ain't er-doin nothin' else but wantin' ter rent hit, Br'er Bear," sez Br'er Rabbit.

"All right, all right, yer kin rent her ergin. But dis time I'se gwine ter hab der tops fer my sheer, en I'se gwine ter hab de bottoms fer my sheer too."

Br'er Rabbit wuz stumped. He didn't know whatter do nex'. But he finally managed to ask, "Br'er Bear, ef yer gits der tops en der bottoms fer yer sheer, what will I git fer my sheer?"

Den ole Br'er Bear laff en say, "Well, yer would git de middles."

Br'er Rabbit he worry en he fret, he plead en he argy, but hit do no good.

Br'er Bear sez, "Take hit er leave hit," en jes' stand pat.

Br'er Rabbit took hit.

Way 'long nex' summer ole Br'er Bear 'cided he would go down to der bottom field en see erbout dat dare sheer crop he had wid Br'er Rabbit. While he wuz er-passin' through de woods on hiz way, he sez to himself, he did:

"De fust year I rents to de ole Rabbit, I makes de tops my sheer, en ole Rabbit planted 'taters; so I gits nothin' but vines. Den I rents ergin, en der Rabbit is to hab de tops, en I de bottoms, en ole Rabbit plants oats; so I gits nothin' but de straw. But I sho is got dat ole Rabbit dis time. I gits both de tops en de bottoms, en de ole Rabbit gits only de middles. I'se bound ter git 'im dis time."

Jes' den de old Bear come ter de field. He stopped. He look at hit. He shet up his fist. He cuss en he say, "Dat derned little scoundrel! He done went en planted dat fiel' in corn."

Buh Owl an Buh Rooster

Buh Owl, him bin a great music-meker. Him an Buh Rooster bin good fren. Heap er bud blan wisit Buh Rooster house fuh yeddy music an fuh dance. Buh Owl, him sing so well an eh pick de banjo so clear, nobody kin listen ter um an keep eh foot still; but eh no wan leh nobody shum wen eh duh sing an play. Buh Rooster, him always blan hab a dark room fuh Buh Owl fuh set in wen eh duh play fuh de bud. Lamp day in day, but eh hab shade on um. Buh Owl kin see de bud wuh duh dance, but de bud, dem cant see Buh Owl. Buh Owl him faid light, and eh yent der bole bud no how.

One ebenin Buh Owl bin a sing an play oncommon well fuh de bud at Buh Rooster house fuh dance. De pahler bin full, but dem yent bin know who dat bin a mek de music. Buh Rooster, him bin prommus Buh Owl dat eh yent guine tell who duh sing an play. Wen dem all bin dance tel dem tired, dem all bague Buh Rooster fuh show dem de man wuh bin mek sich pooty music fuh dance long. Buh Rooster say him cant. Dem keep on bague, tel, at lenk, Buh Rooster gone in de room, an eh tek de shade offer de lamp. Wen dem look pon topper Buh Owl, eh eye so big, an eh yez cock up so high, eh skade de people, an dem all holler an run.

Buh Owl, him berry bex case Buh Rooster broke eh wud, an eh fall out wid Buh Rooster. From dat day Buh Owl hate Buh Rooster, eh wife, an eh chillun. Wenebber, duh night, eh yeddy any er um duh crow er der fix ehself topper eh roose, eh mek fuh de place an eat um up. Eh yent do, in dis wul, fuh man fuh ceive eh fren.

Buh Lion an Buh Goat

Buh Lion bin a hunt, an eh spy Buh Goat duh leddown topper big rock duh wuk eh mout an der chaw. Eh creep up fuh ketch um. Wen eh git close ter um eh notus um good. Buh Goat keep on chaw. Buh Lion try

16

fuh fine out wuh Buh Goat duh eat. Eh yet see nuttin nigh um ceptin de nekked rock wuh eh duh leddown on. Buh Lion stonish. Eh wait topper Buh Goat. Buh Goat keep on chaw, an chaw, an chaw. Buh Lion cant mek de ting out, an eh come close, an eh say: "Hay! Buh Goat, wuh you duh eat?" Buh Goat skade wen Buh Lion rise up befo um, but eh keep er bole harte, an eh mek ansur: "Me duh chaw dis rock, an ef you dont leff, wen me done finish chaw um me guine eat you." Dis big wud sabe Buh Goat. Bole man git outer diffikelty way coward man lose eh life.

Story of a Cow

Now chillun, ef yuh set still an be good, I gwina tells yuh bout two Negroes whut buys a cow.

Soon after de Negroes wus sot free by Mr. Lincoln, two uv-um, by name uv Mose Smiff and Rastus Jones, chuses tuh buys a cow tuhgether, ez da lives on jinen places, an da goes ovah tuh a neighbor, an buys a cow fur twenty dollars an each uv-um tuh pays ten dollars fur his haff.

Comin' on back home, Mose say to Rastus: "Rastus, whut haff uv de cow you wants?"

Rastus he say back: "I wants de front-en uv de cow." Mose say: "All right, I takes de hine-en fur mine." Da turns her in Rastus' clover-patch, whar she main several days.

One mornin', Mose wife wake up an say: "Mose, ain't you an Rastus Jones bought a cow tuther day?" He say: "Yes." She say: "Ain't you done paid fur haff de cow?" He say: "Yes." She say: "What haff uv de cow longs tuh you?" He say: "De hine-en uv de cow." She say "Well era, ef de hine-en longs tuh you, how comes you aint never looks atter yo-en, an milks de cow?" He say: "I hadn't thought uv dat." She say: "Now, you git-up an gits a bucket, an go ovah an melks dat cow, don't I gwina bus yo head wide open wid a boad, nigger!"

Mose gits up and gits a bucket, an goes ovah an says: "Rastus, ain't me-en you bought a cow tuther day?" He say: "Yes." Mose say: "Ain't I done pay fur haff de cow, an tuck de hine-en?" He say: "Yes." Mose say: "Well, era, I wants melk my-en." Rastus say: "I been melkin' de cow." Mose say: "De front-en longs tuh you, and you tuh feeds de cow, an I tuh melks de cow!"

Mary Bronson says: "Uncle Eph, does Mose milk the cow, and does

Rastus continue to feed her?" I says: "De cow she done dead long-go, an ain't givin' no melk now, nur eatin' nuthin' nuther! Look to me lack yuh powful sleepy. Run on an says yuh prars, don't de Devil gwina gits yuh!"

(**Buh Hawss en' Buh Mule**

Buh Hawss' tail long lukkuh willuh switch,
Buh Mule's own stan' lukkuh t'istle.

One time Buh Hawss en' Buh Mule tu'n out duh pastuh duh Sunday. Dem alltwo blonx to high buckruh. Buh Hawss binnuh dribe een buggy, en' Buh Mule binnuh wu'k duh plow. Dem alltwo glad fuh git out en' dem alltwo kick up dem foot en' play 'bout de fiel'. Buh Hawss cantuh. 'E bow 'e neck lukkuh gobluh duh strut, en' 'e tail heng lukkuh willuh switch. Buh Mule trot. 'E 'tretch 'e neck out 'trait lukkuh Muscoby duck duh fly. 'E step high en' 'e tail stan' up lukkuh t'istle. Buh Mule tail oagly, fuh true, but da' duh all de tail wuh 'e got en' 'e berry well sattify 'long um.

Buh Hawss biggin fuh brag. "Look 'puntop oonuh tail," 'e say. "Mekso oonuh ent hab tail lukkuh my own?" 'e ax'um. "Oonuh yent kin switch fly 'long'um 'cause 'e shabe. Shishuh no'count tail ent wut' nuttin'," 'e tell'um. "Me duh buckruh, you duh nigguh!"

Buh Mule biggin fuh shame. 'E yent sattify 'long 'e tail no mo'. Buh Mule cyan' switch fly, fuh true, but 'e skin tough, en' fly don' bodduh'um, but Buh Hawss git'um so agguhnize' een 'e min' 'e fuhgit fuh tell'um duh 'e yent hab cajun fuh switch fly 'long 'e tail, en' 'e heng 'e head en' 'e tail alltwo, en' 'e lef' Buh Hawss en' 'e gone off todduh side de fiel' en' 'e study. Bimeby, 'e look obuh de pastuh, en' todduh side de fench 'e see one las'yeah cawnfiel' weh de nigguh lef' 'nuf sheep buhr duh stan' 'long de cawnstalk. Buh Mule biggin fuh laugh. 'E open 'e mout'. "*Aw-e-Aw-e-Aw-e!*" Buh Hawss cantuh. 'E come close. 'E ax'um 'smattuh mek 'e duh laugh. Buh Mule say 'e laugh 'cause Buh Hawss ent smaa't 'nuf fuh jump de fench en' run'um a race t'ru de cawnfiel'. Buh Hawss tek'um up. 'E jump de fench. 'E behin' foot ketch de top rail en' knock'um off. Buh Mule tumble t'ru. Yuh dem come! Buh Hawss cantuh, Buh Mule trot, up en' down de fiel' t'ru de sheep buhr. Buh Mule tail shabe tell 'e slick. 'E switch'um roun' en' roun' 'mong de buhr but none nebbuh stick. Bimeby, Buh Hawss' tail biggin fuh hebby. 'E ketch full'uh buhr. Dem tanglety een 'e tail 'tell 'e stan' lukkuh timbuh cyaa't rope. 'E duh drag. Eb'ry time 'e switch'um roun' 'e hanch, de buhr sting'um. 'E say to 'eself, "Wuh dis t'ing? Me fuh lick me own self! Me fuh hab spuhr een me own tail! De debble! Me dey een trubble, fuh true!" 'E talk trute. 'E tail lick'um en' spuhr'um alltwo one time.

Buh Mule pass'um. 'E look 'puntop Buh Hawss' tail, en' 'e yent shame no mo'. "Tengk Gawd," 'e say, "fuh shabe tail. Low tree stan' high win'!"

"How Come" and "Why" Tales

Why the Negro Is Black

Another nigger say, "Does you-all know how come we is so black?" Well, God sent Gabriel to get de colored folks an' dey hunted all over till dey found 'em all stretched out 'sleep on de grass under de tree of life. So dey woke 'em an' told 'em God wanted 'em. Dey jumped up an' run, an' dey was so skeered dey might miss something dey begin to push an' shove one another, so God hollered "Git back!" an' dey misunderstood him an' thought he said "Git black!" an' dey been black ever since.

Why the Negro Is Black
(Uncle Remus' Version)

One night, while the little boy was watching Uncle Remus twisting and waxing some shoe-thread, he made what appeared to him to be a very curious discovery. He discovered that the palms of the old man's hands were as white as his own, and the fact was such a source of wonder that he at last made it the subject of remark. The response of Uncle Remus led to the earnest recital of a piece of unwritten history that must prove interesting to ethnologists.

"Tooby sho de pa'm er my han's w'ite, honey," he quietly remarked, "en, w'en it come ter dat, dey wuz a time w'en all de w'ite folks 'uz black —blacker dan me, kaze I done bin yer so long dat I bin sorter bleach out."

The little boy laughed. He thought Uncle Remus was making him the victim of one of his jokes; but the youngster was never more mistaken. The old man was serious. Nevertheless, he failed to rebuke the ill-timed mirth of the child, appearing to be altogether engrossed in his work. After a while, he resumed:

"Yasser. Folks dunner w'at bin yit, let 'lone w'at gwine ter be. Niggers is niggers now, but de time wuz w'en we 'uz all niggers tergedder."

"When was that, Uncle Remus?"

"Way back yander. In dem times we 'uz all on us black; we 'uz all niggers tergedder, en 'cordin' ter all de 'counts w'at I years folks 'uz gittin' 'long 'bout ez well in dem days ez dey is now. But atter w'ile de news come dat dere wuz a pon' er water somers in de neighborhood, w'ich ef dey'd git inter dey'd be wash off nice en w'ite, en den one un um, he fin' de place en make er splunge inter de pon', en come out w'ite ez a town gal. En den, bless gracious! w'en de folks seed it, dey made a break fer de pon', en dem w'at wuz de soopless, dey got in fus' en dey come out w'ite; en dem w'at wuz de nex' soopless, dey got in nex', en dey come out merlatters; en dey wuz sech a crowd un um dat dey mighty nigh use de water up, w'ich w'en dem yuthers come 'long, de morest dey could do wuz ter paddle about wid der foots en dabble in it wid der han's. Dem wuz de niggers, en down ter dis day dey ain't no w'ite 'bout a nigger ceppin' de pa'ms er der han's en de soles er der foot."

The little boy seemed to be very much interested in this new account of the origin of races, and he made some further inquiries, which elicited from Uncle Remus the following additional particulars:

"De Injun en de Chinee got ter be 'counted 'long er de merlatter. I ain't seed no Chinee dat I knows un, but dey tells me dey er sorter 'twix' a brown en a brindle. Dey er all merlatters."

"But mamma says the Chinese have straight hair," the little boy suggested.

"Co'se, honey," the old man unhesitatingly responded, "dem w'at git ter de pon' time nuff fer ter git der head in de water, de water hit onkink der ha'r. Hit bleedzd ter be dat away."

❨ Why the Holy Amen Church Has Two Doors

Dicksonville is the largest colored community in Salisbury, North Carolina, with the largest church. The Holy Amen Church is situated just outside the city limits, and now it has two doors.

Here, as in other Negro churches in the South, it was a common practice to try church members who had committed some act they regarded as sinful. Such a trial took place when Deacon Pennybacker Robinson was accused of "cussing" Holy Amen Church. Following is one account of the incident:

When the prayer was finished and the rustling and craning of necks had subsided and the fanning begun, the meeting was turned over to Deacon Wassail White, who arose and addressed the gathering.

"Brudders an' Sisters, as you all knows, we is assembled here today ter try and 'reak justice on a po', miserable back-slidin' member of dish here church. We is gonna gib 'im er fair tri'l an' effen he has got ennything ter say fer hisself, we is gonna hear 'im through befo' we drives 'im frum de flock. An I don' want no hollerin' at 'im 'twill he gits through.

"Mister Pennybacker Robinson, you has bin 'cused of a most ser'ous crime. You has bin 'cused of cussin' de church. Now nemmine who repo't you an' nemmine what evidence we got ergin you, what has you got to say fer yo'se'f? Is you guilty er not guilty? Answer me dat!"

Pennybacker arose and came forward, proud and unashamed. His head was lifted high. His lanky length seemed to grow under the hostile gaze of his erstwhile friends and neighbors. In his eyes glowed the fire of a martyr.

He was a dignified man. His skin was a dark roan color, somewhat brindled in the darker spots. His grizzled hair, heavy gold-rimmed spectacles, and jim-swinger coat gave him the walk and air of a dusty esthetic. Calmly and in a firm voice he answered his accusers, anonymous though they were.

"Deacon White, Brudders an' Sisters, I don't 'zactly know how ter answer dat question. I is guilty an' yet ergin I ain' guilty. De thing happen lak dis:

"You all, leastways de mos' of you, 'members 'bout er month ago when we was funeralizin' Sister Erferlia Johnson. Well, I knows you also 'members how, when dey opens de kaskit so de family cud hab de las' look, an' when de lid wuz tooken off, er big black cat jump outten de kaskit an start spittin' an' den start runnin' eroun' er tryin' ter git outten here. Well, in de tumult an' de fight at de do', Sis Elby Crawford wuz on mah back, an' Brudder Sam Frisbee was tryin' ter git 'tween my legs, and Sis Peebles wuz er beatin' me ober de haid wid her umbrelly, 'cause I couldn't git outten her way fas' ernuf. . . .

"Well, right den and dare I turn ter Brudder Mose Benson, an' I says ter 'im, sez I, 'Mose, damn a church ennyway dat ain't got but one do'!'"

⸨ Why the Rabbit Has a Short Tail

De kinda tales dat allus suits mah fancy de mo'es' am de tales de ole folks used to tell 'bout de ca'iens on of Brothuh Rabbit. In de early days Ah heerd many an' many a tale 'bout ole Brothuh Rabbit what woke me to de fac' dat hit tecks dis, dat, an' t'othuh to figguh life out—dat you hafto use yo' haid for mo'n a hatrack lack ole Brothuh Rabbit do.

Ole Brothuh Rabbit de smaa'tes' thing Ah done evuh run 'crost in mah whole bawn life. Dere's lots of peoples rat today dat begrudges Brothuh Rabbit de mother-wit he got to help 'im meck his way thoo de worl'. Evuhbody'd lack to be a knowledge man lack Brothuh Rabbit, but dey ain't got dem Judas ways lack Brothuh Rabbit nachul bawn got. Co'se, deys lots of kin's of rabbits, jes' lack peoples. Some rabbits is smaa'ter'n othuh rabbits, but hit's de lazy ones what allus gits de whole bunch in trouble.

De why de rabbit come to hab a short tail rat today am all on 'count of a great big swamp rabbit trawna out-smaa't de alluhgattuh one day down on de rivuh. De swamp rabbit ain't ez pert ez de jack rabbit an' de cottontail—he kinda lazy an' triflin' lack lots of good-for-nothin' Nigguhs is, but he yit got plenty hoss sense. So one day when he meck his way down to de rivuh an' wanna git 'cross to t'othuh side, an' dey ain't no bridge nowhars in sight, he sees a alluhgattuh swimmin' 'roun' in de wadduh, so he holler at 'im an' say, "Oh! Brothuh Alluhgattuh! Ah bet you dey's mo' rabbits in de worl' dan dey is alluhgattuhs."

Brothuh Alluhgattuh yells back, "Not so."

"Well, den," 'low de swamp rabbit, "call up all yo' alluhgattuhs an' line 'em up 'cross de rivuh an' we'll prove what one of us am rat."

So Brothuh Alluhgattuh calls up all de alluhgattuhs, an' dey forms a line from one side of de rivuh to t'othuh one. No sooner'n dey done form de line dan de swamp rabbit jumps from one of dey backs to t'othuh one countin' out loud ez he jump, "One, two, three, fo', five, six, sebun, eight, nine, ten, 'lebun, twelve," and so on, 'til he done plum rech t'othuh side of de rivuh. Ez soon ez his feets hits dry lan', he sets down an' staa'ts to brushin' de wadduh offen his long, bushy white tail.

Whilst he washin' his tail off in de rivuh, Brothuh Alluhgattuh swims up to whar he be an' say, "Now you call all de rabbits an' count 'em; Ah done called out all de alluhgattuhs." When Brothuh Alluhgattuh talk in dis wise, de swamp rabbit jes' crack his sides a-laffin' an' say, "Ah don' in no wise hab no intention of callin' out de rabbits—Ah jes' wanted to git 'cross de rivuh."

Dis heah meck Brothuh Alluhgattuh pow'ful mad, so he dart his haid rail quick to dat paa't de wadduh whar de swamp rabbit am washin' his tail an' bites off de end of hit. An' dat's de why all rabbits, de swamp rabbits, de jack rabbits, an' de cottontails, lackwise, hab a short tail rat today. All of 'em got to suffer for what dat no-good triflin' old swamp rabbit done did. Dey's lots of dem rascals rat 'roun' heah in de Trinity Rivuh Bottoms, now, an' dey's de easies' rabbits in de worl' to ketch—dey's putty nigh too lazy to run.

(Why the Buzzard Has a Red Head

Dar wuz a buzzard en a rabbit en a fox—en de buzzard ax de fox en de rabbit ter go walkin' wid him. Dar wuz a ole holler tree ober in de woods en de buzzard tole de fox dat de one dat go up de holler tree en come down wud live de longes', en de fox he go up en de ole buzzard stop him up, en he go off ev'y day en come back en sing a song ter him:

Bun - gle - toe, bun - gle - toe,

cleav - in' on to yo' life.

An' de fox he say:

Go 'way, Broth-er Big Eye.

He sing it right smart er times en de fox he give de same answer. De buzzard he git louder en de ole fox die en de buzzard eat him up.

When he done git haungry ergin he went on back fer de rabbit en tole him dat de one dat 'ud go up de holler tree fus' en come down 'ud live de longes', en de rabbit tole him to go up, but de buzzard he allus hed a lot uv tricks en he tole *him* to go up, en de rabbit he went up en de buzzard he go off en come back en sing right smart er times. He done git louder en de rabbit he done git weaker en de las' er time de rabbit he git 'way off in one corner. De buzzard he try to pull him out, but de rabbit he done hit him side de head en dat's why de buzzard's hed a red haid ebber sence.

(Granny's Version of the Eagle Who Became a Girl

"De way I hyeah dat," said Granny, "de gal kim in er big rain-drap w'en er stawm wuz gwine on. W'en de drap bustid out she jumped. W'en she tuck up wid de man she lub, she tole 'im plain dat she kyarn' go out do's w'en de sun er de moon wuz a-shinin'. He 'gree dat she go des w'en 'twuz cloudy, but after w'iles he fegit; wunst, w'en he all tuckahed out (tired) arter huntin' he mek 'er go out an' git de game whah he flung hit unneat er ash tree. She don't wanter go, but he mek 'er an' she git de tucky (turkey) an' de piece o' deer meat an' staht back. De moon come out des ez she got ter d' do' an' de man see 'er sail up in de a'r lak er eagle. She drap 'er shoe, dough, and whah hit fall—hit wuz one dem bead shoes dey calls moc'sins—dey grow up flower des lak hit, and dey call hit arter dat name."

(How the Church Came to Be Split Up

"It's too bad that it must be two churches in Eatonville," I commented. "De town's too little. Everybody ought to go to one."

"Dey wouldn't do dat, Zora, and you know better. Fack is, de Christian churches nowhere don't stick together," this from Charlie.

Everybody agreed this was true. So Charlie went on. "Look at all de kind of denominations we got. But de people can't help dat 'cause de church wasn't build on no solid foundation to start wid."

"Oh yes, it 'twas!" Johnnie Mae disputed him. "It was built on solid rock. Didn't Jesus say 'On dis rock Ah build my church'?"

"Yeah," chimed in Auntie Hoyt. "And de song says, 'On Christ de solid rock I stand' and 'Rock of Ages.'"

Charlie was calm and patient. "Yeah, he built it on a rock, but it wasn't solid. It was a pieced-up rock and that's how come de church split up now. Here's de very way it was:

Christ was walkin' long one day wid all his disciples and he said, "We're goin' for a walk today. Everybody pick up a rock and come along." So everybody got their selves a nice big rock 'ceptin' Peter. He was lazy, so he picked up a li'l bit of a pebble and dropped it in his side pocket and come along.

Well, they walked all day long and de other 'leven disciples changed them rocks from one arm to de other but they kept on totin' 'em. Long towards sundown they come 'long by de Sea of Galilee and Jesus tole 'em, "Well, le's fish awhile. Cast in yo' nets right here." They done like he tole 'em and caught a great big mess of fish. Then they cooked 'em and Christ said, "Now, all y'all bring up yo' rocks." So they all brought they rocks and Christ turned 'em into bread and they all had a plenty to eat wid they fish exceptin' Peter. He couldn't hardly make a moufful offa de li'l bread he had and he didn't like dat a bit.

Two or three days after dat Christ went out doors and looked up at de sky and says, "Well, we're goin' for another walk today. Everybody git yo'self a rock and come along."

They all picked up a rock apiece and was ready to go. All but Peter. He went and tore down half a mountain. It was so big he couldn't move it wid his hands. He had to take a pinch-bar to move it. All day long Christ walked and talked to his disciples and Peter sweated and strained wid dat rock of his'n.

Way long in de evenin' Christ went up under a great big ole tree and set down and called all of his disciples around 'im and said, "Now everybody bring up yo' rocks."

So everybody brought theirs but Peter. Peter was about a mile down de road punchin' dat half a mountain he was bringin'. So Christ waited till he got dere. He looked at de rocks dat de other 'leven disciples had, den he seen dis great big mountain dat Peter had and so he got up and walked over to it and put one foot up on it and said, "Why Peter, dis is a fine rock you got here! It's a noble rock! And Peter, on dis rock Ah'm gointer build my church."

Peter says, "Naw you ain't neither. You won't build no church house on *dis* rock. You gointer turn dis rock into bread."

Christ knowed dat Peter meant dat thing so he turnt de hillside into bread and dat mountain is de bread he fed de 5,000 wid. Den he took dem 'leven other rocks and glued 'em together and built his church on it.

26

And that's how come de Christian churches is split up into so many different kinds—cause it's built on pieced-up rock.

There was a storm of laughter following Charlie's tale. "Zora, you come talkin' 'bout puttin' de two churches together and not havin' but one in dis town," Armetta said chidingly. "You know better'n dat. Baptis' and Methdis' always got a pick out at one 'nother. One time two preachers—one Methdis' and de other one Baptis'—wuz on uh train and de engine blowed up and bein' in de colored coach right back of de engine they got blowed up too. When they saw theyself startin' up in de air de Baptis' preacher hollered, 'Ah bet Ah go higher than you!'"

❨ Why There Are So Many Mosquitoes on the East Coast

Well, one Christmas time, God was goin' to Palatka. De Devil was in de neighborhood too and seen God goin' long de big road, so he jumped behind a stump and hid. Not dat he was skeered uh God, but he wanted to git a Christmas present outa God but he didn't wanta give God nothin'.

So he squatted down behind dis stump till God come along and then he jumped up and said, "Christmas gift!"

God just looked back over his shoulder and said, "Take de East Coast," and kept on walkin'. An dat's why we got storms and skeeters—it's de Devil's property.

Tales of Folk Figures

After freedom came, the Negro weaver of tales supplanted Brer Rabbit with "John," the trickster hero of the southern plantation. Like Brer Rabbit, John always comes out victorious in his contests with his "bossman." John tales have been included in several collections of Negro folklore such as Zora Neale Hurston's Mules and Men (1935). The only single collection of them is my John Tales, published in the 1933 yearbook of the Texas Folklore Society.

"John," like Brer Rabbit, is a general folk figure symbolizing an entire group or class. But there is another type of folk figure—the real person, whose odd activities and mannerisms cause him to be talked about extensively by many people in a specific locality. Many American Negroes belong in this category, because of the extraordinary feats they have accomplished or the outstanding distinction they have achieved. Their lives have caused stories to be created about them which have been passed around by word of mouth. In many instances the telling of the stories has reached such widespread proportions that they have transcended local and regional scenes and attained national status.

(John and His Boss-man's Watermelon Patch

Some of the plantation owners in the neighborhood gave their hands an acre of land to raise vegetables, corn and watermelons on, but Colonel Clemons was so mean that he would not let John and the other hands raise any food at all for themselves. He wanted them to buy everything at his commissary.

So it was hard for Colonel Clemons' hands to get a watermelon even in watermelon season. He wouldn't let them have any from his own patch, and he wouldn't give them any money to buy them from other plantations. So John secretly visited the Colonel's patch once or twice a week and took several melons home. David and Joseph, his little boys, always went with him and helped him bring them down to the cabin.

This had been going on for three years now and the Colonel hadn't caught up with them. But one Saturday evening when he was returning from town, he saw John and the little boys leaving his watermelon patch. Each had a melon on each shoulder. The Colonel rode up to them and stopped his horse.

"I've been missing a lot of watermelons out of my patch lately," he said to John. "Lots of tracks lead up this way, and it seems like those watermelons you have may be mine, you thievin' rascal."

"Things ain't always what dey seems, Boss," replied John.

"Well," said the Colonel, "you are coming from the direction of my patch."

"What direction got to do wid a hones' man?" answered John.

The Colonel was so outdone by John's reply that he headed his horse toward the Big-house and went on home.

(John and the Two White Men in Court

One year the boll-weevils got into the cotton crop on Colonel Clemons' plantation and destroyed most of it. This made times very hard for the Colonel, and since he did not make any money, he did not provide sufficient food and clothing for the hands. So naturally they stole anything they could get away with.

Never a week passed that some of the hands were not arrested and carried to jail.

One day the sheriff came out to Colonel Clemons' farm and arrested John. With him were two white hands he had arrested on a neighboring plantation. John and the two white hands were all charged with stealing and they were to be tried on the same day at the same hour.

When John and the two white men were brought in to the court room and arraigned for trial, John was very nervous and was trembling. This was the first time in his life that he had not been able to think of an excuse. He knew, however, that they were going to try the white men first; so he decided to listen to their answers and imitate them when his turn came.

The first case called was that of one of the white hands who was accused of stealing a horse.

"Guilty, or not guilty?" said the Judge.

"Not guilty," replied the man; "I've owned that horse ever since he was a colt." The case was dismissed.

Then the Judge called the second white man to the stand. He was accused of stealing a cow. "Guilty, or not guilty?" asked the Judge.

"Not guilty," replied the defendant; "I've owned that cow ever since she was a calf." The case was dismissed.

Then John was called to the stand. He was accused of stealing a wagon.

"Guilty, or not guilty?" demanded the Judge.

"Not guilty," replied John. "Ah's owned dat wagon ever since it was a wheelbarrow."

Ole Pete

Ole Pete, a huge Negro who died at Port Tampa in 1934 at the age of eighty, might well have been called the "John Henry" of Florida, so remarkable were his deeds, according to local tradition.

His amazing feats, as told by Negroes (and some whites) in Port Tampa, rivaled those of Roark Bradford's fabulous character.

Janitor at a shop office of the Atlantic Coast Line railroad at Port Tampa, his real name was Henry Peterson. The writer knew Ole Pete for five years of Pete's later life, and found him an audible muse of native wisdom, Negro folklore, superstitions and jokes about members of his race. Pete was said to have a skull an inch thick and as hard as iron.

Any old Negro at Port Tampa will tell you of the time a freight car ran over Ole Pete's head. He was asleep in the car repair shed with his head on the track, using the rail as a pillow. A switch engine "kicked" two cars into the shed for repairs. As it is told, the wheels of one passed bumpingly across his head, but his hard skull derailed the other car. Some workmen saw it and ran to pick up Ole Pete's dead body, but Pete was still sound asleep and snoring.

When they woke him up and told him what had happened, Pete rubbed his eyes, then his head, and said sleepily, "Dawgone, mah head does feel kinda funny."

Old waterfront habitués will solemnly admit that Pete once used a ship's anchor for a pickax, that he lifted a derailed locomotive back onto the track, and that he pushed a grounded ship off the bar into the channel.

Port Tampa Negroes all vouch for the fact that Pete would butt horns with any billy goat for four bits a match and that Pete always won.

❲ The Green Runner

Henry felt that he was still almost the equal of the fabulous Green Runner, "who wuz de strongest man I ever heerd tell of on de river. He'd eat half a bar'l er flour an' a middle er meat at one meal, wid a bar'l er greens an' a water-bucket full er syrup. Den w'en he had et dat he stretch an' say to de Cap'n, 'Cap'n, turn off fo' er dese niggers an' I does dey work.' An' de Cap'n turned off fo' mens."

❲ The Sweetheart of Harriet Tubman's Brother

Harriet Tubman, an escaped Negro slave, was widely known as the best conductor on the Underground Railroad, which carried slaves to freedom. Because of the hundreds of slaves that she personally led out of slavery, she was known as General Tubman.

One of Harriet's own brothers, William Henry, had long been attached to a pretty mulatto girl named Catherine, who was owned by another master; but this man had other views for her, and would not let her marry William Henry. Harriet's brother had made up his mind that he would be one of her next party to the North and that Catherine should go also. He went to a tailor's and bought a new suit of clothes for a small person, and concealed them inside the garden fence of Catherine's master. This garden ran down to the bank of a little stream, and Catherine had been notified where to find the clothes. When the time came to get ready, Catherine boldly walked down to the foot of the garden, and took up the bundle. Hiding under the bank, she put on the man's garments and sent her own floating down the stream.

She was soon missed, and all the girls in the house were set to looking for Catherine. Presently they saw coming up from the river a well-dressed little darkey boy, and they all ceased looking for Catherine, and stared at him. He walked directly by them, round the house, and out of the gate, without the slightest suspicion being excited as to who he was. In a few weeks from that time, this party were all safe in Canada.

⟨ King Charley of Albany

What was perhaps the really unique contribution of New York's Dutch to the lore of holidays was the great Negro festival after Whitsunday, or Pinkster. Fortunately we have preserved in the New York State Library one copy of a printed Pinkster ode for the year 1803, together with a somewhat later account from the memory of Dr. Jonathan Eights, Albany's accomplished antiquarian. We must go back to the opening of the nineteenth century, before the beautiful first capitol of the state was erected on Pinkster Hill, just in front of the present Capitol. The festivities now to be described had probably been held annually for more than a century.

Early on Monday morning the children of Albany gathered flowering boughs, sprinkled them with water, hung them over the doors of late sleepers, and waited for the dewy deluge when drowsy citizens came out onto their steps. After a hearty breakfast of *supaan* (cornmeal mush), the children hastened away to Pinkster Hill. Laid out in an oblong were wooden booths where gingerbread, cider, and apple toddy were sold. Everywhere were smiling Negroes in gayest attire enjoying their annual holiday from domestic duties, even though most of them were probably still slaves.

Tuesday was the great day for our black folk. Master of ceremonies for its inauguration was Adam Blake, body servant of the Patroon van Rensselaer, lord of 750,000 acres. At the head of a procession he arrived about ten A.M. at the town house of Mayor Douw. It was not the good burgomaster who emerged, however, but a greater man, Charley of Pinkster Hill, one time Prince of Angola in the Guinea Gulf, master of the revels to Albany. The ode—"printed solely for the purchasers and others"—describes the scene:

Now hark! the banjo, rub-a-dub,
Like a washerwoman's tub;
And hear the drum, 'tis rolling now,
Row-de-dow, row-de-dow.
The pipe and tabor, flute and fife
Shall wake the dullest soul to life.
All beneath the shady tree
There they hold the jubilee.
Charles, the king, will then advance,
Leading on the Guinea dance,
Moving o'er the flow'ring green,
You'll know him by his graceful mien;
You'll know him on the dancing ground,
For where he is folks gather round;
You'll know him by his royal nose,
You'll know him by his Pinkster clothes,
You'll know him by his pleasant face,
And by his hat of yellow lace;
You'll know him by his princely air,
And his politeness to the fair;
And when you know him, then you'll see
A slave whose soul was always free.

If, as the tradition reported by the antiquarian Joel Munsell says, King Charley was 125 years old in 1824 when he died, he must have been a lad of 104 when this ode was composed. Allowing a quarter of a century for exaggeration, he was still close to 80. One of the white children who loved and remembered him later recalled Charley taking him on his shoulder and leaping over a bar more than five feet high. The children were all to remember also his costume of a British brigadier—scarlet coat with gold lace and ribbons, buckskin smallclothes, blue stockings, black shoes with silver buckles, and tricorn hat with pompom.

After parading through the town, the king returned to Pinkster Hill, where from noon till nightfall he presided over the most interesting African folk dance of which I have found record anywhere in early American annals. The principal instrument for establishing rhythm was a drum of which there are various descriptions. One writer recalled an eel pot, covered with sheepskin and beaten by Charley's own hands or by another slave called Jackey Quackenboss, who sat astride it crying "Hi-a-momba, bomba, bomba!" Another description says that the drum was made of a box, that its two heads were both covered with sheepskin, and that Charley himself performed on it, chanting African airs. The Negro women who were not dancing at the moment took up the cry of "Hi-a-bomba!" and clapped with ungloved hands. Usually King Charley led off a dance, sometimes swinging a partner, sometimes performing a double-shuffle-heel-and-toe breakdown. At any rate he was evidently a forerunner of that white entertainer, Daddy Rice of Albany, whose Jim Crow dance and song thrilled the 1830's and prepared an audience for the minstrel troupes of the 1840's.

Except for these pliskies played by Charley, the procedure all afternoon was simple. A dancer simply went on until exhausted, and by nightfall *all* the Negroes were exhausted, while the whites looked on. The Pinkster ode describes *them* too: Dutch, German, Yankee, Vermonter, Indian, French, Scot, Irish, and Welsh, with a dig at the few Englishmen who deigned to attend just to sneer at our barbarities.

After Tuesday the Pinkster week tapered off. On Wednesday there was more dancing on the hill, but the "upper class" of revelers left earlier to attend tea parties and make calls. Thursday and Friday, as Dr. Eights later remembered, were enjoyed by the "humbler classes," and on Friday evening there were usually fights to decide who was champion bully of the city. On Saturday Pinkster Hill was tidied up, broken meats and pastries from the booths were distributed to the poor, and only a few drinking places continued traffic for the "more rude and belligerent."

In April 1811 the Common Council of Albany declared that "boisterous rioting and drunkenness" compelled it to pass an ordinance against the erection of any booth or stalls within the city, "for the purpose of vending any spiritous liquors, beer, mead, or cider, or any kind of meat, fish cakes, or fruit on the days commonly called Pinxter; nor to collect in numbers for the purpose of gambling or dancing or any other amusements . . . or to march or parade, with or without any kind of music, under the penalty of ten dollars or confinement in jail." Perhaps the parades were permitted to continue; an anonymous writer in *Harper's* for 1880 states that the last Pinkster procession in Albany was held considerably later than 1811. At any rate, the memory of the beloved King Charley has never died.—From a paper read by PROFESSOR HAROLD W. THOMPSON of Cornell University before the annual convention of the American Folklore Society, Washington, D.C., December 29, 1949.

(Peg Leg and the Tulsa Race Riot

Many legends have been told about the Tulsa race riot. There are, for example, those about white citizens masking themselves as Negroes to get into the Negro section of the town, those about the KKK burning crosses, and various others. This legend is about Peg Leg.

The Tulsa race riot was brought on when a Negro man had betrusted his white sweetheart. The two worked in a large drugstore in the heart of Tulsa. This drugstore had a storeroom which was on the top floor of the building and which the Negro had charge of. One day while bringing supplies down on the elevator to the drugstore, he and his white sweetheart exchanged heartless words, and she slapped him. This made the Negro angry. He grabbed the girl by the arms and held her very tight. The strength in his bronze muscles caused bruises on her arms.

When they reached the drugstore a group of people were there. The girl, being angry, shouted, "This nigger tried to rape me!" The white people in the drugstore were agitated and tried to seize the Negro. The owner of the store led the Negro to safety, but the Negro was later arrested by the sheriff. The white newspapers played the story up to the extent that both white and colored became very tense. The whites had planned to lynch the Negro, and the Negroes had planned to free him, and so one morning (this was in 1921), a group of Negroes went to the jail on Fourth and Elgin, two blocks from the heart of the downtown district of Tulsa, and freed him. This started the riot.

Peg Leg, a Negro veteran of World War I, lived on First Street, five blocks from where the whites gathered to go into the Negro section and seize the Negro again. Peg Leg had been stealing things from Dick Barton's, a general store that had more ammunition than any other store in town. He slipped in the store and carried away ammunition all day Sunday and until ten o'clock Monday morning, when the white store operators were planning to seize the Negro again. Peg Leg had enough ammunition to hold the whites off while other Negroes looted the store.

Moving to the hill, six blocks from First Street going north, the Negroes made their stand. The whites burned houses, churches, and schools to get the Negroes out in the open, but the Negroes opened fire from the hill and overtook the whites with bullets. Some whites migrated beyond the hill and over the tracks to burn Negro homes. The Negro men on the hill, seeing their homes burn, rushed to save their loved ones, leaving Peg Leg, whose home was south of the hill, alone to battle the mob. He shot round after round of bullets for six hours. He did so much damage that the whites figured the Negroes had reinforcements. So they made a plea to cease fire and offered to let the Negro go free, but the Negroes had a sportsman ask for a franchise for their people. This was granted and the riot ended, but the smell of blood was in the air for months. They carried the bodies of whites away in wagons and threw them in the Arkansas river, south of the Negro district, to keep from revealing how many whites had been killed.

Today in Tulsa the Negroes have a complete section of the city. There everything is operated by Negroes including buses and taxis. Electric-meter readers, water-meter readers, milkmen, department store owners, and theater owners are all Negroes. At one time the Negroes had their own court house, and the building stands today as a living monument to fighting Peg Leg of the Tulsa race riot of 1921.

—CURLEE HACKMON

Nancy Vaughn

Nancy Vaughn said that her story would be written into a book, the Lord had told her so. Now that it appears in print the least of her prophecies finds fulfillment.

The first time that I saw her, Aunt Nancy was seventy-five years old, but she was slim and straight-standing in her cabin door in her starched white prophet robe. She clasped my hand firmly and she looked into my eyes and spoke with the assurance and simplicity of all true prophets. The Lord, she said, had told her I was coming.

The Lord had begun speaking to Nancy Vaughn more than sixty years before our meeting. Her mother, who had belonged to Colonel Irving in Greensboro, had not believed the story that little Nancy heard a voice when there were no people around. So Nancy went on hearing the voice and not telling anybody about it for many years. Indeed she was a grown woman before she knew it was the Lord's voice and understood what it was saying. Then she heard it distinctly:

"Dress yourself in a white robe," said the Lord, "I'll tell you how to make it; and go tell the Pope I say his time is nigh."

"I'll go, Lord," said Nancy, "but I was born in slave time, an' all I been doin' since the war is a little washin' for the white folks here in Eutaw, and I ain't got no money."

"You go and see Sister Jane about that," said the Lord.

So Nancy made herself a white robe according to what the Lord told her and she walked over to see Sister Jane.

"Sis Jane," said Nancy, "the Lord tol' me to dress this way and go tell the Pope his time is nigh. I tol' him I ain't got no money and he say, 'You go see Sister Jane about that.'"

"Well," said Sister Jane, "if the Lord say so, must be so. This is my house and land and maybe we can get enough money from it somehow." . . .

Sister Jane got six hundred dollars for a mortgage on her place and she made herself a white robe, and she and Aunt Nancy went to Rome. They took a steamboat from Mobile, and then a train.

"We got a 'terpreter when we got to the city of Rome," Nancy said, "and he took us to the Pope. 'Course he speak nothin' but Latin an' all we could speak was English, so the 'terpreter had to tell him what I said. First we kneeled down and then the Pope come in an' I riz up an' I said, 'Pope, you ain't been rulin' right an' your time is nigh.'

"The 'terpreter tol' him what I said and then the Pope said somethin' in Latin, I never did know what it was. Then we went away from there an' took a steamboat an' went to Jerusalem an' Japan an' then come on back home. An' by the time we got back to Eutaw the Pope was dead. An' the trip cost the Lord just seven hundred and eighty-eight dollars."

Neither Aunt Nancy nor Sister Jane ever elaborated on the details of their trip so far as I know. This is the story of their journey as they have told it to me again and again and as they have told it to many others. The facts of it have been authenticated.

When Aunt Nancy and Sister Jane came back to the Black Belt, Sister Jane went on with her washing and ironing and planting. She never got her land back. It was sold when the mortgage came due. But Aunt Nancy heard the Lord's voice plainly again. He spoke to her deep down in her heart and told her to go to Birmingham and tell the folks there that they were wicked and a great trouble was coming to destroy them.

A big crowd gathered on Eighteenth Street while the black woman in the white robe was prophesying destruction. Aunt Nancy spoke calmly and certainly, and fear came upon her hearers. Then a policeman forced his way through the people and arrested her.

"They put me in jail, honey. Throngin' the streets was the charge. I tol' 'em one woman couldn't throng the streets but they put me in jail anyhow. An' I tol' 'em, if'n you don't let me out of this here a big wind'll come, bigger'n the tornado that blew the year the stars fell, an' it'll blow the city of Birmingham down. Then in a little while, a black cloud come up. It looked like a storm, an' a man come with some keys an' said he wasn't goin' to take no chances an' he let me out." . . .

After the Birmingham prophecy, Nancy Vaughn wandered the dusty roads of the Black Belt, barefoot, white robed. She stopped at roadside cabins to foretell dire events. She preached against the wicked in the streets of the towns, and the jail doors of Demopolis and Greensboro and Uniontown opened to receive her. When she needed food or clothes she entered white folks' stores and told their owners, "The Lord say to give me this." Usually, since her needs were modest, the suggestion was enough. People laughed at her and made fun of her prophecies, but they were afraid of her, too. Once a storekeeper replied, "Then tell the Lord to send me a dollar for it," but her dignity and her concern over what she considered a sacrilege broke down his resistance.

I saw Aunt Nancy for the last time at the end of a hot Alabama summer day. Her weathered cabin was a golden brown in the mellow light. The white robe stood out against it in sharp relief.

"I tell you, chile, somethin' terrible goin' happen. I don't jes know what 'tis, but hit's goin' to be somethin' awful. So take care of yourself an' behave yourself an' the Lord bless yuh, honey."

She opened her door, standing before the dark interior of the cabin. Her robe was a silver glimmer in the blackness within when I left her.

Now the news has come that Aunt Nancy Vaughn is dead. White folks write me that they miss her on the Black Belt roads, miss her calm, sure voice, her oddly worded prophecies. Her death, they tell me, was as strange as her life. It is something from which to make a religious legend. Had she been a white woman of another age, she might already be destined for sainthood. The white robe, symbol of her devoted life, became a terrible winding sheet. It caught against her stove one night, and Nancy Vaughn left the world she had admonished in a pillar of flame.

(Jim Beckwourth, Frontiersman

In the fall of the year 1829, a small party of hunters from the Crow tribe halted panting and excited at the mouth of a cave in which the quarry, a large bear with several wounds, had sought refuge. There was much discussion and many theories of how to get the bear until at length one member stepped up onto a large boulder and held up his hands for silence.

"Brothers, hear me now," he said. "I, Medicine Calf, would speak." The speaker then waited in silence for assent from the group.

A large muscular man swept his arm outward and answered, "Speak, Medicine Calf."

"We are all great warriors," began Medicine Calf. "All have counted coup many times. Each brave here walks among our people in dignity and honor." He paused, noted nods of agreement and heard their muttered words. "Hoh, Medicine Calf." He continued, "We promise our families meat and skins, we attack 'Old Grandfather' and pursue him to this place. I hear each of my brothers claim he has drawn blood, and now we stop. Here my brothers is a great problem. Do we walk away in defeat and tell our people 'Old Grandfather' is greater than our braves? Do we have our friend trapped or does he have us trapped?" As he paused a new animation appeared on the ring of faces; each brave registered a new interest.

"Speak, Medicine Calf," he heard.

"One among us is great," he continued. "One among us will dance with our 'Grandfather's' head and be warmed with his heavy coat. Now, brothers, who will claim this great honor? I am finished." And Medicine Calf stepped down.

All eyes turned to the cave entrance and with many grunts and 'Hoh's,' the cave was studied. One brave stood erect and recounted many acts of courage in hunt and battle—but finished without offering to enter the cave. Another offered comments on his bravery and shouted into the cave for 'Grandfather' to come out and do battle. Each warrior was well aware that a wounded bear is a dangerous fighter. No one offered to add to his reputation by entering the cave, yet no warrior would chance disgrace by retreat.

Medicine Calf had cannily thought to entice one of the group to enter the cave, but the result was a stalemate.

One among the braves was as crafty as Medicine Calf and he stepped up on the boulder and faced the hunters.

"Our brother Medicine Calf speaks truth, it is great honor to count coup on 'Grandfather' and hear the tale told in long winters to come." He turned his copper face to Medicine Calf. "Although he is not of our birth, the great Medicine Calf is truly our brother. He leads us in battle, he leads us in the hunt; he among us spoke first, and his words asked permission to pursue 'Grandfather'; I do not seek to steal his glory! Medicine Calf, I give my consent." And turning, he inquired, "Do my brothers?"

All faces were relieved. "Hoh, Medicine Calf, Hoh." There was silence and all attention was focused on the great dark warrior who grinned inwardly, knowing his own scheme had placed him in a position of no retreat.

"It is with great honor I hear your words," he said, and he dropped to the ground and studied the bloody trail into the cave with a new interest. So much lost blood might have left 'Grandfather' in a weakened state, thereby the onslaught would be less terrible.

Knowing time was to his advantage Medicine Calf slowly removed his garments and recounted many acts of bravery until he had exhausted considerable time. Then he wrapped a blanket around his left arm, and grasping his knife, he stealthily entered the cave. Soon a terrible din of battle filled the cave and was stilled when Medicine Calf found the great heart with his knife. The huge bear moaned and bawled and died and then there was quiet. Medicine Calf was claw-raked, bloody, and weary with fatigue, yet he kneeled over the bear and spoke softly into the large ear.

"I respect you, 'Grandfather.' You are a great warrior. I am sorry to kill you, but we need your meat for winter. I will wear your skin, we will dance your glory. Now sleep well, oh 'Grandfather.' "

PART I. *Tales*

The Indian mind had spoken. Emerging from the cave he stated simply, "Medicine Calf has defeated our "Grandfather.'"

This was Medicine Calf, Enemy of Horses, Bloody Arm, sub-chief of the Crow Indians. This also was thirty-year-old James P. Beckwourth, a famous American Negro explorer who entrenched himself in the life of the western frontier. He became known and respected as one of the best, as a scout and plainsman of the nineteenth century.

During the first ten years on the frontier he was schooled by experience as a member of various trapping and trading excursions for the famous Sublette. For three or four years he was a constant companion of the noted American scout Jim Bridger, and they remained friends for life.

Jim Beckwourth lived among the Indians for several years and achieved greatness and fame in their midst. He was shrewd, and allowed no opportunity to enlarge on his exploits to pass. His oratory kept the Crows in constant reminder that he, Medicine Calf, Enemy of Horses, was a valuable asset to the tribe. During these years times were good to the Crows. Horse thieving raids were successful, skirmishes with the hated Blackfeet left them victorious.

Beckwourth was also a marrying man, known to have had eight wives during his life, some on the frontier and others in more civilized areas. He spoke often of two sons among the Crows, "Black Panther" and another he referred to as "Little Jim."

The great reputation he held as a trapper and scout pulled him away from his Crow friends. Again, now, he toured the West, shoulder to shoulder at intervals with Jim Bridger, Kit Carson, Jedediah Smith and other noted men of the frontier. For a dozen years—and often as an army scout—he trapped and traded and fought his way through the west, the southwest and to the Pacific Ocean.

An interesting period of his life was during the early gold mining days of California. Beckwourth established a cabin and later a ranch in Sierra Valley, California. While he had a fleeting interest in finding gold, his greatest love was for hunting and exploring. Up and down the Sierra Nevada range he roved, checking each stream and valley. He drifted south a hundred miles and crossed the mountains, roaming the lengths of the great California Valleys. Eventually he found the mining community of Bidwells Bar and spent much time in this area.

At Bidwells Bar his keen sense of direction and geography told him he was immediately westward and below his Sierra Valley ranch. Upon returning to Sierra Valley from a southern route he explored the area to the west, seeking and finding a pass (Beckwourth Pass) he believed could be developed into a route through the mountains, saving many miles and hazards for westbound wagon trains.

Upon discussing the plan of a new Northern Route with an American

40

Valley rancher, Mr. Turner, he was encouraged to continue, and planned for a toll road. Beckwourth the businessman!

Mr. Turner's enthusiasm caused him to help Beckwourth to draw up a subscription list which he headed with a $200 participation.

Full of enthusiasm, Jim Beckwourth moved westward through his pass and emerged at Bidwells Bar. This was the spring of 1850, and excitement about the gold craze was at its peak.

Miners and citizens of the area applauded loudly when Beckwourth told his plan of a new route. The Bidwells Bar Management added several hundred dollars to the fund.

In Marysville, also, his plan was met with enthusiasm, and rightly so, for this city would benefit far more than any other if all westward traffic arrived in Marysville at the end of the road.

The city mayor, Dr. S. M. Miles, and the city council met with Beckwourth and agreed verbally to pay for such a route if he would build it. An amount of $10,000 was mentioned.

Although hesitant to do so without a written contract, Beckwourth received added assurance from the mayor concerning reimbursement. So, using his own funds ($1600) and the subscriptions, he built the road and opened up the pass. It was ready for travel in the spring of 1851, so he traveled to Truckee to lead a wagon train northward to his ranch, then westward through his pass. A wagon train of seventeen vehicles followed Jim down his pass and safely to Marysville. There was wild rejoicing!

A new northern route was established and Beckwourth was assured of payment and reimbursement. It is an extreme irony that due to a severe fire that very night, Marysville was almost burned down and the mayor and his council informed Beckwourth they could not pay. It is on record in the minutes of the council, September 1, 1851, May 9, 1853, and January 1856, that Beckwourth attempted to collect again and again by petition. Eventually he was informed in 1856 that his business transaction and agreement of payment was with members of the city council and management of 1851, and those persons were no longer in office.

During the time he spent in Marysville Beckwourth became acquainted with a writer who was appalled by his experiences and wrote a book of his life.

Beckwourth was popular with the miners and well known for his wild tales. When it became known that a book was written about him, a group of miners in the mountains directed one of their members to purchase a copy of the book when buying supplies. This man could not read and while celebrating in Marysville he tried to buy the book and was instead sold a Bible. When he returned and presented the group with the book they settled around the fire and one opened the book at random and began to read.

"And Sampson went and caught 200 foxes and took firebrands and turned them tail to tail and put a firebrand between two tails, and when he had set the brands on fire, he let them go into the standing corn of the Philistines and burnt up both the shocks and also the standing corn, with the vineyards and olives."

At this point one of the listeners interrupted, "That does it! I'd recognize that as one of Jim Beckwourth's damn lies anywhere."

In his old age Beckwourth was living on a ranch south of Denver where he was contracted and employed by the army to act as a scout through the west, and there to visit the Crow Indians and attempt to pacify them, and keep the peace.

Ultimately Beckwourth rejoined his old friends and hunting companions, and there was great rejoicing and feasting. At this point legend takes over to complete the last chapter of the great American Negro scout, frontiersman and Indian Chief.

Beckwourth's death was due to poisoning. It is believed by some that poison was administered by his friends the Crows. During past days when Medicine Calf, Enemy of Horses, was a chief, the Crows had reigned victorious. After his departure troublesome years followed. They decided—so goes the legend—that this time he would remain. He did.

MEMORIES OF LEAD BELLY

The following stories about Huddie Ledbetter (Lead Belly) were collected in his home town of Mooringsport, Louisiana, from November 1967 to January 1968, by Lynn Butcher and Patricia Rickels of the University of Southwestern Louisiana, Lafayette. The informants were four Negroes: Cynthia Jefferson, about 70, and Maggie Baisley, 71, who first knew Ledbetter as young women in Mooringsport fifty years ago; Maggie's son, Eddie Baisley, 50, who married Ledbetter's daughter Jessie Mae; and Booker T. Washington, 66, who says, "Me and Huddie used to dance and run round together. I used to follow him up. If he was in it, I was in it too."

The informants confirm only partly the image of Lead Belly as a heroic man who could "out-sing, out-drink, out-work, out-love any of his fellows" (Dorson, American Folklore, p. 183): hard-working, hard-drinking people themselves, they do not consider that he excelled in either area. What they remember best and talk about most are his almost uncanny skill as a musician, his power over and appetite for women, his readiness to fight anybody anytime, and the magnificence of his funeral. Incidentally, none of them knew him as Lead Belly. To them he was Huddie (pronounced Yew-dy).

The contributions of each informant are identified by his initials.

(The Power of Huddie's Music

(MB): I *wouldn't* tell you all I *could* tell you—he was so bad. As for the good things, when he began to play was no preacher could keep from movin' his foot. Huddie could beat any bird for singin'. Yes, he could play so. That was a playin' man. His music could make any good Christian move his foot. A good player and a good devil too; women were crazy about that man. I didn't get to but two-three parties where he was round. My husband wouldn't let me. The men sure didn't like him. That Huddie, he would do anything. And I *declare* he could play. Nobody play like that. Well, he naturally could play that guitar. He could *play*, and everyone in the world jumpin'. Now I *know* that about him. And he sing just like a bird. He could naturally sing. He sing by hisself if he didn't have no guitar. Him and that guitar could sing. And the women was *bound* to move they foot. But they watchin' they husbands and scared to move. Lord, I was sittin' up on a little high cheer and he was sittin' there on the floor. I had forgot Oscar [her husband] was sittin' right there. Before I know anything I was just bouncin'. I see him cut that eye at me, like give me a heart attack. No, he didn't like that. But I went on and stopped, because I *did* want to go home that night and go to bed, and if I fuss with Oscar I wasn't gonna get in no bed. No, he didn't like him. Didn't none of the *men* like him. They liked his music all right, but they didn't like their wife havin' nothin' to do with that *movin'* no way on it. They wanted to let her stand still or sit still. And I know *I* sot still. My husband watchin' me. I wanted to go home.

⟨ The Time Huddie Cut Mr. Dick Ellet

(BTW): One time de Salvation Army was playin' uptown for de white folks, and Huddie jine in wid his twelve-string guitar. Flannick an' dem got at him cause de white ladies was laughin' and enjoinin' da music.

(MB): He just thought he was gonna play so well they would accept him with his playin'. That the reason he went in. They didn't invite him in there. Mr. Tom Ellet's brother was the one told him he had to get out of there. He told him he wasn't goin' nowhere. But he did go.

(EB): He went across to the drugstore and bought him a knife and went back and cut Mr. Ellet.

(BTW): Dat man would talk jest as nice an' soft an' easy to you, but he'd cut you up, an' da fust thing you knows you got you entrails in you hands.

(CJ) All da women loved him an' followed him round listenin' to da guitar. We all loved him. I loved him too till I heard he cut people up. He had a mean streak. He come to town an' was walkin' down the street an' Dick Ellett called him a "nigger" an' tried to run him off the street, tellin' him not to come back wid his guitar. An' he pulled out his knife an' cut Dick Ellet all up. You know, he wouldn't take nothin'. He wouldn't let nobody push him around.

(MB): Those white men swore they'd catch him, but they didn't get nothin' but his hat. They hung it on an iron nail and it hung there for a long time. He left town then and didn't come back for a good while. Yes, he was quick to laugh and quick to fight. Got in so much trouble. Caused his mammy and daddy to lose their home, sellin' it to try to help him. But he kept on doin' bad.

⟨ Huddie's Way With Women

(MB): I betcha a heap of marriage was broken up cause of him. If the men wouldn't a said nothin' would a been *all*. The women left they men, cause they was crazy 'bout that music. Now, cause he *was* not pretty— wasn't even good lookin', but they was crazy 'bout his music. They don't care. And he naturally could play.

He was crazy 'bout women. But he had his pick. He didn't take any kinda lookin' woman. He had his *pick*. Cause I know one night he was playin' right up here where Eddie stay—that boy of mine stay up here in that house on the highway. They had a big jump-down up there. And he was *stayin'* with a girl. And both the girl and him were in this room, and she was crazy 'bout him. She was sittin' down with his hat in her lap. He was sittin' here playin'. I wanted to get close to him. I was in the other room, but see I was watchin' my husband. I want to go and scared to go. I went off cross the hall, come out the next door, stand on the porch like I was just lookin', but I try and get in that room. I ease over to the door. I didn't get no further than the door, and I lookin' in. He looked up at me. This girl had his hat, you know, right in her lap, just like this here. He looked up at me and he say to that girl, "Gimme my hat." And told this girl to get up and then me to set down. I declare he done that. I was scared not to set down, and I done set down. And he took his hat and put it in *my* lap. And this girl was standin' in the doorway lookin'. If I'd a been her I never would a stopped till I got to the highway walkin'.

Them men sure were glad Huddie got out from here. They wasn't worry for Huddie when he went to prison. They were glad. They didn't care. If he been goin' to the grave, they wouldn't care. Huddie, they'd kill him, these men. He wasn't pretty. He wasn't good lookin' *at all*. But I declare he had the racket with the women. He had that.

Huddie's Death and Funeral

(BTW): When he died he was singin' a song on his death bed: "Six white horses an' a lion." That was his death song. He knew he was gwinin' to die.

(MB): He was sick then, and after he died, they just sunt him in home. He were put away too. He was in the *nicest* cassit.

(CJ): His body was brought here an' dat man was buried with gold socks an' gold slippers an' his gold guitar.

(MB): And them good-lookin' shoes. He was buried in his Forshun shoes, kind of a reddish color, best-lookin' shoes you ever want to look at. I had never see that befo. And he was lookin' *nice* then. Everybody came what could get in the church. I don't know who were left on the outside—church was full. They knew they were comin' just to see him cause they hadn't see him in *so* long. And they sure see him, cause he ain't change a bit.

(EB): People would get up and say different things 'bout him. There was a lot of them said he was a good man but he had his own ways, just like everybody else. They didn't talk nothin 'bout the lady people.

45

(BTW): Lots of the men didn't say nothin' cause they were glad he was gone, see?

(EB): My daddy wouldn't say nothin', cause he was glad Huddie was dead. He never liked him. Said "If I had to say anything, I'd say he was no good."

Reality-Thinking
Tales

The Negro anecdote, or reality-thinking Negro folk tale portraying real-life situations with human beings as characters, was first collected by William Wells Brown, Negro author and abolitionist lecturer, in 1880, the year Joel Chandler Harris published his first volume of Brer Rabbit stories. Shortly afterward, in 1893, appeared a book of Negro anecdotes by Mrs. A. M. H. Christensen, but not until 1932 was interest in Negro reality-thinking tales revived. In that year the Texas Folklore Society printed in its annual publication a group of slave tales I had collected, and in 1935 a more comprehensive array of these tales formed the bulk of the folk material appearing in Zora Neale Hurston's Mules and Men. The next book of this kind was published in 1945 by the South Carolina Negro Folklore Guild. I was the editor of this collection as well as founder and organizer of the Guild. Next came my The Word on the Brazos, a collection of preacher tales gathered in the Texas Brazos River bottoms (University of Texas Press, 1953). In 1954 I published privately a volume of "snuff-dipping" stories titled Aunt Dicy Tales, in which an elderly Negro matriarch is the heroine.

In 1955 the University of Texas Press published my Dog Ghosts and Other Texas Negro Folk Tales, another group of reality-thinking tales. In 1956 appeared a volume of realistic tales by Richard M. Dorson, Negro

47

Folk Tales in Michigan (*Harvard University Press*), *and in 1958 the same author's* Negro Folk Tales from Pine Bluff, Arkansas, and Calvin, Michigan (*University of Indiana Press*). *My* Worser Days and Better Times, *a collection of practical tales garnered in North Carolina, was published in 1966 by Quadrangle Books.*

The Negro is still busy coining tales of everyday life, folklore in the making—narratives woven into the texture of his times and his environment—like the following:

Two Negroes meet on a street corner in Atlanta, Georgia, and strike up a conversation.

First speaker. *Boy, did you hear 'bout dey gonna move de Rock o' Gibraltar?*

Second speaker. *Man, is you done loose you' mind? You know dey ain't nobody can move de Rock o' Gibraltar but God.*

First speaker. *Yeah, dey is gonna move it, too.*

Second speaker. *Well, who gonna move it?*

First speaker. *Martin Luther King, dat's who.*

Second speaker. *Where he gonna put it?*

GHOST STORIES

(**Little Black Sambo from Guinea**

A long time ago, before the Negroes were freed, there was a slave named Sambo, owned by a planter whose big house was near Gourdvine Creek in Union County, North Carolina.

Now Sambo was no ordinary slave. Others on the plantation were the sons and daughters of slaves. But this Sambo had been smuggled in by a blackbirder who had captured his cargo in Africa.

This little old Sambo looked wild and afraid at the slave market in Fayetteville where the planter bought him. The old folks who tell the story about Sambo say that the planter was a kindhearted man. He felt sorry for the strange black man from Guinea who had come to a strange land. So he didn't work Sambo as a field hand. He let him work in the big house so Sambo could learn the English language from the white folks.

When the bobwhite and the whippoorwill and the red fox would talk from the woods, Sambo would answer them in their own language. He'd often ask the white folks where Guinea was. The white man would take a globe map and tell Sambo that the world was round and that Guinea was on the other side of the earth from Gourdvine Creek.

There was a time when the fever struck whites and Negroes, too. Sambo told the white folks that he was sick of the fever. He said he'd seen a dark man at the edge of the woods—and that the dark man was death.

The white man told Sambo that this was a lot of foolishness, but he wiped the tears away from his eyes when Sambo told him he had to die.

Then Sambo asked his master again where Guinea was. "Is it right straight down, Massa?" he asked.

The planter nodded his head.

Then Sambo said, "Massa, dig my grave way out in the woods, and don't let nobody traipse around it. Bury me on my face, because maybe if I look that way sometime I'll git back to Guinea. If a man yearns for a place maybe he'll get back. Massa, that may take a long time, and that's why I don't want nobody to traipse around my grave."

So when Sambo died the planter had the field hands dig a grave far out into the woods. Then he put out the word that nobody was to traipse around Sambo's grave.

The planter finally died, too, and after freedom came, the planter's family sold the plantation and scattered to the four winds. As the years went by many people forgot that Sambo didn't want anyone to traipse around his grave.

Then strange things began to happen in the woods where Sambo was buried near Gourdvine Creek. The occurrences were told about by fox, coon, and possum hunters. If the hounds chased their quarry into Sambo's woods the dogs would come howling back to their masters, quivering with fear.

Some of the old folks in Union County remembered that they had heard their fathers and grandfathers tell the story about Sambo, who yearned to go back to Guinea. Hunters and hounds feared Sambo's woods for more than a hundred years.

"But today the hounds run fast and free along Gourdvine Creek," said an old man I was talking with recently, who lives near Sambo's woods.

I guess the hounds used to feel little Sambo's homesickness. But now, since the hounds run fast and free, I guess Sambo finally got back to Guinea.

—HEATH THOMAS

⟨ Treasure Hunting Story

One warm summer evening an aged Negress stepped out of her kitchen to the back porch to get a breath of air, and ran right into a white man.

"Hello, Sarah," the white man said. "I want you to meet me behind the milk house at eleven o'clock. I have something for you."

Sarah didn't even answer him. Sarah just opened her mouth and began to scream. She shrieked so loudly that all the other house servants ran out. Then Sarah told them she had met no one but the spirit of her former master, Mr. Mercier.

"It sure was him," Sarah vowed between yells and sobs of terror. "I'd of knowed him anywhere. He done tole me to meet him at eleven o'clock. Just before he vanished, he said he got gold buried behind that milk house. But I don't want no dead man's gold. I don't want to even see no dead man."

Gold! The other Negroes pumped her dry. In a day or two it had spread all through the neighborhood. *Gold!* Even the group's preacher became excited, and finally it was he who led them on a treasure hunt.

They met behind the milk house one night and the preacher took a shovel and began to dig. All of a sudden, as the "reverend" worked away with his shovel he began to yell. He dropped the instrument and sprawled face downward on the earth, crying louder and louder, screaming the Devil had him, that he was dying. The bystanders could hear the sound of a whip lashing through the air, could see the preacher's back begin to cover with thick welts, his shirt darken with blood.

Sarah came running up, fought her way through the paralyzed throng. She shrieked: "Mr. Mercier is whippin' the preacher! I can see him! He's mad 'cause you all went after his gold, and he's whippin' the reverend." No one else could see the wielder of the whip, but they could all see the man, now moaning and writhing in the mud. A few days later he died from the effects of the beating.

⟨ The Sprinkle Man

The longshoreman takes himself very seriously and he takes the river very seriously, with all its ghosts, its legends, and its customs. Every once in a while one of them meets a ghost personally and shines for a long time in his own particular spotlight, for the yarn is never forgotten, but repeated again and again. They never, for instance, forget the fellow who met the Sprinkle Man.

"One day I was walkin' out here," testifies this black laborer, "on my way to work in broad daylight, mindin' strictly to my own affairs. I just happened to turn around and lo and behold! I seen a man sprinklin' dollar bills all over the *banquette*. I know there's no man in his right mind gonna do a thing like that. I called out and asked him why he was doin' that. I begun to think maybe no man in his right mind was gonna see a thing like that. That Sprinkle Man wouldn't answer; he kept right on throwin' them bills around. Then I knew either he was crazy to be doin' that or I was crazy not to do somethin' about it. So I jumped. Man, I jumped right at them bills all over the *banquette*. I jumped and I grabbed. And what do you think I jumped at and what do you think I grabbed at? Leaves. That's what. Nothin' in the world but leaves. All them dollar bills turned into leaves before I could touch 'em. Then that Sprinkle Man stood there and laughed at me. 'See?' he said. 'That's what's the matter with all you people. You puts money first before everything else.' That's how come I know I ain't never gonna be rich. The Sprinkle Man told me so."

A Ghost Voodoo Story

And the riverfront is alive with ghosts, ghosts of murdered seamen and river pirates and stevedores, of great early explorers and of ignominious wharf rats, bad ghosts, good ghosts, and just plain ghosts. Jakie Walker met a ghost one day and the ghost did him a lot of good. Jakie was a roustabout and had been working on the river for more than thirty years, knew most of its secrets and all its tricks, so undoubtedly the story is perfectly true.

Jakie had enjoyed a very hectic evening. He was quite drunk. Now that the party was over and his friends had all drifted homeward, worry of the most profound sort began to seep into his somewhat befogged brain. Mostly on account of his wife. Jakie's wife was one of those strong-minded females with an antipathy to drinking husbands. Sometimes she beat Jakie. That was why he decided not to go home until his condition was less obvious. He started walking and before he realized where he had been drifting he found himself on the wharves where he worked.

"I jest drifted around out there," he explained. "I seen the watchman, but he knowed me, so he didn't say nothin' but, 'Jakie, what you doin' out here lookin' like you sick?' I told him 'bout my woman and he jest laughed and let me alone.

"It felt real good out there, you know, with the wind from the river blowin' in my face and all them nice river smells. I found me a corner and set myself down to rest and try to think what I could tell that woman when I got home. I didn't go to sleep. No, sir. I kept me eyes wide open. Then it happened. Man, I'm tellin' you straight, I can still see that *thing!* It ain't no word of lie, either.

"That *thing* come driftin' right over the top of the river. *It* was shaped jest like a man—only *it* weared a long black gown what dragged behind *it* for a long piece. That *thing* kept comin'. *It* come slowly, too. I wanted to run, but I couldn't. I wanted to holler, but I couldn't. *It* got closer and closer to me. I swear I could feel the heat of that *thing* on my body— that *thing* was burnin' and burnin' right into me. Looked like *it* wanted to crawl through my eyes! And I couldn't do nothin'. I had hell on my hands.

"Then all of a sudden my voice come back. I jest opened my mouth and the words come out.

" 'What I got you want?' I yelled, with that *thing* right there blowin' *its* breath in my face. 'What I got you want?'

"You know that *thing* didn't say nothin' right away? Jest stood there, lookin' at me; and I set there just lookin' at *it*. Then them long arms opened up like a cross and the waves in the water started hummin'. I thought that *thing* was gonna hug me. 'Don't you touch me!' I hollered. 'I ain't got nothin' you want.' Then *it* spoke to me and *its* voice was deep down and awful.

" 'Jakie,' that *thing* said, 'the waves is callin' me back, but I ain't movin' a step until I talks with you. You remembers me, but I ain't tellin' you who I is. I drowned right here in this river. I is a ghost now, Jakie. I is a ghost of the Mississippi River, and I got something to tell you, Jakie. You is gonna leave this here earth soon unless you stops your drinkin'.'

"I didn't say nothin'. I jest looked at that *thing* hard. Scared as I was I was thinkin' even a ghost got nerve to come around and try to rectify my drinkin'.

" 'Jakie,' that *thing* said, 'I done been sent to take you away with me. I done been sent to take you to my watery grave. But you is a good man, Jakie, you really is, outside your drinkin'. All you got to do is stop. Tell me right now, boy, what is your determination in this matter?'

"I thought a minute and I studied a minute.

" 'Ghost,' I said, 'drinkin' is the pleasure of my life. I ain't stoppin' for nobody.'

" 'Jakie,' that *thing* said, 'you knows that ain't my answer.'

" 'Does you know my wife?' I asked that *thing*.

" 'I does,' *it* said, 'an' I knows how you feel, but, Jakie, you gotta stop drinkin'. Now I'm gonna do some of my stuff so as you'll know I mean what I says.'

"Then that *thing* started to do *its* stuff. The waves in the river started rollin' and they started risin'. All of a sudden they makes a noise like I ain't never heared to this day. Then they comes up over that wharf and they was like arms reachin' out for Jakie Walker. Brother, what would you do?

" 'I promises you, ghost,' I said. 'If you will jest go away and take them waves with you, I promises you I ain' never gonna drink again.'

"Then everything was all right. That *thing* turned around and went right away and them waves stopped risin' and stopped rollin' and hollerin' for Jakie Walker. I swear I ain't touched a drop of liquor of no kind since that night. Every payday I totes my money home to my woman and we ain't had much trouble since. And this is the funniest part of it. Do you know that when I got home that night my wife was waitin' for me right in the door? I was scared stiff, but you know what she done? She jest throwed her arms 'round my neck and screams, 'Jakie, honey, I dreamed you was dead. And I sure is glad to see you!' 'Baby,' I says, 'I was almost dead, but I is a new man now.' "

⟨[A Fish Story from Farmville, Virginia

There was once a slave who spent most of his Sundays on the riverbank at a certain famous fishing hole, fishing. This was, of course, against the advice and wishes of his fellow slaves, who assured him that sooner or later some very bad luck would befall him. First they told him that he could not catch any fish on Sunday, " 'cause they wouldn't bite." This prediction, however, proved futile, for Sambo was a very successful fisherman and caught large quantities of fish every Sunday. Sambo's friends then predicted that a fish would kill him if he ate them, but this prophecy failed also, and Sambo still found himself as strong and as healthy as any of his master's slaves. After using every means of persuasion to prevent Sambo's fishing on Sunday, his friends finally decided to apply to their master to stop him, but the master seemed rather indifferent, and said that Sambo had a right to fish on Sunday if he so desired, and that was Sambo's own business.

Finally the young people came to the conclusion that there was no such thing as bad luck, because Sambo was just as lucky as they were, if not more so, but the old people still clung to the idea that "bad luck would sure come to Sambo." Time went on and Sambo's wicked conduct continued. The old people would have nothing to do with such a sinner, while the young people, on the other hand, rather admired him, partly because he was daring and partly because he had apparently proved that the various bad luck theories of the old people were "fogeyism."

But one Sunday, when Sambo was fishing in his usual way, he sat for hours and hours and had not a single bite. He finally noticed a slight quiver of his cork and then he had a bite. He pulled with all his might, and found it difficult to get the fish to the surface. When at last he pulled it out, he discovered that he had caught an animal such as he had never before seen. It had a head like a duck, wings like a bird, and a tail like a fish, and, worse than all, it had a voice like a human being and sang the words it uttered. Sambo was frightened and dropped hook, lines, animal, and everything, and started for the house as fast as his legs could carry him. But the animal sang after him these words:

> "Come back, Sambo,
> Come back, Sambo
> Domie ninky head, Sambo,"

and Sambo came back.

Then the animal sang:

> "Pick me up, Sambo,
> Pick me up, Sambo,
> Domie ninky head, Sambo."

Sambo picked him up.

Then he sang:

> "Carry me home, Sambo,
> Carry me home, Sambo,
> Domie ninky head, Sambo."

Sambo carried him to the house.

Then he sang:

> "Clean and cook me, Sambo,
> Clean and cook me, Sambo,
> Domie ninky head, Sambo."

Sambo cleaned him and put him on to cook, supposing that after he was in the pot he would stop singing commands to him, but he had no such good luck as that, for as soon as Sambo's fish was sufficiently cooked he piped up from the pot in his old musical voice:

"Now take me off, Sambo,
Take me off, Sambo,
Domie ninky head, Sambo."

Sambo took him off.
Then he sang:

"Eat me up, Sambo,
Eat me up, Sambo,
Domie ninky head, Sambo."

Sambo began to eat him up, as he was commanded, but one cannot imagine Sambo as being very hungry under such circumstances, so Sambo ate a mouthful or two and then stopped, but his dinner sang:

"Eat me all, Sambo,
Eat me all, Sambo,
Domie ninky head, Sambo."

Sambo ate him all as he was told.

By this time the slaves from several plantations had gathered, and great consternation and excitement prevailed among the Negroes and white people alike. The old colored people sang and shouted, and many of them said, "I knowed it would come, I knowed; case de Bible said so."

In the meantime, Sambo had swollen to enormous proportions, and he continued to swell till he burst open and the animal came out whole and alive, as he was when caught. He went back to the river singing:

"Don't fish on Sunday,
Don't fish on Sunday,
Domie ninky head, Sambo."

A few minutes after the animal came out, Sambo died.

⟨ Uncle Henry and the Dog Ghost

One Saddy, early in de mawnin' time, Unkuh Henry Bailey rigged up sump'n' 'nothuh to put on an' lef' Clarksville to go down to de big baseball game an' barbecue dey was habin' down to Oak Grove. Unkuh Henry used to eat up baseball when he was a pitchuh on de Clarksville team, so he yit lack to see a good ball game. Dat's de why he was goin' down to Oak Grove dat Saddy mawnin'—to see de Knights of Pythias an' de Odd Fellows play off a twelve innin' tie dey done had de Saddy befo'.

Unkuh Henry rech Oak Grove long 'fo' de game staa't an' gits 'im a good seat on de side on one of de wagons what was stannin' at de fur end of de pastur' whar dey was habin' de barbecue an' ball game. Putty soon de players on bof sides comes lopin' up on dey hosses. Dey ties dey hosses to a fence pos', goes ovuh to de barbecue pit, grabs 'em a big hunk of barbecue, eats hit, an' attuh restin' up a spell, staa'ts to waa'min' up for de game.

But dey was way late gittin' on foot wid de game, attuh all, 'caze one of de pitchuhs dat hab to come from way off somewhar rech Oak Grove 'bout a hour late, an' dis shove de staa'tin' time of de game way back. But Unkuh Henry don' budge till de game am plum' ovuh an' de las' train done lef' for Clarksville. Hit was pitch dark when de game done come to a stop, so de onlies' way dat Unkuh Henry kin git home now is to walk.

Unkuh Henry don' min' walkin' in de daytime, but he don' in no wise relish walkin' down de railroad track in de dark. What pester Unkuh Henry is how is he gonna see whar to walk, dark ez hit done come to be? So he stoops down an' picks up a Coca Cola bottle what layin' on de groun' 'side de wagon he been settin' in an' goes down to de groce'y sto', what yit open, an' buys 'im 'nuff kerosene oil to fill up de bottle. Den he tuck off his neck-tie, folded hit up, an' stuffed hit down in de bottle of kerosene. He struck a match to hit an' ez soon ez hit staa'ted burnin' he lit out to walkin' down de railroad track to'a'ds Clarksville wid de lighted Coca Cola bottle in his han's. Hit was gittin' darker an' darker all de time an' lookin' kinda stormified too, so Unkuh Henry gits rail sho' nuff scairt an' 'magine he sees all kinds of eyes shinin' up at 'im from 'side de railroad track. He fin'ly gits so scairt till he staa'ts to runnin'. He was goin' jes' lack ole numbuh 30 goin' norf, an' 'fo' you c'd say Jack Robinson he done rech Annona, but when he rech it, he stop daid in his tracks, 'caze stannin' rat in fron' of 'im was a great big white dawg wid red eyes. De longer Unkuh Henry eyed de dawg, de bigger de dawg got. "Git back offen me!" yelled Unkuh Henry, hittin' at de dawg, but he cain't dote on de lighted Coca Cola bottle no mo', 'caze he done knocked de necktie outen de bottle on de groun' when he hit at de dawg. So he lit out runnin' down de railroad track again wid de big dawg rat at his heels. Fastuh an' fastuh Unkuh Henry's feet ca'ied 'im to'a'ds Clarksville till fin'ly he reched his house an' falled on de gall'ry limp ez a dishrag, an' jes' a-pantin' for bref. His wife, Aunt Jenny, heerd 'im fall on de gall'ry, so she fetched a oil lamp offen de kitchen table an' comed out on de gall'ry to see what de trouble be wid Unkuh Henry.

When she seed Unkuh Henry stretched out on de gall'ry, she runned in de house an' brung 'im a dipper full of well wadduh. He drunk hit, an' putty soon he set up an' tol' Aunt Jenny all 'bout de big dawg runnin' 'im all de way home from Annona.

Aunt Jenny lissun at Unkuh Henry, an' when he done hab his say, she crack her sides a-laffin'. "Henry, come to think 'bout hit," she say, "you didn't hab to teck no runnin' staa't from dat dawg an' think you was no sho' nuff goner. Dat dawg sperrit was jes' some good Christun frien' what done come back from de grave to bring you good luck an' 'tect you on de way home."

Unkuh Henry was awful sorry dat he done run hisse'f nelly to deaf for nothin', but jes' de same he don' stop short of de dinnuh table whar Aunt Jenny hab him a big dish of collard greens an' neck bones, an' a whole pan full of cracklin' bread waitin' for 'im.

De dawg sperrit didn't mek Unkuh Henry stop goin' to ball games, but he nevuh did stay 'way from home attuh dark no mo'.

❬ The Saturday Night Fiddler

Durin' cotton-pickin' time in de Red Rivuh Bottoms, Saddy was de day dat de cotton-pickuhs what done come from 'way somewhar don' go to baid wid de chickens—'stead, dey buil's 'em plank platfawms on de fawms whar dey's pickin' cotton an' habs 'em a rail break-down ball what las' slap-bang up to de time de roosters staa't to crowin' for daytime Sunday mawnin'.

De fawmuhs cain't in no wise hol' de cotton-pickuhs down neithuh, o' keep 'em from runnin' 'way wid things. Dey hab a sayin' in dat time comin' up de Red Rivuh Bottoms dat "If'n a white man c'd be a nigguh in de Bottoms for jes' one Saddy night he nevuh would wanna be a white man no mo'!"

Dey allus hab a fiddle player to play de music for 'em to dance by evuh Saddy night, an' dey don' do him no dirt 'bout payin' 'im eithuh—he kin allus dote on gittin' 'bout twenny dolluhs for de night, an' dis heah mo'n de schoolteachuh mecks in a couple of weeks. Of a consequence, de news travel 'roun' fas' 'bout de fas' money dat fiddle players meck in de Red Rivuh Bottoms on a Saddy night, so fiddlers from evuhwhichuwhar mecks dey way into de Red Rivuh Bottoms to play for dese Saddy night platfawm dances. Of occasion, a fiddler ebun done come from 'way down in Loozyan-nuh, on t'othuh side of de Red Rivuh, to play for dese Saddy night flang-dangs.

Oncet, one of dese Loozyannuh fiddlers was 'way late gittin' off from Sweespote, an' didn' lan' in de Bottoms till pitch dark. De reason hit was 'way pas' dark when he rech de Bottoms was dat he brung his li'l' brothuh wid 'im. His mama jes' die an' leave his li'l' brothuh, an' de fiddler's de onlies' libin' relative de l'il' boy got, so he hab to tag 'long wid de fiddler wharsumevuh he kin latch on to a job playin' de fiddle.

De fiddler worried a whole heap 'bout gittin' to de Bottoms so late, 'caze he got a extra mouf to feed now. His pocket change rail low, an' he yit don' know if'n he gonna git a job playin' for a platfawm dance dat night. He yit got to go bird-doggin' for a dance to play for, an' his li'l' brothuh's feets is sore, an' his legs achin', an' his tongue hangin' outen his mouf lack a dawg when he been runnin' a rabbit till de fiddler don' wanna meck de li'l' boy walk anothuh-furthuh. So de fiddler looks at his li'l' brothuh rail pitiful lack, 'caze he know how bad de li'l' felluh am farin'. But whar in de name of de Lawd am he gonna leave de li'l' boy while he hunt for a place to play his fiddle? Dat am de questshun what pesterin' 'im now. But jes' den he look up an' seed a white man joggin' 'long de road on a saddle hoss, an' he stop de white man an' ast him do he know whar's de cotton-pickuhs habin' a dance dat Saddy night, an' do he know whar dey's a place he kin leave his li'l' brothuh whilst he go bird-doggin' for a place to play his fiddle. De white man tell him yeah, dat dey was habin' a big dance piece-ways down de road on de rat han' side, an' dat dey's a ole cottonseed house, 'bout ebun wid whar he stannin' rat now on de lef' han' side, whar he kin leave his li'l' brothuh. De fiddler thank de man, den tuck a box of matches outen his pocket, lit one of 'em, an' look cross de barb-wire fence to de lef', an' sho 'nuff, dere was de cotton-seed house jes' lack de white man done tol' 'im. He tickled to deaf 'bout findin' a place to leave his li'l' brothuh, 'caze he know he was moughty haa'd to crowd ez a fiddler, an' he know dat he ain't in no wise gonna hab no trouble landin' a job to play for a dance, if'n he fin' de place what dey's habin' de dance. Se he tecks his li'l' brothuh by one han', his fiddle in t'othuh'n, clams thoo de barb-wire fence wid 'em, an' goes on ovuh to de cottonseed house. Dey's a ladder leadin' to a winduh on one side, so he clams up de ladder, ca'ies de li'l' boy thoo de winduh, tecks de blankets he ca'ien' on his shoulder for 'im an' de li'l' boy to sleep on, spreads one of 'em out for de li'l' boy to stretch hisse'f out on, an' gibs 'im a paper sack wid some cheese an' crackers an' ginger snaps in hit to eat if'n he gits hungry. He den tecks his fiddle, tells his li'l' brothuh, "So long," an' strikes out down de road to see if'n he kin fin' de spot whar dey's habin' de dance.

De cottonseed piled so high in de cottonseed house almos' up to de top of de ceilin' till de li'l' boy barely hab room to stretch hisse'f out, but fin'ly he manage somehow to git hisse'f fixed so he kin lay down an' res' his tiahed limbs. But his big brothuh ain't been gone no mo'n a couple of minutes when de li'l' boy heahs a puffin' noise, an' when he riz his haid up to see what de trouble be, what you reckon he seed?—some smoke comin' thoo de winduh of de li'l' cottonseed house. De li'l' boy so scairt he pull de blanket ovuh his face rail quick an' staa't tremblin' lack a leaf. He lay dere for quite a spell till fin'ly he gits up 'nuff courage to peek out from unnuh de cover, an' what you reckon he seed dis time?—a great big white dawg stannin' up at de foot of his pallet lookin' down at 'im. De li'l' boy so scairt he cain't ebun holler—he jes' lay dere wonderin' if'n de dawg gonna budge from whar he stannin'—but he jes' stan' dere an' look down at de li'l' boy an' don' meck a soun'.

Fin'ly, de li'l' boy see dat de dawg don' ack lack he gonna bite 'im, so he doze off to sleep an' sleep 'bout eight houahs. When he woke up, hit was 'bout five o'clock in de mawnin', an de dawg was still stannin' ovuh 'im jes' lack he was 'fo' he done dozed off to sleep. Putty soon attuh de li'l' boy wake up, he heerd his brothuh comin' down de road playin' his fiddle, an' jes' 'fo' his brothuh reach de cottonseed house, de dawg turnt into smoke again an' went back outen de winduh he done come in. When de fiddler comed in, his li'l' brothuh tol' im what done come to pass, an' de fiddler 'low dat dat dawg was him an' de li'l' boy's mama, what done comed back from de grave to keep a watch ovuh de li'l' felluh whilst he was fiddlin' for de cotton-pickuhs to dance.

◖ The Half-Clad Ghost

"I knew a' ole man once that alluz wo' two paiah o' draw's. But when he died his wife didn' lay out but one paiah foh 'im. Well, after de fune'l, he kep' a-comin' back an' a-comin' back. Evah night he'd come right in dat front do' o' her house. So she moved from dat place, but he jes' kep' on a-comin' de same. She moved fo' o' five times, an' he jes' kep' on a-comin' back evah night o' de worl'. Finely she talked to some o' her frien's. They asked 'er why she don' talk to 'im. She say 'cause she scared to. But they say foh 'er to say 'What in de name o' de Lawd you want?' So dat night he come ag'in.

"This time she walk right up an met 'im an' say, 'What in de name o' de Lawd do you want?'

"He looked at 'er right study foh a long time, but she nevah move, an' she jes' stan' theah; an' finely he say, 'Honey, gimme 'nother paiah o' draw's please.'

"She say, 'Aw right, I'll give 'em to you,' an' from dat day to this he nevah has come back no mo', she say. An' dat's de way it is: When you ask 'em what in de name o' de Lawd they want, an' then tell 'em you'll give it to 'em, they'll go away and leave you alone."

⟨ The Deserted Village

"Dey's a nigguh village in West Texas dat now's got only 'bout three families in it. Dey used to be about two hun'ud cullud families dah, but one time a ghos' in de shape of a cat come dah, an' it had two haids an' eight laigs. He come to evahbody's house all time. Craps wuz fine out dah den; folks 'ud make two an' three bales o' cotton to a' acre. De ghos' would go into de houses o' de folks an' dey'd feed 'im. N'en dey'd tell 'im when dey wanted it to rain, an' hit 'ud rain.

"One day a nigguh gal cotch a little dove an' put it in a cage. De ghos' come dat night an' say, 'Ef'n you don't turn dat fowl out, you'll die on de third day.'"

"Well, she didn' turn it out, an' sho' 'nough, on de third day she died, an' after de fune'al was ovah, dat ghos' come an' stood on her grave. Yas sah, hit suttinly done dat thing, 'cause my pa he wuz dah, an' he seen it!

"Den all dem cullud folks dey 'cided to kill de ghos'. Dey got after it wid dawgs, guns, an' hosses. De dawgs tracked it ahead an' caught it; but—'fo' de folks got to it, de dawgs had done turn it a-loose. Hit nevah did come back no mo'. But de nex' day, all de craps wuz et up by ants, an' in a yeah's time dey wuzn't but three fam'lies livin' dah, an' dey wuz all white 'uns, an' livin' on poultry fahms.'"

⟨ Two Ghost Stories from the Same Section of Virginia

I

There were two slaves who used to pass an old barn at night when they went to visit their wives on a neighboring plantation. The barn seemed to be unused, except that whenever they passed it they saw a young heifer standing outside of it. This heifer, which was apparently a yearling, did not seem to grow any larger as the weeks went by, but it was nice and fat. At last Gibbie, one of the men, made up his mind that if the yearling was not taken by the time they passed the barn again, they would kill her and take the meat home. The next time they went by, there stood the heifer, and Gibbie went up to her and took her by the horns, calling to his chum to help him. The heifer pulled and twisted, so Gibbie jumped up on her back and tried to hold her. The yearling got to jumping and jumped up off the ground. "Hold her, Gibbie," shouted his chum. "I got her," answered Gibbie, and held on. The heifer went on up until she was nearly out of sight. "Hold her, Gibbie," shouted the other man as Gibbie sailed off into the clouds. "I got her, or she got me, one," called Gibbie, as he disappeared entirely from view. That was the last that was ever seen or heard of Gibbie or the heifer.

II

Before railroads were built in Virginia, goods were carried from one inland town to another on wagons. There were a great many men who did this kind of work from one end of the year to the other. One of them, "Uncle Jeter," tells the following story:

A number of wagons were traveling together one afternoon in December. It was extremely cold and about the middle of the afternoon it began to snow. They soon came to an abandoned settlement by the roadside, and decided it would be a good place to camp out of the storm, as there were stalls for their horses and an old dwelling house in which they themselves could stay. When they had nearly finished unhooking their horses a man came along and said that he was the owner of the place and that the men were welcome to stay there as long as they wanted to, but that the house was haunted, and not a single person had staid in it alive for twenty-five years. On hearing this the men immediately moved their camp to a body of woods about one-half mile further up the road. One of them, whose name was Tabb and who was braver than the rest, said that he was not afraid of haunts and that he did not mean to take himself and horses into the woods to perish in the snow, but that he'd stay where he was.

So Tabb staid in the house. He built a big fire, cooked and ate his supper, and rested well through the night without being disturbed. About daybreak he awoke and said, "What fools those other fellows are to have staid in the woods when they might have staid in here, and have been as warm as I am." Just as he had finished speaking he looked up to the ceiling, and there was a large man dressed in white clothes just stretched out under the ceiling and sticking up to it. Before he could get from under the man, the man fell right down upon him, and then commenced a great tussle between Tabb and the man. They made so much noise that the men in the woods heard it and ran to see what was going on. When they looked in at the window and saw the struggle, first Tabb was on top and then the other man. One of them cried, "Hold him, Tabb, hold him!" "You can bet your soul I got him," said Tabb. Soon the man got Tabb up on the roof of the house. "Hold him, Tabb, hold him," said one of the men. "You can bet

your boots I got him," answered Tabb. Finally the man got Tabb up off
the roof into the air. "Hold him, Tabb, hold him," shouted one of the men.
"I got him and he got me too," said Tabb. The man, which was a ghost,
carried Tabb straight up into the air until they were both out of sight.
Nothing was ever seen of him again.

(A Negro Ghost Story

Down in one of the South Atlantic states in a remote, lonely, and dolesome
spot three or four miles from city, town, or village, stands an ageworn and
weather-beaten log cabin which for miles around has long been famous
as the birthplace and residence of all the ghosts of the neighborhood.

This cabin was always a favorite topic of discussion among the country
fellows of that region, and often on hunting expeditions, when caught late
far away from home, one of them would be tempted to lodge there for the
night. Its ill fame, however, would send him plodding wearily on in search
of a more comfortable abode.

A few of the more daring had on certain occasions braved the situation
and entered the cabin, hoping to spend the night. Curiously enough, however, they were always frightened out of their senses about midnight by
loud rumbling, and deep groans and lamentations, and in a very few minutes
placed two or three miles between themselves and the famous log cabin.

One of those unfortunates was once telling his experience to a number of
friends, stating at the same time that he didn't believe there was a man
under the sun who could stay in that cabin from darkness to daylight.

"Yes dah is, too," said one of the listeners, known as "Uncle Sam."

"If you'll gib me fifty dollahs, a chunk o' bread, a fryin' pan, and all de
meat I kin fry an' eat, I'll stay dah, jes as sho as de wol' stan'."

Just for pleasure the party gave Uncle Sam all he asked, and he proceeded
to take up his post for the night. He went alone, entered the building,
started a fire in the rude fireplace, and just before the time for the ghost
to appear, which was usually about twelve o'clock, he put the pan on the
fire and began to fry his meat. He then lit his pipe, took his seat, crossed
his legs, and enjoyed the sweet-smelling savor of that pig.

Suddenly a small, black, formless being about the size of a common hare
ran out on the hearth, spat across the frying pan into the fire beyond, then
turned to Uncle Sam and said,

"There is nobody here but you and me tonight."

Uncle saw and he didn't see, he heard and he didn't hear. His eyes and thoughts were centered on the meat.

The ghost turned and again spat in the fire, this time about an inch from the frying pan. This made Uncle Sam angry, and without the least thought of danger he rushed at the little imp, saying, "Don't you spit in that meat!"

Then as quick as a flash, the ghost kicked the pan of meat into the fire, gave Uncle Sam a claw between the eyes, and again took its place on the hearth, and said,

"There is nobody here but you and me tonight."

Poor Uncle Sam, trembling from head to foot, rose from a dark corner of the room and said in a stammering voice,

"I-I-I'll not be here long."

He then, like his predecessors, made a line for the door, and not a blade of grass grew under his feet.

⟨ Little Nero and the Magic Tea Cakes

You know ole lady Coleman what lib de secon' house from de chu'ch house down by de railroad crossin'? Well, she hab a girl one time what go 'way somewhar an' ma'ie an' hab a li'l' boy name Nero.

When li'l' Nero wasn' no mo'n five yeahs ole, his mama got kilt in a wreck in one dem "starvation buggies," an' his papa brung de li'l' felluh to lib wid ole lady Coleman, an' pay her for his boa'd an' keep. Ole lady Coleman lub de li'l' felluh ver' much, 'caze he de onlies' gran'baby she got in de whole worl'. She do evuhthing unnuh Gawd's sun to please 'im; she git 'im lots of putty li'l' things to play wid, a li'l' red wagon to ride in, a li'l' red rockin' chaih to rock in, an' a cute li'l' baid wid a feather mattress to sleep on. She hab a li'l' blue feather pillow for his baid, too, an' plenty kivver for 'im to kivver hiss'f up wid when hit comed to be wintuhtime.

De onlies' thing dat ole lady Coleman didn' fare too good wid was li'l' Nero's eatin'; he 'speshly hab a sweet toof, an' lack sweet things to eat all day long. But don' gib a keer how many sweet things ole lady Coleman cook 'im—lemon pies, chocolate cakes, sweet 'tater pies, an' peach cobblers—he wouldn' eat mo'n one o' two bites of 'em. He'd jes' sit 'roun' wid his han's unnuh his chin an' look outen de winduh lack his min' in a transom.

Ole lady Coleman was plum' flabbergasted 'bout de way li'l' Nero was ca'ien on, but don' meck no diffunce how much she coax 'im to eat cake an' pie she fix for 'im, he don' budge. He was gittin' all out of han' when hit comed to de eatin' bizniss, an' didn' look ez pert ez he did when his papa done brung 'im to lib wid ole lady Coleman. Her haa't reched out to de li'l' felluh, but she yit couldn' figguh out how to git 'im to eat de sweet things she cook for 'im.

Ole lady Coleman done jes' 'bout rech de end of de rope wid her patience when sump'n' happen one night dat move li'l' Nero's eatin' stumblin' block outen de way. One night 'bout twelve o'clock, li'l Nero felt sumpin' rail hot lack a win' blowin' in his face, so he waked up an' seed a white puff of smoke comin' in de room thoo de winduh. When de smoke done rech li'l' Nero's baid, it turnt into a big white dawg an' staa'ted coughin' up tea cakes on de flo'. When de dawg done coughed up a lots of tea cakes, he turnt hisse'f into some smoke again an' went back outen de winduh. Li'l' Nero was scairt, but he jumped outen his baid rail quick an' picked up some of de tea cakes an' staa'ted eatin' 'em. De tea cakes jes' suit his appetite, so he et 'bout fifteen o' twenny of 'em. He den went out in de kitchen an' fetched a flour sack an' put de tea cakes what was lef' in hit; den he tuck de sack of tea cakes an' hid 'em unnuh de mattress on his baid.

De nex' mawnin' when ole lady Coleman comed in li'l' Nero's room to call 'im to breakfus', he jumped outen de baid a-grinnin' an' actin' so happy dat ole lady Coleman wonduh what done come ovuh 'im. She say, "Nero, Ah sho is glad youse feelin' so good dis mawnin'; huccome youse so happy?" Li'l Nero don' say a word; he jes' teck his gran'ma by de han', lif' up de mattress, an' show her de flour sack full of tea cakes.

"Whar dese tea cakes come from, Nero?" say ole lady Coleman, so li'l' Nero tell her what done come to pass durin' of de night, an' grabs up 'nothuh han'ful of tea cakes an' staa'ts eatin' 'em.

Ole lady Coleman glad dat sump'n' done happen to meck li'l' Nero happy, but she yit doubt what de li'l' boy say. Putty soon, tho', she switch her min' 'roun', 'caze don' keer how many tea cakes li'l' Nero et durin' de day, de nex' mawnin' de flour sack was plum' full of tea cakes again.

One time li'l Nero's papa comed to see 'im an' tuck a peek at de tea cakes, an' say dem's de same kinda tea cakes de li'l' felluh's daid mama used to cook for 'im all de time.

TALES OF RANCH LIFE

(The Red Toro of Hidalgo County

Roun' 'bout de eighteen-eighties, when cattle raisin' in Texas was jes' gittin' off to a good runnin' staa't, dere was a cullud man down in Hidalgo County what comed to be his boss-man's fav'rite. De reports was dat de why he comed to be his boss-man's fav'rite was 'caze he don' nevuh gib his boss-man "down de country," don' gib a keer if'n his boss-man cuss 'im out evuh day de Lawd sen' 'bout sump'n' 'nothuh dat he ain't done did. He de camp cook on de trail, an' de boss-man's handyman at home on de ranch.

He's allus braggin' to de cowhan's 'round de county 'bout what a great cattleman his boss-man be—'bout de fine stock he raise, an' lots of othuh things. But de thing dat he brag about de mo'es' was a red toro dat his boss-man own. Evuh time he'd git 'mongst a bunch of cowhan's offen t'othuh ranches he'd say, "Y'all oughta see dat fine red toro mah boss-man got. He de onlies' red toro Ah done evuh seed, an' he de smaa'tes' toro Ah done evuh laid eyes on, too."

So one fine day, when he come to talk in dis wise 'bout what a fine red toro his boss-man own, one of de cowhan's offen 'nothuh ranch what was settin' dere lissenin' say, "Lissen heah, if'n dat red toro yo' boss-man own be's so fine, huccome you don' gib us leaveway to see 'im?"

De camp cook say dat's awright wid him, so he say, "Ah tells you what; huccome y'all don' come ovuh to mah boss-man's ranch dis nex' comin' Saddy 'bout three o'clock in de evenin' an' Ah'll show you de red toro."

So dat nex' comin' Saddy, all de cowboys comed ovuh to see de red toro. But when dey gits dere dey ain't nary soul dere 'cep'n de camp cook. So one of de cowboys say, "Whar's de red toro?"

So de camp cook hang his haid down low an' say, "You know, Ah's awful put out 'bout dat; de boss-man was forced to meck a trip up to Washin'ton to see de President of de United States an' he tuck de red toro wid 'im."

"How long he done been gone?" say de cowboy.

"He ain't been gone no mo'n ten minutes," 'low de camp cook.

"Well, when he comin' back?" say de cowboy.

"Oh, he ain't gonna be gone long—he'll be back in de nex' ten minutes," 'low de camp cook.

65

"In ten minutes!" yell de cowboy. "What in de worl' he done rid on dat kin fetch 'im back in ten minutes?"

"He rid de red toro," say de camp cook.

⟨ Ropes Cost Money

'Way fur back when dey hab de open range in Texas, an' cattle raisin' was de style of de worl', dey comed to be a lot of cattle rustlers what'd prowl 'roun' in de nighttime an' steal cattle offen de ranches, den teck 'em off 'way somewhars, bran' em wid dey own bran', an' sell 'em.

One of de ranchers whose ranch dey come to raid de mo'es' was a rancher down 'roun' Cuero what hab a lots of cattle, but who was awful tight wid his money, so he don' hire 'nuff han's to herd an' watch ovuh his cattle. Dis de why de cattle thieves meck so many raids on his ranch. De ole man what owned de ranch was Bill Hanley, an' he try to run his ranch wid jes' two cowhan's, one Meskin an' one Nigguh—de Meskin watched ovuh de herd in de daytime, an' de Nigguh watched ovuh hit in de nighttime. But de Nigguh cain't be in all de paa'ts of de ranch at de same time, so de cattle thieves allus know his whar'bouts, an' when dey ketches 'im off guard, dey goes t'othuh side of de ranch, an' steals de cattle.

De boss-man cuss de Nigguh out all de time 'bout lettin' de cattle thieves steal de cows, an' fin'ly one day he says, "Ah's gonna keep watch ovuh de herd mahse'f tonight, an' Ah boun's you dey ain't nobody gonna steal no cows, neithuh." So he keep watch 'stead of de Nigguh, an' dat night, 'long 'bout two o'clock in de mawnin', he heahs lots of stampedin' an' sees de cattle runnin' evuhwhichuwhar, an' some men drivin' 'em off. He lights out attuh de men, but he ain't went but a li'l' piece-ways 'fo' one of de menses stops an' knocks 'im offen his hoss an' tecks a rope an' puts hit 'roun' his neck, an' hangs 'im to a tree limb. But hit so happen dat, jes' 'bout dis time, de Nigguh cowhan' done heerd de noise an' come runnin' outen de house to see what de trouble be. When he gits dere, he sees his boss-man hangin' by de neck from a tree limb, jes' a-gurglin' in his th'oat, so he rech in his pocket rail quick, tuck out his pocketknife, an' cut de rope from 'roun' de boss-man's neck.

De boss-man cain't git his bref for a long time—de rope done putty nigh strangle 'im to deaf—but soon ez he git so he kin talk, he looks up at de Nigguh cowhan', pints his finguh in his face, an' say, "Huccome you cut dat rope in two?—ropes costes' money! Huccome you didn't untie hit?"

❲ The "George West" Steer

You know dat Texas longhorn steer what am mounted in a big glass case in de coa'thouse square in Gawge Wes', Texas? Dey's lots of tales floatin' 'roun' 'bout huccome hit come to be dere. But Ah knows huccome. Dat steer's a runaway steer what was roped by mah gran'pa. Mah gran'pa was de greates' cowboy who evuh libed, black o' white. Gran'pa nevuh got tiahed of tellin' how he roped dat steer. Here's 'zackly de way he done tol' hit to me:

"Long time ago when de cowboys used to drive cattle up from Souf Texas to Kansas, we run 'cross lots of rattlesnakes, Meskin lions, wild bo'-hawgs, an' dangerous steers.

"Oncet we was drivin' 'bout eight hunnuhd haid of cattle up de trail. We rech de Nueces Rivuh 'bout dark one evenin', chowed, an' staa'ted to hit de hay when sump'n' staa'ted de cattle to runnin'. Hit was a turbul thing to see de cattle stampedin'; dey was haidin' norf an' dere was a steep cliff 'bout a half mile ahaid. You know, whenevuh cattle staa'ts to stampedin' de onlies' way to stop 'em is to circle 'em. You has to turn de lead cow an' t'othuhs will turn attuh'im. De lead critter of dis heah herd was a big steer wid de wides' horns Ah evuh seed.

"Ah jumped on my li'l' white pony, th'owed mah six-shooter 'roun' mah wais', an' was off to stop de stampede all by mahself. Ah was ridin' high, shootin' mah gun, an' gainin' on de lead steer all de time. Ah had jes' 'bout caught up wid 'im when he was 'bout fifty feet from de edge of de cliff. Ah was still ridin' full speed. Jes' 'bout de time he reched de cliff, de lead steer jumped. Ah th'owed mah rope an' hit landed square 'roun' de lead steer's neck. He was hangin' off de cliff wid mah lasso 'roun' his neck! Mah hoss's feet was dug in de groun', an' he was pantin' lack a baby, but Ah done saved de herd, 'caze all t'othuh cattle stopped. When de res' of de crew got dere, Ah was jes' yankin' de steer up to de groun'. Dey didn' b'lieve Ah coulda done a thing lack dat, but dere hit was rat 'fo' dey eyes."

Dat steer ovuh dere is de ver' same one mah gran'pa roped ovuh ninety yeahs ago. Gran'pa was sho 'nuff de greates' cowboy who evuh libed.

⟨ The Palacios Rancher and the Preacher

Oncet dey was a cullud cowboy what done go up de trail for a rich rancher 'roun' 'bout Cuero. Of a consequence, he come to be a knowledge man 'bout cattle, an' dey raisin', an' de prices dey brung. So, li'l' by li'l', he buy a bunch of cattle of his own till he done rech de place whar he hab a putty good herd.

He ain't ma'ied, tho', but he meckin' eyes at de daughter of a fawmuh, what hab a li'l' ranch an' fawm rat 'round' Palacios, so he ast de girl to ma'ie 'im one Saddy night, an' dey gits latched an' buys 'em a li'l' spot of lan' rat close to de girl's pappy's fawm, an' staa'ts to raisin' cattle. Dis cowboy a haa'd wuckuh, so dey comes up fas' in de worl', an' in 'bout six yeahs he done come to be one of de bigges' cattle owners in dem paa'ts.

De girl rail proud of de cowboy, but dey's one thing dat she ain't lack 'bout de way he ca'ie hisse'f, an' dat am dat he ain't evuh traced his steps in de chu'ch house. So one night, 'roun' de turn of de week, she tell 'im dat she think he oughta go to chu'ch wid her, since de Lawd done blessed 'im wid a lots of money an' cattle an' lan'. So de cowboy say dat's awright wid him—he don' hab nothin' 'gainst de Lawd! He jes' ain't hab time to go to chu'ch, he been so busy trawna meck a libin' for 'im an' her.

Howbe-evuh, de nex' comin' Sunday, de cowboy puts on his gamblin' stripe pants an' dress coat an' goes to chu'ch up to Edna, Texas, wid his wife. De chu'ch dat dey 'cides to go to am de Mefdis' chu'ch, what was raisin' money to buil' 'em a new chu'ch house. When de preachuh gits thoo wid de servus an' de las' amen done been said, de cowboy walks up to de preachuh an' say, "Revun, you preached a damn good sermon."

"Now, looka here, brothuh," 'low de preachuh; "Ah don' know who you is, o' whar you come from, but Ah wants to tell you rat now, we don' 'low no cussin' in dis chu'ch house."

"Ah! dat's awright; Ah still says you preached a damn good sermon, Revun," 'low de cowboy. "Ah put a hunnuhd-dolluh bill in de colleckshun plate jes' now."

"De hell you did!" yell de preachuh, an' den he look in de colleckshun plate, an' see de hunnuhd-dolluh bill what de ranchuh done dropped in hit, an' he say, "Damn if you didn'!"

AUNT DICY TALES

(Aunt Dicy and the Mailman

When General Granger landed in Galveston, Texas, on June 19, 1865, and issued a proclamation declaring all Negro slaves in the state of Texas free, the plantation owners in Burleson County were greatly disturbed.

The reason they were worried was that it was cotton-chopping season and they needed the slaves they had formerly owned to thin out the hundreds of acres of cotton they had planted. They would need the slave labor again in August, and September too, because the cotton bolls would be open at that time, and the cotton would be ready for picking.

Many of the plantation owners bargained with their former slaves and made contracts with them to pay them a certain sum of money for every acre of cotton they chopped. But there were a few of the freed Negroes who refused to work for the prices offered them for chopping cotton. Among those who would not accept these wages were Uncle June and Aunt Dicy Johnson, of Burleson County. Both Uncle June and Aunt Dicy had been married before. They had had three children born to them as a result of their second marriage—Pomp, a boy aged sixteen, and two girls, Serelia and Samantha, aged fourteen and twelve, respectively.

Uncle June and Aunt Dicy had heard that there was a German community just across the Burleson County line in Lee County where the farm owners wanted to hire Negro families to help them work their farms, so one Saturday morning, about two months after freedom had been declared, Uncle June, Aunt Dicy, and their children bundled up their clothes and put them in an old wheelbarrow they had bought from their former slave master. They walked all day, each taking turns at pushing the wheelbarrow until they finally reached Lee County. They met a white man on horseback soon after they had crossed the Lee County line, and he told them that there was a German by the name of Schultze who lived about four miles farther down the road who wanted to hire a Negro family to work on his farm.

So the Johnson family continued to trudge along until they came to a gate beside the road that had William Schultze's name painted on it. About five hundred yards back on a hill, nestled among a clump of trees, could be seen a large white house, so the Johnson family entered the gate and started walking toward the house. Before they could reach the house, however, a man came forward to meet them. The man was Mr.

Schultze, and he asked Uncle June and Aunt Dicy what they wanted. They told him that they were looking for a job on a farm and that they had been told he was looking for help. Mr. Schultze replied that he certainly was, and right then and there he hired Uncle June and Aunt Dicy to work for him.

Mr. Schultze had a little three-room shack that he let the Johnson family live in. There was a fresh well of water in the back yard and an old woodshed where they could keep their cordwood dry when it rained. Mr. Schultze also allowed them one acre of land free, on which they could raise as many vegetables as they liked, to help provide them with food. There was a big stretch of woods Mr. Schultze owned, too, and he told Uncle June that he could hunt rabbits, squirrels, and doves there, and kill as many of them as he wished any time he liked. He gave Aunt Dicy permission to gather several bucketsful of plums and peaches from the Schultzes' orchard to make preserves for the Johnson family, and he told the Johnson children they could go down into the pecan grove any time they felt like it and get a flour sack full of pecans. So the Johnson family was very happy—that is, all except Aunt Dicy, who was a snuff dipper and was worried because there was no general store near the Schultze farm where she could buy a box of snuff. She was accustomed to receiving a free box of snuff every Saturday from her former master, Mr. Winn, and now that she had used up all the snuff she had brought with her from Burleson County she was very irritable. She whipped Pomp, Serelia, and Samantha nine or ten times every day for no cause whatever.

This kept up for almost a month until one Saturday when Aunt Dicy was out in her front yard. She looked down the lane and saw the mailman from Lexington loping his horse toward Mr. Schultze's mailbox, so she ran as fast as she could toward the mailbox and reached it just in time to catch the mailman before he got back into his buggy and drove off.

"Mister, mister," said Aunt Dicy handing him a dime, panting and almost out of breath from running so fast, "would you mind bringing me a dime box of snuff from Lexington the next time you come to bring the mail?"

"I'd be glad to, Aunty," replied the mailman. So the next Monday morning when he came by the Schultze farm Aunt Dicy met him at the mailbox, and he gave her the box of snuff she had sent for.

Every Saturday from that time on, as long as Aunt Dicy lived on the Schultze farm, she would meet the mailman and give him a dime to bring her a dime box of snuff. Everybody in the little community knew about Aunt Dicy's practice of sending for snuff by the mailman, so they called a meeting one night and decided to call the little community Dime Box of Snuff in honor of Aunt Dicy. They shortened it later to just "Dime Box," and to this day that little community still goes by the name of Dime Box.

¶ Aunt Dicy and the Snuff Salesman

One year a snuff salesman came to Giddings, trying to sell the store owners in Giddings a new kind of snuff. Levi Garrett, the manufacturer of Garrett's snuff, had a son-in-law named Ralph, who had quit working for the Levi Garrett snuff company and had built a snuff factory of his own. He called the snuff he manufactured "Ralph" snuff, and he claimed that he used the original Levi Garrett snuff formula to make it with. This was the kind of snuff the salesman was trying to sell the merchants in Giddings.

The salesman tried as hard as he could to convince the Giddings merchants that Levi Garrett's snuff was no different from Ralph snuff, but the merchants refused to buy even as much as one box of the new kind of snuff he was peddling. They told him that Levi Garrett's snuff was the only kind of snuff the snuff dippers in Lee County would buy, so it would be foolish to buy any other brand of snuff and put it on their shelves.

The salesman was not easily discouraged, however, so he made one of the storekeepers, named Enoch Bergen, a proposition. The proposition was that Mr. Bergen was to get somebody in Lee County who was a snuff dipper to taste some of Levi Garrett's snuff and some Ralph snuff, and see if he could tell the difference between the two. If the person could not tell the difference between them, Mr. Bergen was to buy three cases of Ralph snuff, and if the person making the test could distinguish between the two this person was to receive five large jars of Ralph snuff free of charge. The person was to be blindfolded and given a pinch of each brand of snuff to taste.

Mr. Bergen knew of no better person to make such a test than Aunt Dicy, so he drove out to Dime Box and got her and brought her into Giddings to make the test. He blindfolded Aunt Dicy with an old red bandanna handkerchief so she could not see, and then took a pinch of Ralph snuff and gave it to her to taste. Aunt Dicy took the snuff, put it on the end of her tongue, and tasted it but didn't say anything. Mr. Bergen then took a pinch of Levi Garrett's snuff and gave it to Aunt Dicy to taste. But Aunt Dicy asked Mr. Bergen to bring her a cup of water out of the water barrel before she tasted it. As soon as he handed her the cup of water she took a swallow of it, washed her mouth out real good, and then put the pinch of Levi Garrett's snuff on the tip of her tongue. "Humph! Humph!" exclaimed Aunt Dicy, the moment she put the snuff on the tip of her tongue, "That's old Levi; I'd know old Levi in the dark."

(According to Where the Drop Falls

One Sunday morning about eight months after Aunt Dicy and Uncle June had been living on Mr. Schultze's farm, Aunt Dicy's nephew Hezekiah, who lived in Caldwell, rode up to the little house where Aunt Dicy and Uncle June lived and knocked on the front door. Aunt Dicy was busy cooking Sunday dinner in the kitchen, so Uncle June, who was sitting in an old, rickety straw-bottomed rocking chair in the front bedroom, opened the door and let Hezekiah in.

Hezekiah shook hands with Uncle June, and then asked him where Aunt Dicy was.

"She's in the kitchen cooking Sunday dinner, son," replied Uncle June. "You know how Dicy is about always fixing something extra for me and the children to eat on Sunday."

"I certainly do," said Hezekiah as he made his way to the kitchen, where Aunt Dicy was busy making biscuits.

Aunt Dicy stopped what she was doing as soon as she saw Hezekiah. She ran up to him and gave him a big hug, asking at the same time how Hezekiah's mother, her sister Liza, was. After greeting Hezekiah and inviting him to sit down in the old rawhide chair next to the kitchen stove, Aunt Dicy went to work finishing the biscuits she was making. Her head was directly above the biscuit dough, and every now and then, as she kneaded it, she would take a thumbfull of snuff out of her snuffbox and put it underneath her lip. She was bending over the biscuit dough and some of the snuff juice had begun to trickle down to the end of the hickory toothpick she had in her mouth, forming a little round ball at the end. As Aunt Dicy continued to make the biscuit dough ready for baking, she turned to Hezekiah and said, "Son, how long are you going to be with us?"

"I don't know, Aunt Dicy," replied Hezekiah, watching the small drop of snuff on the end of Aunt Dicy's toothpick as it threatened to jar loose from the stick and fall in the biscuit dough. "It's according to where the drop falls."

(Aunt Dicy and Booker T. Washington's Speech

After remaining on Mr. Schultze's farm for sixteen years, Uncle June and Aunt Dicy had saved enough money to buy them a little fifty-acre farm of their own. The farm they purchased was about two miles south of Mr. Schultze's farm.

Aunt Dicy had learned to love the community in which Mr. Schultze's farm was located so well that she wanted to live in that same neighborhood for the rest of her life, and Uncle June, being a good husband, did not object.

Several of Aunt Dicy's and Uncle June's Negro neighbors who had worked on nearby plantations had also saved enough money to buy farms, so they all bought small farms in the same section of Lee County as Aunt Dicy and Uncle June did, so all of them could still be together.

There were quite a few farms owned by white people that separated the new community of Negroes from Old Dime Box, but Aunt Dicy's friends, remembering that Old Dime Box had been named in her honor, decided to call the new community Dime Box, too.

After Aunt Dicy and Uncle June moved to their new home they bought two buggy horses and five mules, but Uncle June still kept his saddle horse, Old Roan. He only used Old Roan for hunting trips for the most part, however, because he bought a brand-new rubber-tired surrey so he could hitch up the two fine bay horses he had bought and carry Aunt Dicy to church and other public meetings in grand style.

Serelia and Samantha were away attending school at Prairie View College, and Pomp had long since moved to Houston, so Aunt Dicy and Uncle June, being lonesome, traveled quite a bit attending public lectures, camp meetings, and revivals in nearby towns.

One Sunday, about five years after they had moved to their new home, Aunt Dicy read an article in an Austin newspaper announcing the fact that the great Negro leader Booker T. Washington, principal and founder of Tuskegee Institute, Tuskegee, Alabama, was scheduled to speak in Austin on the next Friday night.

Aunt Dicy and Uncle June had heard about Booker T. Washington and his great work, so they decided to go to Austin and hear him speak. When they reached the park where Mr. Washington was scheduled to speak, the crowd was already seated and nearly all the seats were occupied. But Uncle June finally found two vacant seats near the back of the audience, and he and Aunt Dicy sat down. Shortly after they had taken their seats, Booker T. Washington, his secretary, Emmett J. Scott, the mayor of Austin, the members of the city council, and a few Negro preachers mounted the platform that had been built for Mr. Washington to speak from. After the singing of "The Star-Spangled Banner" by the audience and the offering of prayer by one of the Negro ministers the mayor arose and introduced Booker T. Washington.

The subject of Mr. Washington's address was "Great Americans and Their Contributions." He mentioned George Washington and his contributions to the country, Abraham Lincoln and his contributions to the country, Benjamin Franklin and his contributions to the country, Jefferson Davis and his contributions to the country, Sam Houston and his contributions to the country, Thomas Edison and his contributions to the country, John D. Rockefeller and his contributions to the country, Frederick Douglass and his contributions to the country, and many others.

After Mr. Washington had finished his speech, the crowd—Uncle June among them—applauded so much that the great Booker T. Washington had to take several bows. But Aunt Dicy did not join in the hand clapping. So Uncle June turned to her and said, "Dicy, how come you are not clapping for Mr. Washington like everybody else? Didn't you enjoy his speech?"

"Humph! No, I didn't," replied Aunt Dicy. "He ain't said nothing about Levi Garrett—*he* wasn't nobody's fool."

REALITY-THINKING TALES FROM THE NORTH

⟨[　　　　　　　Twelve Days after Christmas

On Christmas Day start to count twelve days, and they will represent the twelve months. And the first day is January, and watch that day the way it changes up, and the month will change the same way. And write it down so you don't forget. And continue that for the twelve days. After the twelve days it will come back to be the regular months. If that Christmas Day is pretty then you're going to have a nice January. They'll all be different; there's going to be twelve changeable days.

When I was a little girl I'd sit down and write on a tablet what happened all day. Then when the month came up I'd say, "Daddy, do such and such, because it's going to be rainy." Just this year I did that, and I said they were going to have a hard time haying. And it was raining so, lots of people lost their hay. It came 99 per cent true. You know just about what the year in front of you is going to be like.

Then on the twelfth day is Old Christmas Day. That night at twelve o'clock the horses (they don't go by this fast time, you know; they go by standard time, and that must be God's time), they get on their knees and moans and groans and prays. Giving God's thanks, I imagine. It was handed down from my parents. My mother would let us stay up till twelve that night, and then those of us that was old enough she and papa took down to the barn. And there were three mules in the barn, and two or three cows, and a heifer, and an old sow. They were all lying down. At twelve o'clock they got up on their knees and groaned—you know how an animal makes a noise. Yes, they was on their knees about two or three minutes, I guess. And they was all groaning at the same time in their own language. The sow was just falling down, to lay down, when I seed her.

I was about ten or eleven when I first seed that. But I've seen it since. I was growed up too. I carried these kiddies here over to see the barn at twelve o'clock. A German woman, Mrs. Crawflin, told my mother about it when I was five. I think that's how these calendar people know; they've heard it around.

—Mrs. E. L. Smith

(The Talking Mule

One day on the Fourth of July, John's Boss-man called him down to the house, told him to hook up old George that morning, and go down and plow up five acres of new ground. Because the day being the Fourth of July, John didn't want to work, he wanted to take off. So he asks his Boss: "Do I have to work today? I'd like to take today off, being the Fourth of July; I'd like to go to town." And so Boss told him, "No, that five acres got to be done today; it might be raining tomorrow and we got to get that corn in."

So John say, "Oh well, all right." So he hooked old George up to the plow, went on down to the five acres of newground and begin to plow. So he plowed about a couple of hours. George, the mule, he stopped and says, "Oh I sure am tired," then started off again. John looked all around, he didn't see nobody; so he kept following the mule. Then George started talking to hisself again. He said, "Ain't it awful, us poor mules and all the niggers have to work all the time, and the white man gets all the money. Don't never get any rest. All we get to eat is beans and hay."

So old John he told George, "Whoa." Looked all around to see who it was talking. He didn't see nobody; so he hit the mule in the side with a rope, told him to git up. The mule started up again. George said, "I get tired of working all the time, don't you, John?" John told him, "Whoa." He still didn't see nobody. So he thought to hisself, well there ain't nobody here but me and George. So he asked George, "George, was that you talking to me?" George says, "Yes, I asked you don't you git tired of working all the time?"

John took off to the house running. When he got to the farmhouse he was just about out of breath. So Old Boss asked him, "John, what's wrong with you?" John says, "Ain't nothing wrong with me; it's George. He's out there talking." Boss says, "Now, John, you know a mule can't talk. I told you you couldn't have the day off; why don't you give up and go on back and plow the five acres?"

But John says "No, sir, Boss; if you want those five acres plowed, you'll have to go and plow it yourself, newground or old ground." So the Boss begins to feel sorry for him, figures he's out of his head, and talks soft to him. "Aw, come on, John, tell Boss, what did George say to you?" "Well, Boss, I can't tell you that; you don't believe me nohow." "O yes, I do, come on now, what did he say?" John tells then, "Oh he just say he's getting damn tired of working all the time, and you getting all the money, and all the good food. He don't ever get any rest, all he gets to eat is hay."

Boss says, "Oh, John, that's just your imagination. You go on back down there and start plowing. I'll be on down in a few minutes. The day's about half gone and you ain't even got started." So John went on down in the field, hit George in the side with the plow line, told him to get up.

George told him, "Yes, you went telling on me to the Boss; you going to get enough of that one of these days." He says, "Yes, you talk too much. And it will get you in a lot of trouble."

So John told George, "Oh, come on, George, I don't want to tell about your talking to the Boss, I wants to get this five acres of newground plowed." George started on off pulling the plow, made three or four rounds, and said, "I sure am tired."

Off John started to the house again. On the way he met Old Boss coming out to the field. So Old Boss asked him what's wrong this time. John says, "Same thing, George is still talking." Old Boss got a little warm, he thought John was kidding him, see. So he says, "You come on back, John, and if that mule don't talk to me I'm going to hang you to-morrow." (He figured he'd scare John to go to work.) So he and John walked on back to where George was, still hooked to the plow. And the Boss told George to get up.

Mule walked on off and Boss plowed him a furrow or two. Then he says, "See that, John? You go ahead and finish this five acres, 'cause I'm getting tired of fooling with you."

So John says, "Well, you doing all right with him, you keep on, 'cause I ain't going to plow George no more." That made Boss hot, John talking to him like that. But he says, "All right, just take George on to the barn and turn him loose, you can have the rest of the day off." So John took George on down to the barn and unhitched him, and gave him his hay and water.

He was still disturbed about his Boss not believing him; he had never lied to his Boss. So he decided to go on up to the house and eavesdrop, to see what his Boss was talking about at dinner. When he got to the window he heard the boss telling his wife about him, that John was losing his mind, he was going crazy. "We'll have to take him out and shoot him." (That's what they did with mules and slaves, so they wouldn't waste no time with them.)

Well he didn't know what to do, that hit him pretty hard, he being loyal to his Boss and all, and all of a sudden his Boss don't believe him. So he moseyed on back to the barn where the mule was. When he sit down on the manger where George was eating his dinner, George told him, "See, I told you you talk too much. I could have told you Old Boss would never have believed it, about what I said, but you never gave me no time."

John didn't say nothing. So George the mule said, "Oh, well, I guess you'll be better off than I am."

—JOHN BLACKAMORE

⟨ Why the Jews Don't Eat Hog

Once Christ was traveling. He could tell a man anything he wanted to know, what he had in his barn, anything at all. So he came into a Jew's house. He told the people they could ask any question, like what was under a pot, and he didn't have to see it, but he could tell them what was under there. So one of 'em takes him in the house and was holding a conversation, while the Jew told his wife, "Slip out there and put our baby under the wash pot and then turn it down bottom upwards, so no one can see it." So he brings Christ out, and ax him, "You can guess everything, now what's under this pot?" Christ said, "It's a hog." Jew says, "No, it's a baby." The people began to laugh and say, "We knowed you couldn't tell nothing. That's our little baby under that pot." Christ told him, "Set the pot up on its legs, the right side." And there was a hog in it instead of a baby. The Jew said, "I'll never eat no more hog."

He believes the hog will turn into a baby. Jews won't use lard or anythings that comes from a hog, in any way, shape, or fashion.

—J. D. SUGGS

❨ The White Quail

Down in Georgia I worked together every day with a fellow, Walt Howard, for the same white man. Howard used to net quail for his boss. By netting the quail he'd catch them so they weren't bruised or hurt. The net is made out of fishing cord, and stakes crooked over hold the middle part up, about a foot off the ground. When the quail comes to your net, he won't fly over it, as long as you don't get off your mule, and he runs right down underneath the net till he gets to the end, which is closed up in kind of a chute. So all you have to do is pull up your stakes and fold the net together, and the quails' heads will be sticking out. Then you just take your thumbnail and press down tight on top of the bird's head, stick it through his brains, and kill him.

Walt's boss, Lee Callaway, told him about a white quail he'd seen, and promised Walt five dollars if he would go down to his place and catch him. Walt went down on Sunday during Christmas, and found the quail in the cornfield on the creek. He put his net down, went back on his mule to where he'd found the white quail, and drove him back to the net, along with the other quails in the bunch. This white one ran into the net first, and Walt was so glad to get him he jumped down from the mule and made all the rest fly. Then he brought him to the house, and his boss gave him the five dollars. Lee Callaway sent it to a neighbor of his, who was a big-shot politician in Washington.

After Christmas that winter Walt took sick. He was lying in the bed, and the white quail 'peared out before him, and told him to "Catch me now." He turned over and laid on his other side. And this quail 'peared over on that side, and told him to "Catch me now." And after that, you couldn't get him to hunt no more on a Sunday. That broke him up hunting on a Sunday.

That's as true, as real as I'm sitting here.

—E. L. Smith

❨ The Detroit Race Riot

One of the nation's first big race riots occurred in Detroit in the year 1942. Some say that the riot started this way:

It was a hot summer day—a good day to go to the park—so a young

Negro lady decided that she would take her young child to the park. Belle Isle wasn't too far away; she could walk there in about twenty minutes, so she left her one-room apartment and started toward Belle Isle. Finally she reached the bridge. She could feel the refreshing wind from the Detroit River. As she was crossing the bridge a white man walked up to her, and looked at her as if he were crazy. She became frightened and began to walk faster. The faster she walked the faster it seemed the white man was walking, and before she knew it she was running as hard as she could. Her baby was locked between her right arm and her side. She didn't know why she was running; she just knew she was afraid and wanted to get away from the man who was following her. After a long pursuit the white man caught up with her and took her baby and threw it in the Detroit River. The man then ran to his parked car, and got away. The Negro lady rolled herself into a ball as she cried on the sidewalk. Her anger got the best of her, and she ran to a Negro bar and shouted, "A white man just threw my baby in the Detroit River!" The bar was in an uproar. Half-drunk Negro men poured from it, throwing rocks and beer bottles at whites as they passed by. This was the beginning of a riot that many Detroiters remember to this day.

—TYRONE BURKETTE

(Pony Moore's Story

It sometimes happens that in making up a story which isn't true, it has such an appeal to the fellow that creates it that it becomes a reality with him.

I am relating one in which I was the subject, and it was told so often in my presence that it had me rather confused.

The incident grew out of a trip from Chicago to Memphis when my traveling companion was the late Pony Moore.

It was in the days when I had prestige and finance, and my contacts were as strong as the shell game. Being a little apprehensive as to what someone might do while I was in Memphis that might not conform to southern rules I made arrangements to identify myself in police circles.

A Chicago lieutenant of police had written a personal letter to the chief of police in Memphis telling him who I was. That put me in line to be shown special favors, and he also furnished me with a police star. In Memphis I became confidential with Pony and explained to him the layout. I had no occasion to use the star.

Everything went along all right in Memphis, but in checking up on the return trip the question arose as to Pullman accommodations.

As we were taking a late train out, we sent a wire to the Pullman conductor asking for reservations for a drawing room. A southern white man who was taking the train with his wife had wired for the same accommodation. When the train arrived the porter, whom we knew, used his influence with the conductor, and we got the preference. It caused some confusion between the conductor and the man who had wired, but the conductor stood pat.

Now that is just what happened, but this is Pony's version of the story:

He said that the conductor, the man, and his wife came to the drawing room and knocked on the door. We had anticipated what was going to happen, and I had the police star on.

When the conductor demanded that we vacate I flashed my star and said to him: "I have this Negro chained in here with leg irons on. He is a desperate criminal. I put in two weeks down here to try to capture him and take him back to Chicago. He is wanted for murder and robbery. The only way anyone can occupy this drawing room is over my dead body."

Pony could tell the story so well that I finally made up my mind that he really believed it happened.—T. Nan Jones, famous Negro gambler and sportsman; told to, and recorded by, the late Lucius Harper, former executive editor of the *Chicago Defender*.

❲ The Coon in the Box

This here fellow was working on a farm. Colored fellow. One night they was sitting outside, boss said, "Sam, what's that over there behind that log?" "I can't see it, boss." He said, "Well, there's a rumor going 'round that you are psychic." He said, "Well, I gather that it's probably nothing but an old rabbit down there." So they went down and they took a peek and it was a rabbit. Said, "What's that behind the tree there?" Sam looked at the tree, "I can't see it, I guess it ain't nothing but an old squirrel. Maybe a black snake done got it." They look around there and a black snake had bit the squirrel.

White man looked and said, "If Sam is psychic, I'ma make some money off of that." So he said, "Sam, I'ma get all the people out here and next week we gonna get something, and you gonna tell us what it is."

So the white man went and bet up all his property, saying Sam could tell them anything they want. So the one guy, he betted him. He said, "I tell you what. I know a thing you can't guess." So he went down an' got a steel box, then he caught a buzzard. They put the buzzard under the box.

So the white man said, "In the morning, Sam, you got to tell us what's in that box, or my land's up against it." Sam said, "All right, boss." But Sam knew he wasn't psychic, he was just guessing. He eased out of the house 'bout four o'clock in the morning, went and peep under the box. Then he went back to bed. That morning he woke up 'bout ten o'clock. Sam come on out. "What's in the box there, Sam?" Sam said, "Hmm, I don't know. Lord, let me see now. Size of the box, I guess you got a buzzard under there." "Sure is. Sure is psychic, ain't he?"

Guy said, "I'ma get you. Next week I'ma get you. Next week I'ma put something under that box, see if you guess it." "All right, captain." So that next Friday night, came out, put a coon under the box. Sam got up 'bout four o'clock, eased out of the house. The guy had two policemen sitting on the box. Sam couldn't see what was under that one. Sam went back in the house, back to bed. White man came 'round, said, "Sam, if you don't win in the morning, I'm broke. Out of business. I'm ruined. And if you don't say what's under that box tomorrow," he said, "you just one hung child." Now Sam was scared.

So morning came, they woke Sam up, 'bout ten o'clock. Sam came outside, he scratched his head, he looked at the box, looked at the people. Guy whispered to his friend, "He'll never guess there's a coon under there." Sam said, "Well, captain, you all finally got the old coon." So he went free just by saying that.

The Big Watermelon

Fellow from Texas, he was telling how big Texas was. "In Texas, we got miles and miles and miles. Nothing but miles and miles and miles. Well, partner, I tell you, in Texas, when you get up in the morning, comb your hair, stick your comb down on the ground and you strike oil. Yes, suh."

So this Southern fellow said, "Well, has you all been up in New York?" "New York?" "Partner, New York is just the northeast side of Texas. That's all it is now." He said, "Gee whiz, wow, that's a big watermelon over there. Must be about fifteen feet in diameter. Must weigh a good bit. Ooh, it's a big watermelon." So the Southern fellow said, "You all talking about that cucumber laying there?"

⟨ Brand-Name Stories

This here little boy was coming out of the store one night. This cop picked him up. The cop told him, "Say, little boy, what's your name?" "Calvin." "What's your father's name?" "J. W." He said, "What's his last name?" "Dant." "What's your mother's name?" "Schenley Vacco." He said, "Where do you live at?" He said, "Well, I live all the way up in Valley Forge." He said, "Where about in Valley Forge?" "Around Four Roses." "Who's in that place with you?" "Must I tell?" He said, "Yeah! I asked you, didn't I?" "Tokay."

Cavalier took a ride across the desert on a Camel, just 'cause he was in love with somebody called Fatima. Phillip was blasting off to Morris. Now Raleigh decided since he had a Lucky Strike he was going down to Chesterfield's. He had a whole pocket full of Old Gold. And so, last but not least, he decided to go on a Holiday.

REALITY-THINKING TALES FROM THE SOUTH

⟨ Jack and Dinah

One time a woman and a man—old slavery people—one was name Dinah, one was name Jack. Jack and Dinah.

Jack and Dinah was staying with a boss-man, so Uncle Jack, he decided one day (he had got in sorta tough) he wanted some money. He study how to get that money. He say "Dinah, I got to have some money! I'se goin' git that money too!"

Living on plantation places, Jack have a boss-man, wife have a different boss-man. So Uncle Jack gone to his boss-man.

"Boss," he say.

"Well, Uncle Jack, how you feelin' this mornin'?"

"Tough, tough, pretty tough, Boss Cap'n."

"What the matter, Jack?"

"Cap'n, Dinah die last night."

"What! What! Dinah die?"

"Yes, Cap'n. I come to see can I get twenty-five dollars to bury Dinah."

"Twenty-five dollars? You can get a hundred dollars. You think twenty-five dollars is enough? I'll put Dinah away myself. You sure twenty-five dollars enough?"

"Oh, yes, Cap'n Boss. Twenty-five dollars all I needin'."

Uncle Jack take the twenty-five dollars and gone on home. He show Dinah the money. He say, "Now mind, Dinah, you dead!

"I tell the cap'n you dead. Cap'n come here, you dead. You best is dead."

Aunt Dinah lis'n, Aunt Dinah study. Dinah study, she study. Then she raise her head, she say,

"Ah, hah! I can get money too!"

Aunt Dinah boss-man see her comin'. She say,

"Mornin', Boss."

"Well, Aunt Dinah, how you feelin'?"

"Sad, sad. Feelin' terrible this mornin'."

"How come that, Mom Dinah?"

"Jack died last night, lose Jack last night. And my business down here is to see can you lend me twenty-five dollars to bury Jack."

The cap'n boss say, "Twenty-five dollars? I'll not lend you, I'll *give* you twenty-five dollars. I'll bury Jack myself."

"No, no, Cap'n. No, no! Twenty-five enough."

Then Aunt Dinah gone on home, say, "Jack, I get twenty-five, too! But, 'member, you dead. My boss come, you better be dead."

Now they got the fifty.

By and by the two boss-mans have a council together. Meet on the road.

One cap'n say, "Looker here, they tell me Uncle Jack dead."

Other cap'n say, "No, they tell me it's Aunt Dinah dead."

Then Jack's cap'n say, "Well, I give Dinah twenty-five dollars to bury Jack."

Dinah's cap'n say, " 'Spose'n we walks over and see 'bout them two old people. Let's us go see who dead."

Jack and Dinah look 'cross the fields and see who comin'.

Uncle Jack say, "Gracious crown, looker who comin'! We'd all better lay down and dead. Here comes boss-mans, talkin', comin' with the walkin' stick."

Now! Now! Well! Well! Both the old people dead! Nobody to tell 'em to come in. Boss-mans walk in, stand 'round there, and look.

"My! My! ain't that a pity?" one cap'n say.

"You know what's the truth? I would give twenty-five dollars to know which one gone fust."

Uncle Jack jump up. "Me, Cap'n! I die fust."

Aunt Dinah jump up. "No, me! I die fust."

So both of the old people die fust and both get the twenty-five dollars and no debt.

❨ Uncle Si, His Boss-Man, and Hell

De han's in de Brazos Bottoms mos' allus drawed envelopes wid a li'l' green-back in 'em or a dolluh or two in change when de time roll 'roun' for dey share of de crops evuh yeah. Dem what drawed envelopes or a li'l' cash was de han's dat hab a wife an' no chilluns. Dem what hab lots of chilluns was de ones what didn't draw no envelopes and didn' git no cash. Unkuh Si Moore was one of dem what didn't draw no envelope and didn't draw no cash. He hab a big bunch of chilluns when he comed to de old Wilson plannuhtation down to Jerusalem an' evuh year since he lit dere his wife Sadie hab a baby. But hit don't meck no diffunce how big Unkuh Si's fam'ly come to be. When Unkuh Si go up to Colonel Wilson's house evuh yeah at settlement time de colonel 'ud say, "Well, Unkuh Si, lemme see. You got fawty gallons of sorghums, 'bout eighty yaa'ds of calico, gingham, an' percale, fifty-eight pair of brogan shoes, twelve pair of duckins, thu'ty-six jars of snuff, six barrels of sugah, fifteen barrels of flour, a hundred plugs of chewin' tabackuh, fo' dozen pair of black cotton stockin's, five dozen pair of socks, ten bottles of castuh oil, 'leben boxes of Black Draf', seventy poun's of dry salt bacon, ten sacks of navy beans, an' 'bout twenty-five work hats."

When de colonel git thoo readin' off his list, he'd say, "Unkuh Si, yo' bill am settled; you don' owe me nothin'."

Unkuh Si moughty tickled evuh yeah, 'caze his bill am settled. So things run on in dis fashion for quite a spell. Ebun down when Unkuh Si hab four gran'chilluns to come and live wid 'im, de colonel still 'low dat Unkuh Si don' owe 'im nothin' evuh yeah when settlin' time come. Unkuh Si lackun de colonel to David dat de Word tell 'bout, who hab a good haa't an' was allus bein' good to somebody. But he don' pay heed to how many han's he furnishin' for de colonel's fawm; he furnishin' de plannuh-tation wid twenty-fo' good han's evuh yeah. He jes' call to min' what de colonel do for 'im, an' he allus goin' 'roun' talkin' 'bout de colonel boun' to hab lub in his haa't for Jesus, 'caze he don' meck 'im pay nothin' for stayin' on de plannuhtation.

Putty soon, though, de colonel staa't to losin' lots of han's, an' he meck Unkuh Si's fam'ly do mo'n dey share of de work on de plannuhtation. He ebun down meck 'em work on a Sunday. Unkuh Si don' lack dis heah Sunday work, 'caze he say dat de Word say de Sabbath ain't no work day. So he sets down an' begins to keep comp'ny wid de Lawd to fin' out if'n he ain't done error 'bout de colonel bein' a good man. So he talks dis thing ovuh in secret wid de Lawd an' switch his min' 'roun' 'bout de colonel.

So de nex' yeah when de time roll 'roun' for de crop settlement, de colonel reads off Unkuh Si's list lack ez usual, an' when he gits thoo readin' hit off, he says lack allus, "Well, Unkuh Si, yo' bill am settled; you don' owe me nothin'."

"Dat's awright, Boss," say Unkuh Si, "but gimme a receipt dat mah bill am settled in full."

"A receipt?" yell de colonel. "Cain't you teck mah word for hit? Ain't Ah been dealin' fair wid you all dese yeahs?"

"Yas, suh, dat's awright," 'low Unkuh Si. "But Ah'm gittin' ole now, an' youse gittin' ole too, an' we mought die fo' nex' yeah dis time, when hit comes to be time for de settlement, an' when Ah gits up to heabun an' St. Peter asts me is mah bills all paid 'fo' he lets me in de heabunly gates, Ah wants a receipt to show 'im! Ah don' wanna be runnin' all ovuh hell lookin' for you."

Uncle Aaron Loses His Home

Oncet dere was a ole man by de name of Unkuh Aaron what hab a nice li'l spot of lan' 'bout eight miles t'othuh side of Luling dat don' nevuh, in no wise, worry 'bout nothin' unnuh Gawd's sun. He meck de bes' outen life, come hell o' high wadduh, an' he done come to be ninety-eight yeahs ole an' jes' ez spry an' pert ez a sixteen yeah ole. He yit cuttin' cordwood, plowin' up his lan', an' nevuh hab a sick day in his life. Lackwise, he ain't de grumblin' kin'. Whatsomevuh come to pass am awright wid him.

Oncet a white man down to Luling what had been knowin' Unkuh Aaron for many a yeah ast 'im de why he kin stay so young an' pert an' don' nevuh hab a sick spell, ole ez he done come to be, so Unkuh Aaron look up at de white man outen de cawnuh of one eye an' say, "Well, Ah tells you de why Ah's still able to git 'roun' lack a sixteen yeah ole—dis de why: Ah don' dig up de pas', an' Ah don' tote de future." An Unkuh Aaron tellin' de gospel truf, too, 'caze he don' 'low nothin', day o' night, to git de bes' of 'im.

One Saddy attuh Unkuh Aaron done rid into Luling on his mule, ole Joe, to sell some eggs an' butter an' some fryin'-size chickens, what his wife,

Aunt Hetty, done tol' 'im to git shed of so he kin buy some meal for her to meck cracklin' bread, an' git some sugar for her an' Unkuh Aaron to sweeten dey coffee wid, some rat smaa't size li'l' ole boys meets Unkuh Aaron in de lane jes' 'fo' he rech his house an' say, "Unkuh Aaron, we come to tell you dat yo' house done burnt down wid all yo' things in hit whilst you was down to Luling."

"Yeah, chilluns, Ah knows," 'low Unkuh Aaron. "Ah ain't worried so much 'bout de house, but Ah sho am sorry for de chinches an' de fleas."

([## Uncle Aaron Goes Fishing

One rail bright sunshiny Sunday, late in de mawnin' time, when springtime was rat 'roun' de cawnuh, an' de bluebonnets was trawna push deyse'fs up thoo de grass, Unkuh Aaron riz his haid up fum de ole rickety rockin' chaih he was settin' in an' tuck a peek at de fishin' pole he hab hangin' up on de raftuhs of his cabin. He tuck a long, ling'rin' look at de pole, an' den reched up an' pulled hit down offen de raftuhs. Attuh he done tied de fishin' cord rail tight 'roun' de pole, he slung hit 'cross his shoulder, put his feet in de road, an' made his way down to a li'l' ole fishin' hole piece-ways down de main road, 'neaf a bridge what runned ovuh de creek.

De sun was way up when Unkuh Aaron landed at de fishin' hole. He ain't been settin' dere no time haa'dly, unnuh a shade tree wid his elbows restin' on his knees holdin' de fishin' pole, 'fo' Revun Black, de Baptis' preachuh, driv pass de bridge wid his hoss an' buggy on de way to chu'ch. He spied Unkuh Aaron settin' down dere on de creek bank.

Revun Black holler at Unkuh Aaron an' say, "What you doin' down dere, Unkuh Aaron—fishin'?"

"Yeah, Ah is," say Unkuh Aaron.

"Well, is you ketched anything yit?" 'low Revun Black.

"Naw, not yit," say Unkuh Aaron.

Revun Black kin jedge from de way Unkuh Aaron pass de time of day dat he ain't in de mood for no long combersashun, so he don't say 'nothuh mumblin' word to 'im; he jes' tecks his buggy whip, whacks his hoss on de shanks, says "Giddy-ap, Nelly," an' trots on down to de chu'ch house.

Unkuh Aaron ain't got nothin' to draw 'im back home in no hurry, so he still settin' dere on de bank of de creek wid his fishin' pole in his han's when Revun Black cross de bridge on his way back home from chu'ch.

Revun Black spies Unkuh Aaron still settin' dere, so he hollers at 'im again, an' says, "Hello dere, Unkuh Aaron; is you still fishin'?"

"Yeah, Ah is," says Unkuh Aaron.

"Well, is you ketched any fish yit?" says Revun Black.

"Naw, Ah ain't," 'low Unkuh Aaron.

"Well, what's de why you ain't ketched none?" say Revun Black. "Ain't you got no bait on yo' hook?"

"Naw, Ah ain't," 'low Unkuh Aaron, "an' dat ain't all: Ah ain't gonna put none on hit. If'n Ah puts bait on de hook dese fishes gonna staa't to worryin' me."

([Uncle Aaron Orders a Baking Pan

De onlies' kinda mail dat Unkuh Aaron an' Aunt Hetty evuh got was what Unkuh Aaron called "wish mail." Dat's what Unkuh Aaron allus tell evuhbody when dey ast 'im 'bout de kinda mail he git, an' if'n dey ast 'im what in de worl' do he mean by "wish mail" he'd jes' crack his sides a-laffin' an' say, "Ah means dem great big thick books you gits from Sears an' Roebucks, an' Montgomery an' Wards, an' what you looks in an' sees de pictures of sump'n' 'nothuh, an' den says, 'Ah wish Ah had dis, an' Ah wish Ah had dat.' "

But Unkuh Aaron done by-pass de wishin' stage of de game oncet, when Aunt Hetty seed a bakin' pan in Sears an' Roebuck's catalogue an' she ast Unkuh Aaron to teck down de number of de pan an' order hit for her. So Unkuh Aaron goes an' gits his ole writin' tablet an' his nub cedar pencil an' scribbles de number of de pan on hit an' mail in a C.O.D. order to Sears an' Roebuck.

In 'roun' 'bout fo' weeks de mailman lef' a notice in Unkuh Aaron's mailbox tellin' 'im to call at de Luling pos' office, dat de bakin' pan he done ordered done come, so Unkuh Aaron saddles ole Joe, his mule, an' rides into Luling to de pos' office, an' han's de pos'master de notice what de mailman done lef' 'im. So de pos'master gits down de package an' asts Unkuh Aaron for de money for hit, but Unkuh Aaron say, "Open de package up fuss an' lemme see if'n dat's de pan Ah done ordered!" So de pos'master unwrops de package so Unkuh Aaron kin see if'n hit's de pan he done ordered. But when he done unwropped hit an' Unkuh Aaron done tuck a peep at de pan, he turnt to de pos'master an' say, "Ah ain't gonna pay for dat pan."

"Huccome you ain't gonna pay for hit?" 'low de pos'master. "Ain't dat de same pan you done ordered?"

"Naw suh, hit ain't," 'low Unkuh Aaron. "De pan Ah ordered had a chicken in hit."

An' you know sump'n'? Unkuh Aaron jes' walks on outen de pos'office an' jump on ole Joe an' ride on back out to his house, an' leave de pos'master stannin' dere holdin' de pan.

⟨ The Woman Hurricane

Many a storm swooped down on Wilmin'ton and nailed it good, dat dey has, but de one dat give it a catchin' in de side de worstes' was dat woman hurricane dey call Hazel. Dat Hazel sho did nail Wilmin'ton good—didn't take jes' one whop at de town—it took two, dat it did. De first time it blowed in, it tore de roof offen our house, blowed down de walls an' de ceilins, an' if'n me an' my mama an' papa an' little six-years-old brother hadn't a runned outen de house an' falled down on de ground, an' laid dere till de storm done gone on 'bout its neverminds, we'd all been kilt, dat we would. If come putty near washin' us out, but it jes' played aroun' wid a old man's house what lived pieceways down de road fum us, dat it did. De first time it hit it took de old man's house wid it, and carried it way up de coast to James City, an' set it down. Den it turnt 'roun' an' comed back an' got de old man's horse what was tied to a tree in de yard an' carried him an' de tree in de yard up to James City, an' set him an' de tree down in de same yard where it done put de house in de first place, dat it did.

⟨ Who's Ready for Who?

It is interesting to note that the national sit-in movement was begun by four A. and T. College students on February 1, 1960, in Greensboro, North Carolina. The youth responsible for the action was formerly a busboy who worked in the kitchen at a Woolworth Department Store. One day he asked the woman who was managing the kitchen for a raise in salary, whereupon she replied, "I can get niggers for a dime a dozen." That afternoon when the youth drew his pay envelope he took two dimes out of the envelope and said, "Here, take these two dimes and buy you two dozen niggers, 'cause

I'm quittin'." Later that evening he returned to the store with three of his schoolmates, sat down with them at the lunch counter, and ordered a meal. They were refused service. Many tales similar to "Who's Ready for Who?" resulted from this incident.

One time dere was a good old man in Winston. Him an' his wife been married for forty years, an' den one day she die. So de old man send for his son what live in New York City to come live wid him so he won't get lonesome all by hisse'f. De son a good son, so he go 'long wid what his papa want an' come on back home to Winston to live wid 'im.

De boy lan's him a good job at de 'bacco factory right off; so he do all right for hisse'f. He ain't married noways; so it fit in good for him an' his papa to be livin' wid one nother. But durin' of de day his papa, what was a retired railroad man, gets lonesome. So he ask his son to see if'n he can't get him somethin' nother to do at de 'bacco factory. De son say all right, he'll see what he can do. So he talk wid de boss-man, an' de boss-man say he can give his papa little somethin' to do. So de old man start to workin' at de 'bacco factory, too. He like dis here fine, 'cause him an' his boy can be together durin' of de daytime.

Dey have a frien' what run a nice café not far from de factory, name de Little Red Hen Café. So ever day dey goes down to de Little Red Hen to eat dinner together. One day, howbesomever, while dey is on de way to de Little Red Hen to eat, dey looks up an' sees a sign on a white café what read like dis here: "Dis restaurant am integrated." So de boy say, "Papa, les' us go in here an' eat dinner today." "Dat awright wid me," say de papa. So dey goes on in de restaurant an' takes a seat at one of de tables. When dey done set down a waitress comed over to where dey was an' ask 'em what dey like to have for dinner, so de old man say, "I'd like to have a plate of collard greens an' chitlins."

"Sorry, but dat ain't on de me an' you," say de waitress.

"Well den," say de old man, "bring me a plate of backbones an' dumplin's."

"Sorry," say de waitress, "but dat ain't on de me an' you neither."

"Den," say de old man, "bring me a plate of cracklin' bread, baked sweet potatoes, fatback, an' pinto beans."

"Sorry," say de waitress, "but dat ain't on de me an' you neither."

"Well den," say de old man, "if'n y'all ain't got none of dat I don't want nothin'; y'all always 'roun' here talkin' 'bout we ain't ready for y'all yet, but it's t'other way 'roun'. Y'all ain't ready for us yet." Then, turnin' to his son, he say, "Come on, boy! Let's go on down to de Little Red Hen and eat."

(A Laugh That Meant Freedom

There were some slaves who had a reputation for keeping out of work because of their wit and humor. These slaves kept their masters laughing most of the time, and were able, if not to keep from working altogether, at least to draw the lighter tasks.

Nehemiah was a clever slave, and no master who had owned him had ever been able to keep him at work, or succeeded in getting him to do heavy work. He would always have some funny story to tell or some humorous remark to make in response to the master's question, or scolding. Because of this faculty for avoiding work, Nehemiah was constantly being transferred from one master to another. As soon as an owner found out that Nehemiah was outwitting him, he sold Nehemiah to some other slaveholder. One day David Wharton, known as the most cruel slave master in Southwest Texas, heard about him.

"I bet I can make that rascal work," said David Wharton, and he went to Nehemiah's master and bargained to buy him.

The morning of the first day after his purchase, David Wharton walked over to where Nehemiah was standing and said, "Now you are going to work, you understand. You are going to pick four hundred pounds of cotton today."

"Wal, Massa, dat's aw right," answered Nehemiah, "but ef Ah meks yuh laff, won' yuh lemme off fo' terday?"

"Well," said David Wharton, who had never been known to laugh, "if you make me laugh, I won't only let you off for today, but I'll give you your freedom."

"Ah decla', Boss," said Nehemiah, "yuh sho' is uh goodlookin' man."

"I am sorry I can't say the same thing about you," retorted David Wharton.

"Oh, yes, Boss, yuh could," Nehemiah laughed out, "yuh could, ef yuh tole ez big uh lie ez Ah did."

David Wharton could not help laughing at this; he laughed before he thought. Nehemiah got his freedom.

(The Cotton-Pickin' Monkeys

I know this story is an out-and-out lie, and it was never told for the truth. Like a lot of folk tales, it was created only to entertain, and I wish that the good old Dr. Brewer could have heard it as I did, from the daddy rabbit of all Negro storytellers, Harrison Neal. This is how Neal told the story:

Way back 'fo' dey built de dam at de narrows, or de Badin pot rooms, likewise, I bound it must of been 'bout de time de gold mines was goin' full blast, an' long 'fo' my papa was kilt in de old Randolph mine, dey was a old Confed'rate granpappy what done lived to be a real ol' man an' had lots of money an' goods in de worl'. Fack, he 'bout de richest man in all dat neck o' de woods 'roun' Anson County.

When de ol' granpappy been a young man he lef' de plantation an' went an' fit in de war wid de Yankees, an' he did a real jam-up job o' fightin', too, from de fus' to de las'. But when he see de Confed'rates was whipped he lit out for home jes' like Moody's goose, an' got home in time to put in a good crop o' cotton an' tobacco. He ain't poke aroun' none. I bound he make dat dirt fly mo' samer'n a dog when he dig out a rat outen de dirt. De ol' man have a heaps o' luck wid his crops, an' de Lord bless him real good, 'cause when he pay off de croppers what hope him he have about two pots o' money lef'. Dat give him a good start. Fack is, he have a runnin' start, an' dat's de way he go atter things de rest o' his natural-born days. Seem like I heerd dat he married 'fo' de war, an' dat he first an' only chap was born de year dat he git home atter the war. Well sir, de ol' granpappy's wife she up an' die de year atter dat, an' de ol' granpappy have to raise de boy by hisse'f. I ain't never in no wise know what de boy's name been, but when he come to be 'bout twenty-one years old he marry up wid a gal what live in dem parts an' dey have a boy chile. 'Twasn't long atter dis 'fo' a runaway team kilt de ol' man's boy an' de yaller fever kilt his wife de nex' year. Dis leave just de ol' granpappy here to take care o' de granbaby an' raise him.

With all de farms, plantations, sawmills, town property, an' two banks dat de old man own, he ain't got but dis one granbaby. Dat's de most onlies' blood-kin he got in de whole wide worl', so he love him more dan all de rest o' de worl', even he ownse'f. So he set out to do de granchile right. He give him whatsomever he heart desire, but de ol' granpappy ain't spoil de chile. He learn him real good, an' he make him hew to de line; so de boy come to be one o' de smartes' young man in dat neck o' de woods. Wid de ol' man bein' so freehearted wid de boy, it ain't in no shape changed his way of bein' stingy wid everybody else. He been more tighter dan de bark on a hick'ry tree. One day, howbesomever, late in de summer time atter all de crops been laid by, de ol' granpappy call he little granchile to him an' talk like unto dis here: "It's 'bout time now dat you go off somewhere to school an' learn 'bout how de rest o' de worl' live, 'cause you done learnt all dat dere be to be learnt 'roun' here."

So long 'fo' de Jack Frost done make de 'cimmons fall, de boy done trace his footsteps outen Anson County well on de way 'long de road to learnin' 'bout de rest o' de worl'. I boun' he learn real good, too, 'cause in roun' 'bout four years he done know all dey is to know in de school where de ol' man sent him. He have a handful o' know-how, an' know-who, an' wid dis he do a real sho-nuff good job. He work way off yonder in Souf Ameriky, but he job don't in no wise trouble de boy.

So he have a lot of time on he hands, but wid all de know-how he got he ain't fergit 'bout what he done learnt on he granpappy farm. He kinda took up wid dat farm life. So he 'cides to show de people down dere how to grow cotton, an' he puts in 'bout a hundred acres of cotton.

Now, de granson, he right smart 'bout learnin' dumb brutes how to do sumpin' nother. He done trained many a dog on he granpappy's plantation, an' when he had a mind to he broke in all de saddle horses for his granpappy. So atter de cotton done growed up an' de bolls done opened up, an' dey ain't nobody in dem parts what knows how to pick cotton, de granson 'cides dat he gonna get him some monkeys an' learn 'em to pick it, an' he do just dat. He gets him two pet monkeys an' learn 'em how to pick cotton. Dey works so fas' dat ain't no time 'fo' de crop on de whole hundred acres done been gathered. De boy so proud o' de monkeys dat he writ his ol' granpappy an' tell him 'bout how fas' de monkeys can pick cotton.

De ol' man gets de letter what he granchile done writ him 'bout his trainin' de cotton-pickin' monkeys, an' he real proud o' what de boy done do, but he don't have no tickler interest in no monkey business. But in de very nex' letter dat de boy write his granpappy he tell him dat he comin' home for a spell, an' dat he have a demonstration he wants him to witness when he done reach dere. It be 'long 'bout cotton-pickin' time when de boy get dere, an' he done brung de two cotton-pickin' monkeys wid him in a big box wid an air-hole cut in it. De ol' granpappy looks at de monkeys an' ask de boy how come he done brung de monkeys wid him.

De boy tell him dat de why he done brung 'em is dat he got a proposition he wanna put to him dat'll make him mo' richer'n what he already be. At de name of money de ol' granpappy prick his years up mo' samer'n dan a mule what done spy a mad dog, an' say, "Le's hear what de proposition be, son."

So de boy say, "Granpappy, if'n you'll 'vance me ten thousand dollars I'll go back to Souf Ameriky an' get some Injuns to catch me some more monkeys, an' I'll get about a hundred monkeys an' give 'em de knowledge how to pick cotton an' you make 'bout fifty pots full o' money, 'cause it don't in no wise cost much money to feed an' house a monkey."

De ol' granpappy say dat don't make no never-mind 'bout dat—dat he don't want to hurt he white an' colored fieldhan's, 'cause dey is easy hurted anyhow. But de boy say, "Granpappy, dey is easy hurted anyways; dey's used to bein' hurt; so what do dey bein' hurted mean to you makin' fifty pots full o' money?" De old granpappy don't like to say "no" to de boy right off; so he say to make a big loan like dat he have to take de matter up wid de board o' directors o' de bank. De boy say dat so much de better, to have de board o' directors come out to de farm an' witness for deyse'f de demonstration, an' when dey sees what de monkeys can do dey boun' to see de why for makin' him de loan o' ten thousand dollars to buy de monkeys an' sen' 'em to his granpappy to pick de cotton he gonna raise, an' if'n de ol' granpappy can get de board to come out to de farm de nex' mornin' real early 'fo' breakfast he gonna put on a demonstration for dem to witness dat they ain't never witness in all dey born days de Lord done give 'em before.

So dat nex' comin' day, very early in de mornin' time 'fo' breakfast, de board o' directors been out to de ol' granpappy's farm to see de demonstration. But 'fo' de demonstration take off to a runnin' start, de ol' granpappy th'ows a big breakfast for de board o' directors. Dey has eight or nine platters o' ham an eggs, a washpot full o' grits, two or three gallon o' red-eye gravy, twelve pans o' biscuits, an' a five-gallon crock o' de bes' peach preserves. An' to cap de climax dey has three washpots o' coffee to wash all dis food down wid. Atter dey done filled dey craws up wid all dis food, dey goes on down to de cotton field where de boy's gettin' de monkeys' middles tied to a pole what go up dey back; an' in front of dey faces, just far nuff out so dey can't reach it, he have a great big banana danglin' 'fore 'em from a string. Den he take de monkeys an' put 'em 'twix' two rows o' cotton, side by side, wid a cotton sack on dey back, an' starts 'em off to pickin' cotton. De monkeys want dat banana swingin' in front of dey little faces, so de hungrier dey gits de more faster dey walks, de more faster dey works, de more cotton dey picks, an' de more de cotton fly. De board members' eyes almost pops out when dey see dat; an' dey 'low dat dis be de out-doin'est demonstration dey done ever witness. So right dere on de spot de board vote to lend de boy de ten thousand dollars to buy some monkeys an' send 'em back to he ol' granpappy's farm to pick cotton. But de ol' granpappy say, "No, no," dat he ain't gonna do no such a t'ing, an' de board dey ain't neither.

But de headknocker of de board confab wid de ol' granpappy lack dis: "You say 'No' an' dat boy bein' as he is your own flesh an' blood. If'n we's got confidence in him, you is bound to have it, too, 'cause you done raised him up an' give him most o' his know-how." But de ol' granpappy answer him dat it ain't de boy, an' it ain't de monkeys, but just de same de answer be "No."

"Den what is it?" de board headknocker wanna know. So de old granpappy say dat it be dem meddlin' damn Yankees, dat what it be. De board members all look s'prised when dey hears dis, so de headknocker of de board say, "Dey ain't no Yankees dis side o' Washington."

De ol' granpappy 'low dat *he* know dat good as *he* do, but he answer to de proposition still be's "No."

But de headknocker of de board insist on havin' de knowledge to know where do de Yankees come in.

At dis here 'joinder de ol' granpappy riz up straight from his chair an' say, "Y'all doesn't know dem meddlin' damn Yankees like I does. Here's where dey comes in—it's just lack dis: Time we gets dem monkeys here, an' we gets to de place where we's makin' some money out o' 'em, dem meddlin' damn Yankees gonna come down here an' free ever one of 'em."

—W. H. BERT ROBERTS

(The Oklahoma Freedman

The Oklahoma freedman some quarter of a century ago was the most discussed, sought after, and exploited Negro in the United States. Given tribal rights by the Creeks, Choctaws, Cherokees, and Seminoles, many of the freedmen went to sleep at night in their rudely constructed cabins on the lands allotted them and awoke the next morning to find black gold gushing from oil wells in their back yards. The efforts of these overnight millionaires to adjust themselves to a progressive civilization have been the inspiration of many humorous stories that reveal a pathetic simplicity.

THEY WENT RIDING SNOW-WHITE HORSES

It was 1905, and Oklahoma had not yet become a state. But Oklahoma freedmen, rolling in their fabulous wealth, were not unaware that a Republican president was to be inaugurated in Washington on March 4. Good Republicans that they were, they felt that the inauguration would be incomplete without their presence, and accordingly plans were made for the trip some thirty days before the date of the inauguration.

The trip was to be made in style, and it was no occasion for the rank and file of Oklahoma freedmen. Only those with substantial bank balances were accepted as members of the party. Bank balances were checked, a special train was chartered, with a special car carrying snow-white horses bought for the inaugural parade, and on this special train these ebony-hued and bronze members of Oklahoma's black aristocracy arrived in Washington—in style. And those who stood on Pennsylvania Avenue on March 4, 1905, and saw the inaugural parade go by say there was much color and some grandeur in the Oklahoma delegation astride their snow-white horses.

A QUEER CONCEPTION OF BEAUTY

Jim Young was a Cherokee half-breed freedman with an allotment of 160 acres of fertile land in the Arkansas River bottoms near Fort Gibson, the oldest town in Oklahoma.

But Jim was not industrious. Work didn't bother Jim, and Jim didn't bother work. He lived with his mother in a two-room shack and raised just enough to keep body and soul together. Jim rarely ever went to Fort Gibson, but he went to the crossroads church on Sunday nights, attended the church suppers about once a month, and made his appearance at all the funerals and "settings-ups" which preceded the funerals. Life to Jim was drab.

Naturally Jim was a bit eager when he was offered a handsome sum for his 160 acres of land, and it took little persuading to get him to Muskogee where the deal was closed. Despite the sound advice offered him, Jim insisted upon being paid in cash, and with his money safely pocketed—more money than he had ever seen before—he started out to buy some of the things he had never had before.

Erelong Jim saw something that he had never seen before—a horse-drawn hearse—the most beautiful thing that he had ever seen. And in less than an hour he had acquired that glass-enclosed carriage, a team of spirited ponies, harness, et al., and was on his way back to the farm of which he had disposed.

Two weeks later Jim was declared incompetent by the courts, and a guardian was appointed to direct the expenditure of what money he had left.

PAID FOR IN PRIVILEGE

To the McIntoshes money meant little, for they had no idea that the day would ever come when theirs would ever run out. The fortune that was theirs had come without effort, and they were too independent to put forth any effort to increase it or even to consider any ways and means of increasing it.

So when the railroad sought to purchase enough land to build a right-of-way through the McIntosh farm not far from Muskogee, Papa McIntosh turned thumbs down on the proposition with fury. He told the agents of the company that he had all the money he needed, he didn't want the "durned thing" running through his farm, and he wasn't interested. Even when an attempt was made to explain to him how convenient facilities for transportation would be for the people of that section, he dismissed the matter with "Let ev'ry tub set on its own bottom."

But Papa McIntosh changed his mind. Thirty days later, with his white guardian, he made a trip on "one of them durned things," and he was quite impressed with its comforts, speed, etc. Upon his return, he instructed his guardian to have the agents of the company get in touch with him.

Came the gentlemen with contract and check, fully confident that the matter would be closed. But Papa McIntosh had different ideas.

"Tear up that contract and check, boys," he said. "I don't need no money. I 'spect I got more money than the railroads. I'm gwine give you that strip of land on one condition, and I want that in the contract. I want me and my famerly to ride free on that train anywhere we wants to go for the rest of our lives, and I wants any train that comes through this farm to stop when they sees us waiting to ride—day or night."

The railroad got the right-of-way, and the McIntosh family got the privilege.

—Horace S. Hughes, Sr.

(**Too Many "Ups"**

Cotton is raised to some extent in a large number of South Carolina counties, but Aiken is one of the leading cotton-producing sections in the entire state. Quite a few white farm owners in this section have Negro sharecroppers working their land. They have found out that this is a profitable system of farming because they clear a large sum of money without doing a lot of work themselves. They always make an effort to keep Negro sharecroppers on their farms. The Negroes, however, get wise occasionally and leave. They move into the city of Aiken and find out that they can make a better living for their families in town than they can on a white man's farm.

Sometimes the white farmers look them up in Aiken and try to get them to leave the city and return to the farms. Rarely, if ever, however, do the Negroes go back.

One time there was a Negro farmer by the name of George Davis, who left the farm he was working on and went into Aiken to work. One Saturday while he was downtown at a grocery store he met his former farm boss.

"George," said the farmer, "how about gittin' you to farm for me again this year?"

"Naw, suh, Cap," replied George, "Ah wouldn't mind it, but dere's too many 'ups' in dat thing."

"What do you mean by too many 'ups'?" inquired the farmer.

"Oh, well," replied George, "when Ah goes to bed at night de first thing in de mawnin' Ah got to wake *up*; then Ah got to git *up*; then Ah got to dress *up*—go to the lot an' feed *up*. When Ah git back to de house Ah got to eat *up* sumpin; time as Ah finish Ah got to go gear *up*—then hitch *up*. Ah cain't let de mule stan' dere, so Ah haf to say 'Git *up*!' Time Ah done work all de summer an' gather *up* mah crop an' sell it, Ah come to you to settle *up*. You gits yo' pencil out an' figger *up* an' say to me, 'Ah'm sorry but you done et it *up*.' Naw, suh, Ah don't think Ah'll try it."

❲ Little Julia and Her Grandmother's Cat

Once upon a time there was a widow woman up in Cherokee County named Mandy. Her husband had deserted her when her youngest daughter was fourteen years old, and she was forced thereafter to make the living for her family, which was composed of three daughters.

The only thing that Mandy's husband had left her was a small twenty-acre farm, but she managed somehow to send her three girls to Avery Institute in Charleston until they graduated. She was a very devoted mother and never married again. After her daughters married and left home she lived alone on her little farm and hired a man to do the work in the fields.

The two older girls married fine, upright, Christian men, who were very intelligent, but the youngest girl, whose name was Georgia, got a job in Columbia in an insurance office shortly after her graduation and fell in love with an ignorant taxi driver. He was a very handsome man who wore expensive clothes and spent his money freely, but he was also a drunkard and a gambler. People told Georgia what kind of a man he was, but she paid no attention to what they said and married him anyhow.

A short while after the marriage Georgia's husband began to pretend that he was sick and that he was unable to work regularly, so she had to pay most of the living expenses for them from that time on.

Georgia had one child, a little girl by the name of Julia, whom she loved very much. When the little girl was six years old Georgia sent her to live with her mother, Mandy, so the little girl could be company for the old lady and also go to the school, which was very close to Mandy's little farmhouse.

Little Julia enjoyed living with her grandmother very much because Mandy was kind to her and did not swear at her when she made mistakes, as her father did. Grandmother Mandy had a beautiful white cat too, which little Julia liked to play with every night after she had finished her lessons. The cat was very playful and enjoyed letting little Julia stroke his fur and roll him over and over again on his back. One night, however, when little Julia tried to play with him, he took his paw and clawed at her and wouldn't allow her to stroke his fur. This made the little girl very angry so she shook her finger in the cat's face and said, "Youse a damn naughty cat."

When the little girl said this, her grandmother, who was seated in a rocking chair sewing, said, "What dat t'ing you say, chile? Don't you know dat been bad talk?"

"Yassum, Ah knows," replied little Julia. "Ah won't say it no mo', mam, but dat be de way Papa talk when he mad."

"Well," said Grandmother Mandy, "ef Ah hears you say de lak o' sich ergin, Ah's gwine switch you good."

The next night when little Julia tried to play with the cat he started clawing at her again, so she pointed her finger in his face just as she had done the night before and, looking shyly up at her grandmother, said, "Youse de same kin' o' cat you was yistiddy."

❨ The Negro Taxi Driver's Trial

A mayor of a low-country town had brought before him for trial some years ago a well-known Negro taxi driver.

The mayor gave the defendant an opportunity to defend himself and the taxi driver said this:

"Yes'uh Boss, I sho was goin' fas' 'cause I was jest behind you and dere was another car jest behind me. When eber you stops, I has to stop, and when you goes, I goes. And Boss, I keeps right up close behind you, too. I was dat proud 'cause I is jest as good a driver as you is."

There were only two courses open to the mayor after that defense, and they were very clear. Either he must arrest himself for speeding or else he must dismiss the case. The case was dismissed.

(A Yellow Bastard

Tad: Who is you an' wuh is you? I ain' 'member to axe you 'fore dis. Who is you an' wuh is you an' wey you come from?

Yellow Jack: You axe me who I is an' wuh I is an' wey I come from. You axe a heap er question all in one, an' I guh axe you a question:

Who business is it who I is an' wuh I is an' wey I come from? Is you care 'bout me? Is you my friend? I ain' think so. Is you my enemy? I ain' think dat neither. Is you axe me jes for talk an' compersation? Maybe you axe me who I is for laugh an' game makin'. Well, it do not matter. It ain't mek no dif-f'ence wuh you reason. I guh tell you who I is an' wuh I is. It ain't matter ef you laugh or cry.

It ain't make no diff'ence, wuh I is I is. An' when dey puts me in de ground, I is wuh everybody is, or guh be is. You axe me wuh I is. Laugh ef you has a mind to. I ain' care. Grin ef you wants to. I ain't to fault, an' I ain' care.

I have thought an' dream, an' I dream beautiful dream, but it seem like I ain' kin tell my dream. I ain' seem rough enough. I ain' seem man enough to make my feelin's known. My dream ain' nothin' but for laughter for other folks, an' my dream is tear for me an' torment. But I dreams—dat's all dere is for me.

You axe who I is an' wuh I is an' wey I come from.

I come from wey de do' is shet an' I come to wey it still is closed. All I got is dreams, an' dey is drownded. I ain' kin make my feelin's known. Laughin' ain' make no diff'ence now. God has overlooked me. I is not strong enough. I ain' kin make my feelin's known.

You axe me wuh I is an' I guh tell you. I is wuh I is. I ain't wuh I mought er been. To my lonesome self I ain' nothin' but a yellow bastard—laugh, I ain' care—a yellow bastard wid no place—wid no place amongst de white folks an' a poorly place amongst de niggers.

De door is shet to me. Hemmed in on every side, I has nothin' but dreams. An' my thoughts is floatin' out, floatin' out above de tall treetops, here an' dere, listenin' to de wind's soft tune above de treetops an' de clouds. Across de stars dey wander for a lonely moment, an' den back again an' down, down, down into de mire. For de door is shet to me. Hemmed in, hemmed in on every side.

I ain' kin make my feelin's known, for I ain' nothin'—nothin' but a yel-low bastard to whites an' blacks alike. I is wuh I is—nothin' but a yellow bastard—an' I ain' kin make my feelin's known. Laugh, I ain' care.

Tad: I hear wuh you say. I ain' guh laugh an' I ain' guh cry. I ain' know wuh you is.

⟮   Tim and Bill from Summerville

Summerville, South Carolina, is one of the beauty spots of the state. It has long been famed as a winter resort, but it is also interesting for another reason. It is the home of a strange group of people of Indian descent who vary greatly in their physical characteristics—from pale white with blue eyes to dark brown with hair of negroid texture. These people are called "Brass Ankles." No one knows what their origin is, but they consider themselves the equals of whites in the communities in which they live.

In Summerville and vicinity they are accorded all the rights and privileges granted the whites, except in a very few instances. For example, white barbers will not cut their hair in their shops, and the city operates a separate school for the Brass Ankles that goes as high as the seventh grade. This school is taught by white teachers. All the Brass Ankle children, regardless of the color of their skin, attend this elementary school that the city has provided for them. After they finish the sixth grade at this school they are permitted to enroll in the white high school or the Negro high school— either one that they may choose to attend. Usually those who can pass for white attend the white high school, and those of darker complexion attend the Negro high school.

Once there were two Brass Ankle brothers by the name of Tim and Bill. Both of them were in the same grade and both finished the Brass Ankle elementary school the same year. One was white, and the other was brown.

When the school term opened the next September, the boys were sent by their parents to enroll in high school. The light boy, who had blue eyes (Tim), enrolled in the white high school, and his brother, with copper-colored skin (Bill), enrolled in the Negro high school.

The teachers at the Negro high school did not know that Bill had a brother attending the white high school. It happened that Bill struck a boy his first day and was told by the principal to remain after school.

"But Ah can't," Bill replied. "Ah got to go up town and meet my brother —he gits his books up to de white school."

⟮   How Uncle Steve Interpreted Spanish

During slavery time in Texas it was the custom among some of the owners of land and slaves to go every year on one or two horse-trading expeditions into old Mexico. If the owner could not speak Spanish, he usually carried along some Mexican living in the vicinity as an interpreter.

Master Phil Potts had his plans all made to leave for the border on a horse-trading expedition the following Monday morning. On Sunday he received word that the Mexican he had engaged to go along as interpreter was sick and could not go. Without an interpreter the trip would be useless. An interpreter had to be found.

Now Steve, a sharp slave, had for a long time wanted to make a trip into Mexico. On more than one occasion he had tried to maneuver his master into taking him along as a hand, but had never succeeded. Here, he thought, was his opportunity. So he hunted up Master Phil and told him he could interpret Spanish. Master Phil was rather surprised to learn of Steve's linguistic accomplishments, but, as there was no choice, agreed to take him.

Everybody in the expedition was in high spirits except Steve, who was wondering what he was going to say when the test came. They traveled all day and did not see a soul until close to sundown. Then, as they approached a water hole, they saw some Mexicans camped there. One of the Mexicans had a very fine-looking bay horse that at once caught the eye of Master Phil.

"Steve," he said, "ask that Mexican how much he will take for that horse."

"Boss," said Steve, "dat Mescan don't wanna sell dat hoss. Mescans don't trade on Mondays, no-how."

"That's all right," answered his master. "Go on and ask him what he wants for the horse."

"Aw right, Boss," agreed Steve, "but Ah jes' knows he ain' gonna sell 'im terday."

"Oh, hombre," called out Steve, "fo' how muchee you sellee de hossy?"

The Mexican, disgusted at Steve's attempt to speak Spanish, replied, "Usted no bueno," which means "You are no good."

"What did he say, Steve?" asked his master.

"He sez," answered Steve, "that he did not want to sell 'im till Wednesday."

"Ah, go on," said the master. "Tell him we will give him a good price, that we really want the horse."

"Aw right, Boss," answered Steve, "Ah'll tell 'im, but Ah done tol' yuh dat Mescans don' trade on Mondays."

"Oh, hombre," said Steve, "no sellee de hossy sho' nuffee?"

"No sabe," answered the Mexican, meaning "I do not understand."

"Well," asked the boss, "what did he say this time, Steve?"

"He sez he don' wanna sell 'im till Sat'day now, Boss. Ah done tol' yuh dese Mescans don't trade on Monday."

"Now," replied the master, "we have just got to have that horse. He is a wonderful animal. Go on and tell him that we will pay him a big price for the horse."

"Aw right, Boss. But yuh sho' is wastin' yo' time, though, 'case Ah knows dat Mescan ain't gwine trade on Monday."

"Oh, hombre," said Steve, "no sellee de hossy fo' biggee de mon?"

The Mexican, who had some wood piled up beside the road, now thought that Steve, who was pointing in its direction, was asking him the price of it, and replied, "Cinco pesos" (five dollars).

"What did he say this time, Steve?" asked his master.

"Boss, he sho' done gone an' talk foolish dis time. He sez sometimes dat hoss is trottin' an' he thinks he's pacin'."

"All right," said his master, "let's go on to Mexico."

(Elvannah's Leave-taking

Two young colored women, meeting on the road to market one morning, entered into the following narrative:

"Wa's de mattuh, Elvannah, yuh ain' workin' in dat w'ite ooman kitchen no mo'?"

"Who, me? N'on deed, chile; I done lef' dat w'ite ooman kitchen too long. N'on deed I done lef' 'uh fo' good. I'm stayin' home takin' k'yeah mah good cittazun se'f an' mah husban' an' baby chile. N'on deed; I an' huh couldn' git long, an' Gawd knows I tried hahd 'nough to please 'uh. I knowed fum de fus' beginnin' I an' huh wasn't gwine pull togethuh 'dout stumblin', when she say she didn' wan' me go home at night to see mah husban' an' baby chile—wan' compel me to sleep on de crevasus. . . .

"N'on deed, dat ooman was too much. Dat ooman was a cross. What I mean by dat, a i-yun cross fo' me to tote. Yassen deed, dat ooman was a buke-tayshun to mah very soul—Chile, I ben had plusey pains in de side; I bin had mizry 'cross de back; I bin 'flickded wid rummatism in de hip; I bin had to pick moss in de swamp an' mud an' watuh up to mah knees— but chile, dat ooman was de wus' cross I evuh had to tote. Who? Yassen deed.

"Chile, yuh know yo' grammah was a mean ole ooman? But lemme tell yuh, yo' grammah ain' nothin' 'long side dat old Judas Oscah. N'on deed— she ain' no people. She ain' bin birthded. She ain' nothin' but a she-line bawn in a ink-abaytuh.

"But I stayed wid' 'uh long's I could, but I lef' 'uh one day when she try to make a natchal pop-a-show out me fo' a whole pack o' w'ite folks at de dinnuh table.

"Chile, yuh know dey had soup fo' dinnuh; an' she had one ole silvuh-lookin' bowl, an' she say she wan' de soup in de bowl in de middle de table 'fo dey all set down.

"Well, chile, I hunt an' hunt fo' de bowl, an' I couldn' fin' it no whah;

an' I commence gittin' oneasy, 'cause I feah'd she comin' in de kitchen to see wa's de mattuh, an' raise a upsetmen' 'fo all dem people—an' yuh know I don' like no loud cahyn' on, so wat I done—I goes to de dinin' room do' to wait tell she turn 'roun' so's I could tell 'uh wat I wan'. An' Lawd, chile, she turn' 'roun' like real respectable people, an' she say to me sof' as silk: 'W'at yo' disposition, Elvannah?'

"I des look at 'uh, 'cause I could read 'uh min' de same's a di'log.

"I des look at 'uh, an' say: 'No, Ma'am, dat ain' wat I come to ax yuh fo'. I come to ax yuh wat yuh done wid de soup sa-winge.'"

(## Gib Morgan's Fight

Gib Morgan was a peaceful and law-abiding man whose motto was "Live and let live." He tried to get along with everybody, and he generally did. In fact during his long career as a tool dresser, driller, pipe liner, production superintendent, and what not, he had only one fight and he wouldn't have had it if he could have helped it.

Gib was working for a pipe-line company bossing a gang of nigger ditch diggers along the Ohio River. They were all fine hands but one. This one was a big buck who thought he knew more than Gib. He wouldn't do his work right, and when Gib would jack him up, he would give him a lot of back talk. Gib saw that he would have to curb him a little bit or he would ruin the whole gang. So one day when he was particularly sassy, Gib corrected him with a pair of forty-eight-inch pipe tongs.

Well, that nigger grabbed Gib around the waist and they both rolled into the Ohio River and sank to the bottom. The next thing Gib knew the nigger had drawn a knife and started to whittle on him. Gib had to protect himself. He drew out his jackknife and started to work on the nigger. Then began the most God-awful battle that ever took place in the United States.

All the men on the gang stopped work and lined up along the riverbank to watch the fight. The news spread and more people came. The railroads ran excursion trains to the scene, and all the steamboats stopped and tied up. The farmers on both sides of the river charged for standing room and cleared over fifty thousand dollars. Tens of thousands of dollars were bet on the outcome of the fight.

The only way the spectators had of knowing how the battle was going was by watching for the pieces of flesh that came to the surface of the water. When there were more pieces of white-skinned flesh than black-skinned flesh coming up, the odds were in favor of the nigger. When there were more pieces of black-skinned than white-skinned flesh coming up, the odds were in favor of Gib. Not all the pieces, however, came up. When the catfish found out what was going on they gathered from miles up and down the river for a big feast. Every once in a while one would swim between Gib and the nigger and get cut to pieces.

No, Gib didn't kill the nigger.

They fought and they fought until finally their knives got so dull they wouldn't cut any more. They agreed to a truce, so they could come up and grind their blades. When they came out they discovered they had been fighting for two weeks, and they were powerfully hungry. They went to a restaurant and each ordered a beefsteak four inches thick. When they had finished eating, they felt so good they called the fight off.

(John Green Peas

English Translation of a Louisiana Creole Folk Tale

An old Negro, called John Green Peas, lived in a cabin by the king's palace. As all the chickens of the king were being stolen he wanted to save his geese, and he asked John to tell him where to put them. John was delighted to tell him, and the geese disappeared in the same way as the chickens. The king asked John to tell him where to put his money, and John told him to put his gold where he had put the geese. The gold disappeared, also. The neighbors then convinced the king that John was a robber, and the king went with his guards to arrest the old man. John knew what was going on, and he placed on the table a goose with a gold coin under its wings. When the king arrived, John showed him the goose and told him that whenever he needed money the goose would give him some, if he played on the fiddle. The king bought the goose, but when he saw how John had deceived him he had him put into a bag to be thrown into the river. The men who were carrying the bag got drunk and left John for some time in the road. John heard a shepherd coming with his flock, and he began crying that he would not marry the king's daughter. The shepherd took John's place in the bag, in order to marry the king's daughter, and the old man went away with the sheep. The king met John, and the latter told him that he had found the sheep and the gold at the bottom of the river.

The king threw himself into the river and was drowned. Poor simple king, to leave a palace to jump into the river.

PART II

❧❧

The Negro's Religion

Tales

Brother Brown's Announcement

In a certain community in Georgia there was a creek running north and south through the town. Most of the inhabitants were of the Baptist persuasion, and there were two Baptist churches known as the East End Church and the West End Church.

Brother Brown, one Sabbath morning, arose and made the following announcement: "Because of bad health, Brother Smith will have a month's vacation. However, his pulpit will be filled by me, and I wish you all to let it be known that during his absence I will in the morning fill my regular appointments at the East End, in the evening at the West End; while children will be baptized at both ends."

(**The Boy Who Played Jesus**

One time a ol' boy what lived out to Pleasant Plains, in Winton Township, what belong to dat "almos'-white" bunch o' folks dey calls "Free Issues," come to learn how to play de organ an' de piana real good, so no sooner'n he done finish up in de high school he tells his mama an' papa dat he wanna go up de road an' come to know mo' 'bout how to play de organ an' de piana. But his mama an' his papa say "No"—dey ain't gonna have him lightin' out from home at no sixteen years ol'.

After dis de boy sit 'roun' de house an' won't open his mouf to his mama an' papa, but dey hol's fas' to what dey says 'bout him not goin' up de road to come to know how to play de organ an' piana better'n he do now.

Howbeevuh, one Saddy when his mama an' papa done drive into Ahoskie to git some tools for de farm, dis ol' boy packs his clothes into a bag an' goes out to de highway to catch him a ride. He gets him a ride as far as Norfolk, an' from dere he catches de train an' goes on to New York.

When he gets to New York he goes down to Harlem, an' rents him a li'l room in a basement. He got a little money dat he kin call his own, so it la's him a li'l while, but putty soon hit 'gin to give out, an' he starts lookin' for a job. But since his folks was land-ownin' farmers an' hire dey help, dis ol' boy don't know nothin' 'bout no work an' he can't fin' nothin' to do.

Dis worry him a lots, 'cause his money 'bout all gone, so one day whilst he was stannin' on de corner thinkin' 'bout he might have to go back home, a man passed him an' say, "Man, you looks like Jesus"—de ol' boy done really growed a beet-nick beard, so when de man tell him dis he hurry down to his li'l room an' look in de lookin'-glass at hisse'f, an' sho nuff, he do look like Jesus. No sooner'n he done peeked at hisse'f in de lookin'-glass he goes down to a Jew store on de corner an' buys him a long white robe. Dat nex' comin' Sunday he puts de robe on an' goes down to a big Baptist Church in Harlem, an' starts walkin' comin' down de aisle towards de pulpit, when de preacher see him an' say, "Hol' de singin' a minnit. Here comes Jesus. Let's take up a collection for him." So dey takes up $200 an' gives it to de ol' boy. Dat nex' comin' Sunday he goes down to a big Catholic Church an' goes in an' starts walkin' down de aisle wid his han's stretched out, so de priest sees him an' say, "Here comes Jesus, let's take up a collection for him." So dey takes up $200 an' gives it to him. De ol' boy say to hisse'f, "I sho got sumpin good workin' for me now." So dat nex' comin' Sunday de ol boy puts on his long white robe again, an' goes down to a Jew synagogue an' starts walkin' down de aisle wid his han's stretched out. Dere was two rabbis 'ductin' de services, so when dey seed de ol' boy walkin' down de aisle one of 'em yells to de other one, "Go an' git de hammer an' nails quick; de fool's off de cross again."

(Witness of the Johnstown Flood in Heaven

In one place they call Johnstown they had a great flood. And so many folks got drowned that it looked jus' like Judgment day.

So some of de folks that got drowned in that flood went one place and some went another. You know, everything that happen, they got to be a nigger in it—and so one of de brothers in black went up to Heben from de flood.

When he got to the gate, Ole Peter let 'im in and made 'im welcome. De colored man was named John, so John ast Peter, says, "Is it dry in dere?"

Ole Peter tole 'im, "Why, yes, it's dry in here. How come you ast that?"

"Well, you know Ah jus' come out of one flood, and Ah don't want to run into no mo'. Ooh, man! You ain't *seen* no water. You just oughter seen dat flood we had at Johnstown."

Peter says, "Yeah, we know all about it. Jus' go wid Gabriel and let him give you some new clothes."

So John went off wid Gabriel and come back all dressed up in brand new clothes and all de time he was changin' his clothes he was tellin' Ole Gabriel all about dat flood, jus' like he didn't know already.

So when he come back from changin' his clothes, they give him a brand new gold harp and handed him to a gold bench and made him welcome. They was so tired of hearing about dat flood they was glad to see him wid his harp 'cause they figgered he'd get to playin' and forget all about it. So Peter tole him, "Now you jus' make yo'self at home and play all de music you please."

John went and took a seat on de bench and commenced to tune up his harp. By dat time, two angels come walkin' by where John was settin' so he throwed down his harp and tackled 'em.

"Say," he hollered, "Y'all want to hear 'bout de big flood Ah was in down on earth? Lawd, Lawd! It sho rained, and talkin' 'bout water!"

Dem two angels hurried off from 'im jus' as quick as they could. He started to tellin' another one and he took to flyin'. Gab'ull went over to 'im and tried to get him to take it easy, but John kept right on stoppin' every angel dat he could find to tell 'im about dat flood of water.

Way after while he went over to Ole Peter and said: "Thought you said everybody would be nice and polite?"

Peter said, "Yeah, Ah said it. Ain't everybody treatin' you right?"

John said, "Naw. Ah jus' walked up to a man as nice and friendly as Ah could be and started to tell 'im 'bout all dat water Ah left back there in Johnstown and instead of him turnin' me a friendly answer he said, 'Shucks! You ain't seen no water!' and walked off and left me standin' by myself."

"Was he a *ole* man wid a crooked walkin' stick?" Peter ast John.
"Yeah."
"Did he have whiskers down to here?" Peter measured down to his waist.
"He sho did," John tol' 'im.
"Aw shucks," Peter tol' 'im. "Dat was Ole Nora (Noah). You can't tell *him* nothin' 'bout no flood."

⟨ Sister Rosie and the African Missionary

In de olden times de preachuh he git lots of he'p from de membuhship when he preachin' a sermon. Dey hab a "amen cawnuh" whar de membuhs squall out all de time when de preachuh put over a good lick agin de Devul. Dey say, "Say yo' lesson, suh," or "Preach de Word, Amen! Amen!" or "Tell hit, tell hit, tell de truf, tell de truf!" Dis been lots of he'p to de preachuh, an' dey hab some pow'ful sermons in de Bottoms in dem days as a consequence.

Ah calls to min' up to McGill Chapel on de Li'l' Brazos Rivuh dere was one sistuh what allus keep up de sperrit for de preachuhs, an' de whole congugation lackwise. Her name was Sistuh Rosie R. Thompson, an' she sump'n lack Naomi dat de Word tell 'bout. She had dat style of faith an' courage dat b'lieve in de Lawd, an' ain't 'fraid to 'knowledge 'im in de public. She meck a big show at de servus, 'caze she nevuh stop he'pin' de preachuh. Evuhtime de preachuh meck a stroke for de Lawd, Sistuh Rosie 'ud squall out, "You sho' is tellin' de truf now. Hab mercy, Lawd, hab mercy." She hones' in her 'pinion too, but of occasion she fall by de wayside.

One time dere was a gambluh what died on de ole Burney plannuhtation an' his mammy b'long to de McGill Chapel Chu'ch. So dey ast Elduh Waters to preach his funeral. He say dat's awright wid 'im. So de Sunday roll 'round for de funeral. Dat's de onlies' day de boss-mens in de Bottoms 'low de han's to hab funerals reckly attuh freedom. If'n you died on a Sunday night dey'd haf to hol' you ovuh till de nex' Sunday, 'caze de boss-mens ain't gonna gib no time off from work durin' de week-a-days. Dey 'low if'n a mule die, buy anothuh one, an' if'n a nigguh die, hire anothuh one.

Anyhow, Elduh Waters gits up de Sunday of de funeral an' staa't to talkin' 'bout what a good boy dis gamblin' boy, Jessie, was; what a good life he live an' what a shinin' light he was for de res' of de folks in de Bottoms. Sister Rosie knows dis heah ain't de truf, so she set dere rail quiet for a long stretch an' don' say a mumblin' word. De people all wonduh huccome Sister Rosie ain't sayin' nothin' today—huccome she ain't talkin' back to de preachuh. So fin'ly, when de preachuh yell out dat Jessie was one o' de bestes' Christuns he evuh seed, Sistuh Rosie cain't hol' her peace no longuh; so she squall out rail loud, "You sho' is a tellin' a lie now; hab mercy, Lawd, hab mercy!"

Sistuh Rosie 'low de preachuh practicin' Bad Religion, but putty soon attuh de funeral a missionary come from Aferkuh to preach at de chu'ch an' Sistuh Rosie fall by de wayside herse'f. De preachuh jes' from Aferkuh whar he been for fo' years; he raisin' money for missionary work for de po' li'l' Aferkuns. In his sermon he tell 'bout how much money de rich white peoples in de Norf done gib de po' li'l' ole Aferkuns an' how much de Christun white folks in de Souf done did for de po' li'l' ole Aferkuns, an' evuh time he tell what done been did for de po' li'l' ole Aferkuns, Sistuh Rosie'd squall out, "Ride, salvation, ride!" Fin'ly de preachuh gits thoo wid his sermon an' he say, "Now brothuhs an' sistuhs, Ah done tole y'all what othuh peoples done did for de po' li'l' ole Aferkuns and now Ah wants evuhbody in dis heah chu'ch house to come up to de table an' lay a dolluh down for de po' li'l' ole Aferkuns."

When de preachuh say dis, Sistuh Rosie th'ow her haid way back, th'ow her han's up in de air rail high, an' squall out loudah dan evuh befo', "Walk, salvation, walk!" Sistuh Rosie ain't 'tickluh 'bout travelin' so fas' when hit come to jarrin' loose from a dolluh herse'f. She lack dey say, "De Nigguh's long on religion, and short on Christ'ainity."

([God Throws a Tree Limb

Hit takes lots of patience to deal wid a sinnuh at de mou'nah's bench. Dey hab a haa'd time comin' thoo, 'caze dey ain't yit ready to jar loose from dey sinful acks. Hit don' matter how pulpitwise a preachuh be, he hab a job on his han's gittin' de haa'd-haated sinnuh man to settle on de chu'ch. Ah calls to min' a han' offen de ole Cole plannuhtation by de name of Pink Jackson. He de bigges' cotton picker on de plannuhtation, but he de rankes' sinnuh, lackwise, an' 'sides dat he kinda simple-minded too.

His wife an' chilluns b'long to de Bethesda Baptis' Chu'ch down to Reagan, an' dey very upset 'bout Pink. He know how to git de cotton to-gethuh for de boss-man, but he cain't hitch hosses wid de Lawd. He know hit bes' to teck one row o' cotton at a time an' to ca'ie a light drag so's to pick de most poun's of cotton, but he don' know you got to hab a clear conscience to git rail converted an' be save. De preachuh work wid Pink evuh way he know how, but Pink don' chance to come thoo.

Fin'ly, one night, though, Revun Randle, de pastuh, pray to de Lawd speshly for Pink. He say, "Gawd, please come down heah an' hope me wid dis heah sinnuh man what goes by de name of Pink. Dis job Ah got for you is too haa'd for a man an' too tedious for de angels." But wid all dis prayin', Pink ain't nevuh chanced to come thoo yit. So fin'ly Revun Randle say, "Pink, Ah tells you what to do, if'n you raily wants to be a true chile of Gawd: Go down in de pasture attuh sundown an' pick yo'se'f out a pos'-oak tree an' light out down dere evuh night. Git down on yo' knees unnuhneaf de tree an' ast de Lawd to convert you."

So Pink goes down to de pasture dat ver' same night, picks him out a pos'-oak tree, gits down on his knees an' say, "Lawd, please convert me! Oh, Lawd, please convert me!"

Dis heah goes on awright for three nights, but while Pink is prayin' on de fo'th night, a dead tree limb falls offen de tree an' almos' hits 'im, so he lights out to runnin'. Hit's about a week attuh dis 'fo' Pink gits up 'nuff courage to go back out to de tree again, but on de Friday night 'fo' de nex' Sunday, Pink goes back out to de tree, kinda sidles up to hit an' say, "Gawd, Ah come out heah to hab a close-up talk wid you 'bout dat tree limb you th'owed at me t'othuh night; you know if'n you had of hit me, dese Nigguhs nevuh would of had no mo' confidence in you."

❨ Brother Gregg Identifies Himself

Ah calls to min' de Gregg fam'ly, what was croppers down on de ole Davis Plannuhtation, what runned jam up to de li'l' Brazos an stretch hitse'f out far ez you could peel yo' eye 'long de banks.

Dey hab a li'l' ole chu'ch house down dere what dey done builded rat attuh freedom done come in a bulge an' hit yit stan'in', cep'n dey cain't in no wise hol' servuses in hit when hit comes a big pour-down, or a northuh. De roof needs shinglin' pow'ful bad, an' some of de planks in de sides of de li'l' ole chu'ch done jarred loose, an' no-count triflin' Brazos Bottom Nigguhs done toted 'em off home for kindlin' wood. Dey calls dis heah li'l' ole chu'ch Li'l' Mount Zion, an' de Gregg fam'ly was one of de fuss fam'lies to jine hit. Dey was four Gregg boys, an' evuh one of 'em hab a whole passel of younguns, what of occasion brung salty tears to dey mammies' an' pappies' sorrowful eyes, 'caze mos' of 'em growed up to be Saddy night gamblers, sloppy drunkards, fas' womens, an' de Lawd in heabun knows what else dese yaps didn't turn out to be.

All de brothuhs cep'n Bud Gregg, de ol'es' brothuh, gits so fed up an' disgusted wid de sinful acks of dey younguns 'til dey done stop tryin' to square accounts wid de Lawd. An' de why dat Bud ain't done got on de "don'-keer" ban' wagon lack his brothuhs am dat he hab a good Christun wife, Carrie, an' a tol'able fair set of younguns. His gals was all married off to hard-workin' croppers an' his boys was all lucky 'nuff to git gals for wives dat could do ez much work on de fawm ez dey could. 'Sides dat, Bud's wife, Carrie, was de stan'by of de fam'ly when hit comed to de chu'ch an' de why an' wharfo' of all de chiliun bein' chu'ch membuhs. Carrie hab a good influence on Bud, lackwise, an' keep a beeline on 'im cep'n Bud don' in no wise 'ten chu'ch services on Sundays. Sistuh Carrie go to chu'ch an' plank herse'f rat down in de "amen cawnuh" evuh Sunday de Lawd sen', but Ole Bud, what was quick ez greased lightnin' wid a shotgun, spen' all his Sundays a huntin' an' a shootin' doves an' plovers an' rabbits evuh time he heah a flip-flappin' in de bushes an' weeds. Ole Bud was jes' a number in de chu'ch book, dat's all. Sistuh Carrie go pieceways wid 'im on de huntin' side of de fence, but she 'low dat de week-a-days am time 'nuff for carryin' on in dis wise. But Ole Bud don' give a whoop how much Sistuh Carrie try to 'suade 'im to go to chu'ch on a Sunday wid her. He jes keep his potato trap shet, an' don' say a mumblin' word when Sistuh Carrie talk to 'im 'bout chu'ch. But dis don' in no wise disencourage Sistuh Carrie; she 'low she b'lieve de Lawd kin still turn a miracle wid his pow'ful awmighty han', so she don' gib up de cross.

Sistuh Carrie ain't in no wise gonna be disappointed neithuh, 'caze 'tain't long 'fo' a nachul-bawn preachuh by de name of Hotwind Johnson comed to de Bottoms to 'duct a 'vivul an' tol' de Brazos Bottom Nigguhs dat de Lawd was gonna lay a heavy han' on 'em if'n dey didn't git shed of dey sinful ways. Dish heah kind of th'owed a scare into Ole Bud, so de nex' comin' Sunday night attuh Hotwind done comed to de Bottoms Bud goes down to de chu'ch house wid Sistuh Carrie an' tecks a seat rat in de "amen cawnuh" whar Sistuh Carrie drop herse'f all de time. Dis de fuss time Bud done set foot in de chu'ch house in ten yeahs, so evuhbody in de ch'uch turnt 'roun' an' look at 'im. Dis meck Ole Bud feel kind of out of place, too, but he try haa'd to brace hisse'f an' ack lack he used to bein' in a chu'ch house. He hol' hisse'f togethuh putty good, too, till Hotwind comed in de pulpit an' raised a song, an', attuh de song done been finish, turnt to whar Sistuh Carrie an' Bud was settin' an' say, p'intin' his finguh at Bud, "Brothuh Gregg, lead us in a word of prayer."

Bud ain't nevuh prayed in his whole life befo', so he tremblin' lack a leaf an' he don' feel lack doin' a jumpin' thing 'bout prayin'. But Sistuh Carrie nudge 'im in de side wid her elbow an' tell 'im to go ahaid an' do lack Hotwind done tole 'im to do, so Ole Bud pays heed to 'er, an' kneels down on de chu'ch house floor. Den he puts his han's ovuh his eyes an' says, "Lawd, Ah reckon Ah bettuh tell you who Ah is befo' Ah staa'ts dis prayer. Ah ain't John Gregg, de one what kin pick eight hunnud poun's of cotton when he teckin' one row at a time. Ah ain't Jim Gregg, de one what plays de fiddle an' de banjo evuh Saddy night for de platform dances, an' Ah ain't Tom Gregg, de one what stealed his boss-man's best pair of mules one Sunday night an runned off way somewhars. Ah'm Ole Man Gregg, de one what shoots de gun so good."

⟨ Why So Many Negroes Are in Heaven

Ah calls to min' durin' of de Worl' War when de flu gits on a rampage in de Bottoms an' staa'ts killin' folks goin' an' comin'. Hit done lay so many low till de doctuhs an' de nusses calls a meetin' down to Calvert so dey kin tell de peoples how to teck keer.

De doctuhs an' de nusses has dey say. Den dey calls on a ole-time cullud preachuh, what go by de name of Unkuh Aaron, to hab a say. Unkuh Aaron a stan'-pat Nigguh wid de white folks, so when dey calls 'im up to de platform, he climbs up de steps, leans ovuh on his ole hick'ry walkin' stick, an' say: "Ah done lissen to all yo' logics an' all yo' isms an' de lack 'bout de flu, but de Lawd's teckin' you white folks outen de worl', 'caze he ain't pleased at de way y'all's treatin' de Nigguhs. Dat's de why he's teckin' so many y'all outen de worl'."

"But, Unkuh Aaron," say one of de doctuhs, "de stisticks shows dat dey's mo' Nigguhs dyin' wid de flu dan dey is white folks."

"Dat's awright," 'low Unkuh Aaron. "Ah still hol's mah p'int. Don' you know huccome de Lawd's teckin' all dem Nigguhs up to heabun? He's teckin' em up dere to testify 'ginst you white folks." An' when Unkuh Aaron say dis, dis was de benediction; de meetin' 'journ' for de night.

⟨ Sister Sadie Washington's Littlest Boy

Sistuh Sadie Washin'ton was a widow woman, but one of de trues' chillun of Gawd dat you gonna evuh run 'cross durin' of a lifetime. Sistuh Sadie hab de record thoo de whole Bottoms of bein' one o' de good uns when hit come to dem what hab paa'lance wid de Lawd, an' she done got dat thing lack de Word say git hit.

But Sistuh Sadie hab one pow'ful regret. She hab a boy, her littlest boy, what go by de name of Pete, what ain't yit jine de chu'ch an' come to be a Christun. Pete now out of his thirteen crowdin' his fo'teen, an' done growed into de shape of a man, so Sistuh Sadie don' feel lack she 'sponsible to Gawd for 'im no mo'.

Don' keer how haa'd Sistuh Sadie an' de membuhship of de Mt. Zion Chu'ch try, dey cain't in no wise toll Pete off to de Christun faith. Sistuh Sadie de mammy of fifteen yaps, an' Pete de onlies' one what ain't come thoo an' be converted; he done rech his own 'sponsibility to de Lawd, an' he ain't 'fessed religion yit. So Sistuh Sadie heah 'bout a rousin' 'vivul dey was habin' up to Bryan 'mongst de Town Nigguhs an' de Pos'-oak Nigguhs, an' she tuck li'l' ole Pete an' dragged 'im out to de meetin' one night. She set 'im down rat by her so de triflin' rascal cain't slip outen de chu'ch house an' "cut buddy short" back home.

Putty soon de preachuh, what come from way somewhars to 'duct de 'vivul, line a hymn for to staa't de servus, an' den staa't blowin' Gawd's word outen his system lack ole Numbuh Three blow steam outen hits smokestack when hit git to de railroad crossin' on de ole Carter plannuhtation. Dat's de plannuhtation whar Sistuh Sadie an' her chilluns all "mecks de day" an' "gits dey pay" from Ole Man Carter what own de plannuhtation. Pete, he de wattuh boy for de han's on de plannuhtation, an' he lackwise beats de sweep for de han's to knock off from work an' come to dinnuh.

De preachuh hab a great big voice, an' weigh 'bout three hunnud pounds. When he walk 'cross de flo', de whole chu'ch house rock an' shake lack a cyclone done hit it. Dis kinda scare li'l' ole Pete. Dis de fuss time in his life he done evuh seed a preachuh dis big what kin shake de flo', so he thinks hit's de Lawd shakin' de flo', an' he goes up to de mou'nah's bench an' meck out he converted. Dat was de secon' Saddy night in de mont', an' de pastuh of de chu'ch set de fo'th Sunday ez de day for baptizin' of de new converts.

Sistuh Sadie so proud dat Pete done come thoo she don' know what to do, so she go all up an' down de whole Bottoms tellin' evuhbody she sees to be at de big baptizin' on de fo'th Sunday, down on de Big Brazos, 'caze Pete gonna be baptized. So de fo'th Sunday comed an' 'bout sebun hunnud Town Nigguhs, Pos'-oak Nigguhs, an' Bottom Nigguhs congugates on bof sides of de Big Brazos, jes' 'fo' hit gits to de fork of de rivuh on de ole Washin'ton plannuhtation, to see de baptizin'. De pastuh an' de 'vangelis' lines up de cannuhdates on de banks of de rivuh. Li'l' Pete was number sebun in de line, an' evuhthing gittin' 'long fine till dey gits to Pete. De converts what baptized 'fo' Pete 'ud all holler, "Ah b'lieves de Lawd done saved mah soul," when de preachuh'd duck 'em under de wattuh; but when dey duck li'l' ole Pete, he don' say nary word, jes' stan' dere in de wattuh an' look. So de preachuh push Pete to one side in de wattuh, an' go on an' duck anothuh convert, an' dis convert, lack all de res' 'cep'n Pete, yell, "Ah b'lieves de Lawd done saved mah soul." Den de preachuh turn 'roun' to Pete, grab 'im an' duck 'im again, but Pete don' say anothin' yet; he jes' stan' dere lack he in a transom or sump'n. So de preachuh shove 'im to one side again an' go on an' duck anothuh convert, an' dis heah convert squall out, jes' lack de res', "Ah b'lieves de Lawd done saved mah soul." Den de preachuh turn· 'roun' and grab li'l' ole Pete an' duck 'im again, an' dis time, when Pete come outen de wattuh, he yell, "Ah b'lieves! Oh! Ah b'lieves!"

Sistuh Sadie was stan'in' on t'othuh side of de rivuh, an' she so happy dat Pete done come thoo an' confess till she yell back at 'im, "What you b'lieve, son? Oh! what you b'lieve?"

"Ah b'lieve," yell Pete, "dat dis damn preachuh tryin' to drown me; dat's what Ah b'lieve."

❨ The Preacher and His Farmer Brother

Of occasion in de Bottoms, in de same fam'ly you kin fin' some of de bestes' preachuhs dat done evuh grace a pulpit, an' a brothuh or a sistuh what ain't nevuh set foot in de ch'ch ez long ez dey live. Ah calls to min' Revun Jeremiah Sol'mon what pastuh de Baptis' chu'ch down to Egypt, on Caney Creek. He done put on de armuh of de Lawd when he rech fo'teen, he come to be a deacon when he rech sixteen, an' dey 'dained 'im for to preach de Word when he turnt to be eighteen. He one of de mos' pow'ful preachuhs dat done evuh grace a Texas pulpit, an' he de moderatuh of de St. John's 'Sociation. But he hab a brothuh, what go by de name of Sid, what ain't nevuh set foot in a chu'ch house in his life.

Sid hab a good spot of lan' 'roun' 'bout Falls, on de Brazos, though; so one time Revun Jeremiah 'cide to pay Sid a visit. Hit been twenty yeah since he laid eyes on 'im; so he driv up to de house an' soon ez he gits thoo shakin' han's wid Sid's wife, Lulu Belle, an' de chilluns, he say, "Ah wants to see yo' fawm, Sid. Le's see what kinda fawmuh you is."

"Sho," say Sid. So he gits his hat on an' dey goes down to de cawn patch an' looks at de cawn Sid done planted an' what nelly 'bout grown, an' de revun looks at hit an' 'low, "Sid, youse got a putty good cotton crop by de he'p of de Lawd." Den dey moseys on down to de sugah cane patch an' when de Revun eye dis, he say, "Sid, youse got a putty good cane patch, by de he'p of de Lawd."

An' when he say dis, Sid eye 'im kinda disgusted lack, an' say, "Yeah, but you oughta seed hit when de Lawd had it by Hisse'f."

116

⟨[A Job for God

Ah calls to min' two han's on de old Babb plannuhtation on de Lowuh Brazos what was cuttin' logs on de wes' side of de rivuh to buil' a bawn on de boss-man's premiuss. Dey cut de cypress trees down on de wes' side an' brung de logs 'cross to de eas' side on a li'l' ole rowboat. Hit wasn't far from de Gulf, an' of occasion a alluhgatuh comed up in de back wattuh, but dey ain't seed one in dese paa'ts for quite a spell. Anyhow, dese two han's, Tim Groce an' Steve Risby, done been to chu'ch de Sunday 'fo' dey staa't to bringin' de logs crost de rivuh, an' dey heahs Elduh Sample, de pastuh of Mothuh Mt. Zion Chu'ch, say, "Gawd so lacked de worl' in sich a way, dat he done sen' de onlies' son he got down to de urf so dat dem what believe on 'im gonna be saved."

Dat sermon stay on Steve's min'. He don' forgit hit. So Tim an' Steve been cuttin' down de cypress trees an' bringin' de logs 'cross de rivuh for four days now, an' dey ain't seed nor heerd tell of no alluhgatuh yit, but when dey staa't back crost de rivuh wid dey las' load dat Friday, what was de thirteenth of de mont'—dat's a bad luck day, you knows—anyways, dey spy sump'n or 'nothuh swimmin' to'a'ds 'em from de Gulf. "What's dat?" say Tim. "Looks lack a alluhgatuh," say Steve. 'N' sho' nuff, 'fo' you c'd say "amen," de alluhgatuh done rech de boat an' turn hit ovuh an' lit out to swimmin' attuh Steve an' Tim. Tim 'bout to git away, but he alluhgatuh gainin' on Steve all de time; so Steve calls to min' what de preachuh say, and he pray:

"Gawd, Ah knows youse got a habit of sen'in' you' son down heah to do yo' work, but Ah wanna tell you rat now, don' you come sen'in' yo' son down heah now. You come down heah you'se'f, 'caze savin' me from dis alluhgatuh is a man's job."

⟨[Little David's Question

Of occasion de preachuh in de Bottoms stretch hisse'f out too far and git hisse'f in a 'dickmint he cain't git outen. One time dey hab a preachuh what hab dis style of ca'iein' on down to de Baptis' chu'ch at Falls, on de Brazos. He allus' jumpin' on de membuhship wid bof feet 'bout tellin' lies. He bawl 'em out all de time 'bout bein' sich big liahs. He say, "A Nigguh'd rathuh tell a lie on a credit dan to tell de truf for cash." He say, "A Nigguh hate de truf worse'n de Devul hate a baptizin'." An' to cap de climax, if'n he didn't git up in de pulpit one Sunday mawnin' an' say, "Brothuhs an' Sistuhs, for mah message tonight, Ah'm gonna preach a sermon on liahs. So Ah wants all y'all to teck yo' Bibles an' read de twenty-fuss chapter of Mark 'fo' you comes back to de chu'ch house tonight."

So dat Sunday night, attuh de song and prayer servus done come to pass, de preachuh gits up, clears his th'oat a li'l', an' says, "Brothuhs and Sistuhs, how many of y'all done read de twenty-fuss chapter of Mark lack Ah done tole you to do 'fo' you comed back to de chu'ch house tonight?" Evuhbody in the chu'ch house hist deyse'f outen dey seat an' stan' up. So de preachuh laff out rail loud rat in de pulpit an' say, "All you liahs set back down. You ain't read no sich a thing, 'caze dey ain't but sixteen chapters in Mark."

De membuhship sho' outdone wid deyse'f, but dey don' lack dis heah fashion of ca'iein' on by de pastuh neither. Dey scairt to call his han', though. 'Staid, dey jes lay his race out 'hin' his back, an' 'roun' de house, but dey an't nevuh git up 'nuff courage to tell 'im to his face dat de style he got of callin' de membuhship liahs evuh Sunday de Lawd sen' don' set good on dey stummicks.

One time, though, a li'l' ole boy go by de name of David, an' what comed to be smaa't by "beatin' de sweep" for de han's on de plannuhtation to knock off from work for dinnuh evuh day, an' what done heerd his mammy complainin' 'roun' de house 'bout de preachuh callin' de membuhship liahs, say he gonna fix de preachuh's bizniss good one of dese days an' break 'im up from callin' de membuhship liahs. So de nex' Sunday mawnin', Elduh Cooper (dat's de preachuh's name) gits up in de pulpit an' staa'ts to callin' de membuhship liahs, lack as allus. Den he lights out to preachin' 'bout Gawd am in de valley, Gawd am on de hillside, Gawd am on de rivers, Gawd am in de clouds, Gawd am in de Pos'-oak districk, Gawd am in de Brazos Bottoms. "Yeah, Gawd am evuhwhars," he says. An' when he talk in dis wise, li'l' David, what am settin' on de front row of de chu'ch house wid his mammy, jumps up rail quick an' yells, "Elduh, is he in mah pocket?"

"Sho', he's in yo' pocket," says Elduh Cooper.

"Youse a liah," say Li'l' David. "Ah ain't ebun done got no pocket."

An' he ain't got no pocket sho' 'nuff, 'caze he wearin' a pair of mammy-made pants his mammy done cut outen a pair of his pappy's ole wore-out britches, an' dey ain't got nary pocket in 'em.

Sermons and Prayers

John G. Williams collected Gullah Negro sermons as early as the year 1895 and called them Elder Coteney's Sermons. In 1908 William E. Hatcher recorded some of the sermons of the renowned Negro folk preacher, John Jasper, and published them under the title From John Jasper. "The Sun Do Move" was the most famous of these sermons. More than three decades later, in 1941, John Henry Faulk presented a group of Texas Negro sermons as a master's thesis at the University of Texas. He gave this collection the general title of Quickened by de Spurit. The first Negro collector of sermons was William H. Pipes, a teacher at Philander Smith College in Little Rock, Arkansas. His book of sermons and prayers, Say Amen! Brother, was published in 1951.

([Why We Come to Church

I'm glad we could come together again to pray and thank God, observing His will, praise His name. The reason we come together is to sing, pray, and talk about God. We come to this house fer de purpose of singing, praying, and knowing that God is the Keeper. Yer hear His word: His word is good. You satisfy ter enjoy home and here, wherever God puts yer.

Yer know, I'm dis way. I believe in doing everything where it ought to be done at. I believe when you have a car, don't put no gas in no radiator; it don't belong dere. Put de water in de radiator and de gas in de tank whar it belong and it'll do good. Put things whar dey don't belong, won't do no good; it'll do harm. Put everything in its own place.

And so as we assemble together, we couldn't honor a better man, greater man than He is. Greatest hero ever sat on the throne. He has great power throughout all ages. And the sweetness of His disposition in the hearts of many have caused us to have hope. He's the only man, . . . only one fer us.

And whatever fer you all this morning, just hold yer cups, and whatever fer yer all, yer git it. Kinda like a mail-carrier or post office; give yer whatever fer you. So jest keep everything waiting and we'll see what's gwine to come ter you.

The Lord say, "Open yer mouth and I'll speak fer you." See what the Spirit gwine do. Tryin' to preach the Word of God. Pray His will be done.

Yer know, when us git hooked up here together, it's like a city and a town—ain't it?—when yer turn on de light. It's down in de corner stores and all behin' 'em and all over the house. It shine everwhar. Child o' God'll shine anywhar you put 'im. Yer may git 'im bowed down, but he gon' shine anyhow! He don't care nothin' 'bout no trouble, child. He gonna shine anyhow! Ain't got no bread, but he'll shine anyhow! Ain't got no clothes, but he'll shine anyhow! Don't care how much yer talk 'bout 'im, he'll shine right on! Lay down at night; yer may, . . . but he'll shine right on! Git up in de mornin' he'll shine everwhar he go! Ever time yer look at 'im, he's shinin'! Ain't dat right?

The Danger of Neglect

I am glad to be present; happy also to see you present, your presence. Regret very much for being somewhat late; however, we hope to work out of this gradually.

We invite your attention to the reading of the Book of Proverbs, the 24th chapter, beginning with the 30th verse:

"I went by the field of the slothful, and by the vineyard of the man void of understanding; and, lo, it was all grown over with thorns, and nettles had covered the face thereof, and the stone wall thereof was broken down. Then I saw, and considered it well; I looked upon it, and received instruction. Yet a little sleep, a little slumber, a little folding of the hands to sleep: So shall thy poverty come as one that travelleth; and thy want as an armed man."

This is our text. . . . From these verses the theme suggesting itself to our minds is this: The Danger of Neglect.

Solomon here is very plainly and clearly bringing to us an observation of the slothful man. He also points out here that where negligence has been made the fields and the walls are all in bad shape. He began here by saying, "I went by the field of the slothful." The sin of slothfulness is a great sin. He said this same slothful man was a man that was void of understanding. It's pathetic to be void of understanding.

He passed by the vineyard; therein the weeds and the thorns and the bushes have grown over and covered the wall over. It simply speaks that vineyard had been neglected. The stone wall was broken down. Solomon saw and considered it well: "I looked on it and received instruction." It's reasonable to look at the negligence of a friend or a neighbor and receive instruction—to see wherein they have failed; to see wherein they neglected their farm and their duties in life. So, therefore, this theme presents itself: The Danger of Neglect.

In thinking of how dangerous it is to neglect, first of all we think most calamities and accidents are all caused by neglect.

When we think of the fameous [sic] flyer Amelia Earhart, who some time ago attempted to fly across the blue waters of the Atlantic Ocean. . . . Something went wrong. That plane went down in some unknown place in the ocean. Millions of dollars was spent in search for her, but until today she's unaccounted for. But it happened because of neglect.

Then I think of the plane that Dr. L. K. Williams, the president of the National Baptist Convention of the United States of America, Incorporated, had taken from Chicago, Illinois, to Detroit, Michigan, where he was slated to make a political speech. Because of unreasonable negligence, that plane caught fire and went down, and Dr. Williams and others met with their death, because of negligence.

Then I think of a few years ago on land, on the Little Southern Railroad, between McDonald and Atlanta. The Southern train wrecked and it wrecked at what we call Camp Creek. And that wreck until now is known as the Camp Creek Wreck. When the train passed through Jenkinsburg, a town back a few miles this side, the engineer was warned there. Because of rain, he was warned that the trestle was in bad condition. The engineer cursed and said, "I'm due in Atlanta in 'so many' minutes." He pulled out. When he came to the trestle, the trestle gave way. More than fifty lives were lost. He was well-warned, but he neglected the warning that he met at Jenkinsburg. So, it's dangerous to neglect.

And then I think of the Titanic, that great ship that started out from Southampton. That ship that had Captain John Smith as its captain and had all of the luxuries that a luxurious heart could desire. Had everything for their pleasure and their comfort thereon. They were well-warned as they left Southampton of the icebergs that were way out there in the ocean. But the reply was that "This ship is sinkproof: no iceberg will be able to sink this ship; this is the Titanic, the greatest ship that this country has ever built or known." But they went on and neglected that warning. But somewhere out near the mountain where those hurge [sic] icebergs had tumbled into the ocean that ship struck those icebergs. And, finally, the water found its way into the ship. Somebody, as they were riding, said, "I believe this ship is sinking here."

They said, "No! This ship is the Titanic; it can't sink."

But finally they said, "Yes, but the lower deck is almost full of water and it's going down." Finally, the captain give out orders to cast out the lifeboats and for the women and children to get on the lifeboats that they might be safe. And that great ship with those valuable things went down in the water, because they neglected to take the warning. Christian friends, it's dangerous to neglect.

Neglect in any way produces a corresponding loss. I might make (a few) examples of a few things where neglect produces a loss. If a merchant neglect his business, he'll go bankrupt. If the gardener neglect to hoe the weeds, the plants will cease to grow; his crop will be cut; he will not be able to get much vegetables wherein he neglected to hoe the weeds. If proper food and clothing is neglected, the health will fail. Too many people go into bad health, because some clothing is necessary for a healthy body. But neglect causes a great loss, loss of health.

Many people go into bad health by improper clothing, and the lack of ventilation. I remember once reading a story of a man who went into a closed room, shut out all of the ventilation, and heated the room at a high degree. Finally, he found himself suffering from heat. Then he opened the ventilators, the doors, and the windows and let all the fresh air in he could. And the consequence were, he developed double pneumonia and died. Then, for sanitation to be neglected, that means the health will fail also.

For the mind to be neglected there will be no education. And where ignorance predominates, there is always a great loss. Solomon said, in Proverbs two—twenty-nine, two, "When the wicked beareth rule, the people mourn." So, then, it produces a great loss.

Where conscience is neglected there will be heathenism, cannibals, and prisons. What do we mean when we say, "Conscience is neglected"? The conscience, to my mind, is a court within itself. We mean by a court within itself that conscience is a thing that will try you, will convict you, and then pass judgment on you. For a conscience is a whole court within itself; we see conscience as a judge in the judgment seat; then we see the prosecution attorney at the bar; then we see the defense attorney at the bar; then we see the solicitor general producing the state evidences on the case; we see the twelve jurors in the box; and then we see both state and defense witnesses taking the stand; and all these make up conscience. Conscience will try you, convict you, and pass judgment on you. Any time you are tempted to go wrong, they all stand close by. Every time you are prompted to commit a sin, they all tell you, "Don't do it."

The soul, neglected, becomes dwarf and dies. You see souls that have lost their spiritual shape. They're out of shape. They—maybe with this illustration you see the condition of a soul that has been neglected. When the basket maker works his white oak around in the yard, under the shade tree, once in a while he'll leave a piece of it laying out in the sunshine and the sunshine will so twist and so dry that piece of oak until it's impossible to put it back in any kind of shape. It was neglected; it wasn't put in the shade or in the water but it was left out in the sunshine. And that's the way it is with a soul that's been neglected. It loses its shape and it soon dies.

Then neglect weakens the power to decide. "I will," said a man one day who promised his companion on a dying bed that he would be saved before he died. He really meant, out of his heart and his soul, that he would be saved, but he put it off and waited too long. (Pray for us.) So, it weakens the power to decide. He neglected the promise that he made to his dying companion. He neglected his soul to the extent that when death laid her hand on him and claimed him and carried him to sleep in the silent city of the dead, his last cry was, "I waited too long!" (Come, Holy Spirit.) The longer we wait, the harder the task becomes.

Neglect produces a loss of sensitiveness. "What you mean by that?" I'm thinking of someone who wants to wake up at a certain time in the morning. They have an alarm clock. They'll set that clock to alarm at a certain hour, and sure enough that clock will alarm and will awaken them out of their sleep. But they'll neglect the alarming of the clock. Not that they didn't hear it, not that it didn't alarm, but they neglect the alarming of the clock and go back to sleep and oversleep themselves and stay there too long and be late getting to their job and lose their job. It's dangerous to neglect.

I think about people who move from the rural section to the city. The first few nights they're in the city (begins accenting rhythmically), they're troubled with the noise, disturbed by the noise. Noisy cars, the trolley, the trains on the rails keep them disturbed for a few nights. Can't sleep sound, but they keep on. After a while, after a few nights have passed, they can just go on to sleep and sleep all night. (Audience answers, "Sleep all night.") Forgot about the noise; they forget about the rumbling and they sleep all right, undisturbed. Procrastination is a thief of time.

Neglect destroys interest. It destroys your interest in school; it destroys your interest in music; it destroys your interest in social affairs; it destroys your interest in the soul of man. And in the word of God (sings it) neglect destroys these things.

Salesman one day had a prospective customer and he failed, he neglected to call on him at the set time and he lost the sale, because he failed to call on him. Neglect in any way causes a great danger. Man one day as he traveled, one cold, icy day, he found a serpent on the ground, that was frozen. And this man had pity on him. He taken the serpent off the ground and said, "I'll be a friend to him. I'll take him and put him in my bosom and warm him." The man taken the serpent, put him in his bosom and got him warm, but he neglected to take the serpent out when he was warm. He bit the man and the man died. It's dangerous to neglect.

A hunter one day been out in the woods, went out hunting in the rain and in the cold. (Come, Holy Spirit.) Went in home as it's customary for huntsmens to do, tired and wet and hungry. And as he went in, he sat his gun in a corner by the fireplace and neglected to take the load out of his gun. And, finally, a little three-year-old child, playing about in the house, knocked the gun down and the gun discharged and shot the little child in the head, and it died. It's dangerous to neglect. Neglect leads to ruin. Neglect lead to damnation. Neglect lead to loss.

Ah, I saw another man neglect to learn to swim. Stood on the banks of a river one day, saw all the child he had drown, because he neglected to learn to swim. Neglect will lead in the road of ruin to both time and eternity.

I can hear Paul saying one day in the Book of Hebrews, "How shall we escape"—ah—"If we neglect so great a Salvation?" Here's what he meant. He meant: "Is it any way around it?"

I can hear somebody answer 'im and say, "No! No! Ain't no way around it." I could hear Job saying one day, "There's no way to escape death, because your bounds been struck and you can't go 'round." Ahhhhhhhh, Glory! Dangerous to neglect, my friends. Then I hear him say, "Well, how will we get 'round then if we neglect to express Salvation?"

He said, "Well, it's so high, you can't get over; so wide, you can't go around; then it's so deep down, you just can't turn under it; no way 'round it." No way around this Salvation. Well, what do you mean now? Salvation said one day, "I am the way, the truth, and the light." He said, "I am an open door; I am a door no man can shut, but you must come in by Me." He said to another crowd one day, "If any man come any other way, he cometh as a thief and a robber." My Lord. No way around Salvation. But I just kept on reading where He said to Nicodemus, "You must be born again." My Lord!

I said, "Well, now, men escape from the county chain, then," I said; "men escape sometimes from the jail houses; they escape from the state prisons sometimes and then, every once in a while, somebody escape from the federal prison." My Lord!

But I could hear the word of my God ringing in my soul, ringing in my heart, good news and glad tidings, saying, "It ain't no way around Salvation. If you neglect this Salvation, ain't no way 'round it." No way around.

Dangerous to neglect. Somebody neglect their spiritual activity and they get cold and they get lukewarm. One reason why, one reason why we can't all cry the same cry is—er—(audience moans) we neglect our spirit (moans) and we get lukewarm. We neither cold nor hot and the Spirit can't find its way into our soul. I tell you, I tell you, if you let the Spirit find its way into your heart, it'll move in your heart and then it'll make you move. Ahhhhhhhh, Glory! Jeremiah said, "It's like fire shut up in my bones," and then, then, then he said, "It's like a mighty hammer." Oh, Glory! But I'll tell you what it'll do for you: It'll make an old man feel like a young man; if you are tired, it'll make you move anyhow. I tell you what it'll do for you: It'll make you forget about your burden; it'll make you forget about your heavy crosses; it'll make you forget about your trials. And then you'll say: "Whatever it takes (loud accent by striking the speaker's stand rhythmically), I'm going on; I'm going in Jesus.". . . Going on in Jesus.

Now my spiritual strength renewed, then I am going to remember that Salvation is free for all. It's dangerous to neglect it; it's dangerous to go by heedlessly. Salvation is to all men; Salvation is to men and mankind. And if we neglect this great Salvation, there is no way of escape.

May the Lord bless us, may He help us, and may He save us when it comes our time to die. Amen!

(De Progicul Son

Well, amen. Ah'm goin' to take mah tex' outen Luke tonight. Ah'm goin' to preach on de progicul son, iffen de Lawd's willin'. Ah knows mos' de chu'ch has heahed 'bout de progicul son, an' heahed me preach on 'im befo', but dey's still a lot mo' to heah 'bout 'im, an' a lot mo' to say 'bout 'im. Dat's why Ah 'cided to preach on 'im tonight. We still got progicul sons with us. Yes, we has. Dey's plenty of progicul sons right heah t'day, and long as we got progicul sons, de Lawd goin' to want 'em preached to. Amen!

Now, Luke tell us a suhtun man had two sons, but he nevuh call de man's name. Why he call dat man a suhtun man? A suhtun man! What de wul' is a *suhtun* man? A *suhtun* man is a special sawt of a man, co'se he is. Den ol' man Luke weren't writin' 'bout no evuhday man; he was writin' 'bout a *suhtun, special* man. An' de Lawd was de suhtunes' man dey was in dem days. Well, amen, co'se he was. Den ol' man Luke mus' of been writin' about de Lawd. Amen!

An' he say dat dis heah suhtun man have two sons. Well, now, de onlies' two sons de Lawd evuh had was Adam an' Jesus, an' ol' man Luke knowed hit. Whut Ah'm trying to show you is dat all de wul' ol' Luke was talkin' 'bout was de Lawd an' his two boys, Adam an' Jesus. Ol' Luke go on to say dat one o' dese sons was a cuttuh an' a smawt-aleck. Dis son he took all he had comin' an lef' home. Now, which one was dat?

Well, we know de sawt of boy Jesus was. Jesus love de Lawd, an' do His bes' to he'p 'im out. Jesus nevuh studied 'bout nuthin' but wuckin' an' prayin'. Jesus'd gid out in de fiel' by daylight an' nevuh look up from de row 'til dinnuhtime. Jesus was a wuckuh. Amen. Hit's so.

But nevuh heahed of ol' Adam hittin' a lick of wuck! Adam was a high steppuh. If de Lawd evuh git 'im in de fiel' a-tall, he'd drap his hoe an' strike out fur de shade de minute de Lawd tuhned His back. Co'se he would. Adam was a show-off. He set 'round studyin' 'bout his po'tion all day. Amen.

Well, de day come when Adam 'cided he done had 'nough sittin' 'round tryin' to keep out of wuck. He walk hisse'f up to de Lawd an' say, "Papa, give me mah po'tion of de goods what Ah got comin'. Ah wants to go fo'th."

Well, de Lawd say, "Son, you ol' 'nough now to have good sense; Ah's done de bes' Ah knows how by you. Ah's tried to set yo' feet in de path of righteousness. Hit don't seem like nothin' will do you but to leave home. So heah's yo' po'tion dat falls to you. Try to make hit las'."

Ah kin see Adam now, stickin' his money in his pocket, takin' his b'longin's, an' struttin' off. Oh, but he was de bigges' thing dat evuh happen! An dere was his po' ol' daddy a-standin' dere at de gate, a-shakin' his haid an' sayin' goodbye. He knowed Adam nevuh had sense enough to come outen de rain. An' He knowed couldn't nobody tell Adam nothin'! Adam goin' to have to fin' out fuh hisse'f. Amen.

Yes, Ah kin see 'im now. Oh, yonduh he go—mawchin' 'long de road callin' hisse'f big. Ah sees 'im come walkin' up to Pahradise. Set down his grip an' fan hisse'f. "Dis looks good to me; think Ah'll stay awhile," he say. Folks in Pahradise say, "Who is dis heah strange man?" Adam step out befo' 'em an' 'low, "Ah's Adam, de Lawd's younges' boy. An' Ah's de ol' Bo' coon 'long dis heah rivuh. Ah's de ol' tush hawg in dese heah woods. Uh-huh, uh-huh. Done come down heah to see de sights." Had to show hisse'f off.

Well, hit weren't no time 'til de wuhd got 'round dat dey was smart-aleck with money in town, an' dat's just what ol' Satan's always watchin' fuh. Ol' Satan come up an' take Adam's han' an' say, "So glad to see you, Adam. Ah ain' seed you since ah lef' Heab'n, an' you was jes' a little shirt-tail young 'un den. Lawdy, but you sho' made a fine man!"

Adam swell up an' look proud. Othuh folks come 'roun' 'im jes' a-helloin' 'im an a-pattin' 'im on de back. Adam swell hisse'f 'til he nigh on bus', an' say, "Let's spen' some money. Come on, boys, hit's all on me. Ah got mo' money dan de gov'mint, an' Ah kin git mo' whah dis come from."

Oh, he was ridin' high and talkin' big. An' dat's jes' whut ol' Satan love. When ol' Satan git a man to actin' high an talkin' big, he know he got 'im den. Oh, yes, he do. Satan know he got dat man den, don' he?

Well, dey gallivanted all night an' slep' all day. He nevuh had to look fuh nobody to he'p him spen' his money an' carry on his sinnin'. Ol' Satan seen to hit dat dey was always plenty of dat sawt 'roun'. You kin always fin' plenty bad comp'ny when you looks fuh hit. Ol' Satan see to dat. Yes, Lawd.

Ah kin see Adam now; he jes' had to show off. He say, "Looky heah, Satan, Ah likes dis sinnin' fine, but hit's too slow fuh me. Ah's a fas' man, an' Ah needs fas' comp'ny. Ain' dey no women folks 'round heah?" Dat was all ol' Satan was waitin' fuh. He cock his haid to one side an' cackle, "Co'se dey's gals heah, boy, but you got to spen' yo' money fas' to keep 'em happy. You don' want to mess 'roun' none dese heah Pahradise women. You liable to git yo'se'f run ovuh, boy." Den he laugh agin. Well, well, well, well, well—uh-huh, uh-huh. He had Adam goin' his way.

Adam slam down a big hunnud-dollah bill an say, "Le's git stawted, Satan. You ain' waitin' on me." Ol' Satan hunted up Eve, an' say, "Gal, heah's whut we been waitin' fuh. A great big ol' smawt-aleck boy dat think he got mo' sense dan his own daddy. He got his pocket full of money an' his min' full of sin. Come on, honey, we'll pick dis ol' roostuh clean."

Well, hit weren't no time 'fo' Adam was co'tin Miss Eve. He co'ted huh so hawd dat he ax huh to marry. But Miss Eve had huh min' on money. She weren't studyin' 'bout marryin' nobody. De onlies' puhsun she evuh thought 'bout was Miss Eve. She'd jes' laugh an' slap Adam when he talk 'bout marryin'.

By de time ol' Satan an' Eve got through takin' Adam 'roun', Adam was cleanuh dan a scraped possum. He run his han' in his pocket an' he nevuh felt nothin' but bottom. He sawt of smile an' say, "Well, now Ah jes' 'clah, iffen Ah ain' done gone an' spent evuh las' cent Ah had. Satan, would you loan me a little 'til Ah gets holt of some mo'?"

Ol' Satan look at 'im fuh a minute, den he slap his laig an' laugh real big. He say, "W'y, boy, Ah thought you was *so rich*. Ah got plenty of money, but Ah ain' len'in' none of hit to no ol' no-count, woman-chasin', drinkin' thing like you. If you done run out of money, Ah'm leavin' you." Dat's ol' Satan fuh you.

Well, Ah kin see Adam now. He tuhn 'roun' to Eve an' ax huh fuh a place to stay 'til he could git some money. She jes' laugh in his face an' go a-switchin' off. Lef' Adam stan'in' dere. Uh-huh, uh-huh. Mmmm. . . .

Well, Ah kin see po' Adam now. He got mighty hongry, but nobody ax him to eat. Ol' Satan an' Eve was off foolin' 'roun' wid some othuh po' sinnuh. Adam went down to de hawg pen an' et de huskies dat de hawg was eatin'. He'd lived mighty high, but he'd done sin hisse'f out.

Den he stawted studyin' 'bout Eve an' Satan an' de hawg pen. Dey's boys right heah now dat had bettuh stawt studyin' 'bout Eve an' Satan an' de hawg pen. Oh, yes, dey had. Dey bettuh stawt right now. Uh-huh, uh-huh.

Well, Ah kin see 'im rise up in de mawnin' an' say, "Looky heah, even de hawgs at home gits bettuh dan Ah's gittin' now. Ah done sin agin mah fathuh. An' Ah's sorry fur hit. Ah'm goin' to go back to mah po' ol' daddy an' go down on my knees an' beg fur fuhgiveness. Ah's too mean to live, an' Ah ain' fittin' to die. Ah'm goin' to go back dere an' try to pray mahse'f outen dis mess. Ah's goin' to go back dere an' live like a Christian man. Oh, Lawd! Oh, Lawd! Yes, yes, yes.

Well, Ah kin see 'im rise up in de mawnin' an' say, "Looky heah." He stawt limpin' back to his fathuh's house. Oh, de road was long, an' de way was rough, but he kep' right on. Limpin' 'long an' studyin' 'bout ol' Satan an' Eve an' sin. Goin' back to his daddy's home. Oh, yes! Oh, yes!

When he git 'bout dere, de Lawd look off down de lane an' see 'im comin'. "Well, Ah jes' 'clah, if dere don' come mah po' little Adam! Go git 'im some good clothes an' kill de fattes' calf in de lot. Mah son whut was los' has done been foun' agin. Mah Adam done come home to his ol' daddy agin." He run an' flung his awms 'roun' Adam's neck. He jes' had to cry 'cause he was so happy.

Adam stawted cryin' an' say, "Pappa, Ah ain't fittin' to sit 'roun' yo' table. Ah has sinned agin you an' all de disciples, an' Jesus too. Ah ain' fit to 'sociate with nothin' but hawgs!"

Well, de Lawd jes' hug 'im a little tightuh an' say, "Hush, chile, come on, we goin' to have a feas'." An' dey had a feas'. Uh-huh, uh-huh. Dey had a feas'.

Now dey's progicul sons sittin' out heah 'fo' me right now. Oh, po' progicul sons, how much longuh you goin' to wait 'fo' you rises up an' goes back to de Lawd? He's always lookin' an' waitin' fuh you. How much longuh you goin' to have 'im wait? Oh chillun, chillun! Why don' you change yo' sinful ways an' come to de Lawd tonight? De feas' is waitin'! Won' you come tonight? De Lawd's at de gate waitin' fuh his sons to come home. Oh, won' you come tonight? Won' you come home tonight? Amen.—JOHN HENRY FAULK, "Quickened by de Spurit," master's thesis, University of Texas.

❮ De Tetter Wine Christun*

A Gullah Dialect Sermon of the South Carolina Negro

But wha kinder Christun dat? We yeddy 'bout all kinder Christun, but neber yeddy befo' ter night 'bout tetter wine Christun. Well, I gwine tell you. I gwine take de tetter wine fur a parable, an' I want yunner all fur keep you eye open an' lissin good, an' ef you ent mine I'le show befo' I get tru dat some yunner yer—ternight da tetter wine Christun.

Wen de groun' berry rich de tetter wine grow berry rank an' kibber de groun' tell you can't shun an' hide de tetter bed. Well, now, wen de time come fur dig tetter, an' de wuk berry tight, an' bittle berry skase, an' you so glad dat tetter-diggin' time come, fur nigger berry lub tetter, an' you tek you hoe an' go to de tetter feel, an' wen you see de wine so big an' rank, 'e mek you laff, an' you say: "Tetter da yer, oh 'e da yer, brudder." But mine you ent da joice an' brag too soon! An' now you tek de wine off de bed, an' dig de bed down, but de tetter you bin speck fur fine ent da. De tetter all gone to wine—nutt'n pum de wine but string an' scrap tetter. All on de outside de bed an' nutt'n in de inside. An' now you tetter spectashun tun to disappint, an' you laff tun to bex. De tetter wine fool you; e promis you heap, an' ent gib you nutt'n. (Yes, we shun dat way heaper time.)

Well, now, yunner mus'n shet yo' eye an' ent see de parable. ("De Lawd gib we sperityul understandin' yer tonight, dat we mout hab ecnolig ob de parable ob de tetter wine Christun.") Now dis is de parable in de tetter wine.

De chuch is de Lawd tetter feel. An' de chuch member is de tetter de Lawd plant in 'e tetter feel to mek de tetter ob good wuks. An' de Lawd watch ober dat feel, an' culterwate dat feel, an' send de sezuns pun dat feel, dat 'e mout bring fote heaper tetter of good wuks to de glory of Him great name, an' fur bless de wul. De chuch is de tetter feel outer wich de wul is to feed an' lib. But I berry 'fraid dat de chuch stahbe de wul mo' dan 'e feed um. But de time will come wen de Lawd will come to dig him tetter—to see wha pun de wine ob chuch membership an' perfeshun. Oh brudder an' sister, dat's gwine to be a time—dat diggin' time—ef tetter da, time ob rejoicin'—ef tetter ent da, time of great trouble an' lemuntashun.

Wen yunner come to dig tetter, ent de tetter wine you come fur, but de tetter pun de wine. An' de same wid de Lawd wen 'e come in det an' judgment—dem da him tetter diggin' time, an' 'e want nutt'n but de

* "The Potato Vine Christian."

tetter ob grace in de haht an' de tetter ob good wuks in de life. 'E ent gwine ask ef you chuch member, ef you baptize, ef you tek de commun-eyun, how much money you been gib to de chuch, ef you Baptis', ef you Metodis', ef you Prisbeteriun, ef you 'Piscopul.

No, 'e ent gwine ask no sich questun as dem. But 'e gwine do jes like you do wen you go fur dig tetter—dig de bed down an ta um all to peeces an' see ef any tetter da. An' so de Lawd in de diggin' day ent gwine stop to look at dem outside ting dat we mek de morest ob, but 'e gwine open de haht, like you dig open de tetter bed, to see ef 'e kin fine de tetter ob fait' an' lub an' grace to all dat wine ob perfeshun on de outside.

An I berry 'fraid dat menny wen de Lawd dig dem will fine to be all wine an' no tetter. Like de barrun fig tree, dat de Sabeyur cuss, dat mek a great show, but ent hab no fig—nutt'n but leaf. An' de parable ob de barrun fig tree an' de parable ob de barrun "tetter wine" all de same. Oh dat barrun is a wicket ting befo' de Lawd an' a berry danjerus ting. An' de barrun chu'ch member is de wust ob all barrun ting—kase wid dem bar-run, dem is hippercrit an liar. Like de barrun fig tree, an' de barrun tetter wine, kibber wid lead an' so rank an' flourishin', dem say dem hab fig an' tetter, wen dem ent hab none an' jes da fool you. No wunder dat de Sabeyur bex wid dat barrun fig tree an' cuss um dat 'e dead. W'y 'e mek de Sabeyur tink 'e hab fig on um? An' lemme tell yunner dat satefy so long is you baptize, an' chuch member an' hab de name of Christun, an' ent da try fur be Christun, but had on de Lawd unifohm an da fight in de debil ahmy, you ent de fool de Lawd, but you da fool youself an' is de biggest fool in de wul. De open sinner ent sich fool as de chuch member sinner, because him know dat tetter wine an' fig leaf is wutless widout de tetter an' de fig.

But mebbe you ax, is tetter wine a bad ting? No, I say, tetter wine is a good ting. You can't hab tetter widout de tetter wine. Dat wha' tetter wine fur—to mek tetter. But dat tetter wine dat ent mek tetter, dat's a bad tetter wine kase 'e barrun tetter wine. 'E wine but do 'e look like tetter wine, 'e ent tetter wine, or e'd ba tetter. You kin be chu'ch member an' de barrun tetter wine, but you can't be Christun, de true tetter wine, an' not hab de tetter ob delijun. E's de juty ob de Christun to jine de chuch an' baptize an' mek perfeshun ob delijun befo' de wul. But wha' good 'e gwine do you to perfess—delijun ent gwine gib you delijun. An' dats de rez'n de wul full you today wid so much trashy an' wuthless Christun. De debil fool dem to tek de name an perfeshun of delijun, fur de delijun 'eself, an' dat mek de wul full up wid chuch member but hab berry few true Christun in um—heaper wine but berry little tetter.

Wen you talk to dese tetter wine Christuns, dem talk berry well, an' say dem hab fait', but dem fait' is a dead fait', kase 'e ent ba de tetter ob good wuks. "Fait' widout wuk," de scriptur say, "is dead, and wuthless—same like wine widout tetter." But if 'e jes bin dat dese dead-fait' Christuns, like barrun tetter wine, ent ba no tetter ob good wuk, dat would be bad nuff. But dem barrun to da good wuk, dem ent barrun, but berry fruitful to ba bad wuks. Dem cuss, dem lie, dem teel, dem dance, an' frolic de whole night, dem eyes are bunt, an' dem dultrify, an' de only diffrunce between dem an' de udder sinner is dat dem hab de tetter wine ob de perfeshun ob delijun an' de udder ent. Dat all de diffrunce, an' dat mek dem wuss dan de perfess sinner dat ent mek no perfeshun. Kase now dem fool to tek de perfeshun fur delijun an' de perfeshun dem mek wen dem so wickit an' da lib in sin mek dem to be stumblin' block befo' de sinner dat dem stumble ober intertawment.

But, brudder an' sister, de true gospel fait' wen 'e plant in de haht nebber fail to bring fote de tetter ob good wuks. 'E ent all tetter wine now. Now de perfeshun wut sump'n. Grace in de haht mek grace in de life. Befo' 'e been de tetter wine ob "dead wuks," nutt'n but jine chuch an' baptize, an gib money mabbe, an' go right on in sin. But wen grace come inter de haht, de fait' is a libbin fait', an libbin fait' mek libbin wuks. 'E ent no tetter wine delijun now, fur de wine ob perfeshun heng full an' hebby wid de tetter ob "good wuks," like wen you dig tetter de groun' full of tetter, an' dem ole yam tetter too, de tetter dat nigger lub de morest ob all tetter.

An' now I wanter tell you 'bout some ob dese gospel tetter, dat de Lawd put grace in we haht to mek we ba an' bring fote fruit in we life, an' dat ef we ent ba, we ain't nutt'n but tetter wine Christun to condem in de day of judgment. Dese is some ob de gospel tetter ent en furgit um lub fur de Sabeyur, lub fur de brudder an' sister, an' lub fur de po' sinner to pray fur him, an' try fur bring um to de Sabeyur to sabe 'e. Dat's wun ob de gospel tetter. Yo da ba, like tetter wine, dat wun. Obejuns to all de Sabeyur commandiments, dat's annudder wun ob de gospel tetter. You da bey de Lawd. O dat obejuns to de Sabeyur, to do what he tell we fur do, an' ent do what 'e say you muss'n do. Oh, brudder an' sister, de wine of perfeshun ent nutt'n ef 'e ent had de tetter ob obejuns da heng to um. An' da's de tetter ob puow haht an' good an' holy life. Christun ent fur wohk in de flesh an' git drunk, an' dultrify, an' teel, an' tell lie, an fur mix up 'eself wid sinner in all dem sin an' ebil way. Do yunner mine de tetter ob puow an' holy life, an' member dat widout dat weddin' gahment de do' ob heb'n will neber open to you. Dat's de tetter de Sabeyur will dig fur an' 'quire wen 'e come in de judgment.

But I ent hav time to tell you 'bout all de gospel tetter, but I'll hab to tell you 'bout dis wun, an' dat is all do all de good yo' kin in de wul, 'cordin to you opperchunity an' you talunt, an' to mek yo'self nuseful an' a blessin' to de wul. What tetter put yer fur, but fur de good ob de wul? An dat's wha' de Christun yer fur. De gospel an' sister Christuns is de greatest blessin' dat de wul hab. An' so brudder an' sister, member—ent furget um—dat ef you ent a blessin' to de wul, an' de wul ent better fur you bein in um—den you tetter wine an' ent tetter.

Oh, I berry 'fraid dat heaper dem chuch member is nutt'n but tetter wine Christun, an' heap of de delijun in de wul is nutt'n but tetter wine delijun. An dat I mout be fait'ful wid you ternight lemme tell you who some dem tetter wine Christun is. De hippercrit is wun ob dem; 'e all wine an' no tetter. Ef 'e been Christun 'e wouldn't haffer try so hahd to mek 'eself out wun. Wen yo' see a man da try fur walk straight dat show drunk. Sober man ain't haffer try to walk straight. De hippercrit is same like de cheap, wutless hickry stripe homespun de shopkeeper sell to we niggers. De cloht so t'in an' light dat dey full um up an' mek um stiff wid stahch to hide de tinness, an' mek um hebby an' fool we to buy um. I ent like to buy cloht dat stiff wid stahch, an' I ent like dem chuch member dat stahch stiff wid delijun—dem berry apt to be hippercrit. Ef delijun been in dem so much is dey mek out de wouldn't hab to put so much delijun on dem.

Annuder tetter wine Christun is de man or 'oman dat jine de chuch but ent jine de Sabeyur. Dem trus' in de chuch in de baptize, but dem ent trus' in de Sabeyur. An de's heaper dem kind ob tetter wine Christun.

De man dat sich powerful Baptis', an' sich powerful Metodis', an' sich powerful Prisbeteriun, an' sich powerful 'Piscopul, dat dem ent beleebe dat none but dem own chuch gwine to hebin, dem's ginuwine tetter wine Christun. Dem big Baptis' an' Metodis', but I feel dem berry little scrappy Christun, ef dem Christun 'tal. De Baptis' wine and de Metodis' wine, and de Prisbeteriun and de 'Piscopul wine berry rank and flourishin', but de tetter ob puow an' undefile delijun ent da—dem delijun gone inter de Baptis' wine an' de Metodis' wine an' dem tudder wine. Da's too menny ob dem 'Piscopul an' Prisbeteriun an' Metodis' and Baptis' tetter wine, an' dat mek de wul ent no better.

But one udder tetter wine Christun dat I beleege to tell yo' 'bout is de man dat calls 'eself morrul man. Him ent chuch member kase 'e say 'e better dan de chuch member an' de chuch ent good nuff fur em. 'E say 'e pay all jes' det, 'e ent git drunk, 'e ent dultrify, an' 'e berry 'spectible, which 'e say is more dan heaper chuch member is. But ef all de good ting de morrul man say 'bout 'eself is true, 'e guilty all de same ob de wust of all sin. 'E wont beleebe in de Sabeyur an' jeck um, kase 'e say 'e good nuff an' ent need de Sabeyur.

Oh, wha' bad, wicket haht some dem morrul an' self-rightyus man hab. Some dem is wus sinner befo' God dan some dem sinner dem spise an tink demself better dan dem. De old Pharisee been wusser sinner dan de Publikin dat 'e spise. De self-rightyus man, 'e sin lay deep in 'e haht, like measles dat neber bruk out an' den sho to kell you. Oh, I'd redder be one dem sinner wid dem sin, dan one dem self-rightyus sinner sick unto det wid sin, but dem ent feel de sin an' ent see de sin. But God shum.

Brudder an' sister hahky to me. Dem self-rightyus man an' 'oman dat too good to come to de Sabeyur an' trus' in Him, dem is tetter wine Christun, an' in dem haht da ent no differunt between dem an' de tetter wine Christun dat baptize, jine chuch, an' mek big perfeshun, an' git drunk an' teel an' dultrify an' lib in sin. De lack wid dem all is de grace ob God an' de rightyusness ob Christ in dem haht. Self-rightyus stroy de soul an' is jes as bad as unrightyus.

De self-rightyus man is like one dem bran' new purty counterfit bill. Yo tink sho 'e good money an' you tek 'em, but wen yo' gib um to de sto'keeper fur pay um fur wha' you buy, 'e look at um an' zamun um berry close, an' den 'e say: "Wa you git dis money? 'E berry purty, but 'e ent wut nutt'n; 'e counterfit." De quikenin ob de sperit, an' de lub of Christ in 'e haht—dat w'at mek de jenuwine Christun, an' ef 'e ent hab dot, morrul man or immorrul chuch member—'e's all de same, a tetter wine Christun.

Better to'be ole ragged bill dat is money dan to be new an' purty bill dat counterfit an' ent no money 'tall. I redder be one dem po' stumblin' Christun, like de ole raggid money, dan to be one dem morrul man dat like de purty new bill, lack de wun ting dat mek um Christun. 'E may pass wid man, but not wid God.

But mebbee you ax, "How come so menny tetter wine Christun in de wul dat mek perfeshun, but neber ba de tetter ob delijun?" Well, I tink one rez'n is dat de debil fool heaper dem to tink dat de perfeshun am de name will sabe dem. De debil kin mek people beleebe tings in delijun dat 'e couldn't mek dem beleebe wid all 'e tryin' in nutt'n else.

An' anudder ting, I tink dat mek so much tetter wine Christun dat berry barrun, or ba berry leetle fruit, is dat heaper Christun hab too good a time in dis wul. Some time de lan' so rich, an' de sezun so high—so much rain—dat de groth so rapid dat 'e gone into de wine instid ob inter de tetter. An' dat de way wid heaper Christun. Dem rich, de budd'n ob life ent hebby pun dem, dem neber sick nor hab trouble, an' dat mek dem nigleck fur pray an' fight dem sin, an' keep dem frum libbin close to de Sabeyur, an' mek dem nigleck dem juty, an' den de wul tek de feel ob dem haht, an' den dem delijun is berry leetle mo' dan de wine ob perfeshun. De Christun can't hab too high a sezun ob grace to ba de tetter of delijun, but 'e kin hab too much wully food, ef heaper grace ent go wid um. In de triul and flicksuns ob de Christun mebbe de ent so much wine, but mo' dan dat, mo' tetter. Yunner all 'member an' ent furgit de parable ob de "Tetter Wine Christun."

(A Negro's Version of Heaven and Hell

A *Mississippi Folk Sermon*

One Sunday night in the month of August, some years ago, I was passing by Mount Ever Rest colored church. The doors and windows were open and the congregation was singing:

> God showed Noah by the rainbow sign,
> No more water, but the fire next time.

And as they finished the last stanza, the Rev. George W. Flowers, a minister of ebony hue, and who was an acquaintance of mine, arose and began to address them, as follows:

"Bretheren, and sisteren, my discourse dis even am gwine to be on the beautifulness of heav'n, and de horrifulness of hell, and one or de other of dem two things ought to reach every man, woman, and child in this vast assembliment.

"My text am like de brains of most of our hearers here tonight, somewhat scatterin', but de thought dat I wishes to convey to you am gwine to be more constimated and to de pint.

"My text am scattered all through dis good old book from kiver to kiver, like chicken feed in de straw, and if any of you smart-alecks doubts anything dat I has to say here to you here tonight, you can take dis book down and search out dis vital trufe for yourselves, after I am through wid my expostulations.

"I wishes to further say, dat I sees in dis congregation, a big flock of black sheep without a shepherd: one in which de bline am 'temptin' to lead de bline. De very openin' song dat you has just sung show dat you am followin' after false doctrine. And I mought just as well tell you now as any other time, by way of introductatory, dat my remarks to you on dis auspicious occasion am not gwine to be long de old and well-beaten path followed by all of my prepossessors, but am gwine to be entirely new to de most of you.

"Now hear me, people, and give your ears over to understandin'. De Bible specifies dat all flesh am not de same; dat dare am one kine of flesh of men; another kine of birds; and still another of fish and fowls; and it mought have further said dat all flesh of men am not de same kine of meat, for we has de flesh of de white folks; de flesh of de nigger; de flesh of de Injun; and at last, de flesh of de Chinaman, all differin' in glory de same as one star differs from another star in glory.

Sermons and Prayers

"Listen now, and hear me, people. All heavens and all hells am not duh same kine either.

"Listen now, and hear me. (I am gwine to ax de brother dat is settin' de closest to dat dawg to please kick him out of dis sanctuary 'fore I proceeds any further, and I wants to agin call de attention to all of you to dat scripture dat says, 'Cast not your pearls before a hawg, nor feed holy things to er dawg.' Dat am de third time now dat I has seed dat same dawg trying to lif' dat kiver from off dat Sacrament board, and I am going to ax you once more to leave dem dawgs at home in de future.—Thank you, my brother, be seated.)

"Now hear me, people, and hearken unto my voice. Don't you all know dat dare am seven heavens; and don't you all further know dat wid all dat room dat dey ain't gwine to be anyways crowded; and dat dare will be plenty of room widout mixin' up de different races?

"All you niggers what think you gwine to set down and eat wid de white people at de feast of de Lamb am gwine to be disappointed. De white folks ain't gwine to stand for nothin' like dat, and 'sides dat, if you was in dare, de way they am gwine to have dare grub cooked wouldn't suit you nohow, and you mought just as well gid dat off you mine, for you ain't gwine to be dare.

"De New Jerusalem ain't gwine to be no 'coon town, and it ain't gwine to have no ile mills or compresses in it; and dare ain't gwine to be no fruit stands or lunch counters on dem golden streets. Dat town am gwine to be strictly for de white folks, and no nigger is goin' to have a chance to git any further in dat town dan Paradise Alley.

"De nigger settlement in heaven am gwine to be some miles out, on de east side of de River of Life, and hear me, people, and give heed to my supplication, de catfish in dat river am gwine to be as big as a whale—'cording to de size of de whale, of course—and de watermelons and sweet 'taters am gwine to grow wile and spontaneous all up and down dat fertile valley.

"Oh, my bretheren, methinks I see dat place now, dimly in de distance, through de twilight; and I thinks I can see wid my mine eye a twelve-pound possum wid his tail twined 'round a 'simmon limb; and a young Plymouth Rock roostin' on de lot fence.—Glory be to God in the highest. Amen.

"But brethren, hear me now, and despise not de messenger of de Lord, what am you gwine to do on dat awful day of judgment; dat day when de Lord of Lords and King of Kings comes down in all his glory to judge dis old world? Dat am not gwine to be any perlice court trial. False swearin' ain't gwine to git you nothin' dare. Dat am gwine to be one time when you am gwine to git all dat is comin' to you and den some, even to de uttermost farthin'—whatsumever dat mought be.

"Oh my bretheren, it makes me tremble, tremble, when I thinks of what

135

you gwine to do when dat trial is over; and when de good Shepherd 'gins to separate de goats from de sheeps. Oh, my brother, I 'magines I can hear him saying now, 'Depart from me, you big bobtail billy goat from Riverside Plantation. Git off the exhibition ground altogether; I never knewed you.' Den dare will be weepin', wailin', and gnashin' of teeth; and de wicked will be cast out into outer darkness widout so much as a two-bit three-burner headlight on; and on down into dat awful region where de sun never shines, and where de thermometer stand fifty degrees below zero on de Fourth of July.

"Oh, my bretheren and sisteren, I beseeches you to beware of dat awful place where hell is frez over all de year round, and where de devil am gwine to roll you in de snow through de countless ages of eternity.

"Oh, my brother, think about what you gwine to do when dem awful icicles go slidin' down your back. Oh, what am you gwine to do in dat awful hour? De North Pole, what Dr. Cook has done told so many horrifying and conflicktin' tales about, am a plumb tropical climate 'side dat awful region.

"Oh, my bretheren, de very words in your mouf am gwine to freeze hard and drap down on dat icy floor and rattle like tinklin' brass and clashin' symbles, when you tries to cry out in your agony. De very breath of your nostrils am gwine to freeze, and beat you in de face like a snowstorm; and hail and sleet am gwine to blow and beat on dat old leaky roof of hell continuously.

"Oh, my bretheren, let me 'monish you to quit your cussin', lyin', stealin', crap shottin', whiskey drinkin', and backbitin' one another to de white folks, and prepare yourselves for dat awful day what am bound to come.

"And now may de good Lord have mercy on your poor ignited souls 'fore it is everlastin'ly too late, shall be my prayer.

"Now bretheren, and sisteren, while de congregation stands, I am gwine to ax all of you to jine me in singin':

> It rains and it hails,
> And it is cold and stormy weather;
> De people weeps, and dey wails,
> And Lord, I flees to Thee for shelter."

On the following morning, I saw George, and said, "Reverend Flowers, what sort of a hell was that you were telling your people about last night?"

"Who, me?"

"Yes, you. I happened to be passing Mount Ever Rest last night and stopped outside and listened to you preach for a while."

"Oh, pshaw, Capt'n," said George, with a broad smile on his face, "I know dat de Bible say dat hell am a lake of fire and blue stone, but den you knows a nigger well enough to know dat it don't do no good to try to skeer him wid hot weather, 'n' dat if you wants to git next to him, you got to threaten him wid cold."

([

"Dem Sebun Wimmin"

Negro Folk Sermon by John Jasper

"Did you ebur git yer mine on what Iz'er say in chapter fo' an' vurs wun? Listen to hiz wurds: 'An' sebun wimmin shall tek hol' uv wun man in dat day, sayin' we will eat our own bread an' mek our own 'parrel; only let us be called by Thy name; tek Thou erway our reproach!' De profit is furloserfizin' 'bout de matter uv wimmin—spechully wen dar is sebun in de lan' wen wars done thin out de men an' de wimmins feels de strings and' bites uv reproach. I tell yer to stan' it. Shure ez yer settin' on dat bench she will fly erway an' hide herself, or she will fly at yer, an' den, ole fellus, yer had bettur be pullin' out fer de tall timbur fast. Gord done settled it dat wun 'omun iz noff fer a man, an' two iz er war on yer hans —bless yer, it is.

"But dar kums times wen it goze hard wid wimmin. Dey iz lef' out uv de lottery uv heavun; dey draws blanks an' dey gits to be a laughin' stock ub de ungodly. Not dat dey is crazy ter marry, an' not dat dey is uv dat flautin', slatturn lot dat allus gallavantin' eroun' er-tryin' ter git a man ter s'port' um. Dey wuz square, all right wimmin. Wurk wud not skeer um. Dey wuz willin' ter mek dere bread an' cloes, ter pay dere own way, purvided dey ud be Mrs. Sumbody, an' in dat way 'skape de dev'lish jeers an' slights uv base men. Fur my part, I feels quite sorry fur dat class uv ladiz, an' I kinder feels my blud gittin' up when I finds folks castin' reproachiz on dere fair names.

"But my mastur in de skies! Dis pikshur here uv de profit iz too much fer me. It mek me feel like tekin' ter de woods, in quick order. Lord, what would I do ef I wuz pursued by er army uv sebun wimmin, axin' me ter 'low each wun ev um to be called Mrs. Jasper? It may be dat each wun wuz fer hersef ter de limit, an' hoped ter shet out de udder six an hev de man ter hersef; an' ef she wuz ter hev 'im ertall she ort ter hev all uv 'im. Dar is not nuff ter d'vide, I tell yer dar ain't, an' wen yer git er haf interest in er man yer iz po' indeed, an ef only wun sevunth iz yourn, yer had es well start on ter de po' house 'fo' yer git yer dinner.

"A gud 'oman can' byar ter be oberluked. It ain't her nature, an' it iz a site fer de anguls ter see wat sort uv men sum wimmin will tek sooner dan be lef' out inti'ly.

"But what gits me arter all iz a man. I see 'im in de quiet uv de day, de Sabuth day. He teks a stroll fer de koolin' uv hiz mine, er-wearin' uv hiz nice cloes, an feelin' like a new man in de City Kounsil; de fust thing he know'd a lady glide up ter 'im an' put her han' light on hiz arm. He jump 'roun' an' she say, mighty flush'd up, 'Skuse me!'

"He see at wunst she er lady, but he wuz kinder lo' in hiz sperrit, an' yit he wish in hiz hart dat she had gone ter de udder en' uv de rode, but he want ter hear her out.

"She tell 'im de sight uv a man wuz medsin fer bad eyes, dat nurly all uv 'em wuz out down in de war an' dat in konsequens it wuz er lonesum time fer wimmin; dey hav nobody—no ringin' de do' bells in de eb'nin; nobody sendin' 'em flowers an' fekshuns; no sweetarts tekin' 'em walkin' on Sunday arternoons, an' weddin's gwine out er fashun. 'An' dis ain't de wust uv it. It mek us shamed. De wives, dey purrades 'roun' an' brags 'bout dere ole man, an' cuts dere eye at us scornful; an' de husban's iz mighty nigh es bad, er-pokin' fun at us an' axin' erbout de chillun.'

"She say, 'Yer needn' think we're crazy ter marry; tain't dat, an' tain't dat we want yer ter s'port us, no, no! We hev money an' kin funnish our own vittuls an cloes, an' we kin wuk; but it iz dere reproach dey kas' on us, de wear an' tear uv bein' laff'd at dat cuts us so deep. If I cud be Mrs. Sumbody, had sum proof dat I had de name uv sumun—sumthin' ter rub off de reproach. Dat's it, dis ding-dongin' dey pokes at me.'

"De man wuz pale es linnin, an' wuz hopin' ter ansur, but 'fo' de wuds floo from his lips ernudder 'oman hooked 'im in de udder side. Mursy uv de Lord! Two uv 'em had 'im an' it luk like de fus' wun an' tetter wun was gwine to rip 'im in tew an' each tek a haf. De las' wun tell her tale jes' like de fus't wun an' wuss. She bring in tears es part uv her argurmint, an' de udder wun got frerred an' used wuds dat would 'a' konkured 'im ef jes' den two mo'—mine yer mekin' fo' in all—hed not kum up an' git er grip on de gemmun, an hiz eyes luk like dey'd pop out his hed; wun on each side an' it seems he gwine ter faint.

" 'Yer ladiz,' he says, 'may be right in yer 'thuzasm, but yer iz too menny. Up ter dis time I hav bin shy uv wimmin, but ef I cud be erlowed ter choose jes' wun I might try it.'

"Den de fo' wimmins begun ter git shaky wen a nu wun sailed in—dat's five; den ernudder—dat's six; an' den wun mo'—*sebun!*

"Luk, will yer! Sebun got wun man. It izn't sed wedder de wimmin wuz fer a partnurship, wid de man es de kapertul, or wedder each uv 'em hoped ter beat out de udder six; but wun thing we know, an' dat iz dat de po' man iz in de low grounds uv sorrur. Ter my mine, de pikshur iz mighty serus, eben do it mek us smile. Fur my po' part, I iz glad we lives in fairer times. In our day mens iz awful plen'ful, tho' I kinnot say dat de quality iz fust class in vey menny. But I thanks de Lord mos' enny nice leddy kin git married in dese times ef dey choose, an' dat widout gwine out sparkin' fer de man. I notis dat ef she stay ter home, ten' ter her busnis, mine her mudder, an' not sweep de streets off'n wid her skirts, in de long run her modes' sperrit will win de day.

"I ubsurv ernudder thing; de unmerrid lady, de ole maid is sum calls her, need not hang her haid. Jes' let her be quiet an' surv de Lord; jes' not fret 'bout wat fools say. Dey duz er heap uv talkin', but it iz like de cracklin' uv de burnin' sticks under de pot—a big fuss an' a littul heat. Fer my part, I honors de 'oman dat b'haves herself, briduls her tongue, duz her wuk, an' sings es she goes erlong. Her contendid sperrit beats a lazy husban' ebry time an' mighty off'n brings er gud husband erlong.

"Es fer dese folks dat flurts an' scouts at de ole maid, dey ain't fitten ter live, an' ort ter be in de bottum uv Jeems Rivur, 'cept'n dey'd spile de watur. No gennum nur no lady wud do it.

"No, dis iz my wud 'bout de wimmin, an' I hope yer like it, but if yer doan't, jes' 'member dat Jasper sed it, an' will stand by it, 'til de cows in de lo'er fiel' kums home.

(Prayers

THE WHITE MAN'S PRAYER

It had been a long dry spell in Florida, and everybody had been worried about the crops, so they thought they had better hold a prayer meeting about it and ask God for some rain. So they asked Brother John to send up the prayer because everybody said that he was really a good old man, if there was one in the country. So Brother John got down on his knees in the meeting and began to pray, and this is how he prayed:

"O Lahd, the first thing I want you to understand is that it is a white man talking to you. This ain't no nigger whooping and hollering for something and then don't know what to do with it after he gets it. This is a white man talking to you, and I want you to pay some attention. Now, in the first place, Lahd, we would like a little rain. It's been powerful dry around here, and we needs rain mighty bad. But don't come in no storm like you did last year. Come ca'm and gentle and water our crops.

"And now another thing, Lahd—don't let these niggers be as sassy this coming year as they have been in the past. That's all, Lahd. Amen."

THE NEGRO'S PRAYER

A white minister was conducting a revival series in a colored church. After exercising a bit, he asked an old colored deacon to lead in prayer.

According to the *Roanoke News*, this is the appeal which the brother in black offered for his brother in white:

"Oh Lawd, gib him de eye ob de eagle, dat he may spy out sin afar off, weave his hands to de gospel plow, tie his tongue to de limbs ob truth, nail his ear to de South Pole. Bow his head away down between his knees, and his knees way down in some lonesome dark and narrow valley where prayer is much wanted to be made. 'Noint him wid de kerosene oil of salvation and set him on fire."

PRAYER

"O, Lord, here it is again and again and one time more that your weak, unprofitable servant has come, knee bent and body bowed, this evening, to call upon your darling name. And we ask you, our Father, while your servant pertemps to bow, to please do not let him bow for form nor for fashion nor cloak before dis unfrendly world, for Jesus' sake. But we will ask you to bow my head below my knees, and my knees 'way down in some lonesome valley of humiliation where you promised to hear and answer prayer in every time of need and every distressful hour, for Jesus' sake. Didn't you say in your forewritten and divine word where there was two, three, or ever so many of your royal blood bought purchase from hell, and their blood has ransomed and their names truly cut on the chief cornerstone that lay 'way in the court of Mount Zina, that thou would be a prayer-hearing God, and the chieftest among the number? Here is the number, my Father, too many to be lost and not enough to be saved, and unless you will come this way our work will be in vain. O Lord! There is work to be done in this part of our moral vineyard, too hard for man to do, and angels can't do it, so we ask thee to come this way and lend us a helping hand. In thy mighty coming, please don't come in wrath nor in strick judgment, but come over many hills, gills, and poverlications, with darling love in one hand and free grace in the other, healing up all our back-sliding ways and loving our little souls freely, once more for Jesus' sake.

"Didn't you say that you was a rock in the weary land, a shelter in a mighty storm, a stronghold in the day of trouble, and a cave in thy temple? We believe that you are a manna to the hungry soul and to the weary you will give rest, that you will make the wounded conscience whole and calm the troubled breast. We ask you to lift high your dorman windows of heaven this evening and take a gentle peep over Joshua's high white wall, 'way down in the low grounds of sorrow, and see what sin and flesh is doing with your people.

"We ask thee to remember sinners in a special manner. They are like wild horses in a furious battle, fearing not God and dreading not hell. Make bars out of your mighty arms and stop them in their wild career and flighty condition. Hammer hard on their hard rock hearts with the hammer of Jeremiah and break their hearts in ten thousand pieces. We ask you to catch them, shake them, and shake them over hell; let mercy forbid their fall, for Jesus' sake. Amen."

PART III

❧ ❧

Songs

Spirituals

Negro spirituals, which had always fascinated and delighted the people who heard them sung by Negroes on plantations and on battlefields, were the first Negro folk gems to be recorded and published. Charlotte Forten, who had heard them sung by Negroes on St. Helena Island, South Carolina, wrote down a few in 1864. Thomas Wentworth Higginson was deeply impressed during the Civil War with the spirituals sung by Negro soldiers in his regiment as they sat around the campfires in the evening, and in 1867 he collected a group of them and had them published in the Atlantic Monthly magazine. In the same year the first systematic and well-organized collection of Negro spirituals, titled Slave Songs in the United States, was published, edited by William F. Allen, Charles P. Ware, and Lucy McKim Garrison.

Spirituals were further popularized in 1871 by a group of singers at Fisk University, Nashville, Tennessee. Calling themselves the Jubilee Singers, they sang these songs to large audiences in America and in European countries as well. The second major collection of Negro spirituals was published in one section of a volume labeled The Story of the Jubilee Singers with Their Songs, written by J. B. T. Marsh in the year 1880. Later on, a few representative collections were compiled by Negroes, chief among them being Folk Songs of the American Negro, by Frederick J. Work, in 1915, and Folk Songs of the Negro as Sung at Hampton Institute, by Nathaniel Dett, eminent Negro musician and composer. The most comprehensive volume of Negro spirituals was assembled and edited by the distinguished *author and scholar James Weldon Johnson and his brother J. Rosamond Johnson, noted composer.* This work, The Book of Negro Spirituals, *published in 1925, was followed in 1926 by a companion volume,* The Second Book of Negro Spirituals.

The spiritual reflects the Negro slave's characteristic philosophy—that heaven was his home and the world only a temporary abode. This other-worldly view of life helped him endure the hardships and trials of slavery cheerfully, even optimistically. While the themes of most of the spirituals reflect that philosophy, some of them reveal a certain practicality, an acceptance of conditions as they are. The songs belonging to this second category express what might be termed "reality-thinking." A third type of Negro spiritual simply relates a portion of some Bible story.

The popularity of Negro spirituals has not waned. They have stood the test of time and are still sung by talented soloists and famous singing groups.

Swing Low, Sweet Chariot

Swing low, sweet char-i-ot, Coming for to car-ry me home

Swing low, sweet char-i-ot, Coming for to car-ry me home.

1. I looked o - ver Jor-dan and what did I see,
2. If you get there be - fore I do,
3. The bright-est day that ev - er I saw,
4. I'm some-times up and some-times down,

Com-ing for to car-ry me home? A band of an-gels
Com-ing for to car-ry me home, Tell all my friends I'm
Com-ing for to car-ry me home, When Je-sus wash'd my
Com-ing for to car-ry me home, But still my soul feels

Com-ing af-ter me, Com-ing for to car-ry me home.
com - ing too, Com-ing for to car-ry me home.
sins a - way, Com-ing for to car-ry me home.
heaven - ly bound, Com-ing for to car-ry me home.

Steal Away

Steal a-way, steal a-way, steal a-way to Je-sus!

Steal a-way, steal a-way home, I hain't got long to stay here.

1. My Lord ___ calls me, He calls me by the
2. Green trees are bend-ing, Poor sin-ners stand ___

thun - der; The trum-pet sounds it
trem - bling; The trum-pet sounds it

in my soul: I hain't got long to stay here.

3. My Lord calls me,
   He calls me by the lightning;
The trumpet sounds it in my soul:
   I hain't got long to stay here.
   Cho.—Steal away, &c.

4. Tombstones are bursting,
   Poor sinners are trembling;
The trumpet sounds it in my soul:
   I hain't got long to stay here.
   Cho.—Steal away, &c.

148

Old Ship of Zion

What ___ ship is that a - sail-ing, Hal - le -
1. 'Tis the old ___ ship of Zi - on, Hal - le -
Do you think that ___ she is a - ble, Hal - le -

lu - jah, What ___ ship is that a -
lu - jah, 'Tis ___ the old ship of
lu - jah, Do ___ you think that she is

Repeat twice for first verse.

sail - ing, Hal - le - lu.⎫
Zi - on, Hal - le - lu.⎬   Do   you
a - ble, Hal - le - lu.⎭

think that she is a - ble, For to car-ry us all ___

home. O ___ glo - ry, Hal - le - lu.

In singing the last two verses the music is not to be repeated.

2. She has landed many a thousand, Hallelujah,
   She has landed many a thousand, Hallelu,
   She has landed many a thousand,
   And will land as many a more. O glory, Hallelu.

3. She is loaded down with angels, Hallelujah,
   She is loaded down with angels, Hallelu,
   And King Jesus is the Captain,
   And he'll carry us all home. O glory, Hallelu.

The Gospel Train

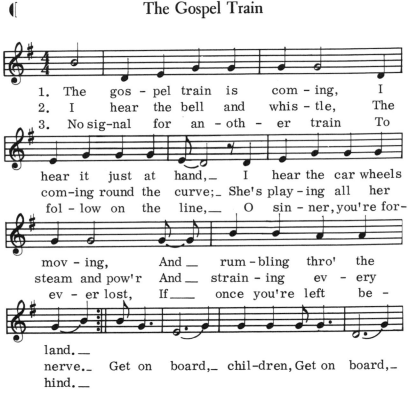

1. The gos - pel train is com - ing, I
2. I hear the bell and whis - tle, The
3. No sig-nal for an - oth - er train To

hear it just at hand,— I hear the car wheels
com-ing round the curve;— She's play - ing all her
fol - low on the line,— O sin - ner, you're for-

mov - ing, And — rum - bling thro' the
steam and pow'r And — strain - ing ev - ery
ev - er lost, If — once you're left be -

land. —
nerve. — Get on board,— chil-dren, Get on board,—
hind. —

chil - dren, Get on board,＿ chil-dren, For there's

room for man-y a more.＿ more.

4. This is the Christian banner,
   The motto's new and old,
   Salvation and Repentance
   Are burnished there in gold.
       Cho.—Get on board, children, &c.

5. She's nearing now the station,
   O, sinner, don't be vain,
   But come and get your ticket,
   And be ready for the train.
       Cho.—Get on board, children, &c.

6. The fare is cheap and all can go,
   The rich and poor are there,
   No second-class on board the train,
   No difference in the fare.
       Cho.—Get on board, children, &c.

This Old Time Religion

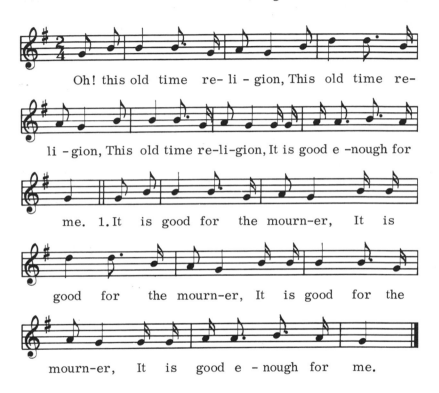

Oh! this old time re-li-gion, This old time re-li-gion, This old time re-li-gion, It is good e-nough for me. 1. It is good for the mourn-er, It is good for the mourn-er, It is good for the mourn-er, It is good e-nough for me.

2. It will carry you home to heaven,
   It will carry you home to heaven,
   It will carry you home to heaven,
     It is good enough for me.
       Cho.—Oh, this old time religion, &c.

3. It brought me out of bondage, &c.
       Cho.—Oh, this old time religion, &c.

4. It is good when you are in trouble, &c.
       Cho.—Oh, this old time religion, &c.

Lord, I Wish I Had a Come

1. Lord, I wish I had a come when you
2. There's no temp - ta - tions in the
3. My fa - ther and my mo - ther in the

call'd me, Lord, I wish I had a come when you
hea - vens, There's no temp - ta - tions in the
hea - vens, My fa - ther and my mo - ther in the

call'd me, Lord, I wish I had a come when you
hea - vens, There's no temp - ta - tions in the
hea - vens, My fa - ther and my mo - ther in the

call'd me,
hea - vens, Sit - ting by the side of my Je - sus.
hea - vens,

Way o - ver in the hea - vens, Way o - ver in the

hea - vens, Way o - ver in the hea - vens,

Sit - ing by the side of my Je - sus.

Did Not Old Pharaoh Get Lost?

1. I-saac a ran-som, while he lay Upon an al-tar bound, Mo-ses, an in-fant
cast a-way, By Pha-raoh's_ daugh-ter found. Did
not old Pha-raoh get lost, get lost, get lost, Did
not old Pha-raoh get lost in the Red Sea?

2. Joseph, by his false brethren
   sold,
   God raised above them all;
   To Hannah's child the Lord
   foretold
   How Eli's house should fall.
   Cho.—Did not old Phar-
   aoh, &c.

3. The Lord said unto Moses,
   Go unto Pharaoh now,
   For I have hardened Pharaoh's
   heart,
   To me he will not bow.
   Cho.—Did not old Phar-
   aoh, &c.

4. Then Moses and Aaron
   To Pharaoh did go,
   Thus says the God of Israel,
   Let my people go.
   Cho.—Did not old Pharaoh, &c.

5. Old Pharaoh said who is the
   Lord,
   That I should Him obey?
   His name it is Jehovah,
   For he hears his people pray.
   Cho.—Did not old Pharaoh, &c.

6. Then Moses numbered Israel,
   Through all the land abroad,
   Saying, children, do not murmur,
   But hear the word of God.
   Cho.—Did not old Pharaoh, &c.

7. Hark! hear the children murmur,
   They cried aloud for bread,
   Down came the hidden manna,
   The hungry soldiers fed.
   Cho.—Did not old Pharaoh, &c.

8. Then Moses said to Israel,
   As they stood along the
   shore,
   Your enemies you see to-day,
   You will never see no more.
   Cho.—Did not old Pharaoh, &c.

9. Then down came raging Pharaoh,
   That you may plainly see,
   Old Pharaoh and his host,
   Got lost in the Red Sea.
   Cho.—Did not old Pharaoh, &c.

10. Then men, and women, and
    children
    To Moses they did flock;
    They cried aloud for water,
    And Moses smote the rock.
    Cho.—Did not old Pharaoh, &c.

11. And the Lord spoke to Moses,
    From Sinai's smoking top,
    Saying, Moses, lead the people,
    Till I shall bid you stop.
    Cho.—Did not old Pharaoh, &c.

When Moses Smote the Water

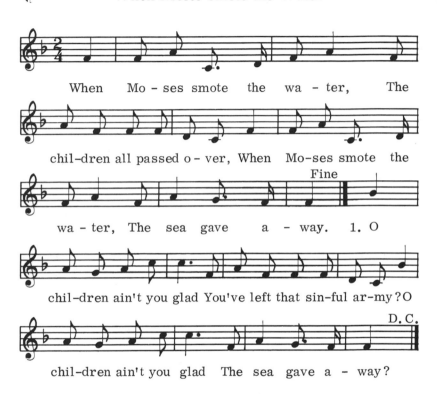

When Mo - ses smote the wa - ter, The
chil-dren all passed o - ver, When Mo-ses smote the
wa - ter, The sea gave a - way. 1. O
chil-dren ain't you glad You've left that sin-ful ar-my? O
chil-dren ain't you glad The sea gave a - way?

2. O Christians ain't you glad
   You've left that sinful army?
   O Christians ain't you glad
   The sea gave away?
   Cho.—When Moses smote, &c.

3. O brothers ain't you glad
   You've left that sinful army?
   O brothers ain't you glad
   The sea gave away?
   Cho.—When Moses smote, &c.

Didn't My Lord Deliver Daniel?

Did - n't   my   Lord   de - liv - er

Dan - iel, ___ D'liv-er Dan - iel, ___ d'liv-er

Dan - iel, Did-n't   my Lord   de - liv - er

Dan - iel, ___ And why not   a ev-er-y   man?

1st Verse

He de - liv-er'd Dan-iel from the li - on's den,

Jo -nah from the bel-ly   of   the   whale,   And the

He-brew chil-dren from the fie - ry   fur - nace, And

why not ev - er - y man?

Did-n't my Lord de - liv - er Dan - iel,— D'liv-er

Dan - iel,— d'liv-er Dan - iel, Did - n't

my Lord de - liv - er Dan - iel,— And

why not a ev - er - y man?

2nd Verse

The moon run down in a pur-ple stream, The

sun for - bear to shine, And ev-er - y star—

D.C. "Didn't my Lord"

dis - ap - pear,— King Je - sus shall— be mine.

3rd Verse

The wind blows East and the wind blows West, It blows like the judg - ment day, And ev - ery poor soul_ that nev - er did pray,_ 'll be glad to pray____ that day.

D.C. "Didn't my Lord"

4th Verse

I set my foot on the Gos - pel ship, And the ship it be - gin to sail, It land - ed me o - ver on Ca - naan's shore,_ And I'll nev - er come back_ a - ny more.

D.C. "Didn't my Lord"

He Rose from the Dead

Lord shall bear his chil - dren home. 1. The

Jews cru-ci-fied Him, and nail'd Him to the tree. The

Jews cru-ci-fied Him, and nail'd Him to the tree, The

Jews cru-ci-fied Him, and nail'd Him to the tree, And the

Lord shall bear His chil - dren home.

2. Joseph begged His body, and laid it in the tomb,
   And the Lord shall bear His children home.

3. Down came an angel, and rolled the stone away,
   And the Lord shall bear His children home.

4. Mary, she came weeping, her Lord for to see,
   But Christ had gone to Galilee.

My Good Lord's Been Here

My good Lord's been here, been here, been here. My good Lord's been here, And he's blessed my soul and gone. 1. O broth - ers, where were you, broth-ers, where were you, broth-ers, where were you When my good Lord was here?

2. O sinners, where were you, &c.
   Cho.—My good Lord's been here, &c.

3. O Christians, where were you, &c.
   Cho.—My good Lord's been here, &c.

4. O mourners, where were you, &c.
   Cho.—My good Lord's been here, &c.

Show Me the Way

1. Bro- ther, have you come to show me the
2. Sis - ter, have you come to show me the
3. Yes, ___ my good Lord, ___ show me the

way? Bro - ther, have you come to
way? Sis - ter, have you come to
way? Yes, ___ my good Lord, ___

show me the way, Show me the

way how to watch and ___ pray.

Nobody Knows the Trouble I See, Lord!

No - bod - y knows the trou-ble I see, Lord,

No - bod - y knows the trou - ble I see,

No - bod - y knows the trou - ble I see, Lord,

Fine

No - bod - y knows like Je - sus. 1. Brothers, will you

pray for me, Broth- ers will you pray for me,

And

D. C.

Broth-ers, will you pray for me,

help me to drive old Sa - tan a - way.

2. Sisters, will you pray for me, &c.

3. Mothers, will you pray for me, &c.

4. Preachers, will you pray for me, &c.

I Ain't Got Weary Yet

And I ain't got wea-ry yet, And I
ain't got wea-ry yet; Been down in the val-ley
so long, And I ain't got wea-ry yet. 1. Been
pray-ing for the sin-ner so long, And I ain't got wea-ry
yet; Been pray-ing for the sin-ner
so long, And I ain't got wea-ry yet.

2. Been praying for the mourner so long, &c.

3. Been going to the sitting-up so long, &c.

I'm a Rolling

I'm a roll - ing, I'm a roll - ing, I'm a-

roll-ing_ thro'an un-friend-ly world, I'm a roll -ing, I'm a

roll - ing thro' an un - friend - ly world.

1. O broth-ers, won't you help me, O broth-ers, won't you
2. O sis-ters, won't you help me, O sis-ters, won't you
3. O preach-ers, won't you help me, O preachers, won't you

help me to pray? O brothers, won't you
help me to pray? O sis-ters, won't you help me, Won't you
help me to fight? O preachers, won't you

D.C.

help me in the ser - vice of the Lord?___

All the Time

A Modern Gospel Song

The — Lord — look — up - on — me, And I'll

praise Him all the time. — I love my

Lord, — I'll love Him all the time. And I'll

fol - low ev -'ry day, and I'll fol - low in ev -'ry

way. Yes, the Lord — looks up - on me,

All — the time. —

Chorus

Well, all the time; _____ All the
time. _____ Oh, yes, my Lord __
watch-es all the time. _____ He's my
moth-er, He's my fa-ther, He's my
sis-ter and my broth-er. Oh,
yes, my Lord __ watch-es all the time. _____

Get Right, Stay Right

A Shout Song

The Negro "shout song" originated on St. Helena Island, off the coast of South Carolina. It was one of the major activities of a religious institution called the "praise house." The praise house was established by Negro slaves living on the various island plantations for the purpose of religious worship. It was non-denominational, open to all those who wished to praise God, render him thanks, and pray to him.

The shout song, sometimes referred to as the "running spiritual" and believed to antedate the traditional spiritual, usually accompanied the "shout," a religious dance performed by members of the praise house at the close of a meeting. Several members would stand up, beat time with their feet, clap their hands, and sing a song based upon a rather fragmentary knowledge of the scriptures, yet full of religious fervor. Other members of the group would begin walking around in a ring, in single file, while joining their comrades in singing the song. Sometimes the dancers stepped to the same melody for as long as half an hour. Usually they stopped briefly at the last note of each stanza, stamping with one foot while bringing the other foot forward at the same time. Then they started singing the next stanza.

Get right and stay right, Be
rea-dy when my Je-sus come,(oh yes I'm goin' to)
Get right and stay right, Be

rea - dy when my Je - sus come.

Verse - Soprano

1. I feel I am a Christian,
2. When I meet my neigh - bor,
3. I may be at church preaching,

Ev - ry day I tries,__ Dere's
We talk and have a good time, But
Or home down on my knees, Dis

Some - bo - dy watch-ing an' a - wait-ing to
I am al - ways wor-ried for
worl' is__ so__ two __- faced__ Dere's

break my heart wid lies! D.C.
fear dere's trouble be - hind!
some body talking 'bout me.

2. When I meet my neighbor
   We talk and have a good time
   But I'm always worried
   For fear dere's trouble behind!

3. I may be at church preaching
   Or home down on my knee,
   Dis worl' is so two-faceded
   Dere's somebody talking 'bout
   me.

Folk Blues

The "blues" represent the second major contribution of the Negro to the American folk song. Unlike the highly imaginative spirituals, which stress escape from reality, the blues face life as it is, with its disappointments, heartaches, and losses, especially the loss of a lover. Blues are plaintive sorrow songs lamenting the inability of the wooer to capture the love of the one he loves, or to keep this love once it has been secured. Some blues condemn certain types of jobs at which the Negro labors—jobs that cause him to become the victim of some incurable disease, like "The Silicosis Blues," composed by folk singer Josh White. (But this song, like the "St. Louis Blues" and "Memphis Blues," by the famous composer W. C. Handy, is not authentic folk blues.)

In spite of the fact that folk blues have been in the living tradition of the Negro for many decades, no collection of them was published until Folk Blues, compiled and edited by Jerry Silverman, appeared in 1958.

Lonesome Blues

I woke up this morn-in' feel-in' sad and blue. Ba-by done quit me, what am I gon-na do?_ You know I'm lone - some, and the blues is in my way. _____ I may be down and out to-day, but I'll __ be up some day. _____

Arrangement by Jerry Silverman, © 1958. From *Folk Blues* by Jerry Silverman, published by the Macmillan Company and used by permission.

Folk Blues

Boys, ain't it hard lovin' another man's girl friend?
Can't see her when you want to, got to see her when you can.
Chorus

I got to walk by myself, sleep by myself,
While the woman I love she's lovin' somebody else.
Chorus

My baby left me, she left me broken down,
Said, "Goodbye, daddy, I'll meet you in another town."
Chorus

I wake up in the morning, 'bout the break of day,
Reach against the pillow where my baby used to lay.
Chorus

Worried Blues

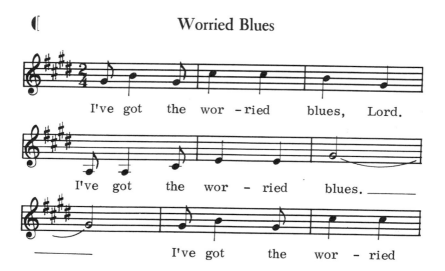

I've got the wor - ried blues, Lord.

I've got the wor - ried blues. _____

_____ I've got the wor - ried

Arrangement by Jerry Silverman, © 1958. From *Folk Blues* by Jerry Silverman, published by the Macmillan Company and used by permission.

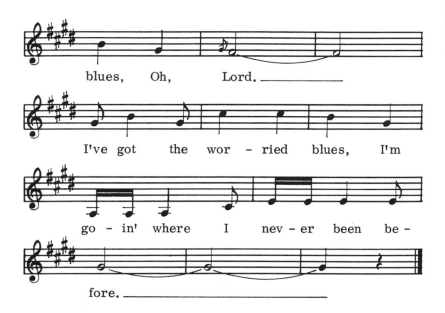

blues, Oh, Lord. _____

I've got the wor - ried blues, I'm

go - in' where I nev - er been be -

fore. _____

Goin' where I never been beat, I'm
  goin' where the chilly winds don't
  blow,
Goin' where I never been beat, oh,
  Lord,
Goin' where I never been beat, I'm
  goin' where the chilly winds don't
  blow.

Honey baby, don't leave me now, oh,
  honey baby, don't leave me now,
Honey baby, don't leave me now, oh,
  Lord God,
Honey baby, don't leave me now,
  well I've got trouble in my mind.

Goin' where the orange blossoms
  bloom, I'm goin' where the chilly
  winds don't blow,
Goin' where the orange blossoms
  bloom, oh, Lord,
Goin' where the orange blossoms
  bloom, I'm goin' where I never
  been before.

I've got the worried blues, Lord, I've
  got the worried blues,
I've got the worried blues, oh, oh,
  Lord,
I've got the worried blues, I'm goin'
  where I never been before.

Careless Love

Words and music by Huddie Ledbetter
Collected and adapted by John A. Lomax and Alan Lomax

A sweet, slow blues

An' you see what care-less love ___ have done, An' you see what care-less ___ love ___ have done, ___ An' you see what care-less ___ love ___ have ___ done, made me love you, now your man ___ done come. 2. When I wo' my ap - 'on

low,   When   I   wo'   my   ap - 'on

low, _____   When   I   wo'   my

ap - 'on ___   low,   Dad - dy, you   drove   me,

hon - ey,   f'om ___   yo'   do'.

1. An' you see what careless love have done,
   An' you see what careless love have done,
   An' you see what careless love have done,
   Made me love you, now your man done come.

2. When I wo' my ap'on low, (3)
   Daddy, you drove me, honey, f'om yo' do'.

3. Now, I wears my ap'on high, (3)
   You looks at me and passes by.

4. I'm wearin' my ap'on up under my chin, (3)
   You pass my do', an' you wouldn' come in.

5. Now, you see what careless love will do, (3)
   Make you kill yourself an' your sweetheart, too.

6. Lawd, you see what careless love have done, (3)
   Make your grandma marry her oldes' son.

7. Lawd, have mercy on me. (3)
   You see, Lawd, baby, don' you see?

Good Mornin' Blues

New words and music by Huddie Ledbettter
Edited with new additional material by Alan Lomax

Good morn - in', blues, blues, how do you

do?__ Good morn - in', blues,

blues, how do you do. I'm

doin' all right, good morn-in', how'r are you?

I lay down last night, turn-in' from side to

side, ___ Aw, ___

turn-in' from side to side._ I

was not sick, but I was just dis - sat-is - fied.

(Spoken)

Now this is Good Mornin'
Blues,
An' I'll tell you about the blues.
All Negroes like blues.
Why?
Because they was born with the
blues.
And now, everybody have the
blues.
Sometimes they don't know
what it is.
But when you lay down at night,
turn from one side of the bed
all night to the other
And can't sleep,
What's the matter? Blues got
you.
You don't want no talk out of
mornin', sit on side of yo'
bed—
May have a mother or father,
sister an' brother,
Boy-friend or girl-friend, or hus-
band or wife around—
You don't want no talk out of
um.
They ain't done you nothin',
you ain't done them nothin'—
but what's the matter?
Blues got you.
Well, you get up and shev your
feet down under the table
and look down in your plate—
May have chicken and rice, take

my advice, you walk away and
shake your head,
You say, "Lord have mercy. I
can't eat an' I can't sleep."
What's the matter?
Blues has still got you.
They want to talk to you.
You got to tell um something.

(Sung)

1. "Good mornin', blues, blues
how do you do? (Come on)
Good mornin', blues, blues how
do you do?"
"I'm doin' all right, good mornin'
how'r are you?"

2. I lay down last night, turnin'
from side to side,
(What's the matter?)
Aw, turnin' from side to side,
I was not sick, but I was just
dissatisfied.

3. When I got up this mornin',
blues walkin' 'round my bed,
Aw, de blues walkin' 'round my
bed,
I went to eat my breakfast, the
blues was all in my bread.

4. I got a new way of spelling
Memphis, Tennessee, (Go
ahead and spell it to the
people)
Aw, Memphis, Tennessee, (now
you can spell it to me)
Double E, double T, Lord,
Double N, X, Y, Z.

Frankie Blues

Frank - ie was a good wom-an,____

Ev - 'ry-bo - dy knows, Gave

for - ty - one dol - lars to buy

Al - bert ____ a suit of clothes;____

"Yes, he's my man,_____

____ but he done me wrong."_____

1. Frankie was a good woman,
   Ev'rybody knows,
   Gave forty-one dollars to buy
   Albert
   A suit of clothes:
   "Yes, he's my man, but he done
   me wrong."

2. Frankie went to the corner,
   Took a forty-four gun,
   Shot her Albert a-rooty-to-toot,
   And away he tried to run:
   "He was my man, but he done
   me wrong."

3. "Roll me over easy,
   Roll me over slow,
   Roll me over on my right side,
   'Cause the bullet hurt me so;
   I was your man, but I done you
   wrong."

4. Frankie sit in a parlor,
   Cool herself with a fan,
   Tell all the other women and
   girls,
   "Don't trust any doggone man,
   He'll do you wrong, he'll do you
   wrong."

Michigan Water Blues

Mich-i-gan wa-ter ___ tastes like sher - ry wine, (sweet sher - ry wine). Oh, ___ Mis - si - sip-pi wa - ter ___ tastes like tur - pen - tine. Mich - i - gan wa - ter tastes like sher - ry wine. ___

Arrangement by Jerry Silverman, © 1958. From *Folk Blues* by Jerry Silverman, published by the Macmillan Company and used by permission.

Ash-es to ash - es and   dust to dust,   if I

don't leave   here some-thing's bound to   bust.

Mich – i – gan   wa - ter   tastes   like   sher - ry

wine,   Mich - i - gan   wa - ter

tastes like sher - ry   wine.

I. I believe to my soul I've got to
   leave this place,
  Goin' away where the folks don't
   know my face.
  Michigan water tastes like sherry
   wine.

II. Gal in Lou'siana—one in Maine,
   Got one in Mississippi, scared to
    call her name.
  Michigan water tastes like sherry
   wine,
  Michigan water tastes like sherry
   wine.

Slave Seculars
and Work Songs

A compilation of Negro folksongs would not be complete without the inclusion of two other branches of this important segment of American culture. Although not as plentiful as other types of Negro folk songs, the slave seculars and work songs of Negro origin provide interesting innovations in the field.

The slave seculars were varied—some of them love songs, a few of them complaints about the slave's status, others expressing humility. The work songs of the Negro are, for the most part, about experiences on chain gangs and work on rock quarries. The general theme of these narratives is one of protest against the treatment of workers and prisoners by the guards and foremen, whom the Negroes refer to as "Cap'n."

⦗ Foller de Drinkin' Gou'd

"One of my great-uncles, who was connected with the railroad movement, remembered that in the records of the Anti-Slavery Society there
was a story of a peg-leg sailor, known as Peg-Leg Joe, who made a number of
trips through the South and induced young Negroes to run away and
escape. . . . The main scene of his activities was in the country north of
Mobile, and the trail described in the song followed northward to the head-
waters of the Tombigbee River, thence over the divide and down the Ohio
River to Ohio. . . . The peg-leg sailor would . . . teach this song to the young
slaves and show them the mark of his natural left foot and the round hole
made by his peg-leg. He would then go ahead of them northward and leave
a print made with charcoal and mud of the outline of a human left foot
and a round spot in place of the right foot. . . . Nothing more could be
found relative to the man. . . . 'Drinkin' gou'd' is the Great Dipper. . . .
'The grea' big un,' the Ohio."—H. B. Parks in Volume VII of the *Publications of the Texas Folk-Lore Society.*

Fol - ler de drink - in' gou'd. Fol - ler de

drink - in' gou'd. For de ol' man

say, "Fol - ler de drink - in' gou'd."

When de sun come back,
When de firs' quail call,
Den de time is come—
Foller de drinkin' gou'd.

Chorus:
    Foller de drinkin' gou'd,
    Foller de drinkin' gou'd;
    For de ol' man say,
    "Foller de drinkin' gou'd."

De riva's bank am a very good road,
De dead trees show de way;
Lef' foot, peg foot goin' on,
Foller de drinkin' gou'd. (*Chorus.*)

De river ends atween two hills,
Foller de drinkin' gou'd;
'Nother river on de other side,
Foller de drinkin' gou'd. (*Chorus.*)

Wha de little river
Meet de gre' big un,
De ol' man waits—
Foller de drinkin' gou'd. (*Chorus.*)

Aurore Pradère

A Creole Song from St. Charles Parish, Louisiana

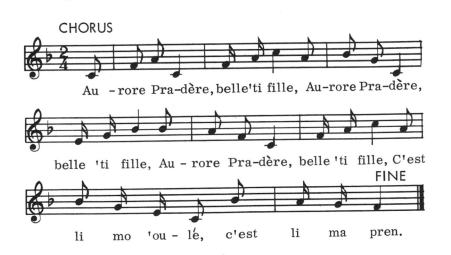

CHORUS

Au - rore Pra-dère, belle 'ti fille, Au-rore Pra-dère,

belle 'ti fille, Au - rore Pra-dère, belle 'ti fille, C'est

FINE

li mo 'ou - lé, c'est li ma pren.

SOLO

Li pas man-dé robe mous - se -line, Li pas man-dé des bas bro-dé, Li pas mon-dé sou-

D.C.

liers prin-elle, C'est li mo 'ou-lé, c'est li ma pren.

Aurore Pradère, belle 'ti fille, (ter)
C'est li mo 'oulé, c'est li ma pren.
Li pas mandé robe mousseline,
Li pas mandé des bas brodés,
Li pas mandé souliers prinelle;
C'est li mo 'oulé, c'est li ma pren.

Aurore Pradère, belle 'ti fille, (ter)
C'est li mo 'oulé, c'est li ma pren.
Ya moun qui dit li trop zolie;
Ya moun qui dit li pas polie;
Tout ça ya dit (Sia!) bin fou bin,
C'est li mo 'oulé, c'est li ma pren.

Translation

Aurore Pradère, pretty maid,
She's just what I want and her I'll
   have.
A muslin gown she does not choose,
She doesn't ask for 'broidered hose,
She doesn't want prunella shoes;
Oh, she's what I want and her I'll
   have.

Aurore Pradère, pretty maid,
She's what I want and her I'll have.
Some folks say she's too pretty
   quite;
Some folks say she's not polite,
All this they say—Psha-a-ah!
More fool am I!
For she's what I want and her I'll
   have.

Aurore Pradère, pretty maid,
She's what I want and her I'll have.
Some say she's going to the bad;
Some say her mama went mad;
All this they say—Psha-a-ah!
More fool am I!
For she's what I want and her I'll
   have.

Reprinted by permission of the publishers from Dorothy Scarborough, *On the Trail of Negro Folk Songs*. Cambridge, Mass.: Harvard University Press. Copyright © 1925, 1953.

Many T'ousand Go

No more peck o' corn for me, No more, no more, No more peck o' corn for me, Man - y t'ou - sand go.

No more peck of corn for me, no more, no more;
No more peck of corn for me, many t'ousand go.
No more driver's lash for me, etc.
No more pint of salt for me, etc.
No more hundred lash for me, etc.
No more mistress' call for me, etc.

Lay Dis Body Down

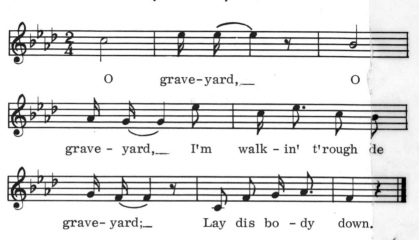

O grave-yard,— O grave-yard,— I'm walk-in' t'rough de grave-yard;— Lay dis bo-dy down.

O graveyard,
O graveyard,
I'm walkin' t'rough de graveyard;
Lay dis body down.

I know moonlight,
I know starlight,
I'm walkin' t'rough de starlight;
Lay dis body down.

I lay in de grave
An' stretch out my arms,
I'm layin' in de graveyard;
Lay dis body down.

I Went to Atlanta

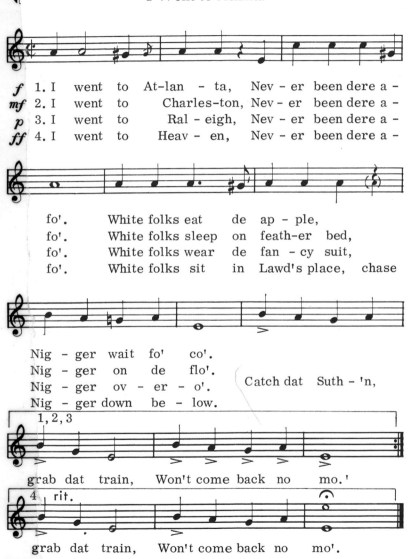

f 1. I went to At-lan - ta, Nev - er been dere a -
mf 2. I went to Charles-ton, Nev - er been dere a -
p 3. I went to Ral - eigh, Nev - er been dere a -
ff 4. I went to Heav - en, Nev - er been dere a -

fo'. White folks eat de ap - ple,
fo'. White folks sleep on feath-er bed,
fo'. White folks wear de fan - cy suit,
fo'. White folks sit in Lawd's place, chase

Nig - ger wait fo' co'.
Nig - ger on de flo'.
Nig - ger ov - er - o'.   Catch dat Suth - 'n,
Nig - ger down be - low.

1, 2, 3
grab dat train, Won't come back no mo.'

4 rit.
grab dat train, Won't come back no mo'.

Workin' on de Railroad

1. Work - in' on de rail - road, _____
2. Trou - ble ne - ver lay- in dead on de
3. Help to build dat rail - road, can't af-

fif - ty cents a day. De
bot - tom dis here worl'.
ford no ri - din' tag.

boss _____ at de comp' - ny sto' sign
Ev - ry thin' _____ you can see _____
Mo - ney talks but my bits ain't _____

all I makes a - way. _____
shin - in' ain't no gol'. _____
bits e - nough to wag. _____

Mam - my po' - ly write, "Please
Rail - road it com-ple - ted, cars a
Walk -in' 'long side de track,

sen' some mon - ey, son."
run - ning on de track.
hun - gry, wan - tin' to eat.

But I ain't____ got ____ no
No mo' work____ for me
Dog dead tired, _____

rea - dy made mo ____- ney, But
here____ a - bouts,____
Shoes____ wore out,____

I ain't got ____ no
No more work for me ____
Dog dead tired,____

rea - dy made mo-ney,___ my God damn
here ___ a - bouts. ___ Time for
Shoes wore out, _____ an Lawd,

black soul I can't
pack - ing up de ol'
bur - nin' blis - ters

send her none. _____
rag - ge - dy grip sack. _____
on my feet. _____

Levee Moan

Ah'm go - in' whah no-bod-y knows ma name. Lawd, Lawd,

Lawd, Lawd! Ah'm go - in' whah no-bod-y knows ma name.

Ah'm go - in' whah no - bod - y knows ma name!

2. Ah'm goin' whah dey don't shovel no snow, Lawd, Lawd, Lawd, Lawd!
Ah'm goin' whah dey don't shovel no snow, Ah'm goin' whah dey don't shovel no snow!

3. Ah'm goin' whah de chilly wind don't blow, Lawd, Lawd, Lawd, Lawd!
Ah'm goin' whah de chilly wind don't blow, Ah'm goin' whah de chilly wind don't blow!

Note: Those who so choose may use the following "K. C. line" couplet in place of one of the above stanzas; or the El Paso version (B) below.

Ah'm goin' on dat ol' K. C. line, Lawd, Lawd, Lawd, Lawd!
Ah'm goin' on dat ol' K. C. line, Ah'm goin' on dat ol' K. C. line!

B

1. O baby, where you been so long? Lord, Lord, Lord, Lord,
O baby, where you been so long? O baby, where you been so long?

2. O honey, let your hair hang down, Lord, Lord, Lord, Lord,
O honey, let your hair hang down, O honey, let your hair hang down.

3. O honey, your hair grows too long, Lord, Lord, Lord, Lord,
O honey, your hair grows too long, O honey, your hair grows too long.

193

Dis Ole Rock Mine

Sung by Johnny Workman and recorded in Greensboro, North Carolina

Lord I done got tired of the

way I bin fal - lin' in

dis ole rock mine I done got tired of

way I bin fal - lin' in dis ole rock mine

Oh Lord I start to fal - lin'

when I wuz young try - in' to get my

day's work done. I done got tired of

way I'm fal- lin' in dis ole rock mine. I

ask my cap'-n for nine pound ham-mer an' he
give me twelve. I ask my cap'-n for
nine pound ham-mer an' he give me twelve.
Oh Lord ask my cap'-n for
nine pound ham-mer an' he so hard heart-ed he
give me twelve. Dis ole ham-mer that
I bin us-in' is kil-lin' me.

Take dis ole hammer an' carry it
   to the cap'n
And tell him I'm gone.
If he ask you was I runnin', tell him,
   no, I was might' near flyin'.
Take dis ole hammer an' carry it to
   the Cap'n and tell him I'm gone.

Dis ole hammer that I bin usin'
It ring like steel.
Dis ole hammer it must be loaded
Cause it's bearin' down on me.
Dis ole hammer that I bin usin'
Is killing me, oh, yes!

195

Sweet Mamie Chadman

Sung by Johnny Workman and recorded in Greensboro, North Carolina

Sweet Ma-mie Chad-man Chad-man dat's the girl I

love. ____ She got hair like her

mo - ther an' teeth like a light - ning ____

bug. ____ I went up

Church ___ Street ho - ney an' I turned down

Main. ____ Den the chief po -

lice ___ man ___ he want to know my ___

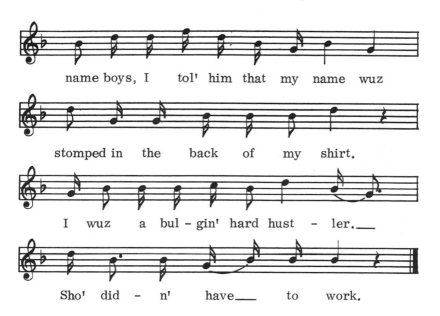

name boys, I tol' him that my name wuz

stomped in the back of my shirt.

I wuz a bul - gin' hard hust - ler.__

Sho' did - n' have__ to work.

Boys, den he took me,
Took me down to the courthouse.
Boys, den he stood me
'Fo that lonesome judge.

Oh, the judge he want know, boys,
What might be my fine.
He said, "A pick an' a shovel;
Go make ninety-nine."

My buddy make a hundred;
I can make ninety-nine;
My buddy make a hundred;
I can make ninety-nine.

Oh, you know that's enough to
Change any po' man's mind,
Lord to be double shackled
An' be all governed down!

Dere's some on the chain gang,
Chain gang, some on the farm.
I see some on the right of way,
Right of way, an' some goin'
home.

When I was a little boy,
Little boy thinking 'bout strolling.
Know what my mother tol' me?
"Too young, son, don't go!"

Now I made myself hardheaded;
Hard head lissen to the other boys.
Now don't you see what
Hard head brought me to?

Lord, don't talk about it,
'Bout it, if you do, I'll cry.
Lord, I want to see my baby
One mo' time 'fo I die.

Carry Me Back to Old Virginny

A *Plantation Melody*
Words and Music by James Bland

1. Car- ry me back to old Vir - gin- ny,
2. Car- ry me back to old Vir - gin- ny,

There's where the cot-tonand the corn and taters grow,
There let me live till I with-er and de-cay,

There's where the birds war-ble sweet in the spring-time,
Long by the old Dis - mal Swamp have I wan -dered,

There's where the old dar - key's heart am longed to go.
There's where the old dar - key's life will pass a way.

There's where I la-bored so hard for old Mas-sa,
Mas- sa and Mis-sis have long gone be-fore me,

Day af - ter day in the field of yel-low corn,
Soon we will meet on that bright and golden shore,

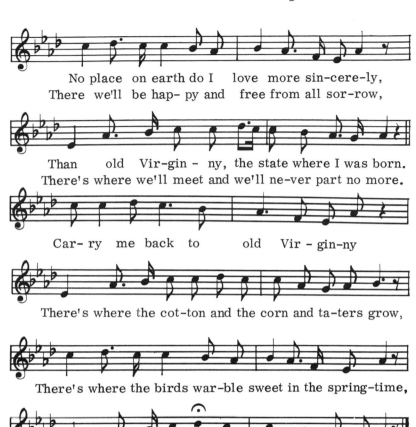

No place on earth do I love more sin-cere-ly,
There we'll be hap- py and free from all sor-row,

Than old Vir-gin - ny, the state where I was born.
There's where we'll meet and we'll ne-ver part no more.

Car- ry me back to old Vir - gin-ny

There's where the cot-ton and the corn and ta-ters grow,

There's where the birds war-ble sweet in the spring-time,

There's where the old dar-key's heart am long'd to go.

Ballads

The Negro has not been very prolific in composing ballads. By far his most popular ballad is "John Henry," about the steel-driving man who is not only a folk hero in the American Negro tradition, but one of the most famous folk heroes in all America. Two other Negro ballads are "Frankie and Johnny" and "Ella Speed," and worthy of mention also are such novelties as "De Ballit of de Boll Weevil" and "De Grey Goose."

In addition to popular ballads invented by the Negro, he created versions of English and Scottish ballads brought to this country by European tradition bearers and culture carriers—primarily masters and mistresses who sang these songs where the Negro slaves could hear them.

John Henry

John_ Hen - ry tol'_ his cap' - n' Dat a

man wuz a na - tu - ral man, An' be -

fo'- he'd let dat steam drill beat him

down He'd fall dead wid a ham - mer

in his han', He'd fall dead wid a ham-mer in his han'.

1. John Henry tol' his cap'n
   Dat a man wuz a natural man,
   An' befo' he'd let dat steam drill
   run him down,
   He'd fall dead wid a hammer in
   his han',
   He'd fall dead wid a hammer in
   his han'.

2. Cap'n he sez to John Henry:
   "Gonna bring me a steam drill
   'round;
   Take that steel drill out on the
   job,
   Gonna whop that steel on down,
   Gonna whop that steel on
   down."

3. John Henry sez to his cap'n:
   "Send me a twelve-poun' ham-
      mer aroun',
   A twelve-poun' hammer wid a
      fo'-foot handle,
   An' I beat yo' steam drill down,
   An' I beat yo' steam drill down."

4. John Henry sez to his shaker:
   "Niggah, why don' yo' sing?
   I'm throwin' twelve poun' from
      my hips on down,
   Jes' lissen to de col' steel ring,
   Jes' lissen to de col' steel ring!"

5. John Henry went down de rail-
      road
   Wid a twelve-poun' hammer by
      his side,
   He walked down de track but he
      didn' come back,
   'Cause he laid down his ham-
      mer an' he died,
   'Cause he laid down his ham-
      mer an' he died.

6. John Henry hammered in de
      mountains,
   De mountains wuz so high.
   De las' words I heard de pore
      boy say:
   "Gimme a cool drink o' watah
      fo' I die,
   Gimme a cool drink o' watah
      fo' I die!"

7. John Henry had a little baby,
   Hel' him in de palm of his han'.
   De las' words I heard de pore
      boy say:
   "Son, yo're gonna be a steel-
      drivin' man,
   Son, yo're gonna be a steel-
      drivin' man!"

8. John Henry had a 'ooman,
   De dress she wo' wuz blue.
   De las' words I heard de pore
      gal say:
   "John Henry, I ben true to yo',
   John Henry, I ben true to yo'."

9. John Henry had a li'l 'ooman,
   De dress she wo' wuz brown.
   De las' words I heard de pore
      gal say:
   "I'm goin' w'eah mah man went
      down,
   I'm goin' w'eah mah man went
      down!"

10. John Henry had anothah 'ooman,
   De dress she wo' wuz red.
   De las' words I heard de pore
      gal say:
   "I'm goin' w'eah mah man
      drapt daid,
   I'm goin' w'eah mah man drapt
      daid!"

11. John Henry had a li'l 'ooman,
   Her name wuz Polly Ann.
   On de day John Henry he drap
      daid
   Polly Ann hammered steel like
      a man,
   Polly Ann hammered steel like
      a man.

12. W'eah did yo' git dat dress!
   W'eah did you git dose shoes so
      fine?
   Got dat dress f'm off a railroad
      man,
   An' shoes f'm a driver in a mine,
   An' shoes f'm a driver in a mine.

Ella Speed

Words and music by Huddie Ledbetter
Collected and adapted by John A. Lomax and Alan Lomax

Come all__ and take heed,__ Just re-
mem-ber the death of__ El-la Speed.__ Come all
__ and take__ heed Just re-
mem-ber__ the death of El-la Speed.

1. Come all and take heed,
   Just remember the death of
   Ella Speed.
   Come all and take heed,
   Just remember the death of
   Ella Speed.

2. Ella Speed was downtown,
   havin' her lovin' fun,
   'Long come Bill Martin wid his
   cold 41.
   Ella Speed was downtown,
   havin' her lovin' fun,
   'Long come Bill Martin wid
   his cold 41.

3. Th' deed that Bill Martin done
   Was cold-blooded murder wid
       his cold 41.
   Th' deed that Bill Martin done
   Was cold-blooded murder wid
       his cold 41.

4. The womens was all singin' wid
       a doneful soun',
   When Bill Martin shot de
       woman down.
   The womens was all singin' wid
       a doneful soun',
   When Bill Martin shot de
       woman down.

5. They looked all over de heart
       of that town,
   Lookin' for that bully, but he
       couldn' be foun'.
   They looked all over de heart
       of that town,
   Lookin' for that bully, but he
       couldn' be foun'.

6. Bill Martin, he was long an'
       slender,
   Better known by bein' a bar-
       tender.
   Bill Martin, he was long an'
       slender,
   Better known by bein' a bar-
       tender.

7. When he was 'rested an' locked
       up in jail,
   Judge says, "Bill Martin, I never
       fail."
   When he was 'rested an' locked
       up in jail,
   Judge says, "Bill Martin, I never
       fail."

8. "De deed, Bill Martin, that you
       done,
   Your sentence—you know you
       oughta be hung.
   De deed, Bill Martin, that you
       done,
   Your sentence—you know you
       oughta be hung."

9. Bill Martin fell down upon his
       knees,
   Cryin', "Judge, have mercy on
       me."
   Bill Martin fell down upon his
       knees,
   Cryin', "Judge, have mercy on
       me."

10. Bill Martin wring his han's an'
        he started to cryin'.
    Judge said, "I won' hang you,
        but I'll give you life-time."
    Bill Martin wring his han's an'
        he started to cryin'.
    Judge said, "I won' hang you,
        but I'll give you life-time."

11. "Think about your dirty deed—
        Cold-blooded—murderin' the
        po' girl, Ella Speed.
    Think about your dirty deed—
        Cold-blooded—murderin' the
        po' girl, Ella Speed."

12. Bill Martin sat down to play
        cooncan,
    Po' boy couldn' half play his
        han',
    Thinkin' 'bout de woman that
        he murdered,
    Had gone away to some far, dis-
        tant lan'.

13. They taken Bill Martin to de
    freight depot,
    The train come on easin' by;
    Waved his han' at de woman
    that he murdered,
    Po' boy hung down his head
    an' he cry:

14. "She's gone, she's gone, she's
    gone,
    An' cryin' won' bring her back.
    She's the onlies' woman dat I
    ever loved.
    She's gone down some lone-
    some railroad track.

15. "I love Ella Speed six feet in
    the groun',
    Lawd, Lawd, an' they ain' no
    hangin' aroun'.
    I love Ella Speed six feet in
    the groun',
    Lawd, Lawd, an' they ain' no
    hangin' aroun'."

16. De women all heard dat Ella
    Speed was dead.
    They all went home an' they
    re-ragged in red.
    De women all heard Ella Speed
    was dead,
    They all went home an' they
    re-ragged in red.

17. They taken Ella Speed to the
    buryin' groun',
    They was all singin' wid a done-
    ful soun'.
    They taken Ella Speed to the
    buryin' groun',
    They was all singin' wid a done-
    ful soun'.

De Ballit of de Boll Weevil

Words and music by Huddie Ledbetter
Collected and adapted by John A. Lomax and Alan Lomax

Talk a-bout de la-tes', De la-tes' of this

song, Dese dev-il-ish boll weev-ils, Dey gon-na

rob you of a home, Dey look-in' for a home,

Dey look-in for a home,____

I'll have a home,____ I'll have a home,

____ I'll have a home,____

Ballads

I'll   have   a   home._____

1. Talk about de lates',
   De lates' of this song,
   Dese devilish boll weevils,
   Dey gonna rob you of a home,
   Dey lookin' for a home,
   Dey lookin' for a home.

2. The first time I seed him,
   He was settin' on de square,
   The nex' time I seed him,
   He was spreadin' ev'ywhere—
   He was lookin' for a home,
   He was lookin' for a home.

3. Farmer taken the boll weevil,
   Put him in de san',
   Boll weevil said to de farmer,
   "Dis is treatin' me like a man—
   I have a home,
   I have a home."

4. Farmer taken the boll weevil,
   Put him in de ice,
   Boll weevil said to de farmer,
   "Dis is treatin' me mighty
      nice—
   I'll have a home,
   I'll have a home."

5. The farmer an' his ol' lady
   Went out 'cross de fiel'.
   The farmer said to de ol' lady:
   "I found a lotta meat an' meal—
   I'll have a home,
   I'll have a home."

6. Ol' lady said to de ol' man:
   "I'm tryin' my level bes',
   To keep dese devilish boll wee-
      vils
   Outa my ol' cotton dress—
   It's full of holes,
   It's full of holes."

7. Farmer said to de ol' lady:
   "What do you think of that?
   I got some devilish boll weevils
   In my ol' Stetson hat—
   It's full of holes,
   It's full of holes."

8. Farmer tol' de merchant,
   "I didn't make but one bale,
   Before I let you have that one,
   I'll suffer an' die in jail—
   I'll have a home,
   I'll have a home."

De Grey Goose

Words and music by Huddie Ledbetter
Collected and adapted by John A. Lomax and Alan Lomax

Preach-er went a-hunt-in', Lawd, Lawd, Lawd,

Preach-er went a hunt-in Lawd, Lawd, Lawd! He was

7. Then they
11. Well I
Stanzas 10, 17, and 20
12. So dey

Great God! Great God! Lawd, Lawd, Lawd, Great

God! Great God! Lawd, Lawd, Lawd!

1. Preacher went a-huntin',
   Lawd, Lawd, Lawd;
   Preacher went a-huntin',
   Lawd, Lawd, Lawd!

2. Carried 'long his shotgun,

3. 'Long came a grey goose,

4. Gun went "a-boo-loo!"

5. Down came a grey goose,

6. He was six weeks a fallin',

7. Then they give a feather-pickin',

8. Yo' wife an' my wife,

9. They was six weeks a-pickin',

10. Great God! Great God!

11. Well, I wonder what's de matter,

12. So dey put him on to parboil,

13. He was six weeks a-boilin',

14. So dey put him on de table,

15. Fork couldn't stick him,

16. Knife couldn't cut him,

17. Great God, it's a grey goose!

18. So dey taken him to de hogpen,

19. Broke the sow's teeth out,

20. Great God, it's a grey goose.

Bob-ree Allin

The Virginia Negro Version of "Barbara Allan"

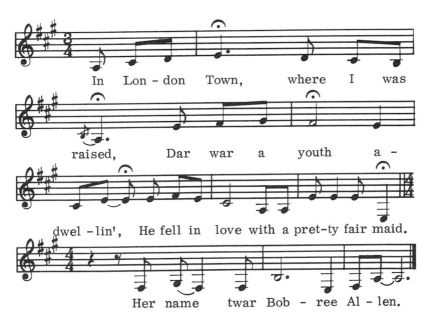

In Lon - don Town, where I was

raised, Dar war a youth a -

dwel -lin', He fell in love with a pret-ty fair maid.

Her name twar Bob - ree Al - len.

Reprinted by permission of the publishers from Dorothy Scarborough, *On the Trail of Negro Folk Songs.* Cambridge, Mass.: Harvard University Press. Copyright © 1925, 1953.

In London town, whar I was raised,
Dar war a youth a-dwellin',
He fell in love wid a putty fair
maid,
Her name 'twar Bob-ree Allin.

He co'ted her for seben long years;
She said she would not marry;
Poor Willie went home an' war
taken sick,
And ve'y likely died.

He den sen' out his waitin' boy
Wid a note for Bob-ree Allin
So close, ah, she read, so slow, ah
she walk;
"Go tell him I'm a-comin'."

She den step up into his room
An' stood an' looked upon him.
He stretched to her his pale white
hands
"Oh, won't you tell me howdy?"

"Have you forgot de udder day,
When we war in de pawlor,
You drank your health to de gals
around,
An' slighted Bob-ree Allin?"

"Oh, no, oh, no, my dear young
miss;
I think you is mistaken;
Ef I drink my healt' to de gals
around,
It war love for Bob-ree Allin.

"An' now I'm ve'y sick
An' on my death bed lyin';
One kiss or two from you, my dear,
Would take away dis dyin'."

"Dat kiss or two you will not git,
Not ef your heart was breakin';
I cannot keep you from death,
So farewell," said Bob-ree Allin.

He tu'n his pale face to de wall,
An' den began er cryin';
An' every tear he shed appeared
Hard-hearted Bob-ree Allin.

She walked across de fiel's nex' day
An' heard de birds a-singin',
An' every note dey seemed to say,
"Hard-hearted Bob-ree Allin."

She war walkin' across de fiel's nex'
day
An' spied his pale corpse comin';
"Oh, lay him down upon de groun',
An' let me look upon him."

As she war walkin' down de street
She heard de deathbells ringin'
And every tone dey seemed to say,
"Hard-hearted Bob-ree Allin."

"Oh, fader, fader, dig-a my grave,
An' dig it long an' narrow;
My true love he have died today,
An' I mus' die tomorrow."

Sweet Willie war buried in de new
churchyard
An' Bob-ree Allin beside him,
Outen his grave sprang a putty red
rose,
An' Bob-ree Allin's briar.

Dey grew as high as de steeple top,
An' couldn't grow no higher;
An' den dey tied a true-love knot,
De sweet rose roun' de briar.

The Kosciusko Bootlegger's Gripe

I am over a hundred miles from home
    In the jail of Aberdeen.
I decided to compose a few words
    Concerning Mr. Skeen.

Skeen bought some whiskey in bottles,
    And he bought some whiskey in jars.
He turned it over to Mr. Blanton,
    And he locked us behind the bars.

We thought it was a mighty dirty trick
    That was played on us by Skeen,
But Mr. Blanton turned us over to revenue men,
    And they brought us to Aberdeen.

They treated us all mighty bad,
    And some would rather be dying
Than to rede out from the jail house yard
    And leave our family crying.

Skeen he gambles mighty well,
    And his dice did not crap;
He framed on all us honest men
    And caught us in his trap.

Throughout the state of Mississippi
    These federal men they roam.
They made a raid on Kosciusko
    And carried twenty-eight men from home.

They framed on Bertha and Willie Mae
    And me and Price, you know,
And Percy Dodd and many others,
    And poor little Johnnie Moore.

They have brought us a hundred miles from home.
  The town is Aberdeen.
There is nothing else that I can do
  But talk about old Skeen.

Of course Skeen did not trap us all.
  Guinn, he trapped his part
And turned our name in to the sheriff,
  The man without a heart.

He said on Wednesday the fifteenth of March,
  "You boys must all be tried."
And they loaded us in five Chevrolet cars
  And taken us for a ride.

Guinn after doing the dirty trick
  He stood around and looked pale;
But Skeen got Mr. Bailey's car
  And brought some of his men to jail.

Some of us wore overalls
  And some of us wore serge,
But none of us knows what will happen
  Until we go before the judge.

We don't get no lemonade to drink
  And is never served no punch,
But all that I can say for us,
  We are a badly messed-up bunch.

There is men from everywhere in jail.
  Some of them have jake legs,
And men of all descriptions,
  And one man is on a peg.

If you-all could see inside this jail
  You would think it a crying shame,
But the men that caused us to be here
  I have already told their name.

Mr. Dudley is our jailer's name,
  And he treats us mighty well,
But when you are locked up in this jail
  You feel like you are in hell.

Ballads

He does everything he can for us
    And helps us get our mail,
But the thing I want him to do for me
    Is turn me out of this jail.

I hope the judge don't say six months.
    God knows I am not lying,
Because when I left home to come up here
    Poor Hattie May was crying.

I promised her that I would return.
    That promise I must keep true,
For I believe deep down in my heart
    That she really hope I do.

They got old Fuller Wilson here;
    They taken him off the road.
I am sure the girls miss John H. Moore
    From riding them in his Ford.

William Rimmer cannot play ball in jail.
    There is nothing to do but rest.
John H. have no bricks to lay,
    And Percy have no clothes to press.

The longest stick that's in the jail
    Is the handle of the broom.
I must not forget to tell Will Cox
    That we miss his old poolroom.

And, too, I must tell Howard Huffman
    We miss his café, too.
We would love to play his radio,
    For there is nothing else to do.

We cannot see no picture shows;
    We have no magazines to read.
This jail house is a lonesome place,
    A lonesome place indeed.

I know every man loves his wife,
    For I loved my baby dear,
But I want to tell all my Kosciusko friends
    To keep away from here.

(The Death of Brock

October the sixth was one most terrible night;
That was the last day that Brock saw the light.
He left Six Street about a quarter to eight,
Going over Eleventh Street in a Ford V eight.

He pulled up to Louis' place, where they were having their fun;
He felt kinder hankety and he felt for his gun.
He walked to the bar and ask if they had whiskey for sell.
"If so, bring me a pint, and make it snappy than hell."

There was a spruce stood standing by, ask if could have him a glass.
"Get back, M.F., before I kick your G-d.A."

His partner was standing by with a dirk in his hand;
His whole heart desire was to kill him a man.
He said, "Kicking and A.'s has been your past;
If you kick that boy, you kick your G-d. last."

Brock was hankety and was right on the alert;
Before he could move he got hit with that dirk.
He pulled his gun and he began to cuss;
You should have seen the people trying to get thin dust.

He made three shots inside of the place,
And walked ten steps and fell on his face.
The ambulance began howling and the sirens whined,
Said some noted rider must be dying.

They pulled up to Curve Street and stopped,
One jumps out and said "Bedam if it ain't Brock.
Say what hospital must we carry him to?"
Someone said, "Take him to the undertaker,
Because it is not any use."

They carried him to Fuller's, but he couldn't be seen
Because he belonged to an undertaker by the name of King.
The day of the funeral everybody was sad,
Excepting old Ice House; he was the only one glad.

Ballads

There was little Red Georgia, and Dallas Chatt,
Essie Mae from Houston, and the Fast Black.
There was Florence Jones in a powdered blue,
B. D., Lessie Lee, and Jackie Lue.

Minnie ask Rosie Lee,
"What can I do?
I know he was your man,
And he was my man too."

There was Ty Ty Lewis, and Kool Goose Slim,
Little Death Alley standing next to him.
There was Pass Picking Roe, and Squabbling Ned,
Lamp Globing Ike, and Big Head Ed.

Everybody stopping and began to stare;
They were looking around to see if Cup Grease was there.
The gamblers had come near and far;
Up drive Buddie Marshall driving Cup Grease's car.

The preacher read a scripture before he knelt to pray;
Ask if any of his friends had anything to say.
They said, "Good-by, Brock, we hate to see you go,
But the good book tells you, that you must reap what you sow."

The Ballad of Harrison Neal

Set down, frien', an' pour you a dram,
While I sing you a song 'bout a big black man.
Wid a heart of gold an' muscles of steel,
He been knowed far an' wide as Harrison Neal.

He live on de farm till he been nine,
Den he pappy got kilt in de Randolph mine.
Den he mammy say, "Dear Lawd, help me.
Cain't feed my chaps nuttin' but cawnbread, 'lasses, an'
    sassyfras tea."

Neal he say, "Mammy, don' you sell de mule or de cow,
'Cause we gwine to make it anyhow.
Keep dese chaps workin' dis lan';
Make a crop, den I come back an' give you a han.'

"I's gwine down de river where dey buil'in' de dam,
An' get me a job from de corntractin' man.
Save mos' my money an' bring it to you,
Mo' samer dan a good boy ought to do."

So Neal he set out 'fo' de break of day,
Dark an' stormy wid de lightnin' showin' him de way.
He reach de river 'bout seven o'clock,
Say, "Gimme a job drillin' dis rock."

Straw boss say, "Mister Ben been gone;
Got a full crew, can't put you on.
But, boy, I kind of likes yo' spunk,
So I make you water boy, if you don' get drunk."

So Neal say, "Yassuh, I's been dat befo';
I know how de water-totin' racket go."
So he grabs up some buckets an' runs like hell,
An' brings de men's water from de company well.

He do his job good, an' he make de day,
An' hold on fast till he gets his pay.
Den' when de rock pile ain't no mo',
He goes back home an' knocks on de do'.

Say, "Mama, dis heah's yo' gone-son Neal,
What come back to help you in de 'bacco fiel'.
I's got lots of money in my pockets, too,
Dat I done brung home to de chaps and you."

So his mammy grab Neal an' she hug him tight,
Say, "Neal, I knowed you'd turn out right.
Come on in, boy, an' rest yo'self,
While I fetches some ham offen' de smokehouse shelf."

From dat day on, for many a year,
Neal stayed home, didn't go nowhere.
Stayed right dere till time run by;
An' his po' ol' mammy laid down an' die.

Some Other Songs

A Sea Chantey

Still Sung by North Carolina Negro Fishermen

Sweet Rosie Ann, Sweet Rosie Ann,
Bye, bye, Sweet Rosie Ann;
I thought I heard my baby say,
"I won't be back tomorrow."

The steamboat's comin' roun' the bend,
Bye, bye, Sweet Rosie Ann,
It's loaded wid dat high-bred gin;
"I won't be home tomorrow."

Tone de Bell Easy

When you hear dat Ise__ a - dy - in', I

don' want no -bo- dy to moan. All__

I want my frien's__ to do____ Is

REFRAIN give__ dat bell a tone,_____

Well, well, well, tone de __ bell eas- y,

Well, well, well, tone de__ bell eas- y,

Well, well, well, tone de__ bell eas- y,

Je -sus gon- na make up my dy- in' bed.

Honey Bee

Sung by Harvey Reaves and recorded in Greensboro, North Carolina

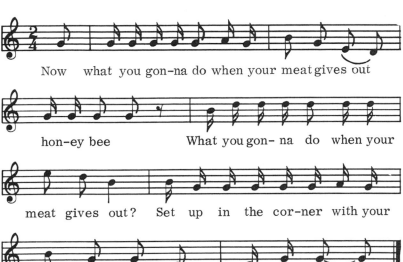

Now what you gon-na do when your meat gives out hon-ey bee What you gon-na do when your meat gives out? Set up in the cor-ner with your mouth poked out hon - ey bee.

I got on de dummy, I didn't have
no fare, my honey.
Got on de dummy, didn't have no
fare;
Conductor ast me what I'm doin'
on dere, my honey.

I don't have no money, but I'm
gonna have some, my honey.
I don't have no money, but I will
have some,
Soon as dat eas'-boun' train it come,
my honey.

219

Katie an' the Jim Lee Had a Race*
A Ballad of Steamboating Days

Ka - tie an' the Jim Lee had a race,

Ah, that same song,

Ka - tie throwed the wa-tuh in the Jim Lee's face,

Ah, that same song.

Tain't no lie, Tain't no tale, Ah, that same song,

Ka - tie made the Jim Lee leave her mail,

Ah, that same song.

Melody: First tetrachord of major scale.

* Two mail-carrying steamboats on the Ohio River: the *James Lee* and the *Kate Adams*.

We Shall Overcome

We shall o-ver come, We shall o-ver come,—

We shall o-ver come some day!_____ Oh,

Deep in my heart, I do be - lieve,

We shall o - ver come some day!____

Rosie

Collected, adapted, and arranged by John A. Lomax and Alan Lomax

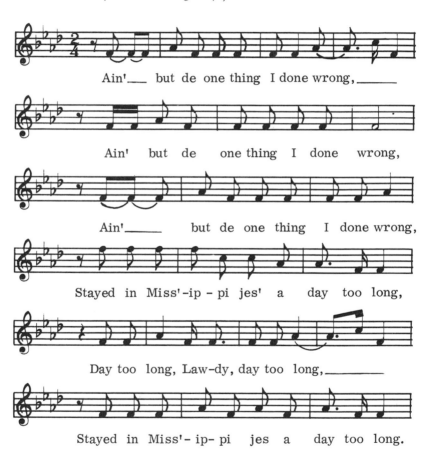

Ain'___ but de one thing I done wrong,_____

Ain' but de one thing I done wrong,

Ain'_____ but de one thing I done wrong,

Stayed in Miss'-ip-pi jes' a day too long,

Day too long, Law-dy, day too long,_____

Stayed in Miss'-ip-pi jes a day too long.

Some Other Songs

Oh, Ros-ie, O - ho, Oh Ros-ie, Oh, Lawd, gal!

Oh, Ros-ie, O - ho, Oh, Ros-ie, Oh, Lawd, gal!

Ain' but de one thing I done wrong,
Ain' but de one thing I done wrong,
Ain' but de one thing I done wrong,
Stayed in Mis'sippi jes' a day too
long,
Day too long, Lawdy, day too long,
Stayed in Mis'sippi jes' a day too
long.

Chorus:
> O Rosie, oho,
> O Rosie, oh, Lawd, gal.
> O Rosie, oho,
> O Rosie, oh, Lawd, gal.

I'm in trouble down on de farm,
I'm in trouble down on de farm,
I'm in trouble down on de farm,
I'm in trouble, Lawdy, all day long,
All day long, honey, all day long,
I'm in trouble, honey, all day long.

Chorus:
> O Rosie, oho,
> O Rosie, oh, Lawd, gal.
> O Rosie, oho,
> O Rosie, oh, Lawd, gal.

Think I'll jump in forty foot of
water,
Over my head, Lawdy, over my head.

You needn' worry, you kin take yo'
time,
Kin give me ninety an' still have
nine [years].

Oh, I wonder who get de sergeant
Down on me, Lawdy, down on me.

Some ol' snitcher mus' got de sergeant
Down on me, Lawdy, down on me.

Ef I don' kill him, I'm gonna fix him
so
He won' be snitchin' on me no mo'.

Lil baby Franklin wasn' but nine
days ol',
Stuck his finger in a crawfish hole;

Crawfish back back an' he wunk
one eye,
"Lil baby Franklin, you is born to
die."

Ain' but de one thing worries my
min',
My cheatin' woman an' my grea'
long time.

She says she loves me, but I b'lieve
she's lyin',
Hasn' been to see me in a grea' long
time.

Well, this keepin' Rosie sho is hard,
Dress she wo' it cos' a dollar a yard.

Wake up, Rosie, an' turn up yo'
  clo'es,
May be de las' time, I don't know.

I don' wan' ev'ything I see,
Jes' want dat lil bit you promised
  me.

If they mistreat me, tell you what
  I'll do,
I'll cut dis steel an' bring it home
  to you.

Come an' git me an' a-take me
  home,
Dese lifetime devils, dey won't let
  me 'lone.

Well, I come in here wid a hundred years,
Tree fall on me, I don' bit mo' keer.

Axes a-walkin', chipses a-talkin',
All day long, honey, all day long.

    O Rosie, oho,
    O Rosie, oh, Lawd, gal.

PART IV

❦

Personal Experiences

Slavery Time

Professor John B. Cade, of Prairie View College, Prairie View, Texas, was the first to recognize the value of the slave narrative, or individual experience, as a branch of the Negro folk tradition possessing a distinctive and unique folk flavor. He aroused the interest of historians and folklorists alike in this genre when he read a paper at an annual meeting of the Association for the Study of Negro Life and History. Carter G. Woodson, founder of the Association, was deeply impressed with this presentation, "Out of the Mouths of Ex-Slaves," and published it in the Journal of Negro History *for July 1935. In 1945 B. A. Botkin, chief of the Archive of Folk Song at the Library of Congress, selected a group of slave narratives from a massive quantity collected by Federal Writers Project units and housed in the Library. These were published under the title* Lay My Burden Down. *That same year the noted sociologist Charles S. Johnson, chairman of the Social Science Division at Fisk University, published two thick mimeographed volumes of slave experiences and religious conversion experiences related by ex-slaves.*

❪ "I Can't Forgive Her, the Way She Used to Beat Us"

I don't know anything 'cept what happened when I was a child. I know I was born in slavery, and I know they was awful mean. I was born in 1855, and the War started in '61. My white folks was awful bad and mean. I'm telling you what I know; they was mean; they beat us till the blood run down our legs. When we left here we was naked; my sister was the weaver and she was weaving some clothes for us, and old Mistress took that stuff off the loom and took it upstairs and hid it. We went away naked. . . .

You know chillen get into mischief, and they get whipped for it. I often told my mother time after time that I didn't blame old Mistress for whipping us, but she didn't need to kill us; she coulda just whipped us. We didn't have on but one piece winter or summer, and she would pull it over our head and whip us till the blood run down, and we was dasn't to holler. I can't remember now like I can back yonder; but I can remember that just as plain as day. We stayed there a year after freedom 'cause we didn't have sense enough to know we was free. My mother took care of the chillen and washing and ironing, and she took me with her to wash socks and hand-kerchiefs. They used to keep her hired out 'cause she wouldn't let her (mistress) whip her; so they hired her out and finally sold her. But she come back 'cause they said she only had two chillen and she was sound, and they found out that she had had fourteen chillen, and when she was a girl she had knocked her toe out of place, and she was a little cripple; so they had to take her back. You know if you sold stock and it wasn't sound like you said it was, you would have to take it back; so that's the way they did. I seen Mistress come in there with a bucket of hot water to throw on my mother, and mother grabbed the bucket and threw it on her, and the old woman hollered murder and all the chillen come running in with sticks and things; then the old woman said she wasn't mad, she was just happy in her soul. One of the boys took the stick he had and hit me a lick or two, but they wouldn't let him hurt me; and he wouldn't touch mother.

You know that old woman was mean. When she was dying she said she was all right, and I said to mother, "Yes, she is all right: all right for hell." Mother said I ought to forgive, but I can't forgive her, the way she used to beat us. Ain't no child what don't deserve a whipping. We'd eat green apples, eat dirt and things like that, and if she caught us we would hide it behind us, and if she asked what we had, we'd say "Nothing"; you see we done tole a lie right there and she would whip you. I'm telling you the truth; I can't lie 'cause I got to go before my God, and she's dead and can't speak for herself; but she beat me till the blood run down to my heels. Mother said when she was sold she had a baby in her arms, and her other boy next to the baby was standing by the fence crying. When she come back, she had me. I was her baby. My father was a Bailey, but mother and father separated before I was born. I was born in '55 and that was in slavery time. In '61 I was six years old, and that's when the War started. No, they didn't sell him; he and mother just got mad in a quarrel and separated. He tried to get her back and the white folks tried to get her to take him back, but she wouldn't do it, 'cause he drawed back to hit her with a chair, and he'd never done that before. He woulda hit her too if her brother hadn't been there and stopped him.

Mother was put on the block three times after that; but they couldn't sell her. They tried to bid her off for a dime, but nobody would give it. I don't know why they wouldn't but I just know nobody would. Why, in them days they would sell a baby from its mother and a mother from her baby, like cows and calves, and think no more of it.

No'm, we didn't have plenty to eat. The chillen never did get no meat. We had bean soup, cabbage soup, and milk, with mush or bread in it. The grown folks got a little meat 'cause they had to work, but we didn't. Once a man brought some old hog heads and pieces of fresh meat like that to old Mistress in a barrel, to make soap with, and the things was just floating on top; and she got mad 'cause the grown folks (slaves) wouldn't eat it. She give it to us chillen, and 'course we was glad to get it, 'cause it was meat, and we eat it till it made us sick, and they couldn't give us any more. Mr. ———— (the man who had given the meat) came by and found out what she had done, and he said, "I just brought that meat here 'cause I thought you might want it to make soap. I didn't know you was going to make nobody eat it. I wouldn't give it to my dogs." You know she was mean. When I heared she was dead I couldn't help but laugh, and I was grown then and had a child. She ought not to do me that way.

Marse Jack Barbee, he was so good to we chillen. He jerked her off of us many a time, and he'd say, "Plague take you, you trying to kill that little baby." If he found any of the old rawhides she'd use, he'd cut 'em up and take 'em out to the woodpile and burn 'em. Then she'd go to them old sprouts in the yard. Sometimes I'd rather it been the cowhide, 'cause sometimes the sprouts would have thorns on 'em.

My aunt, she'd slip meat skins through the crack to us chillen till that hole would get right greasy. She had a little hole in the floor that she could use; and we would go down to the orchard and broil them or cook 'em some way. We'd put the little ones in the henhouse, through the hole they left for the hens; and they'd come out with an apron full of eggs, and we'd take them out to the woods and cook 'em some way; and we would steal chickens too. Me and sister Lottie was the biggest ones in the bunch, and we was real little. The white chillen would help us eat 'em too, and they would go to the house and get salt, you know.

(When Mistress would whip her) I'd squall and squall, and she'd shake me, and tell me to hush; then I'd just jump. I had to do something. I'd go round back of the chimney and cry easy. My mother never did whip me over twice, and I would mind her; I was 'fraid of her, and I always did what she told me. She was part Indian, you know. I said to her after freedom, "It's funny you wouldn't let Mistress whip you and yet you let her whip us chillen all the time." She said, "If I'd started that they woulda sent me away and I never woulda seen you no more."

Yes, when we left there we had our dresses pulled round in front to hide our nakedness. Many's the time I had to ask the white chillen for bread, and they'd slip and get us bread, and meat too. God my deliverer! I despised her! One of her daughters was dying, and I was going to a picnic, and mother said, "You ought to go by and see Miss ———, she's dying," and I told mother I didn't want to go, but you know I had been brought up to obey, and I was grown but I never could tell her I wasn't going. I just left like I was going in that direction, but I went on where I was going and I never did say no more to mother about it. When we was little, she used to whip us and then make us kiss the switch. She was the meanest one of the daughters. . . .

I seed one of our young marsters take an old colored woman and pull her clothes down to her waist and whip her with a cowhide. It's a strange thing to me that they would never try to whip my mammy, but I think that old Marster Jack was the cause of that. 'Cause she just had trouble with Mistress, and he said he wished they might try to help her out, 'cause she was a woman and Nancy was a woman. . . .

I'm seventy-seven now; I've been here to hear it thunder.

⟨ If All Slaves Had Belonged to White Folks like Ours

I was big enough to remember well us coming back from Texas after we refugeed there when the fighting of the war was so bad at St. Charles. We stayed in Texas till the surrender, then we all come back in lots of wagons. I was sick, but they put me on a little bed, and me and all the little children rode in a "Jersey" that one of the old Negro mammies drove, along behind the wagons, and our young master, Colonel Bob Chaney, rode a great big black horse. Oh! he nice-looking on that horse! Every once and a while he'd ride back to the last wagon to see if everything was all right. I remember how scared us children was when we crossed the Red River. Aunt Mandy said, "We crossing you old Red River today, but we not going to cross you any more, 'cause we are going home now, back to Arkansas." That day when we stopped to cook our dinner I picked up a lot little blackjack acorns, and when my mammy saw them she said, "Throw them things down, child. They'll make you wormy." I cried because I thought they were chinquapins. I begged my daddy to let's go back to Texas, but he said, "No! No! We going with our white folks." My mammy and daddy belonged to Colonel Jesse Chaney, much of a gentleman, and his wife, Miss Sallie, was the best mistress anybody ever had. She was a Christian. I can hear her praying yet! She wouldn't let one of her slaves hit a tap on Sunday. They must rest and go to church. They had preaching at the cabin of some one of the slaves, and in the summertime sometimes they had it out in the shade under the trees. Yes, and the slaves on each plantation had their own church. They didn't go gallivanting over the neighborhood or country like niggers do now. Colonel Chaney had lots and lots of slaves, and all their houses were in a row, all one-room cabins. Everything happened in that one room— birth, sickness, death, and everything, but in them days niggers kept their houses clean and their door yards too. These houses where they lived was called "the quarters." I used to love to walk down by that row of houses. It looked like a town, and late of an evening as you'd go by the doors you could smell meat a-frying, coffee making, and good things cooking. We were fed good and had plenty clothes to keep us dry and warm.

Along about time for the surrender, Colonel Jess, our master, took sick and died with some kind of head trouble. Then Colonel Bob, our young master, took care of his mama and the slaves. All the grown folks went to the field to work, and the little children would be left at a big room called the nursing-home. All us little ones would be nursed and fed by an old mammy, Aunt Mandy. She was too old to go to the field, you know. We wouldn't see our mammy and daddy from early in the morning till night when their work was done, then they'd go by Aunt Mandy's and get their children and go home till work time in the morning.

Some of the slaves were house Negroes. They didn't go to work in the fields. They each one had their own job around the house, barn, orchard, milkhouse, and things like that.

When washday come, Lord, the pretty white clothes! It would take three or four women a-washing all day.

When two of the slaves wanted to get married, they'd dress up nice as they could and go up to the big house, and the master would marry them. They'd stand up before him, and he'd read out of a book called *The Discipline* and say, "Thou shalt love the Lord thy God with all thy heart, all thy strength, with all thy might and thy neighbor as thyself." Then he'd say they were man and wife and tell them to live right and be honest and kind to each other. All the slaves would be there too, seeing the wedding.

Our Miss Sallie was the sweetest best thing in the world! She was so good and kind to everybody, and she loved her slaves, too. I can remember when

231

Uncle Tony died how she cried! Uncle Tony Wadd was Miss Sallie's favorite servant. He stayed in a little house in the yard and made fires for her, brought in wood and water, and just waited on the house. He was a little black man and white-headed as cotton, when he died. Miss Sallie told the niggers when they come to take him to the graveyard, to let her know when they got him in his coffin, and when they sent and told her she come out with all the little white children, her little grandchildren, to see Uncle Tony. She just cried and stood for a long time looking at him, then she said, "Tony, you have been a good and faithful servant." Then the Negro men walked and carried him to the graveyard out in a big grove in the field. Every plantation had its own graveyard and buried its own folks and slaves right on the place.

If all slaves had belonged to white folks like ours, there wouldn't been any freedom wanted.

(Out of the Mouths of Ex-Slaves

Mrs. Mary Frances, an ex-slave woman about ninety years of age, states that during slavery time many of the slaves endured all kinds of torture in order to escape the hard punishments inflicted upon them. She tells of an instance when an uncle of hers resisted one of the overseers and struck his master a severe blow when the master attempted to beat him with a cowhide whip for not working fast enough for him. After having this encounter with the master the poor slave knew that it meant death if he remained on the place and that if he ran away the hounds would be sent in pursuit. Thus, he had to think fast of a means to escape.

Immediately he set out for the woods. After crossing a small stream in a dense forest he came to a spot where there was a large hole in the ground. This was the place for him. He took trees, leaves, and branches to cover it over in order that he might be protected from wild animals and storms. He made a bed of leaves upon which he slept and kept near him a large club which was his only weapon. He killed birds and game and other wild animals of this forest for food. He seized every opportunity to slip back to the plantation to visit the cabin in which his mother lived, so as to stay in touch with her and the family. No one knew of his whereabouts but her, and she kept it strictly a secret. This particular slave remained in the forest until the hair covered his body and he looked like the animals about him.

When freedom came, he revealed himself, went to his wife and children, who to their utmost surprise, and fright, greeted him, although they were not thoroughly convinced that he was whom he claimed to be. . . .

During the time of slavery, there were two women by the name of Betty and Molly. Molly was tall with coal black hair, about the age of thirty. Betty was a slave brought from Alabama and sold in Louisiana. She was very high-tempered. She weighed about one hundred and eighty-five pounds. Betty was treated very cruelly by the overseer on account of her temper. On one occasion, her punishment was to be whipped every morning for one month. This she thought horrible. She was the mother of one child named Simon.

One day Aunt Betty and Molly got into a dispute over a cotton row in a field where they were chopping cotton. Betty struck Molly with her hoe, cutting the flesh from her face. Her punishment was too severe, so she decided that she would stand it no longer. She threw her little son, Simon, in the well. They whipped her terribly about the disappearance of the child. She would never tell where the child was. There was one old slave who felt sorry for her and begged her to tell where the child was because he had heard the overseer say that night would be the last time to whip her because he was going to kill her. So she told this old slave man where her little son was. He rushed to the lot where the well was and pulled him out.

Aunt Betty was brought to Homer and tried by the court and was condemned to die.

On the day that she was hanged they asked her what she had to say. She only said, "I want to eat breakfast in hell tomorrow morning with Molly McAmore!" . . .

Usually when a slave holder gave a big festival, slaves from all neighboring farms would be invited. At times, festivals would be given for the sole benefit of the slaves of one slave holder. At this festival, the Negroes would sing and dance. Some would march and dance by the music of a banjo, others by the beating of a tin pan. The ladies would dress in white towel dresses, with white rags on their heads. The men would dress in white duckings and shirts. Their pantaloons would be rolled up to the knees, and all would dance barefooted.

The slaves were allowed to have socials or balls occasionally. At times, the mistress and master would come out to see the Negroes dance and enjoy themselves; the dances that were done in those days were the quadrille and other square dances. An accordion often furnished the music. On rare occasions, there were fiddles, fifes, and sometimes drums. This same music was often carried to the home of the master when company came.

Frequently, these slaves were permitted to have a ball or dance. Some would play ring plays, such as "Git around, Napper, and git out ob de way" or "Where yo gwine, buzzard, where you gwine, crow? Ise gwine down to de new groun' to jump Jim Crow. Wheel aroun' and turn aroun' and do jes so. Ev'y time you turn aroun', you jump Jim Crow." . . .

On a plantation in Franklin Parish, Louisiana, the children of the plantation were fed in a long trough with all their food put in at one time mixed together. The food consisted of vegetables, cornbread, and milk. These troughs were located in the back yard of the master's house near the big kitchen.

The children of the plantation were fed by some old woman who was too old for field work. They were fed in a trough or dug-out made from the body of a tree. These poor little children ate with their hands or fingers and put their little heads down into the trough to sip up the milk or pot licker.

We children ate at the big house. Our food was put in one big trough together; syrup, milk, and other odd food were mixed in this trough and we children stood around eating like little pigs. Sometimes we would go to the creek and get mussel shells for spoons.

❪ Kicked Around like a Mule

I was in the Civil War. Mighty rough time, I tell you. My marster sold me. I was in Georgia, then they brought me to Tennessee. I was on the northern side. The man that bought me brought me from Atlanta to Knoxville; right at the Knoxville Branch the Yankees met us and made him give me up; so he lost me.

I got a discharge all right, but after the War I was met one night out in the woods, and some robbers robbed me of all the money I had, which was $2.00, and took my discharge papers. I never thought much about it then, but I have never been able to get a pension on account of not having them papers. Several people have tried for me, but I never could tell what regiment I was with. The regiment was from Wisconsin; I remember that all right, and I remember two names of officers. They were Lieutenant Parker and Lieutenant Hughes. I am eighty-seven years old. The year the Civil War commenced I was a fifteen-year-old boy.

I left 'long about chopping cotton time. The man who sold me was a speculator in slaves. Buy them just like mules. The Yankees took up I don't know how many boys. I waited on two officers. I kept their clothes clean, boots shined, and would bring water. I was standing right 'side of them when they give the discharge papers out, and I would be all right now if I coulda just kept them papers. But I just never was able to get on to getting anything. A old lady in Gallatin told me she was going to write about it for me; but I knowed the old heifer wasn't going to do it.

One old man in Gallatin, 'fore I come down here, told me he got $3,000, and said I sure ought to get something out of it.

Well, . . . I can't tell you nothing 'cept I was treated pretty bad— knocked and kicked around like I was a mule. They would tie you up to a tree, tie your hands and feet down, and whip you. They was awful mean in Georgia. You never was allowed to have a piece of paper to look at. They would whip you for that, 'cause they didn't want you to learn anything. When they would whip you they would tear your back all to pieces. Child, they didn't care for you. We had to stand in fear of them; we had no protection. They would take your clothes off and whip you like you was no more than mules.

When Civil War commenced, marster went and stayed two months, but it rained so much he come back. The man who bought me, the Yankees cut him off at Knoxville. That's how I got to Tennessee. I reckon my marster had something like fifteen or sixteen grown people on his place. Some of them had a hundred men on their farm at once. They would see children and give them candy; if they looked healthy they would buy them and raise them up. They would look at them and say, "That's a mighty fine nigger." Mighty few of them had marsters that would treat them right. The niggers was mighty glad to have the Yankees take them; they wanted to get out from under that rough treatment. Georgia was about the meanest place in the world. They would knock and kick you around just like you was dogs.

You couldn't raise no corn or hogs in Georgia to do no good; the hogs woulda been poor, for they didn't have anything to eat. Nothing there but rocks. Sometimes you could grow a little corn near a stream. But it was so hilly and rocky that you couldn't do nothing but raise cotton. It was a terribly ugly country. I never been back since I left. I never have seen my mother since I left, or my sister or brother. Diana was my mother's only girl. They wouldn't make no difference in the half-white slaves. They would get whippings just like we would.

I never seen any colored people who couldn't talk English. I have been as far as Ohio. They talk so curious I just couldn't understand them.

We had to go to the white folks' church, and a white man would preach to us. We always sit in the back of the church. My mother had me in her arms and a white man sprinkled me. He put water on my head. They didn't mind sprinkling then. Colored folks would go to the woods sometimes and have a meeting. Whenever they wanted to marry all you had to do was go ask old marster if you could have so-and-so, and that was all to it. They didn't allow you no license. They wouldn't allow you to carry a book; reckon they was 'fraid you would learn something.

They would let them have parties sometimes on Saturday nights. But the white folks would have to tell the padderollers that we was going to have something, so they wouldn't bother us. In corn shucking time, no padderollers would ever bother you. We would have a big time at corn shuckings. They would call up the crowd and line the men up and give them a drink. I was a corn general—would stand out high above everybody, giving out corn songs and throwing down corn to them. There would be two sides of them, one side trying to out-shuck the other. Such times we did have. I never will forget one night the niggers got to fighting and tore down a whole rail fence pulling the rails off, fighting with them. They was full of whiskey then. The ladies would wait on us and give us cakes and pies and all kind of good things to eat. That was the only enjoyment we had, but we sure had a good time then. When we wanted to have a dance, we had to ask marster. They would have a fiddler, and we would tromp around mightily.

You would always have to ask marster and mistress every time you wanted to do anything at all. At Christmas time they would give you something— shoes, hat, and one thing and another. Some would do it, and some wouldn't.

The man who owned us was right clever to us. He gave my mother a little patch to raise cotton, and when he would sell it he would always give her the money. Heap of them was too lazy to work a patch. He would give her a half-day on Saturday to work her crop. On moonlight nights we would work it too. Every family had a cabin to theirself. Hogs was wild; they just roved about in the woods trying to find something to eat. It was a mighty poor country then. There was plenty of grapes, plums, and watermelons. Georgia is the greatest place in the world for big watermelons. We would eat them all through the cotton patch. We used to pack watermelons in straw, and when Christmas would come we would be eating watermelons for Christmas day.

When a nigger would run away and be caught they would take you and whip you good, and sell you right away; some of them would keep them after they run away.

I didn't get religion until about three or four years ago. I was pretty tough, I guess. I thought I heard something; it look like I heard a voice speak to me when I was seeking religion. Things come like a dream to me sometimes. I feel a change in the body. I tries to do what's right, for I want to get to heaven when I die. I am satisfied to let the world go, so I get to heaven. We got to wait until He come and call, but I want to be ready when He comes.

I hope to join the army by and by;
I hope to join the army by and by;
Little bells ringing for the Christians;
Hope to join the army by and by.

All these old-time songs, I can't think of them now. My mind is short. I am looking most any time to be called. My time ain't long here.

They used to give us roots boiled for medicine. For a sore throat they had something called Mobile. It tasted mighty bad, and it would make you holler, but it was good for sore throat. I always wanted to do something. I was raised to it. My mother would make us wash every Monday night. Her name was Sara. She worked all the time. She would go about with her knitting in her pockets, and if she had to walk from the cabin to the house she would always knit wherever she walked to. Sometimes she would sit on top of the mule on her way to the field, knitting. She never got tired of knitting. Sometimes she would whip us for nothing. We always washed the things after she knit them. Marster would take and sell them for her, and give mother the money. He was a right good man in that way. . . .

When it come time for soldiers to kill a man, twelve of them would have guns, and one would be loaded, and that way none of them would know which one did the killing. Some of the soldiers would be on one side, and if things got too hot for him, he would go over on the other side. Once we was trying to get to a little town; men was laying out on the battlefield like cornstalks. We was in a little place called Lowden. The niggers come down with the cannons. Little bullets was flying through the woods; niggers was standing on that hill. One man went back and said, "Hell done broke loose in Georgia." We went to a place called Sweetwater. Democrats wanted to take us, but the niggers started running, and Lord have mercy, they never did stop. You could hear men all over the battlefield, crying, "Water, water, somebody please give me water." The ambulance would come and get them and try to do something for them, but they couldn't get them fast enough. It was terrible. That was the bloodiest war I ever saw. I believe gunpowder made them mean. They didn't bit more mind shooting you down than they did a partridge.

(["Master Got Good When War Come Up"

Yes, I was here in slavery. I will be 86 years old the 15th of August. My master had 47 slaves. We all lived right in the yard below the white people's house. There was about eight or nine cabins. My mother had eight children; all of us stayed at home. None of us was sold from her. Sometimes they was good, and again they was mean. If you didn't do to suit them they would whip you. I have got a many beating over my head with a stick, cowhide, or anything that they could lay their hands on. I was so sassy. I would sass them to the very last. They would knock and beat me again, but I would sass them again. They would whip me 'cause I didn't mind. We would pick wool and have us all sitting around in the house, and I would go to sleep. Old mistress got sick and I would fan her with a brush, to keep the flies off her. After a while I would get a lick on my head for going to sleep. I would hit her all in the face; sometimes I would make out I was asleep and beat her in the face. She was so sick she couldn't sleep much, and couldn't talk, and when old master come in the house she would try to tell him on me, but he thought she meant I would just go to sleep. Then he would tell me to go out in the yard and wake up. She couldn't tell him that I had been hitting her all in the face. I done that woman bad. She was so mean to me.

Well, she died and all the slaves come in the house just a hollering and crying and holding their hands over their eyes, just hollering for all they could. Soon as they got outside of the house they would say "Old God-damn-son-of-a-bitch, she gone on down to hell." My mother said she believed I cussed too, but I didn't. They sho was mean. On Monday morning old master would get up on a big block that was out in the yard and holler for eggs; he would have the niggers bring him all the eggs that was gathered. They would carry you down to the trundle house to whip you. Four niggers was killed in that neighborhood. Old Uncle Henry was hit right in the forehead, and he fell down and never did come to. A woman named Charlotte had real long hair, and they cut one side of her hair off and left the other side long. They whipped her one evening for the longest, and told her to get over the barb-wire fence, and she said she couldn't, and he jerked her through by the hair, and she never did come to. She was a corpse in ten minutes after they jerked her through. I never did know how come her to be beat up like that. But they would beat you for anything.

Old mistress had two daughters named Ellen and Nancy; old lady died and Ellen told mother to fix the bed, for since her mother died she believed she was going to die too. Mother fixed the bed, and she was dead in five minutes.

When the Yankees come I saw them way off in the field, and I didn't know what they was. I run and told master the field was full of buzzards. He filled up a wagon full of bedclothes and things to eat and was fixing to go away, but the Yankees came up there and set fire to that wagon and burned up every one of them bedclothes, and caught old master and tried to make him tell where his money was, but he never did tell that; he never opened his mouth. He didn't even holler.

Slavery Time

That was right there in Arlington where we lived. And them slaves was killed right on the next farm from ours at old Payne Buchanan's place. I never been back there but once since I left. I have been here twenty years. When slaves would die they would dig a hole and put you in a box, and take you up to the woods and bury you. They would bury white and colored in the same graveyard, but the white folks was in the upper part and the colored folks was in the low end. When the white folks would die the slaves would all stand around and 'tend like they was crying, but after they would get outside they would say, "They going on to hell like a damn barrelful of nails."

One thing, they give us plenty something to eat and plenty warm clothes. We had red flannel clothes in the winter. In the summer we went about with not a God's thing on but a "shimmy." We always went in our "shimmy-tails" in the summer. We had our food put on a table in a kitchen right back of the white folks'. They did feed us good and give us good clothes.

We never did go to no church. White woman took me to church one day with her baby, and I liked to tore them white folks' church up shouting. The preacher said, "Let her shout; she is a Christian and got religion." But they never did carry me back no more. They left me home with the baby after that.

One day I was at church here, and a woman come by and give me a awful lick with her fist; she didn't like me nohow, and I knowed she tried to do it, so I just hit her back. She had good sense. Nobody don't get foolish when they are shouting; they just putting on.

The War went on four years, and I stayed single, and I was 'gaged to marry the man I did. I never went out with anybody else, for I didn't think it was right since I was 'gaged to him. We got married after he come back. They courted then just like they do now. Only they wasn't fast like they are now. I never in all my born days went out at night by myself and stayed out like these young folks do now. When I went out I always had company.

Whenever a girl had a baby in slavery they never paid no 'tention to it, 'cause they knowed they would have more slaves the more babies they got. Sam Patton come driving up one day with two women in his carriage, and they had veils over they face, and master thought they was white, and he went out to help them and found out they was colored. He run them niggers away from there. Sam Patton was really married to them. We had a girl on the place running out all times of night. I knowed something bad was gonna follow her. You could hear the soldiers after her, and you could hear her scream. They just killed her.

When that happened, mother didn't tell us. I didn't know what had happened to me. I went running to the branch and washed myself. I come on up the road just naked, done been to the branch washing. It never did hurt me, though. The Lord certainly has blessed me.

The white folks would let them sing all they wanted to in the houses. One night they come down and there was three dozen eggs in the fire which they done stole. Mother give me a look, and looked over to the bed, and that meant for me to get up and go to bed; I better had went too. The fire was hot, and one of them eggs popped. Old master looked around trying to see what it was. My mother looked at me, for she was scared I was gonna tell. But master didn't stay long, but if he had he would have heard all them eggs. Soon as he left they began pulling eggs out and such a feast they did have. One Saturday night my father and uncle killed a great big mutton. They cooked that mutton and dug a great big hole and put paper over it and put plank across over it and put the mutton there and covered it up. And such another time they did have. They invited company in to help eat it up. They give us nothing, for they didn't want us to know about it, but we knowed it all the time but we knowed better than to tell it. They would kill shoats and have company way in the night. We children would get together and laff about it. They'd a-killed us if we had told.

One day I asked my mother where babies come from; she said the doctor brought it. One day I crawled up under the house when a girl was fixing to have a baby; I heard her holler and after a while I heard the baby crying. I asked my mother why the girl hollered if the doctor brought the baby; she told me to get out of there or she would kill me.

After slavery old master was sitting in the house crying, and he wouldn't tell us we was free, but he sent for his nephew to tell us. The nephew told us to get out, but old master told us we wasn't going to leave. We stayed there four years after slavery. He fed us just like he always did. He sold my father a place right off his place. He fed us and give us clothes just like he always done. He never was mean to us after freedom. He was 'fraid the niggers might kill him. After war come up he got just as good.

I remember once when one of the white folks died old Uncle Albert keeled over on the floor and was just a-crying, but when he saw nobody was looking he was just a-dying laughing. The soldiers would come and steal all of our butter; we had great buckets of butter in the spring, but the soldiers would come and steal it.

Once they had a runaway nigger, and when they caught him they put a piece of long chain tied onto his ankle and locked it and at night they would put him upstairs. One night old Payne Buchanan come along and put him up, for old master was sick, but he said he saw him go upstairs, but he didn't, for that nigger got away and stayed away a long time before anybody found him. The flesh was swollen all over that chain when they found him, and it had to be sawed off. He died. Nothing was never done about that.

One night there was a man come and had a little string about a foot long, and he had something on the end of it, and he was swinging it along and when it got to my father it stopped just as still. He said father was going to get whipped the next morning but he would keep him from getting the whipping. Sure enough the next morning they come got him, but they never touched him. They couldn't, for that man had fixed it so they couldn't whip him. This man was a runaway nigger. He just went around keeping people from getting killed. My mother wouldn't let nobody whip her. Old mistress couldn't do nothing with her. She would have the men tie her, and after she was tied they was 'fraid to whip her.

I remember once a mulatto woman was on the block to be sold and the women would say, "I don't want that mulatto bitch here." Finally one of the brothers bought her. After the War two of her brothers come through, and they carried her away. We had plenty of good food, but at the farm next to us you would see cornbread and meat out on the fence; the slaves would have to get it and eat it the best they could and keep working. He was so mean to them. His name was old Claybrooks. We had a kitchen to eat in, and they just had to eat the best they could. He would make them grab hot dog irons from the fire, and beat them if they wouldn't. Their hands would be so sore from grabbing them that they couldn't open them. He was just mean.

I had eight cards to spin every day. I was good at that. All of us had to spin eight, and sometimes they would be spinning way in the night, and I would be through before night. We made clothes all the time. I used to make the prettiest bedspreads. Men used to shuck corn, but the women wasn't there. They would get about forty or fifty men and shuck corn, and they would sing all kinds of songs. We never did have nothing like parties. They would 'low us to make our own quilts.

I got a whipping by my mother every night; I was so bad. Then the children would tell things on me and then I would get another whipping. One day my brother was coming from the spring with a bucket of water, and he said he was sick. I went on up to the house and picked up some rabbit pills that the rabbits had dropped and carried them to him and told him the master said take them and he would get well. He swallowed them all like a fool. I didn't think I was going to get a whipping for that, but he told mother I had brought him some pills that master sent him. I got a whipping. I used to pick 150 pounds of cotton every day. We would pick cotton and sing, pick and sing all day. A girl would wet in the basket to make her cotton heavier, and she would put rocks in the bottom of it. I told on her, for I didn't want her to beat me. I have been a good worker, but I ain't no good now.

When they wanted to marry they just asked old master, and the squire would marry them. Sometimes they would slip and sleep with the women and wouldn't marry at all. They would slip just like they do now. They would let us have company, but they couldn't stay no longer than ten o'clock. They couldn't stay until one and two o'clock like they do now.

❲ Mulatto Whom Owners Treated like a Family Member

My grandmother was stole from Spain and brought here, and they made a slave out of her. I remember mother crying and Mistress got in bed with her. She slept right with mother. We had trundle beds then. My mother was kind of the boss around there about things around the house. Mistress' daughter-in-law didn't like it a bit, 'cause mother was bossing things. Mistress finally picked out a place for us and built us a house. We stayed there until after the War come up. We didn't know nothing about hard slavery. We stayed right where Mistress did. I was named for her, Margaret Lavine; they call me Maggie now. I was kinda small and I can't remember very much, but I know we didn't have no hard time. I played with the white children all the time.

I can remember when the men was getting ready to go to war, and seeing mother and Mistress going off crying. Me and the white children wanted to cry too, so we wet rags with spit and rubbed it on our eyes to make tears.

Mistress' son had six fine horses. A poor white boy came riding by and said, "The Yankees will be here in a few minutes." We was all sitting down on the porch. We didn't pay no attention to him, but Mistress got up and looked over the hill and saw them coming. Mother grabbed me in her arms. They had blue coats with shiny buttons, and they had on blue caps, and the coats had capes on the back of them. The soldiers took the horses, cows, and everything they could, trying to starve us out. The son kept one horse bridled and hid, so that if the Yankees did come he could run. When he saw them coming over the hill he run and got on his horse that he kept bridled. He had a hundred-acre field to run through, and the Yankees saw him and fired shot after shot at him. But they didn't get him. He went to Ringold, Georgia, not far from Chattanooga. That's where the rebel soldiers camped. The soldiers got everything they could and carried it to Chattanooga. The old master wasn't dead then. He sent the family to Murfreesboro, out of the way of the war. We went to Murfreesboro, or we started for it. We didn't know what she was going to do. A man saw us on the train and told mother that the superintendent of the L. and N. wanted a cook and somebody to keep house for him. We had never been used to no rough life and mother was glad to get that job, for she didn't know what she was going to do. That man was M. H. Smith. He told mother he would give us a home. We stayed there until peace was declared. . . .

I used to play with white children all the time when we was at Mistress' house. She used to tell me not to play with the colored children so much 'cause I wasn't like they was. They said my mother was half Spanish and half Indian. She helped drive the Indians away. My father was a white man, of course. I just remember seeing him one time, driving by on a horse. When the Yankees come up to our house Mistress cried, and Master didn't want them to bother us. They said, "God damn, these must be your grand-children, the way you are carrying on about them." We always had every-thing the white folks did. Mother was kind of the overseer of things. She hired hands, and would see about food and everything. One day a man come by with a pretty clock for sale. Mistress wanted it so bad, and mother told her to get it. She said she would but she didn't have the money. The clock was $12.00, and mother went to her bed and looked under the pillow and got the money and gave it to her. Mistress didn't even know mother had it, and mother had sold milk and things like that, and it really belonged to Mistress. But she hadn't even asked her for the money. So you see we didn't know about hard slavery time. Our Mistress treated us just like we was in the family. We could have gone back to them after the War, but we didn't do it.

(The Negro Slave's Pride

Strangers to the institution of slavery, and its effects upon its victims, would frequently speak with astonishment of the pride that slaves would show in regard to their own value in the market. This was especially so at auction sales where town or city servants were sold. Conversations between slaves who were to be auctioned off could often be heard, like the following:

"What did your marster pay for you?"

"Eight hundred dollars."

"Eight hundred dollars! Ha, ha! Well, ef I didn't sell for mo' dan eight hundred dollars, I'd neber show my head agin 'mong 'spectable people."

"You got so much to say 'bout me sellin' cheap, now I want to know how much your boss paid fer you?"

"My boss paid fifteen hundred dollars, cash, for me; an' it was a rainy day, an' not many out to de auction, or he'd had to pay a heap mo', let me tell you. I'm none of your cheap niggers, I ain't."

"Hy, uncle. Did dey sell you 'isterday? I see you down dar to de market."

"Yes, dey sole me."

"How much did you fetch?"

"Eighteen hundred dollars."

"Dat was putty smart fer man like you, ain't it?"

"Well, I dunno; it's no mo' dan I is wuf; fer you muss' 'member, I was raised by de Christys. I'm none of yer common niggers, sellin' fer a picayune. I tink my new boss got me mighty cheap."

Harriet Parker on Slavery

De day de Yankees comed I seed 'em comin', an' didn't know who dey was, so I snuck out of de house an' run out to de loom house, an' slam de door, an' den climb up de ladder to de loft an' peeped out de left-hand window. My old missus seed me run out of de house, so she comed out to de loom house whar I was, an' bade me to open de door. I opened it, an' she ast me how come me to run out of de house. I told her dat I didn't know who dem men wid dem blue coats on an' guns slung over dey shoulders was, so she say, "Git down from dere an' come on back in de house wid me; dem men ain't gonna bother hide nor hair on you; dey's come to clear you." So I paid my missus some "never mind" an' come down outen de loft, an' followed her back in de house.

When de Yankees gits dere dey takes some grub out of de house an' takes my old massa's best horse outen de stable. He points a pistol at 'em, an' tries to stop 'em from takin' de horse, but dey takes 'im off anyways.

When I was a little bitty girl dey used to make a scarecrow outen me; dey'd make me git up fo' daybreak an' go out into de cornfields an' set dere till way pas' dark so's to keep de crows from diggin' up de young corn what was just peepin' hits head 'bove de groun'. A heap of mornin's de fros' fros'-bit my feet, an' when hit come time to go back to de cabin I could hardly walk, my feet was so sore. I used to go wid my mama to milk de cows, too—in de dead of winter when de groun' was all froze over an' even cows' titties had ice all hangin' down on 'em. It was so cold dat me an' mama's feet busted open, 'cause we didn't have no shoes to wear an' had to walk on de ice barefooted.

De old place is just three miles from here, an' de whole time I was dere dey never gimme a nickel.

Reconstruction Days

(Dorie Boyd on Freedom and Reconstruction

I was born in Catawba County in 1856; dat was my "maiden station." De Yankees comed an' set us free. Dey rid up on about one hundred an' fifty horses, went to de barn whar de corn was stacked, an' prized de door open so all de corn could run down de hill an' dey could git all dey wanted to of it. Den dey told my gran'pa to go an' fetch 'em all de hams outen de old massa's smokehouse, dat dey didn't want nothin' to eat cep'n ham. So my gran'pa went an' fetched all de hams, an' dey all et ham for supper an' for breakfast de nex' mornin'. Den dey tuck de hams what was left an' give em to de slaves, an' told 'em dey better not git scared an' give 'em back to dey masters, 'cause dey couldn't whip 'em no more now.

Dey never destroyed nothin'. Dey just et all de ham dey could, carried off all dey could wid 'em, an' rid on off.

De secret of de colored man's mind ain't never been knowed. If it had of been, North Car'lina would have been the richest state in the Union. Right after slavery time when dey started sharecroppin', de colored people didn't have much use for dese dollars. Dey raised ever'thing dey needed, wove yarn an' made dey clothes, so dey didn't do nothin' wid dey money but save it.

When you does bad you' conscience will sho' check you. I was raised wid some mighty good black folks. When you gits converted it's just lack sumpin' moves off of you. You done whipped de Devil, so all you have to do is just pray on. De old people wouldn't go fishin' on Sunday in dem days. Nowadays Sunday is de main day fer fishin'. If a nigger'd just pray lack he sings an' dances he'd sho' go to Heaven anyhow. When I was twelve years old I heard a .preacher preach the best sermon I ever heard. It was about "Death's in de Pot." If you gamble, "death's in de pot"; if you steal, "death's in de pot."

Yassuh, de Yankees didn't do us no harm; dey just told us, "You all is loosed now."

De old folks used to sing a little song, "Do, re, me, fa, so, la, te, do" and back down again, "Do, te, la, so, fa, me, re, do."

And I used to sing after 'em, but I could just catch the first part, "Do re me, do re me!" So that's how they come to call me that. The old master named me Do-Re. Only I spell it D-o-r-i-e.

'Nother thing, I never was scared of no hants. Wasn't no need to be, 'cause I knowed if I couldn't whip 'em, I could sho' outrun 'em. I did have a kind of a scare one time, though. When I got to be courtin' age I started over to my girl's house one night, and had to go through a swamp to git dere. I had a pistol, so I tuck it along wid me in case I runned into sumpin' I didn't know nothin' 'bout. When I got 'bout midways de swamp I seed a light keep on poppin' off an' on in front of me 'bout quarter a mile away, so I says to myself, "Maybe dey's sumpin' to dis heah hant stuff after all." So I tuck out my pistol, an' put it in my right han' an' started walkin' to'a'ds where I seed de light. I started to go back home first, but I said to myself, "What would my girl think if I let sumpin' 'nother stan' in de way of my comin' to see her? She wouldn't think much of me if I let sumpin' throw a scare into me an' keep me from comin' to her house." So I kep' on walkin' to'a'ds the thing, an' when I got close enough to shoot at it, I fired my gun at it. An' it falled an' hit de ground, but it kep' on lightin' up an' going on an' off. I slipped up to where it was poppin' off an' on, looked down an' seen it wasn't nothin' but a lightnin' bug. Wouldn't dat a-been sumpin' if'n I had let a lightnin' bug keep me from goin' to see my girl?

(Reconstruction Was a Mighty Hard Pull

I was born in Edgefield County, South Carolina. I am eighty-five years old. I was born a slave of George Strauter. I remembers hearing them say, "Thank God, I's free as a jay bird." My ma was a slave in the field. I was eleven years old when freedom was declared. When I was little, Mr. Strauter whipped my ma. It hurt me bad as it did her. I hated him. She was crying. I chunked him with rocks. He run after me, but he didn't catch me. There was twenty-five or thirty hands that worked in the field. They raised wheat, corn, oats, barley, and cotton. All the children that couldn't work stayed at one house. Aunt Mat kept the babies and small children that couldn't go to the field. He had a gin and a shop. The shop was at the fork of the roads. When the war come on, my papa went to build forts. He quit Ma and took another woman. When the war close, Ma took her four children, bundled 'em up and went to Augusta. The government give out rations there. My ma washed and ironed. People died in piles. I don't know till yet what was the matter. They said it was the change of living. I seen five or six wooden, painted coffins piled up on wagons pass by our house. Loads passed every day like you see cotton pass here. Some said it was cholera and some took consumption. Lots of the colored people nearly starved. Not much to get to do and not much houseroom. Several families had to live in one house. Lots of the colored folks went up North and froze to death. They couldn't stand the cold. They wrote back about them dying. No, they never sent them back. I heard some sent for money to come back. I heard plenty 'bout the Ku Klux. They scared the folks to death. People left Augusta in droves. About a thousand would all meet and walk going to hunt work and new homes. Some of them died. I had a sister and brother lost that way. I had another sister come to Louisiana that way. She wrote back.

I don't think the colored folks looked for a share of land. They never got nothing 'cause the white folks didn't have nothing but barren hills left. About all the mules was wore out hauling provisions in the army. Some folks say they ought to done more for the colored folks when they left, but they say they was broke. Freeing all the slaves left 'em broke.

That reconstruction was a mighty hard pull. Me and Ma couldn't live. A man paid our ways to Carlisle, Arkansas, and we come. We started working for Mr. Emenson. He had a big store, teams, and land. We liked it fine, and I been here fifty-six years now. There was so much wild game, living was not so hard. If a fellow could get a little bread and a place to stay, he was all right. After I come to this state, I voted some. I have farmed and worked at odd jobs. I farmed mostly. Ma went back to her old master. He persuaded her to come back home. Me and her went back and run a farm four or five years before she died. Then I come back here.

(# Ku Klux

I

I never will forget when they hung Cy Guy. They hung him for a scandalous insult to a white woman, and they comed after him a hundred strong.

They tries him there in the woods, and they scratches Cy's arm to git some blood, and with that blood they writes that he shall hang 'tween the heavens and the earth till he am dead, dead, dead, and that any nigger what takes down the body shall be hung too.

Well, sir, the next morning there he hung, right over the road, and the sentence hanging over his head. Nobody'd bother with that body for four days, and there it hung, swinging in the wind, but the fourth day the sheriff comes and takes it down.

There was Ed and Cindy, who 'fore the war belonged to Mr. Lynch, and after the war he told 'em to move. He gives 'em a month, and they ain't gone, so the Ku Kluxes gits 'em.

It was on a cold night when they comed and drugged the niggers outen bed. They carried 'em down in the woods and whup them, then they throws 'em in the pond, their bodies breaking the ice. Ed come out and come to our house, but Cindy ain't been seed since.

Sam Allen in Caswell County was told to move, and after a month the hundred Ku Klux come a-toting his casket, and they tells him that his time has come and iffen he want to tell his wife goodbye and say his prayers hurry up.

They set the coffin on two chairs, and Sam kisses his old woman who am a-crying, then he kneels down side of his bed with his head on the pillow and his arms throwed out front of him.

He sets there for a minute and when he riz he had a long knife in his hand. 'Fore he could be grabbed he done kill two of the Ku Kluxes with the knife, and he done gone outen the door. They ain't catch him neither, and the next night when they comed back, 'termined to git him, they shot another nigger by accident.

I know one time Miss Hendon inherits a thousand dollars from her pappy's 'state, and that night she goes with her sweetheart to the gate, and on her way back to the house she gits knocked in the head with a axe. She screams, and her two nigger servants, Jim and Sam, runs and saves her, but she am robbed.

Then she tells the folkses that Jim and Sam am the guilty parties, but her little sister swears that they ain't, so they gits out of it.

Reconstruction Days

After that they finds out that it am five mens—Atwater, Edwards, Andrews, Davis, and Markham. The preacher comes down to where they am hanging to preach their funeral, and he stands there while lightning plays round the dead men's heads and the wind blows the trees, and he preaches such a sermon as I ain't never heard before.

Bob Boylan falls in love with another woman, so he burns his wife and four young-uns up in their house.

The Ku Kluxes gits him, of course, and they hangs him high on the old red oak on the Hillsboro road. After they hunged him, his lawyer says to us boys, "Bury him good, boys, just as good as you'd bury me iffen I was dead."

I shook hands with Bob 'fore they hunged him, and I helped to bury him too, and we bury him nice, and we all hopes that he done gone to glory.

II

After us colored folks was 'sidered free and turned loose, the Ku Klux broke out. Some colored people started to farming, like I told you, and gathered the old stock. If they got so they made good money and had a good farm, the Ku Klux would come and murder 'em. The government builded schoolhouses, and the Ku Klux went to work and burned 'em down. They'd go to the jails and take the colored men out and knock their brains out and break their necks and throw 'em in the river.

There was a colored man they taken, his name was Jim Freeman. They taken him and destroyed his stuff and him 'cause he was making some money. Hung him on a tree in his front yard, right in front of his cabin.

There was some colored young men went to the schools they'd opened by the government. Some white woman said someone had stole something of hers, so they put them young men in jail. The Ku Klux went to the jail and took 'em out and killed 'em. That happened the second year after the war.

After the Ku Kluxes got so strong the colored men got together and made the complaint before the law. The governor told the law to give 'em the old guns in the commissary, what the Southern soldiers had used, so they issued the colored men old muskets and said protect themselves. They got together and organized the militia and had leaders like regular soldiers. They didn't meet 'cept when they heared the Ku Kluxes was coming to get some colored folks. Then they was ready for 'em. They'd hide in the cabins, and then's when they found out who a lot of them Ku Kluxes was, 'cause a lot of 'em was kilt. They wore long sheets and covered the hosses with sheets so you couldn't recognize 'em. Men you thought was your friend was Ku Kluxes, and you'd deal with 'em in stores in the daytime, and at night they'd come out to your house and kill you. I never took part in none of the fights, but I heared the others talk 'bout them, but not where them Ku Klux could hear 'em.

One time they had twelve men in jail, 'cused of robbing white folks. All was white in jail but one, and he was colored. The Ku Kluxes went to the jailor's house and got the jail key and got them men out and carried 'em to the river bridge, in the middle. Then they knocked their brains out and threw 'em in the river.

III

The Ku Klux got after Uncle Will once. He was a brave man. He had a little mare that was a race horse. Will rode right through the bunch before they ever realized that it was him. He got on the other side of them. She [i.e., the mare] was gone! They kept on after him. They went down to his house one night. He wouldn't run for nothing. He shot two of them, and they went away. Then he was out of ammunition. People urged him to leave, for they knew he didn't have no more bullets; but he wouldn't, and they came back and killed him.

They came down to Hancock County one night, and the boys hid on both sides of the bridge. When they got in the middle of the bridge, the boys commenced to fire on them from both sides, and they jumped into the river. The darkies went on home when they got through shooting at them; but there wasn't no more Ku Klux in Hancock County. The better-thinking white folks got together and stopped it.

The Ku Klux kept the niggers scared. They cowed them down so that they wouldn't go to the polls. I stood there one night when they were counting ballots. I belonged to the County Central Committee. I went in and stood and looked. Our ballot was long; theirs was short. I stood and seen Clait Turner calling their names from our ballots. I went out and got Rube Turner, and then we both went back. They couldn't call the votes that they had put down they had. Rube saw it.

Then they said, "Are you going to contest this?"

Rube said, "Yes." But he didn't because it would have cost too much money. Rube was chairman of the committee.

The Ku Klux did a whole lot to keep the niggers away from the polls in Washington and Baldwin counties. They killed a many a nigger down there.

They hanged a Ku Klux for killing his wife, and he said he didn't mind being hung, but he didn't want a damn nigger to see him die.

But they couldn't keep the niggers in Hancock County away from the polls. There was too many of them.

(Little but "Way Out in Front"

If we believe that the tales of our nurseries are as important factors in forming the characters of our children as the theological dogmas of maturer years, we of the New South cannot wish our children to pore long over these pages, which certainly could not have been approved by Froebel.

But such legends as these must always be interesting to all students of folklore (Beaufort, South Carolina, November 1891):

"You see, Missus, I is small man myself; but I ain't nebber 'low no one for to git 'head o' me. I allers use my sense for help me 'long, jes' like Brer Rabbit. 'Fo' de wah, ol' Marse Heywood mek me he driber on de place, an' so I ain't hab for work so hard as de res'; same time I git mo' ration ebery mont' an' mo' shoe when dey share out de cloes at Chris'mus time. Well, dat come from usin' my sense. An' den when I ben a-courtin' I nebber 'lowed no man to git de benefit ob me in dat. I allers carry off de purties' gal, 'cause, you see, Missus, I know how to play de fiddle an' aller had to go to ebery dance to play de fiddle for dem."

(The Reverend Matthew N. McRae on "The Closest I Evuh Come to Bein' Robbed"

I b'lieve I do remember one thing that happened while I was a wagoner that done stuck with me. It was the time I was drivin' for John Q. A. Henry, in Montgomery County, who runned a gen'ul store next to Aldredge's mill down there.

Well, it happened like this: One mornin' me and John Q. A. Henry loaded my shut wagon with new shingles, fresh hogs, jus'-kilt rabbits, partridges, and squirrels, and I set out for Old Salem to take the goods to a storekeeper there.

Evuht'ing got along all right on the trip up to Old Salem, and after I done unloaded the goods I brought, he gimme four hun'red dollars of budget money in cash to pay for the goods. When he handed me the money there was a big bearded man stan'in' in the store what seed him gimme the money, but I didn't pay him no mind at the time. Howbe-evuh, after I started back to Montgomery County on the old Plank Road what went from Troy to Fayetteville, seemed like to me I could hear the beats of hosses' hoofs travelin' behind me. There was a lots of robbin' and stealin' goin' on 'roun' them parts in them days; sometimes wagoners was robbed and kilt, and the money they had on 'em took off of 'em, and they never could find out who 'twas was doin' the stealin' and killin'. So after I heard the beats of the hosses' hoofs I took the four hun'red dollars out of my pocket and put it down in the food box what I was sittin' on and what retched all the way 'cross the front of the wagon. The food box had a lot of sumpin' to eat in it, and some bones from some neck bones I'd been chawin' on from a lunch I brought with me. I thought in case that somebody really tried to steal the money it'd be safer in the food box, and harder to git to. After I put the money in the food box I retched down in the corner of the box and took out a old British bulldog pistol I always carried with me on trips, and there was Old Bill, a big shepherd dog what always went with me and walked along 'side the wagon. So I thought with Old Bill and the British bulldog pistol I'd be able to take care of myself if the bearded man tried to rob me.

I kept on driving down the road, but ever' now and then it still seemed like to me I could hear the beat of some hosses' feet in the back of me. Then, too, Old Bill would run back behind the wagon and bark evuh now and then like he knowed somebody was followin' us. This kept up till nightfall begin to come on.

I recollected that a white friend of John Q. A. Henry's lived about four miles off the road a li'l' further down from High Point, so I decided to ast 'em to let me spend the night with 'em that night.

When I got there it was already pitch dark, but I drove my horses up to the gate, and got down from the wagon, and went in and knocked on the door of the house, and they come to the door to see who it was. They recognized me, and I told 'em I thought a bearded man I seed down to High Point was followin' me to rob me, and ast 'em if I could spend the night with 'em. They said sho' I could, and they'd be glad to have me, and they knowed John Q. A. Henry'd be grateful to 'em. So I told 'em I had four hun'red dollars worth of budget money in the wagon that I wanted 'em to keep for me till next mornin'. So she set down, and I counted out the four hun'red dollars and give it to her, and then she counted it out again, and took it and hid it in a room some place. When I got up the next mornin' she brought the money out, and counted it out, and the whole four hun'red was there. Then she took out four one-dollar bills and told me to put 'em in my pocket and spread the other three hun'red and ninety-six dollars out over the food in the food box. She said if the bearded man caught up with me and tried to rob me to give him my purse with the four dollars in it, and then while he was scramblin' 'roun' in the food box tryin' to find the other three hun'red ninety-six dollars I could be doin' sumpin' else like hittin' him over the head with the butt of my old British bulldog pistol, or shootin' him. So I thanked her and left, and in about two-thirds of a day's ride I was back at John Q. A. Henry's store with the budget money all safe. This is the closest that I knows of I evuh come to bein' robbed, and I drove many a trip with my shut wagon after that, too.

Religious Conversion

(Hooked in the Heart

Before God can use a man that man must be hooked in the heart. By this I mean that he has to feel converted. And once God stirs up a man's pure mind and makes him see the folly of his ways he is wishing for God to take him and use him. From this time on it is up to God and if He has ever started a work He will not stop until it is finished and finished once and for all times. He spoke to me once after I had prayed and prayed trying to hurry Him and get a religion. He said, "I am a time-God. Behold, I work after the counsel of my own will and in due time I will visit whomsoever I will."

He showed me many things before He turned me around and then gave me my orders. I was a great musician and at times, after I had spent seasons at fasting and praying, I would get tired of it and go back to the ways of the world. You see the devil knows how to tempt a man. He always reminds him of the things he likes best and in this way he can get his attention.

God started on me when I was a little boy. I used to grieve a lot over my mother. She had been sold away from me and taken a long way off. One evening I was going through the woods to get the cows. I was walking along thinking about mama and crying. Then a voice spoke to me and said, "Blessed art thou. An obedient child shall live out the fullness of his days." I got scared because I did not know who it was that spoke nor what he meant. But from this time on I thought more about God and my soul and started to praying as best I knew how. It went on this way until I was about grown. I would pray a while and then stop and forget God. Finally, one day I was plowing in a field. There was a stump at one end and as I came to the end and turned around I heard a mourning behind the stump. I turned around and sat on the plow-handle and looked but didn't see anything. Yet the voice kept on mourning. I went on about my plowing feeling sad and wondering what it all meant. The voice said nothing but just mourned. Later God revealed to me that it was my soul crying out for deliverance. The voice was within me all the time but it sounded like it was behind the stump. From this time on He began to show me things.

Once while I was sick I saw in a vision three people and one was a woman. They looked at me and said, "He is sick." The woman said, "I can cure him." So speaking she took out a little silver vial, held it before me, and vanished.

At another time I saw myself traveling down a big, broad road. I came to three marks across my path and it was revealed to me that those marks represented the number of times I had started to find God and turned back.

After this, one day, I was putting a top on our little log house that I was building. It was broad open day and I was as wide awake as ever I was in this world. I had just got in position to fit on the first rafters when a voice called my name three distinct times. It called, "O William! O William! O William!" I hollered and answered, "Hey!" but nobody answered. I looked all around and began to wonder about the voice. It sounded so strange. It seemed to come from afar off and still it seemed to be right at me. I never have been able to find out what it meant.

I started to praying again. That night I went to my regular praying-place. I usually prayed behind a big beech-tree, a little distance from the house, and often during the night when I would feel to pray, I would get out of bed and go to this tree. That night I said, "Lord, if I am praying right, let me hear a dove mourn three times." While I was praying I went off in a trance and I saw myself going up a broad, hilly road through the woods. When I was nearly to the top I saw a big dog. I got scared and started to run back but something urged me on. The dog was chained to a big block, I found out when I got closer, and though she tried to get to me I passed out of her reach. I came then to a tree like a willow and there I heard a dove mourn three times.

But in spite of this it wasn't long before I was serving the devil again. I was serving him outwardly but my soul was pleading with God. I turned back several times because the devil stayed so hot on my trail. Whenever a man tries to do right and seek God then the devil gets busy. I used to go to my praying-place and it just looked like the devil would take me whether or no. I would see him with my spiritual eye as some great monster coming down out of the tree to tear me to pieces and devour me. Or else I would recall all the good times I had had. Such temptations are the first that a man goes through before he becomes purified and fit for God's kingdom.

You can't serve two masters. You either got to be on the one side or the other. Before any man hires another to work for him he tries to find out something about that man—what kind of a worker he is; how much interest he will take in his work and how much time he can give. If that man finds out that you cannot give his job the proper time and interest, no matter how good a worker you may be, he can't use you. The same is true with God. If we don't meet his requirements he can't use us. He calls us and gives us our orders, and until a man gets orders from God he is not ready to serve him.

When God called me I had applied in hell but my name wasn't on the roll. I saw a sharp-eyed looking man and he seemed to be walking back and forth from one end of a workshop to the other and looking at a time-book. I went to ask him if my name was in the book and he snapped back, "No!" It was from here that God delivered my soul, turned me around, and gave me my orders. I saw myself on the same broad road I had seen so much of in the spirit. As I went along a voice called out, "O William! O William! O William!" When He said that He turned me around out of the big road into a little path, my face being toward the east. He spoke again and said, "Go preach my Gospel to every creature and fear not for I am with you, an everlasting prop. Amen."

⟨[Everything Just Fits

I am now about sixty-seven years old. I was born in the year the Civil War started, in June. I had six brothers and seven sisters. My mother was a Baptist and I often used to see her sit alone knitting and singing. She would often get happy and shout. When she died I was only about ten years old. I used to hear her say, "I am so glad I am free." I did not know then what she was talking about. I thought she meant freedom from slavery.

I went to church and tried to get a religion because I wanted to shout like Mama.

The first time I heard the voice I was in the cotton patch. A voice said,

"Behold, I move you by the still waters." The voice was like muttering thunder. I kept on praying and the next time I heard the voice it was many years later. I had married and had five children. I had been going to dances but continued always to feel the desire to pray. The voice said to me, "I am a spirit and am to be worshiped in spirit and truth."

The first time I ever saw a vision I saw myself a little body, pure white, and flying along a beautiful stream that flowed from the east.

Later I was chased by the devil. He chased me in a broad and rocky road but he kept a good distance from me. I traveled in a western direction, but when my soul was freed I traveled eastward. I always prayed and the prayer was on the inside crying, "Mercy, Lord."

I still did not join the church and a little later I had my soul fixed up. I saw myself standing on a pretty white rock with nothing around it. I was afraid I was going to fall into the deep pit. It seemed that there was nothing to pity me. I was a little image and my body was standing beside me. While I stood there a little man came before me and said, "Don't you know that you will be devoured in here?" With this he took me in his arms and journeyed on a narrow white path that seemed no wider than a spider web. I saw three devils, one very large, one smaller, etc. They threw three large balls at me and I cried and said, "Lord, if those balls should hit me they would tear me to pieces." We journeyed on and saw two lions lying by the side of the path. They were cream-colored. They did not move as we passed.

We journeyed on and came to a beautiful green pasture with beautiful green grass. Every spring seemed even. There was a beautiful willow tree and every limb seemed even. We came finally to heaven. My guide put me down and said, "I leave you in the hands of the mother." She arose—a very tall woman—and began to dress me. She had on a long white robe and she dressed me the same way, and when she was through she said, "Everything just fits." I then began to shout and praise God with the rest of the angels.

We must see, feel, and hear something, for our God talks to His children. I joined the church after nearly ten years of experience and I rejoice ever in the love of God. The love of God is beyond understanding. It makes you love everybody.

⟨ Jesus Handed Me a Ticket

Before I begin I want to say that I don't know what other people have heard and seen in the spirit nor do I know whether it is necessary for everybody to see and hear what I have experienced, for God knows what is best.

It may be that some people do not need to see or hear anything. I say this because I do not want anyone to feel that I think God deals with everybody in the same way. The secret is with Him and He reveals things to whomever He wills and as He wills.

My first experience came one night just after I had gone to bed. I was twelve years old at the time and it had never occurred to me that I had to die. In fact, I had never given it a thought until that night. I was not asleep but had just closed my eyes when I saw, in a vision, a beautiful little white chariot floating through the air and I was in it. There was no one with me nor was I guiding the chariot, but it just went along sailing through the air. In time it passed through a dark tunnel or dungeon and here I saw a lot of devils. They all seemed to be working but as I passed through they stopped and threw things at me. I sailed on unafraid.

After some time I came to heaven. I saw God sitting in a large armchair, His head up and looking into space. He neither moved nor spoke. He wore a full armor, and across His chest was a breast protector that shone as if it was made of bars of gold. My mother was standing there and she showed me my two brothers who had died. I looked around and saw hosts of angels around two long tables and they were shouting and clapping their hands. The tables were covered with white cloth that hung evenly all around and nearly touched the ground, which was covered with beautiful green grass. The angels would come up to the table, take one mouthful of food, and go away shouting and rejoicing, saying, "Praise God."

From this time on I was made to know that I had to die. On another night, not long afterwards, I saw my two oldest brothers sailing through the air and going towards the east. The younger brother was in front. I did not know at that time what it meant, but about five years ago I lost the younger of the two brothers and two years later the older one died.

A few years after I saw my first vision I became sick and was tormented by old Satan nearly every day. He would seem to come in my room and make faces at me and beckon me to the ballroom. I seemed to be looking through the wall of my room into a large ballroom where dancing and all kinds of amusements were going on. How the devil entered my room I don't know, but he would suddenly appear before me with his clawlike hand, beckon to me, and then enter the other room. He kept worrying me until I decided to pray.

One day while lying there in bed I saw a star. It came and rested right on the window sash where the pieces that hold the panes of glass cross one another. I looked through that star and saw the heavens open and a sword came out and was laid on my bed beside me. A voice said to me, "When Satan comes, show him this sword." He came back and started towards me, but when he saw the sword he vanished and I never saw him again.

At another time something that looked like a blackboard flashed before my eyes and on it were my sins. There was no writing but I was made to know that they were my sins. A voice said, "Though your sins be as scarlet, I will wash you as white as snow; though they be heaped up like a mountain, I will roll them away as a scroll."

When I was about eighteen years old I began to think seriously about the salvation of my soul and I began to pray, saying, "Lord, show me if I am right." Not long after this I saw in a vision three heads side by side, one just a little above the other—the Father, the Son, and the Holy Ghost. A voice spoke to me and said, "My little one, thy faith hath made thee whole. Amen." I shouted for joy.

Once again I saw, as it were, a ladder. It was more like a pole with rungs on it let down from heaven, and it reached from heaven to earth. I was on the bottom rung and somebody was on every rung climbing upward but no one seemed to be in a hurry.

Once I saw two men and I was made to know that one of them was Jesus and I wanted to speak to Him. I hurriedly came up to Him but I was ashamed for I wanted to speak to Him privately. While I stood hesitating another man came up in great haste and handed a ticket through the window and passed out to a platform to take a train. My knees got weak and I knelt to pray. As I knelt Jesus handed me a ticket. It was all signed with my name. I arose to my feet and handed it in at the window and was told to take my place with the three men standing on the platform and wait.

One other time I saw Jesus in a vision and this time it was a warning of death. I saw in the west one evening a cloud and in it I first saw a man's foot but as I looked I saw the head exposed at another point in the cloud. I began to cry and shout for joy because for some reason I was made to feel glad. About a month after this a very dear uncle of mine died and I think that this vision was a warning.

This is the way the Lord has dealt with me. Seldom does anything happen in my family but that I get a warning.

God knows what He is about, and the best that any of us can do is to follow as He directs us through the spirit.

What is good for one person may not be suitable for another. God is the judge.

Wartime Experiences

Negroes in the Civil War

The aristocracy of all those Southern Negroes who engaged in military activities were the personal attendants . . . of the white soldiers. During the early days of the war the number of these attendants, or body servants as they were generally called, was considerable. A large proportion of the early volunteers belonged to the gentry class. On the plantation the young gentlemen had been attended, in most cases, by personal servants who looked after their clothing, groomed their horses, and cared for their hounds. When they volunteered for military service, these scions of aristocratic families naturally took their servants along with them to look after their needs in camp and on the field.

During the first part of the war, many private soldiers were attended by servants. In one South Carolina company there were twenty-five men with servants. Two years later there were no Negro servants except a few in the service of the higher officers.

The duties of the body servants varied greatly. In the early part of the

260

war some of the volunteers seemed to have the idea that they might call on their black helpers to perform duties assigned to them which were not to their liking.

The ordinary responsibilities of the servant of an officer were to keep the quarters clean, to wash clothes, shine shoes, brush uniforms, polish swords, buckles, and spurs, to run errands, to go to the commissary and get rations, and to prepare them for the master's table.

A few of the body servants were sometimes called on to act as musicians for the units to which their masters were attached. The servants had opportunities to earn money on the side by various methods; they made small charges for washing socks and shirts for members of the company and for running errands. Bill Yopp, servant of Captain Yopp, Fourteenth Georgia Regiment, made a standard charge of ten cents for every task which was performed for a soldier, whether it was washing a pair of socks or running a five-mile errand. His consistency in making this charge won him the sobriquet of "Ten-cent Bill," which followed him till his death in 1936.

The Negroes had also been buying whiskey at five dollars per gallon and then selling it to the soldiers for fifty cents for a drink of one-eighth of a pint.

The life of the body servant was, generally, not a hard one. He had the best of food obtainable in the army. The joviality and lightheartedness of the Negroes were important factors in keeping up the spirit of the camp.

One Negro, when asked by his master if he were frightened by the bullets, responded: "No, Sah, but I was terribly demoralized."

The body servants sometimes took part in the fighting. A newspaper correspondent reporting on the early engagements of the war said that a serv't named Levi Graham refused to stay in camp during the fight, but obtained a musket, "fought manfully," and "killed four of the Yankees."

The enjoyment which the Negro derived from his army activities is indicated in a letter said to have been written by the servant of General Bates to his sister in South Carolina:

"I've bin havin' a good time ginerally—see a heap of fine country and a plenty of purty gals. . . . I have also bin on the battlefields and heard the bullets whiz. When the Yankees run, I . . . got more clothes, blankets, overcoats, and razors than I could tote. I've got an injun rubber cloke with two brass eyes, keeps the rain off like a meetin' house. I'm a made man since the battle, and cockt and primed to try it again. If I kin kill a Yankee and git a gold watch, and a pair of boots, my trip will be made. How other niggers do stay at home, while we soldiers are havin' such a good time, is more than I can tell."

❨[

He Wanted to Ask a Question

Time: Sunday morning, May 1918
Place: Headquarters, U.S. troops, A.P.O. 741
Somewhere in France

I had just come in from church services and was writing a letter home when I heard three gentle knocks on the door of my little shack.

I said, "Come in." In response, a rather small, very black, bowlegged Negro soldier entered. From the standpoint of neatness his rating was fine. His O.D. uniform was nicely pressed, his wrapped leggins properly adjusted, and his hobnailed shoes were polished to perfection. Cracking his heels together, he saluted. Acknowledging the salute, I asked, "What do you want?"

"Is you de boss?" he queried. I replied, "Yes, I guess so. I am the commanding officer of this post." "Well, I's got er piece er paper fer yer." Saying this, he unbuttoned the flap on his blouse pocket. Taking the paper out and rebuttoning the flap, he again saluted and handed me the "piece of paper." It contained the following:

"Headquarters 525 Engnrs., A.E.F.
A.P.O. 741, May 1918

Private ——— has permission to speak to the Commanding Officer.

W. L. Glazer, Major Engrs.
Commanding Officer, 525 Engineers."

After reading the permit, I gave my acquiescence by saying, "You have permission to speak. What do you wish to talk about?" For reply, he began, "Boss, I's wun er dem drafted niggers. Yer did'n know dat, did yer?" I affirmed, "Yes, I knew you were drafted." "Yas, suh, I sho is," he stated. "Dey drafted me at Deridder—Luzy Anner. Yer doan know whar dat is, does yer?" I asserted that I did, continuing, "It's where the Long Bell Lumber Company has a big sawmill. It is about sixty miles north of Lake Charles."

His confirmatory words were forthcoming. "Yas, sah, hit sho is. After dey drafted us, dey tuck us ter Camp Pike, Arkansaw, en kep' us dere t'ree er fo' mumfs tryin' ter make sojers outen us."

Thinking it again necessary to test my knowledge of geography, he reiterated the question, "Yer doan know whar dat is, does yer?" and still being able to give an affirmative answer, I responded, "Yes, it is near Little Rock."

"Yas, sah, hit sho is." Then, going on, he added, "Atter dey done wid us at Camp Pike, dey puts us on er train one mornin' en de mornin'. Den dey tuck us offen de train en fed us. We walked er-roun' some tell dinner, den dey fed us ergin en put us back on de train. We trabbled all dat night, all nex' day, en all de nex' night. We did'n stop but t'ree times ter eat. At las' de train stopped at er plaze name Tenerfly, Noo Jersey. I did'n know whar we'd bin all dis time, but somebody's say we's at Cam' Meh'it."

Assured no doubt that it would certainly be necessary to give me information regarding the location of what had been, for him, so distant a place as "Cam' Meh'it," his stock interrogation was repeated, "Yer don' know whar dat is, does yer?" "Yes, I took the first troops to Camp Merritt, and took the first troops from there for duty with the A.E.F. in France," I returned. To my remarks he assented with the simple statement, "Yas, sah," proceeding with, "Dat's de bigges' camp in de wuld. Hit's seben mile long en erbout er mile en er half wide frum Tenerfly on one side ter Dumon' on de udder. I don' know w'y dey got two railroads so close tergedder, but dey's dere. One on bofe sides er dat long, flat ridge wat Cam' Meh'it's on. Well, we stayed at Cam' Meh'it erbout er week. Den one mornin' dey gits up at fo' er-clock en march us down ter de depot biffo' er train backed up fer us ter git on. Dey put us on de train en we rode about twelve er thirteen miles ter er plaze dey called Weehawk'n en tole us ter git off. Den dey march us down er big wide street erbout two miles ter de ribber. Dey say dat plaze is name Hobok'n. I don' know whar Weehawk'n quit en Hobok'n begin bicuz hit wuz jes' one straight street all de way. Dat wuz a mighty big ribber, mos' ez big ez de Missersippey. Dey's er big town 'cross de ribber from whar we wuz. Dey say hit Nu Yawk. I don' know but knows dey's lots er mighty big houses ober dere. Atter we got ter de ribber en stood er-roun' er w'ile dey put us on er boat en march us way down mos' ter hits bottom, en shet up de holes we come t'rough. Dey says hit wuz ter keep folks from knowin' we wuz on dat boat. Dat look mighty foolis' ter me, kaze we done march right down dat wide street en onter de boat in plain daylight. I jes' b'lieves ef ennybody wan' ter know we wuz on dat boat hit wan' no trubble ter fin' hit out.

"We lef' Cam' Meh'it 'fo' brekfus', but we did'n git ter eat dat day. Sometime dat night our boat pulls out, en nex' mornin' our cap'n comes down w'ere we wuz en sez, 'Yer boiz, git outen hyah. Come out on deck en git some fres' air biffo' brekfus'.'

"W'en we got on da dock, yer reckon wot we saw?" My knowledge of geography not being at stake, I did not hesitate to confess my ignorance and ask for information. The answer came, "Wotter, jes' wotter. Nuthin' but wotter, en hit er-rollin' en er-tumblin' jes' ever w'icher way. W'en I see all dat wotter, I begin ter git sick, en I gits sicker en sicker. I t'ought I's gon'er die. En dat night I's so sick, I got so I wan' eben 'fraid ter die. I don' know how long we wuz on dat boat, but finely we landed at er plaze dey call

Breas'. I don' know whut dey call it dat fer. Cap'n say we's a goin' out ter er res' camp fer er few days, en I says, 'Thank Gawd! I sho needs hit.' W'en we got up dere, wot yer reckon dat res' camp wuz?"

Probably his question was to learn whether or not I was following him. I was attending. For answer I asked, "What was it?" He explained, "Jes' er little patch 'bout ha'f er acre wid er mud fence erbout t'ree foot high er-roun' hit, en de mud inside wuz deep, en ez sauf' ez soap. We stay dere 'bout er week, en dey put us on er train ergin ober Sunday, en we got hyah on Wenzdy, en dis is Sunday ergin. Now wot I wan's to ax yer is dis. W'en we git done ober hyah, kin I go home by Newer Leens, en up de Missersip- pey Ribber, so's not to cross dat ole ocean ergin?"

They Speak of
Many Things

(Experiences of a Chimney Sweeper

John Junior began to talk. "Me, I'm a chimney sweep from way back—a chimney sweeper havin' a holiday. My pa was a chimney sweeper. . . . my ma was a chimney sweeper. Ask Susie." He wanted to say more about his mother and father but Emma interrupted him to remind him that his mother wasn't a chimney sweeper, but was a washwoman. "Shut up," John Junior said.

"I was born in Westwego. Took after my pa and ma. She born me in whiskey. My pa drank whiskey like the tank that bottles it. He was a laborer in the Round House of the T. P. My ma didn't work at all. She was a good-time woman. But when she married my pa she settled down. She got into an argument with some people and bore me to prove she could have a baby. I'm sho glad of it. No, my ma didn't have to work. She had enough to do takin' care of my pa when he got drunk."

He moved away from the post and eased himself down on the step. "I ain't got no education. Went to the third grade. That was enough fo' me. My pa stopped me, made me get a job on a milk truck. I was makin' two dollars a week. What I did with my money? I had a good time, that's what.

Sho, school is all right fo' them who wants it, but I figures all you got to know is how to read and write, then nobody can cheat you out of nothin'. Ain't figures enough?

"I believe my pa and ma liked large families, but they tell me—now I don't know—but they tell me my ma had such a time bringin' me she swore she wasn't goin' bring no more. She and pa drank so much they don't even remember how it all started, to tell the truth. Sho, I drank, too. Pa used to make me drunk, half the time. I've always liked whiskey and who don't like the way I do, they know what they can do.

"I quit the milk truck, couldn't have my fun like I wanted to. Had to get up too early. I was only ten years old then. What I didn't like about the milk truck was I couldn't be wid that sweet little gal next door long enough. Then, I got me a job ridin' a bike. Three-fifty a week. I went to work so I could buy the clothes I wanted. My pa and ma wouldn't give me nothin'. I always did like to be dressed up. I like it now but my money ain't right. That's all a po' man can do—dress up, and have a good time."

Susie reminded John Junior that he spent three hundred dollars of his bonus on clothes for himself and his women.

But John had a defense: "Ain't we got to look fine when we walk down the street?" Susie reminded him that he pawned most of his clothes for whiskey, which encouraged John Junior to shout back: "A good bottle of whiskey is worth a suit in pawn any day. Then agin, a man as ugly as me is got to spend money on women. Ain't that right? It ain't no need fo' me to fool myself. I always did spend money on women and I'm goin' to keep on doin' it.

"Sho, I done other jobs besides workin' on a milk truck and ridin' a bike. I worked at the Round House when I was a man. Made twenty-one fifty. Used every bit of it up, that's right. Man, I used to buy mo' fun than a chicken had feathers. They used to call me lil John Junior. A chip off his daddy's block. I was a mess. Had women shakin' down and doin' the Eagle Rock wid dollar bills in their hands. Have fun, live. You don't live but once. When you die, square up the Devil. No, indeed! There never was a Christian in my family, we don't believe in that stuff. My pa used to say, 'Get me a bucket full of wine I'll join the church.' Spare time? Man, I ain't had no spare time. Don't have none now. In my spare time I have my fun!

"I came to this part of town when I was about twenty. Bought so much stuff I had to go back on the other side. The policeman says: 'Boy, go back where you b'long. You is got these womens jumpin' naked.'

"Well, I tell you. There ain't nothin' wrong with being a chimney sweeper. The work might be dirty but the money is sho clean and long. Yes suh! You get bucks when you clean chimneys! SWEEPER! ROOAP, ROOAP, SWEEPER! CHIMNEY SWEEPER! GET 'UM CLEAN

266

'FORE YOU SCREAM. . . . FIRE! ROOAP! ROOAP! SWEEPER! I charge some people two dollars, and some two dollars and a half, mostly two and a half. I charge by the day and by the chimney. Jews make their own prices. You can't jew them up. The only thing I don't like about cleanin' chimneys is when them womens hang around me. They sho can give orders. What they know about cleanin' chimneys won't fill a book, but they hang around you. Sometimes I feel like tellin' um, 'Don't cry around me, lady, I'm not the fireman.'

"How I started cleanin' chimneys? Let me see. Say, you wants to know everything. Well, I was friendly with a fellow named Jeff Scott. He's dead. Jeff was makin' plenty money and needed help. So, me and him made up as partners. We used to make as high as twenty dollars a day fo' both of us. Wasn't bad, eh? Them was the days. Ain't no money in it now. Everybody is usin' gas and electric lights. And then again, nobody wants to pay. Can't make but about four or five dollars a day in the season . . . that in the winter time. Some say 'Let's get a union' but not me. I don't want no union. Fo' what? Fo' a bunch of black bastards to land in jail.

"How we get our jobs? Well, most of 'em is from our customers. They send us to people. And the fire stations send us lots of business too. But, we just go along the street hollerin'. The reason why the fire stations wants to give us work because it saves them from a lot of work. See?

"It feels all right to clean chimneys. It's a job. And a good job. Sho, I'm proud of it. All them people who laughs at us is crazy. I used to make mo' money in a day cleanin' chimneys than some people who laugh at us make in a week. Money was just that good. Then agin, there is a lot of places that feed you. Everybody likes a chimney sweeper. People think we is Mardi Gras. We don't care. We pick up a lot of tips like that.

"This is how we clean a chimney: We take them long corn vines and tie 'um together and sweep the soot down from top. It takes two men to do it. We draw down a small fire in the chimney by throwin' salt up the chimney. Salt is a strong-actin' agent fo' fire. It can't stand salt.

"I don't know why we wears beaver hats and them kind of clothes. I believes them is the uniforms because they don't look dirty. Nobody minds dirty clothes gettin' dirty. Does they? A white man gave me my beaver. The coat and pants is mine. We tie rope around our waist because we have to use it sometimes, to pull ourselves up and down the roof. We use that rope like a ladder. Man, sometimes we almost go down in one of them chimneys. I seen the time when I was in one of 'um like Santa Claus, reachin' down in there like a baby reachin' for candy. We take our pads, rags, salt and stuff and wrap them up in a bundle.

"The trouble with this business is that them bastards cuts the prices all the time. Some of them womens tell you, 'The other man said he'd clean my chimney fo' fifty cents.' All that dust and stuff gets in your eyes.

Man, that's dangerous. Suppose you get consumption? Cleanin' chimneys is bad on your lungs. I drink milk and liquor to keep from losin' my lungs. No, I ain't never been sick in my life.

"There ain't no mo' money in cleanin' chimneys, ain't nothin' to it. Everything is modern and streamline. I'm tryin' to be streamline myself." He laughed and the women laughed with him. "I was so streamline I fell off a woman's roof one mornin'. The woman had done said, 'What you goin' do way up there?' I said, 'I'm goin' to examine things.' She had to examine my head.

"Say man, them chimneys make you so dirty that when you get home you got to take a bath in kerosene. Everything on you gets black. That work makes you nervous. A white man sho could never be no chimney sweeper. He would look like he was carryin' his shadow aroun'.

"Some white folks like to talk with you, especially them from the North. They say they ain't never seen nothin' like us. They wants to know where we live and how we live. One white lady ain't had nothin' fo' us to do, she just called us in and gave us wine and two dollars to talk with us. Man, we ain't told that woman nothin'. I ain't goin' to never let nobody know all my business. 'Specially no white folks. We get cigarettes, clothes and things from people. All in all we do all right. But, we don't take things instead of money. Some of them white folks try to get you to do that, but not me. I tells them to pay me money, sumpin' I can use. I can get bread, clothes, and what I wants with my money. It ain't coneyfit.

"I strictly haves my fun. No, I ain't tendin' bein' no Christian. That's the trouble with niggers now. They pray too damn much. Everytime you look around you see some nigger on his knees and the white man figurin' at his desk. What in the world is they prayin' fo'? Tryin' to get to heaven? They is goin' to get there anyhow. There ain't no other hell but this one down here. Look at me. I'm catchin' hell right now. I'm drunk and I ain't got no money.

"If I had some? Man, don't ask me no question like that. What else is I'm goin' to do but have my fun. I pay my rent, give my old lady what she takes to pay the insurance, buy food, and get her sumpin' and that's all. What I'm goin' to do? Ain't no need fo' me to save nothin'. I ain't never been able to save nothin' in my life. I don't want to save nothin'. You want me to have troubles?

"I went to war—didn't get killed. Come on back—got my bonus. And then got me a load of womens and threw it away. Ain't that bein' a sucker? When you spend your money you ain't got nothin' to show fo' it. When you spend your money on whiskey you got whiskey to show fo' it.

"My wife is a good woman. She ain't had to work in two years. I took her out the white folks' kitchen. She wasn't makin' but three dollars a week, anyhow. That ain't no money. Sho, she brought the pots and pans home. But what was in 'um? A lot of leftovers. Man, as long as I can make a dollar sweepin' chimneys I ain't goin' to eat nobody's leftovers. I can buy what I want and I'm my own boss. Do you know that I been sweepin' chimneys off and on fo' eighteen years? Before I did that I used to be a common laborer. If I can help it I'll never be a common laborer agin. I likes to be my own boss. Don't want no white folks hollerin' at me.

"I fo'got to tell you that sweepin' chimneys is a hard thing in the wintertime, it's mighty cold five o'clock in the mornin'. I'll never fo'get. Man, I went hollerin' under a politician's window one mornin'. ROOAP . . . ROO . . . AP . . . ROOO . . . OAP! CHIMNEY SWEEPER . . . RO . . . ROOAP . . . REEE . . . REE . . . ROOAP . . . CHIMNEY! Man, the politician poked his head out of his window and told me, 'Say, you black bastard, if you don't get the hell away from here I'm comin' out there and rope your damn neck to one of them trees!' His wife stuck her head out the window and just laughed. It was early in the mornin' too. She just laughed, and said, 'Darlin', leave him alone. I think he's cute.' The man looked at her and looked at me; I was ready to make haste. He started cussin' agin, 'You black bastard, if you don't get goin' you'll be cute. You won't have no damn head.' Then, he looked at his wife. 'Cute hell. You run your damn trap all night and here comes that chimney man runnin' his mouth early in the mornin' and you say he's cute. I'll kill that nigger.' Man, did I leave from away from there! That's why we don't go out early in the mornin' no mo'."

The man with the bottle said, "Come on, John, quit talkin' and let's go to that saloon on Washington Avenue."

Emma said, "John."

He looked at her and said: "Baby, get my dinner ready. I'll be back."

But the woman knew that he was off with his friends. Old Susie was angry; she shrugged her shoulders and said, "Damn fool, there he goes bummin' with rats when he has a nice gent'man to talk with."

A black man called to John Junior from a passing automobile, "Where you goin'?"

He flipped his fingers and shouted back, "I'm goin' make some women shake down and show their linen. Everybody is worrin' about John. Can't a man have a holiday?"

Emma was "plum disgusted" with John. "All he knows is work, more work, fun and more fun. That fool has more holidays than the President. He ain't never had nothin' . . . ain't got nothin' and ain't goin' to never have nothin'. He's the best money-circulator in the whole round world."

(New Orleans' First "Baby Doll"

"I was the first Baby Doll," Beatrice Hill asserted firmly, when questioned about the history of the organization. "Liberty and Perdido Streets were red hot back in 1912, when that idea started. Women danced on bars with green money in their stockings, and sometimes they danced naked. They used to lie on the floor and shake their bellies while the mens fed them candy. You didn't need no system to work uptown. It wasn't like the downtown red-light district, where they made more money, but paid more graft. You had to put on the ritz downtown, which some of the gals didn't like. You did what you wanted uptown."

Uptown prostitutes got high on marijuana and "snow." They still do. Beatrice is fifty-two and is about beat out now. Her arms and legs are thickly spotted with black needle holes. She still uses drugs, and admits it. Also, she goes to Charity Hospital and takes treatment for syphilis. Back in 1912 she made fifty to seventy-five dollars a day hustling and stealing. Her man, Jelly Beans, got most of it, and they blew the rest "gettin' their kicks." Beatrice is all bad and proud of it. She's been to jail for murder, shooting, stealing, and prostitution. She boasts of her hectic past with gusto and vanity.

"Them downtown bitches thought their behinds was solid silver," she recalls contemptuously, "but they didn't never have any more money than we did. We was just as good lookers and had just as much money. Me, I was workin' right there on Gravier and Franklin Streets.

"We gals around my house got along fine. Them downtown gals tried to get the police to go up on our graft, but they wouldn't do it. Does you remember Clara Clay, who had all them houses downtown? Well, we was makin' good money and used to buy up some fun. All of us uptown had nothin' but good-lookin' men. We used to send them downtown 'round them whores and make 'em get all their money until they found out and had 'em beat up. Then we stopped. I'm tellin' you that was a war worse'n the Civil War. All the time we was tryin' to outdo them downtown gals.

"I knew a lady, name was Peggy Bry; she used to live at 231 Basin Street. Well, anyhow, Miss Bry gave a ball for the nigger bitches in the downtown district at the Entertainers' Café, and she said she didn't want no uptown whore there. All them gals was dressed to kill in silks and satins and they had all their mens dressed up, too. That was goin' to be some ball. We heared about it long before. So, we figures and figures how we could go and show them whores up with our frocks. I told all my friends to get their clothes ready and to dress up their mens, 'cause we was goin' to that ball.

"Everybody got to gettin' ready, buyin' up some clothes. Sam Bonart was askin' the mens what was the matter and Canal Street was lookin' up at us niggers like we was the moon. We was ready, I'm tellin' you. I figures and figures. So, I figures what we would do. I got hold of a captain, the baddest dick on the force, and I tells him what was what. I tells him a white whore is givin' a ball for niggers and didn't want us to come. He says, 'Is it a public hall?' And I says it is. He tells us to get ready to do our stuff and go to that ball. You see, the Captain knows we is in a war with them downtown bitches. Me, I figures he was kiddin', so I went to him and told him if he'd come downtown with us I'd give him a hundred dollars. He says, sure he would.

"Child, we got the news around for the gals to get ready. And was they ready! Is the sun shinin'? It was a Monday night and Louie Armstrong and his Hot Five and Buddy Petit was gonna be playin' at that ball. We called up Geddes and Moss and hired black limousines. You know them whores was livin' their lives! All the houses was shut down, and the Captain was out there in front. I'm tellin' you when that uptown brigade rode up to the Entertainers' Café, all the bitches came runnin' out. Then they saw the Captain and they all started runnin' back inside. We just strutted up and filed in and filled the joint. I'm tellin' you, that was somethin'!

"The first thing I did was to order one hundred and four dollars' worth of champagne, and the house couldn't fill the order. The bartender said, 'You got me.' I took all the place had, and the band starts playin' 'Shake That Thing,' and dedicates it to me. This white bitch, Miss Bry, comes runnin' up to me and says, 'Look here, this is my party for my friends.' I says: 'Miss Bry, I'm the one showed you how to put silk teddies on your tail. Who is you? What's your racket?' Then the Captain walks up, lookin' hard, and he says: 'Miss Bry, you ain't got no right in this public dance. If you don't shut your trap, I'll pull you in.' Man, would you keep quiet? Well, that's what she did.

"One of my gals—I think it was Julia Ford—got up on a table and started shakin' it on down. We took off all her clothes, and the owner of the place started chargin' admission to come in to the dance. Miss Bry raised particular hell about this, then went on home. We broke up that joint for true. The Entertainers ain't never seen a party like that one.

"Let me tell you, and this ain't no lie: Every girl with me had no less than one hundred dollars on her. We called that the hundred-dollar party. Say, niggers was under the tables tryin' to find the money we was wastin' on the floor. I remembers one nigger trying to tear my stockings open to get at my money till my man hit him over his head with a chair, and that nigger went to the hospital. 'Course it all ended in a big fight and we all went to jail.

"It wasn't long after that when a downtown gal named Susie Brown come to see me. She says she wants to work uptown, so we give her a chance. She got to makin' money, and soon she was called the best-dressed gal in Gravier Street. I didn't mind, me. She was workin' in my house, and her bed percentage was fine. I done seen time when I made fifty dollars in a day just waitin' for Susie to get done turnin' tricks.

"Shux, that wasn't nothing. When them ships come in, that's when I made money. All them sailors wanted a brownie. High yellows fared poorly then, unless they got in them freakish shows. When I took in fifty dollars in them days it was a bad day. I was rentin' rooms, payin' me a dollar every time a gal turned a trick. Then I had two gals stealin' for me, and I was turnin' tricks myself.

"Lights was low around my house and some awful things was done right in the streets. The police? Shux, does you know what we was payin' the law? Every gal paid three bucks a day and the landlady paid three and a half, but we didn't mind at all, 'cause we made that with a smile.

"Everywhere we went like the Silver Platter, the Élite, the Black and Tan and so on, people used to say, 'Look at them whores!' We was always dressed down and carried our money in our stockings. See like around Mardi Gras Day? We used to break up the Zulu Ball with money, used to buy the King champagne by the case. That's another thing, we had the Zulus with us. Shux, we took Mardi Gras by storm. No, we wasn't the Baby Dolls then; I'm talkin' about before that.

"In 1912, Ida Jackson, Millie Barnes and Sallie Gail and a few other gals downtown was makin' up to mask on Mardi Gras Day. No, I don't know how they was goin' to mask, but they was goin' to mask. We was all sittin' around about three o'clock in the morning in my house. A gal named Althea Brown jumps up and she says, 'Let's be ourselves. Let's be Baby Dolls. That's what the pimps always calls us.' We started comin' up with the money, but Leola says: 'Hold your horses. Let every tub stand on its own bottom.' That suited everybody fine and the tubs stood.

"Everybody agreed to have fifty dollars in her stocking, and that we could see who had the most money. Somebody says, 'What's the name of this here organization?' And we decided to call ourselves the Million-Dollar Baby Dolls, and be red hot. Johnny Metoyer wanted us to come along with the Zulus, but we said nothin' doin'. We told Johnny we was out to get some fun in our own way and we was not stoppin' at nothin'.

"Some of us made our dresses and some had 'em made. We was all lookin' sharp. There was thirty of us—the best whores in town. We was all good-lookin' and had our stuff with us. Man, I'm tellin' you, we had money all over us, even in our bloomers, and they didn't have no zippers.

"And that Mardi Gras Day came and we hit the streets. I'm tellin' you, we hit the streets lookin' forty, fine and mellow. We got out 'bout ten o'clock. We had stacks of dollars in our stockings and in our hands. We went to the Sam Bonart playground on Rampart and Poydras and bucked against each other to see who had the most money. Leola had the most—she had one hundred and two dollars. I had ninety-six dollars and I was second, but I had more home in case I ran out. There wasn't a woman in the bunch who had less than fifty dollars. We had all the niggers from everywhere followin' us. They liked the way we shook our behinds and we shook 'em like we wanted to.

"Know what? We went on downtown, and talk about puttin' on the ritz! We showed them whores how to put it on. Boy, we was smokin' cigars and flingin' ten- and twenty-dollar bills through the air. Sho, we used to sing, and boy, did we shake it on down. We sang 'When the Sun Goes Down' and 'When the Saints Come Marchin' Through I Want to Be in That Number.' We wore them wide hats, but they was seldom worn, 'cause when we got to heatin' we pulled 'em off. When them Baby Dolls strutted, they strutted. We showed our linen that day, I'm tellin' you.

"When we hit downtown all them gals had to admit we was stuff. Man, when we started pitchin' dollars around, we had their mens fallin' on their faces tryin' to get that money. And there you have the startin' of the Baby Dolls. Yeah, peace was made. All them gals got together."

A Wife Longs for the Town

Albert O'Neal is a laborer in a log mill, earning seven dollars a week. He has held this job seven years and he makes a point of keeping his wife at home. They have been married eight years and seem happy. But she is bored with the life of the community. Said she:

"I love my husband but it seems like he has such a hard time keeping up his family. I married in 1923. I was going ter school and my father had died and I had to take care of myself. My mother just died last year. She had pellagacy. I stayed with my godmother in Milstead. I never did stay with my mother. She left and went to Louisiana and never did return. She left papa. She never could git along. I met my husband and we married in Godmother's house. We done been going tergether when we married 'bout three years. I uster like the farm all right tel they wasn't gittin' nothin' for cotton.

"We would be living in town but my husband can't git nothin' ter do up there. I gits tired out here sometimes. I wish I was in town. I'm tired of picnics and suppers and ball games. That's 'bout all we hafta do. My husband goes to work wid sunrise ever' morning and works tel dark. I git up 'fo day and cooks his breakfast. He don't come back home ter dinner 'cause hit's so far. Hit's 'bout seven miles from home. He comes home 'bout dark, half dead. Then we eat supper and 'round a hour he's sleep."

(A Farm Wife Tells of Her Children

In this family neither of the parents can read and write. And none of the children has passed through the fourth grade in school. The parents wanted the children to be educated but even education was less important than living decent. The mother is the stronger element of the family, and has pronounced notions about morality and respectability. The attitude of the family is unique in its revolt against commonplace practices in the community. Having seven children ranging in ages from eight to twenty years, they live in a five-room cottage which they are attempting to buy. The house has never been painted, has half the windows out and is " 'bout to fall down," according to Mrs. Frank Grice. They are cotton farmers and have tried to make a living off the thirty acres of questionable land that they rent:

"Yes, I's the mother of seven children and every last one of dem belongs to Frank Grice. I ain't stuck on dese stolen chillun; dat's why I married in my mother's house 'fore I broke my virtue. I just got 'omanish and nothin' would do me but to marry. Out of all dem, I ain't got but one bad un. He ain't just say bad, but he wanders away. Been away now 'bout three year, and the last time I heard from him he was in Union Springs. No, he don't get into no trouble, 'cept last year he got into trouble for carryin' a gun. He didn't shoot nobody, but hit's 'gainst de law to have one. He got out of it all right because we have mighty good white friends.

"No, hit's been some time now since I's been to church. In my condition I can't go. I'm lookin' for the baby in September. I's shame to go to church lookin' like dis. You know yourself everybody would be lookin' at me with my stomach so big. Maybe if I could get me a loose dress I'd go. I 'speck this will be my last time to come around. Eliza Rose, the midwife, tells me the time come, but she said, too, dey would be twins. I wish dey would come twins, and den I knows I would be done for all time, 'cause I's just about tired of having chillun. Every time I look out de door I's like dis. I's so thankful for one thing: my oldest boy is such a good child."

(A Negro Cowboy: J. H. Brewer

When I was eighteen years old I was awful little and real skinny and kind of sickly, so a Goliad doctor told me I would have to work out in the open as much as possible if I wanted to be healthy and strong. He advised me to get work on a ranch and become a cowhand.

Luckily it was not hard to follow his advice, because Mama did day work in town sometimes for a ranch owner by the name of Dillard Fant. Colonel Fant and his family thought a whole lot of Mama, so when she asked him to give me a job as a cowhand on one of his ranches he said "All right, Martha (that was Mama's name), I'll give the boy a job if you want him to have it." So Colonel Fant loaded me on a wagon one Saturday morning with some more Goliad men he had hired as cowhands and carried me out to one of his ranches. The name of the ranch was the Santa Rosa, or Media-Luna (Halfmoon) Ranch, and it was located about fifty miles north of the Rio Grande River and twenty-five miles on the other side of the King Ranch. Part of it was in Hidalgo County, and part of it was in Cameron County.

Colonel Fant had a contract with the government to furnish beef for the Indians in the Indian Territory, so he employed about a hundred Negroes and Mexicans to drive his herds up the trail every year or work the cattle he sold and shipped by train to Ardmore, Oklahoma.

The year I started working for Colonel Fant was 1887, and I didn't get very far up the trail that first trip. We had barely got started; the fact of it is we hardly reached Live Oak County when our whole herd was sold to another ranch owner by the name of George West. So instead of using our crew to drive cattle up the trail that year, Colonel Fant had us to build a water tank on one of his ranches in Live Oak County. We started building the tank in April and finished it on August 12, but a cyclone came along on August 13, and it was blown to pieces—over a hundred days of hard work by twenty-five men wrecked in just a few minutes.

But it was the year 1888 that I remember most, because that was my first year to really go all the way up the trail. The reason I remember my first full trip up the trail so well is because of some trouble I had with a trail boss named Jim Myers. Jim was about thirty years old, five feet and seven inches tall, and so light in complexion he could have passed for white. But he was an ill-tempered and overbearing man. Colonel Fant had made me second trail boss and Jim first trail boss. The Colonel said that the reason he made me second trail boss was that I had a level head and knew better how to get along with the other cowhands than Jim did. Jim didn't say nothing to Colonel Fant before we left the Media-Luna, but I could tell by the way he acted and the look on his face when he looked at me after we got started up the trail that he didn't like it about Colonel Fant making me second trail boss.

I didn't see much of Jim because, as I'm sure you already know, the duty of a trail boss was to ride ahead and find a suitable bedding place for the cattle sleeping area every night and to locate water where the herds could drink. So Jim spent very little time with the herd and the rest of the crew. But whenever he was with us he would look at me in a way that I knew meant trouble ahead. I didn't know in what form the trouble was gonna come, but I kept my eyes on Jim whenever he was around and watched his every move.

The trouble came one morning after we had been on the trail about five weeks—about the first week in May 1888. It usually took about three months to reach Colonel Fant's headquarters ranch in the Indian Territory, and we had started driving the herd up the trail about the last week in March, so we were about halfway to the headquarters ranch when me and Jim had it out. The way it happened was like this: The camp cook was having calf steaks for breakfast that morning, an occasion that was always looked forward to with great pleasure by the cowhands because it wasn't often that a calf was killed and they had an opportunity to enjoy this trail driver's delicacy.

We were all seated around on the ground in a circle when Jim drove up, got down off of his horse, and took a seat among us. I was just taking a nice, juicy calf steak out of the pan with my fork when Jim sat down. As soon as he sat down he looked at me with an angry scowl on his face and said, "John, git up out of that pan and pass that pan of meat over here to me."

"Git up out of that pan of meat?" I said, glaring back at him. "I knew I was small, but I didn't know I was little enough to git in a pan. And now, do you want this meat?" So I took my foot and kicked the pan over to where Jim was sitting, and when I did this he jumped to his feet, pointed his finger in my face, and yelled, "What's the matter with you, John? Do you think I'm a dog?"

"I don't know, but you sho do act like one," I replied. And when I said this Jim yelled, "I've had enough of this!" and started for his gun. But when he started for it I put my hand on my gun right quick and said, "If you put your hands on that gun, Jim, I'll kill you." This took Jim by surprise because he had borrowed what he thought was my only pistol about three weeks before, and he had no idea that I had another gun. So looking at me he said, "Where'd you git that gun? I thought you loaned me the only gun you had."

"Yeah, I know that's what you thought," I replied, "but I had two instead of one."

"Well, what's the matter with you?" Jim continued.

"Nothing," I replied in return. "Something's wrong with you." He never said any more, so I finished eating my calf steak and got on my horse and rode out to where the cattle were grazing and told Bill McKenzie, one of the cowhands who had been watching the cattle all night, to ride into camp and get his breakfast—that I'd relieve him. So Bill got on his horse and rode into camp for his breakfast like I told him to do. But when Bill rode into camp and sat down and started eating, Jim jumped up and said, "Who told you to leave that herd and come in here and eat?" All the cowhands called me "the little one" because I was the smallest as well as the youngest man in the crew, so Bill looked up at Jim and said, "The little one told me to come in an' get my breakfast 'cause we have to make a big drive today an' oughta get started early."

"The little one ain't got no right to tell you to do nothin'," said Jim. "Now you go right back on out there and start watching them cattle again like you was doin'."

"I ain't gonna do no such a thing," said Bill, rising to his feet an' drawing his pistol on Jim. "The little one told me to come in here an' git my breakfast an' that's what I'm gonna do. You don't know how to treat a man nohow; if it hadn't been for the little one we would of all quit the trail weeks ago when you acted a fool with us. The little one got us to stay on, an' we gonna do what he says do."

When Bill said this, Jim jumped on his horse and rode out where I was watching the herd and said "John, what's the matter with you?" I still had my hand on my pistol, so I said, "Nothin', Jim; there must be something wrong with you." So he said, "Well, I reckon it is me, John. I have to deal with so much confusion, riding ahead by myself all day without anybody to talk to, so I reckon I am a little quick on the trigger when it comes to gittin' mad, so let's shake hands and furgit it." So I told Jim that was all right with me and we shook hands and didn't have no more trouble all the way to Fort Supply.

After we delivered the cattle I never saw Jim no more. Reports had it that he married a German girl, bought him a farm in the Indian Territory, and settled down and raised a family.

The other cowhands went on back to the Media-Luna, but I stayed on so I could come back on the train with the horses. The train that I came back on had one car full of barrels of whiskey being shipped into Texas and had a wreck after we started off. Some Indians came and took away the broken barrels of whiskey and got drunk. I drank some of the whiskey, too, but I didn't get drunk. About a week later I was back on the Santa Rosa ranch getting ready for another trail drive.

One thing more I forgot to tell you was about the horse races they always had at Fort Supply every July Fourth. The horse races were one of the main attractions of the day. They always had four horses in the races—an army horse, a civilian horse, an Indian horse, and a cowboy horse.

The same year that me and Jim Myers had that trouble I was selected to ride the cowboy horse in the race because I was light in weight and jockey size. We got started when the gun went off, and I was in the lead until we got within fifty yards of the finishing line. Then all of a sudden the Indian who was right in behind me let out a whoop, threw his hands up in the air, and his horse shot past me like a streak of lightning. Of course he won the race.

Note. The late J. H. Brewer, father of the editor of this anthology, eventually became a barber. Until he died on May 26, 1961, at the age of ninety-two, he was still barbering with a steady hand.

❨ Trabbler Man

I had been uh trabbler. I trabbel 'most all ober de wuld 'cept I ain't been to Jerusalem. I talk with white man who been ter Jerusalem, dough. He tell me de place far off. It way past New York, an' dat's uh long way. I know all 'bout New York, 'cause I lib dere five year. Yas suh, I well 'quainted wid Lexington Avenue an' Forty-second Street. I lib between Forty-second Street an' Coney Island—right down dere in de Juck between dem big hotel an' de bathing beach. Dey had me in Barnum and Bailey Circus ter pick de banjo for nigger to dance. Coney Island an' Forty-second Street been near togedder. . . . I ain't know how de ground stand now; I ain't been dere fer nineteen years.

During de World War the gover'ment hire me ter build airship down in Florida. Dey had anudder colored man build de engine an' I tack on de wing. I get tired of dat kin' ob wuk, an' move ter North Charleston, so I can handle mule an' help run de steam shovel. Uncle Sam say he willing ter double my salary if I come back to Flordia, but I done mek up my mind ter move an' I move.

One time I been down ter Cuba. I been dere most six year. No, I ain't wuk in de cane patch. I know too much fer dat. I obersaw uh big army of nigger. I crack de lasser, an' dey jump. I get in fight dere 'bout uh woman, an' I ketch uh train ter Mexico City. Some people ain't know dat train run from Cuba to Mexico City, but they ain't trabbling man like me.

You see me kinda ragged, but I got plenty of clothes in Beaufort—de best kind. I got frocк coat an' black pants; I got uh high beaver an' red coat wid long tail. I store um wid my sister when I come ter South Carolina. I leave my clothes an' ninety acre of land an' two wife in Beaufort. She tell you, she tell you dat Robert Samuel ain't no liar.

I leave my last wife 'cause she too yaller. I marry she one Christmas an' leabe she Easter Day. I been study 'bout de matter er long time. I say to myself, "Robert, you do wrong, ain't fer marry er yaller wife. One day she goin' ter reproach you 'bout bein' black an' den you goin' get mad and cut her t'roat wid de sha'ap razor your Grandpa leabe you. Den people goin' ter say you ain't uh true Christian an' you goin' ter feel dat insult. Better leabe she now, 'fore trouble sta'at." So I clear out de house an' nebber once blew back.

I been around Meggett fer t'ree year, ter wuk with Mr. Smoak an' fish fer myself. I meet Rebecca dere an' take up wid she. We mek 'greement dat I ter fish an' knock 'round an' put some grocery in de house, Rebecca ter wash fer me an' cook t'ree hot meals eber' day, an' help me wid my crop an' go out an' do day labor. W'en de white man call, I sorry I eber meet dat 'ooman. I ain't 'nuse ter lib common. I want me hot meal, t'ree time eber' day, an' sometimes she ain't cook but two. I come ter Edisto on a fishing trip, an' I like de place an' decide ter stay uh wile. I can tum my hand ter most anything. You t'ink I didn't work nary time, but I work w'en I got my mind ter. I kin get up likker still. I know how to mek fine likker. I oughter still fer de gover'ment fer six year in Kentucky. Dat's where I lernt ter cure corn likker. I tell you de secret: you ain't got to 'nuse pot and copper ter coil, no, suh. Jest drap copper cent in de pot an' likker come out like syrup. He taste like he two year old.

Dese Edisto nigger fool; dey ain't wuth sha'ak gravy. I different. I raise in white man house an' I trabbled all ober de wuld. Dey ain't know what wisdom I got store im my head. I kin outwuk an' outfish all ob dem. Dey say I lie, but I kin prove everyt'ing I say. You ain't hear I bin great songster? I don't sing 'round here, 'cause I mek all dese nigger shame. I ain't 'tend church on Edisto eider. If I go to church, I sure interrup' de preacher, 'cause I been preacher nine year in Florida. I done quit dat trail 'long time ago, an' I ain't want to hear any Edisto man tangle he'self up wid de Bible.

I fust-class carpenter too. I begin uh carpenter in Jacksonville goin' on nine year, but I stop 'cause I find I know more dan de head man, an' I ain't draw 'nough money. Fom dere I walk over ter Savannah an' soon as I git ter de city uh w'ile, a man stop me an' say, "You look like uh good man. I been look fer night watchman. You git eight dollar a week an' all you eat."

I tuk de job an' I watch at de biggest warehouse in Savannah fer nine year. De boss man 'most cry when I go, but I done tired ob de job. Got ter move 'long on an' go places, so I walk up to New York an' stay dere till de circus broke up. I spend nine year after dat out West. I been in Chicago an' Milwaukee. I been in 'most eber' place in de West. You see my hair gray on top of my head. Dat's from worr'ation. You t'ink I old, but you mek mistake. I forty-seven come December. He write down in de big family

Bible in my sister house in Beaufort an' fin' dat I tell de truth. Everybody know me in Beaufort.

I kin go back to New York or Cuba any time I get ready, but I goin' ter stay 'round South Carolina fer a w'ile an' ketch my health. Uh man get tired trabbel all de time.

⟨ No Money, but Provisions

The following testimony was reported to have been made by one of the islanders (South Carolina sea islands) who managed to remain at home in spite of the boll weevil:

De las' time I talk fr'm dis platform, I talk 'bout Mr. Cotton, but dis time I'm goin' to talk 'bout prowision. I raise good cotton, too. . . . Wen my cotton ain't stan' no mo' I say, "Look yuh! wut yo' goin' to do 'bout de animul an' de chillun?"

Fust I study 'bout de animul. Got two horse and a half to feed, so I 'cide to plant me some oats. Den I tek five task o' lan' (a task is one fourth of an acre), an' plow it an' harrow it, an' I plush dat lan'. An' den it ain't suit me an' I plush um again. Den I tek bough outen de woods an' trail um ober de lan' fo' help cover de seed. An' it ain't been long fo' I look yonder an' I see de oats sta't fo' sprout up in de fiel'.

An' my frien's, wen de time come, I cut eight wagon load off dat fiel', an' my animul, dey live on um fr'm dat dey to dis!

Well, dat fix de horses, but how 'bout de chillun? I fix to plant corn fo' de chillun. You know some people tink yo' kin raise crop outen de lan' an' yo' ain't raise um mo' dan dat high. An den de white people say yo' kin raise crop wid de fertilizer, but I cyant raise my crop dat-a-way, 'cause I cyant buy de fertilizer. But I go in de wood an' I rake me trash, an' I go in de crick an' I cut me ma'sh. Hab dem long kin' of boats dat fetch me up yuh, an' I had manure in de shed n' I pit um all on de lan'. An' I raise me a crop too! Ain't got no cotton, but I got oats fo' de horses, an' co'n and peas and sweet potatoes fo' de chillun, an' den a few head ob hog to pit 'long wid dat.

Now de people go to Savannah an' alla bout fo' wuk-out money. Wuk-out money is all right, but wuk-out money's like las' night rain—run in one han' an' run out de udder. I ain't got no money but I got de prowision!

([Jim Finn on Calling Up the Devil

Cross my heart, here's my hand, an' I hopes to never git up off of dis rock if dis ain't true. You can ask my wife an' my four sons, an' dey'll tell you de same thing. I knows how to call up de Devil an' make 'im learn me how to do things.

Now here's what you has to do if'n you wants to call up de Devil: De first thing you have to do is to take one of yo' old shoes an' take de inner sole outen it. Den you waits till a Sunday mornin' rocks 'roun', an' you goes out to de forks of de road an' draws a big circle. When you done drawed de circle you gits in de middle of it, an' den takes de inner sole out of yo' pocket an' throws it outside de circle. Den you calls de Devil three times, an' tells 'im you wanna give 'im yo' soul for comin' an' learnin' you how to do sumpin' nothuh.

De first time I called 'im up was to learn me how to play de guitar. Dey was havin' a lots of Saturday night parties in Gaston county, an' dey needed guitar pickers bad to play for 'em. So I went out to de forks of de road one Sunday mornin', took my shoes off, an' took out de inner sole of one of 'em an' drawed me a big circle, got in de middle of it, an' throwed de inner sole of my shoe out of de circle. Den I called de Devil three times, an' told 'im I wanted to give 'im my soul for learnin' me how to play de guitar. He didn't put in his appearance on dat first Sunday. So I went back de nex' Sunday an' tried to call 'im again, an' he didn't show dis Sunday neither; but I kept my hand on de railin' an' didn't give up. I went back de third Sunday an' called 'im up, an' putty soon I see sumpin' look like smoke comin' up de road whar I was stannin' an' when it get close to me it turn into de shape of de Devil, walked up to me, an' asked me what it c'd do for me. So I tells 'im dat I want to gi' 'im my soul for learnin' me how to play de guitar. So I had my guitar wid me, an' he tuck it outen my hand an' started playin' de box an' I took it on home wid me. Dat nex' comin' Saddy night me an' my Buddy went an' played for a party, an' evuhbody wanna know when I learn how to pick a box. I ain't tellin' 'em nothin'; I jus' played on; an' dat night when I got back home I hung de box on a nail on de wall, an' no sooner'n I hung it up it started to playin' by itself jus' like somebody was pickin' it. I gi' de Devil my soul an' made 'im learn me how to play de guitar, but I sho has had to pay high for it. I was havin' enough bad luck 'fo' I gi' de Devil my soul, but gi'en 'im my soul runned it up double.

I was even 'cused of murderin' a man one Saddy night, an' put in jail an' tried for it. Evuh time I thinks about de hard times I done had since I gi' de Devil my soul I gits eye water to cry wid.

Now if you evuh wanna call up de Devil, don't furgit dat he gonna test you out good an' dat he ain't gonna show up de first Sunday you goes out to de forks of de road an' calls 'im; he ain't gonna show up no sooner'n de third time you calls 'im an' maybe not den.

(Luster an' de Devil

I ain't been dere but I been told bout dem mean folkses down yander in de swampy lands.

Meanest swamper ever live was name Luster. He so ugly an black dat at de high noontime hit look like midnight faw half a mile around him. An mean! Laws! Luster so mean dat nothin but pizen toadstools would grow in his footsteps.

Well, hit was jes one thing in de worl dat trouble Luster. Dem swampers see him roamin round lookin grum wid his lip hangin down a foot.

"Whut ail you, Luster?" dey say.

"My feets," say Luster. "I can whup any man dat come up, but I can't git my feet warm. I wears sheep wool socks, summer and winter, but my big old feets is always cold as blue spring-mud."

"Whyn't you warm 'em at de fire?" dey say.

"Aw, hit ain't no use," say Luster. "I try dat. My feets is so cold dat dey puts out de fire if I shoves em close enough to do some good. Jes freeze up dat fire 'til hit's nothin but a nest of red ice."

"Hit's de damp do hit," dey say. "Hit's dis here ol wet swamp, Luster. Whyn't you dreen de swamp? You's big an strong. If anybody can dreen de swamp, hit's Ol Luster."

"Doggone!" say Luster. "Gimme a pick an gimme a shovel, folkses." "Yeah," say Luster, "I gwine dreen dis ol swamp!"

So Luster got de pick an shovel. He spit on his hands and swung de pick—*unh-unh-unh!* Every time he *unh!* de pick loosen ten feet of dirt, so he digged faw a week dere. Every time he throw out a shovel of dirt, hit look like dynamite goin off.

One day Luster taken off to eat him little somethin. He fixin to take a bite when a black man, blacker dan Luster, pop out of de hole and come scootin up de slope like a rabbit. He was kind of smokin an he smell like a hot iron.

De black man look mad. Sparks was jes spittin from his ears an some little red flames was curlin out of his nose. "Whut de devil you think you is doin, Luster?" he say.

"Who want to know?" say Luster, reachin faw his shovel.

"De Devil, dat who!"

"Huh," say Luster. "You is split from de ground to de belly-band, ain't you?"

"Yeah, Luster, but I ain't a man. I's de Devil straight from Hell. An Hell's back yard is whut you's jes befo bustin into. I was layin out dere takin a nap when a clod of dirt hit me smack on de nose. I look up and see de pick point stickin through de roof. Luster, I ain't gwine put up wid you makin de roof of Hell leaky! Wid dat low-grade coal we has to use hit's hard enough keepin de fires goin widout lettin no water in!"

"Aw, shet yo tater-trap, black man! You ain't no Devil!"

"Now, Luster, look at me good. Don't I look like de Devil to you?"

"Naw, black man! I knows a preacher man look mo like de Devil dan you."

"Come on now, Luster!" say de black man, gittin so upset dat he begun sweatin little streams of runnin fire. "You got to admit I got a tail. Take a look, Luster."

"Hunh," say Luster. "I knows a man born wid a tail an two extry fingers an toes. But he ain't no Devil. He jes a Methodist."

Black man stomp his foot an fire spout up.

"But I is de simon pure true blue Devil, Luster! Cross my heart!"

Luster jes laugh. "Prove hit. Yea, prove you is de Devil!"

"Now you is talkin sense," say de black man. "How do you want me to prove hit?"

Dat jes whut ol smart Luster waitin to hear. He say, "Well, my feets is sort of cold an if you's de Devil sho enough, why, supposin you jes give em a little whiff of de fire of Hell to warm em up."

So de Devil run back to Hell and dip up a gourd full out of de hottest core an come back to where Luster was settin. So Luster taken off his shoes an his sheep wool socks an stuck out his big ol feets.

"You sho got a pair of feets, Luster," say de Devil. "My land!" he say. "Look at dat frost on em!"

"Yeah," say Luster, "de minute dey hits de air, hit's frost all over em. Hurry wid dat hellfire, black man!"

So de Devil po some of de gourd of fire on Luster's feets.

"Ah!" say Luster. "Dat feel good. Dey's gittin warmish. Po some mo, Brother Devil."

So de Devil jes splash de whole gourd of fire on Luster's feets.

"Didn't I tell you I's de Devil, Luster?" he say.

"Sho did. My, dat feel fine!"

Den Luster yell, "Ouch! You black son-of-a-gun, you blister my ankle!" An den he jump up and lam de Devil over de haid wid his shovel and de Devil drap daid in his tracks.

So Luster throwed de Devil back in de hole and went on off wid his warm feets. "Dese is real feets now!" say Luster. An so when hit come de next rain de hole fill up wid water.

An ever since den, folkses call hit de Hellfeets Lake. An if you don't believe dat, you can go dere any day in de year and see dat lake!

❨ A Harlem Jive Spiel

Looka here, Babes, I'm too busy to spiel too long to any one hen. But I wanna put it down for you once and for all I'm too hipped for any small beg acts, and I ain't never in the mood to be so crude as to drop my gold on a chick that's bold. I'm a CI. I ain't no GI, so get on the right track and stay till I get back cause I'm a hustler, a rustler, the solid hipster they all boost, and the King of the Robber's Roost. I've put down issues and solid action for the whole world's complete satisfaction, from the Golden West to the Righteous East! I'm a cool fool, to say the least. I've got chicks and hens, fryers and broilers, bantams and pullets and some that are spoilers.

They all gotta give for me to let 'em live. I'm the stud who wears one good boot, in the toe of which is all my loot. I'm also mean and dirty, rotten, lowdown, bad, and thirty. Yep, I went around one day to see my Uncle Sam, but that stud didn't want me because of what I am. I'm really BAD, Babes. I'm rough and I'm tough. I've climbed the Rocky Mountains, fought the grizzly bear; I've trailed the wild panther to his hidden lair. I've crossed the great Sahara Desert, Babes, I've swam the Rio Grande; I fought with Pancho Villa and his bloodthirsty band.

I've robbed groceries, held up stores; broken out windows and knocked down doors. I've killed elephants and some gorillas, too; I've walked through Hell with a boot and a shoe; I use tiger teeth for toothpicks, drink lion's blood for my soup—I'm a player and a parlayer when I see a chicken coop. Only yesterday, Babes, a rattlesnake bit me, crawled away and died, and you know, Honeychile, your papa never lied! Remember last week when that cyclone and hurricane came through New York City? Well, Babes, me, your ace stud, was driving it! So that's the kind of stud you're trying to jive. Go get me something, chick!!

—Dan Burley

PART V

❧❦

Superstitions

The best study of Negro superstitions was made in 1926 by Newbell Niles Puckett, but no volume of Negro superstitions has yet appeared. Various folklore collections do contain sections on superstitions; the most substantial listing of them is found in a book of New Orleans folklore titled Gumbo Ya Ya, *by Lyle Saxon, with Edward Dreyer and Robert Tallant (1945). The Southern Workman, a magazine published by Hampton Institute, Hampton, Virginia, also devoted quite a bit of space to superstitions in its "Folklore and Ethnology" section, especially in the years 1896 and 1897.*

Superstitions exist wherever Negroes live. They are one of the major inheritances from the Negro's African ancestry, as well as the most consistent branch of American Negro lore. There may be localities where groups of Negroes have no tales, songs, or rhymes in their living tradition, but not so with superstition: it is omnipresent in all Negro communities.

Negroes refer to superstitions as "signs" and use them to condition their daily living. "Signs" for curing and preventing illnesses, for succeeding in undertakings, for warding off dangers, and for predicting the weather are prevalent today even among urban Negroes. Rural Negroes still plant in the "moon" rather than in the "ground," observing strictly the belief that if the fruit of the plant grows above the ground, it must be planted on the "light" of the moon; if the fruit grows beneath the ground, it must be planted on the "dark" of the moon. In this age of science, this belief almost always brings satisfactory results.

⟨ Bad Luck Signs

When you hear duh screech owl, honey, in de sweet-gum tree
Hits a sign as sho's yuh bawn, a deaf is boun' tuh be;
Onless yuh put de shovel in de fiah mighty quick
Fur tuh cunjer dat ol' screech owl, 'n kyar de one dat's sick.

Sumpin's gonna happen ef uh dawg outside de do
Gits tuh howlin'—Dat's uh sign somebody's dead, dat's so.

Ef duh rheumatiz has cropped all thoo yo' jints an' sockets,
Don' fuhgit to tote er I'sh tater in yo' pocket.

For a teethin' baby, honey, you mus' take duh pains
To apply, whilst good an' warm, a fresh-killed rabbit's brains.

Ef you don' want bad luck, mah chile, don' nevuh take a hoe
Thoo duh house, or sho's you live, bad luck'll follow, sho!

Hit's duh wustes' sort o' luck tuh raise yo' parasol
In duh house—now some folks says dat dis is folderol;
But you bettuh not be 'sperimentin'; you'll sorry be,
Caze I'll tell yuh 'bout duh pesky luck dat come to me!
Liza Jane, my daughter, was er fixin fer tuh marry;
An she bought er highferlutin' parasol to carry.
She raised it in duh parlor on de day befo' de weddin',
An' fo' de Lawd, dat night de groom, he 'loped wid Tildy Reddin'.
So you bettuh listen, honey, don't tamper wid uh sign;
Er bad luck's bound tuh foller you, ten times out o' nine.

⟨ Birds of Ill Omen

There is common to all southern bayous and creeks a small blue heron,
known as the skypoke. It is ungainly, timid, and harmless. It has an infre-
quent cry that has something of the resonance of the bittern, though on a
much weaker scale. This bird, which inhabits the depths of swamps and flies
above morasses, the Negroes have invested with familiarity with the Evil
One. To some of them it is known as the "devil's doctor," and it is supposed
to have a satanic knowledge of the virtues of herbs. It never eats herbs, living
entirely upon minnows and small frogs, yet it is supposed to take them when
sick, and its gizzard and liver when dried and powdered are taken as specifics
for many complaints. Skypoke feathers are common ornaments in Negro
cabins. If a housewife can get a duster made of its wings she is happy.

Another devil's bird is the yellowhammer, the large, beautifully colored
woodpecker of brown, red, and gold that is common in all southern forests.
The yellowhammer is not a familiar like the jaybird, . . . but it is believed
to be under the protection of Satan, and any man who slays it is marked
out for especial machinations on the part of the Prince of Darkness. He will
be made ill, or he may die. In any case, he will be so tempted that he will
be certain to fall and then punishment will follow. The yellowhammer

builds nests in the hollows of trees and its eggs are richly marked, but little Negro boys who are habitual robbers of nests will not disturb its home. They are taught from their cradle that there is no surer way to evil fortune. . . .

The purple grackle, which is a frequenter of barnyards and fond of the company of cows and horses, is looked upon with special aversion, and a Negro will waste an hour which should be devoted to work endeavoring to force one of these birds to leave the premises and stay away. Magpies, starlings, and black martins are all objects of aversion. . . . The magpie is disliked and believed to be an ill-luck bird as much because it is an irreformable thief as because of its inky cloak.

All of this crowd of flyers that partake of the nature of the Evil One are classed among his subjects. On the contrary, redbirds, cardinals, bluebirds, tanagers, many of the green vireos, and even the awkward pink flamingo are viewed with pleasure, and their presence is welcomed about a cabin clearing.

([Gambling Superstitions, Among Others

Few bolita players will admit a woman into the house on Monday, if she is the first person who has called that day.

Play the age and number of someone who is dead. It is believed that the spirit of the dead will cause these numbers to fall.

Powdering your face at bedtime and burning the soles of your shoes are thought to be conducive to clear dreams.

All numbers dreamed of should be played for three days.

It is considered bad luck to burn bolita tickets. (Alleys and trash cans are strewn with them.)

If a house is haunted, a piece of new lumber should be nailed in a conspicuous place; ghosts hate new things.

There is always some hesitancy about giving a child the name of a deceased child.

A baby born near midnight will be able to see ghosts.

Babies born in the full of the moon will be larger than those born at other times.

Hang pants over the bed at night for easy delivery.

Never step over a baby less than a year old, as this stunts its growth.

If the child's fingernails are cut before he is one year old, he will be a thief.

I brought Henrietta her wages in bills and called to her that I had laid it on the table.
"Put something on it, please ma'am," she replied from the basement.
"Why?" I asked.
"'Cause paper money crawls," she replied.

A piece of money tied around the ankle will insure the wearer against poverty.

Bringing a hoe in the house is bad luck.

Never kill a toad. It will cause your cow to give bloody milk.

Scrapings from a cow's horn made into a tea will cure fever.

([**Popular Beliefs and Superstitions**

TENNESSEE

If one starts pickin' cotton in a row an' leave it unfinished to pick another row one is sure to be bit by a snake.
If one takes cotton to a gin widout covering it, de owner will be robbed.
Pick five hundred pounds a day or de debbil will come and carry you away.
When us have a bright Christmas, hit de sign white folks gwine to die, and lots of 'em. When us have a dark Christmas, hit de sign Niggers is sho gwine to die.

ALABAMA

If the tongue is sore you have told a lie.
Thunder before seven, hit will rain before 'leven.
An egg laid on Good Friday will not spoil. Can be put away and kept for years in a loose bag; the contents will turn to wax.

Popular Beliefs and Superstitions

If you cannot raise your children, bury on its face the last one to die, and those coming after will live.

If you go to a cow lot on Christmas morning, you will find all the cows on their knees praying.

If you set out a tree and name it after a large person, it will grow to be a large tree.

If you burn wood in your house that has been struck by lightning, the lightning will strike your house (again).

FLORIDA

Keep way from me, hoodooin' witch,
Leave my paf from de poorhouse gate,
Ah pines for the golden harps and such;
Oh, Lord, I'll jest set and wait.

If a light goes out full of oil, hit's a sign of bad luck.

De scripture say a slip of de tongue ain't no strain on de backbone, and dey say dat every Friday de jaybird visit he'll be takin' kin'lin' wood and sand on a drop of water to de devil. De sand am a ransom fo' de ones in hell who can't come out until all de sand on de surface of de earth has been carried below. And de devil uses de sand to blind people and dey sing:

Did you ever see de devil with his iron handle shovel?
He scrapes up de sand in his ole tin pan,
He cuts up funny, he steals all yo' money,
He blinds yo' with sand, and he's trying to get you, man.

Grass is green, grass is hard.
An' de rooster in de yard,
Say, "So long, nigger, go 'long, I say.
Yo' don't get none o' my money till nex' pay day."

TEXAS

If you sing before making bread, you will cry before it is eaten.

If you go to bed without cleaning the table, the youngest in the family will not sleep well.

To sneeze in the morning tells that misfortune is near you.

Washing in the same basin of water with another will cause a fuss.

PART V. *Superstitions*

If your shoestring comes untied, somebody is talking about you.

It is a sign of disappointment to brush or comb the hair after dark.

An itching of the lips signifies that someone is slandering you.

Don't twirl a chair on one leg; you are turning friends from you.

If in stirring your tea, the leaves or stalks keep in the middle of your cup, it is a sign that you will soon be married, or talk to a stranger or an absent friend.

When bread or cake or pie burns in spite of you, your husband or lover is angry.

To forget to put coffee or tea in the pot is a sure sign that company is coming.

If you are deeply depressed in spirits, it is a sure sign that you will hear good news.

If you put on your right shoe first, you will be fortunate all day.

May is an unlucky month to marry in.

Nose bleeding is a sign of bad luck.

If your left foot itches, you will take an unfortunate journey.

If your stomach itches, you will be invited to a feast.

It is bad luck to destroy spiders.

If a slat falls out of a bed, it is a sign of coming riches.

If you forget something, never go back home for it, or you will have bad luck.

If a task is started on a Friday and not finished, it will take a long time to finish it.

It is bad luck for two persons to look in a mirror at the same time.

It is a sign of death for a dog to howl.

A dream of marriage is a sign of death. To dream of death is a sign of marriage.

To see silver money in your dream is the sign of trouble.

If a rooster crows at your window, it is a sign of death. If a rooster crows on your front or back porch, a stranger is coming.

You will have bad luck if you leave a sealed letter in the house overnight.

Always go out of the same door you go in, if you have never been to that place before, to prevent bad luck.

It is a sign of company if your nostrils itch.

If a spider swings down on a web, company is coming.

If you drop a dishcloth, it is a sign of bad luck.

It is very unlucky to remove a long-worn ring from the finger.

It is unlucky to pick up an old glove.

Never tell a dream until you have broken your fast.

A dark person coming into the house at the beginning of a new year is a sign of bad luck.

Sudden or shooting pains in the body are signs of bad news.

If the crown of your head itches, you will soon be advanced to a more honorable position.

If bees settle in a house, it is a sure sign of fire or other disaster.

The event of death in the family can be made known to the bees by jingling keys or beating on a small pan; otherwise another death will occur within a year.

When you move, take all your furniture, etc., at one time. It is bad luck to go back a second time; you will not stay long in your new home.

It is bad luck to postpone marriage.

It is bad luck to pass a sharp instrument to another person.

If you sweep someone's feet, he will run off.

If you step over a fishing pole, you will have bad luck.

You will never have good luck if you grow an ivy plant in your house.

If you are touched or hit with a broom, always spit on it or you will go to jail.

When passing a graveyard always cross your fingers; if you don't you will die.

If you cross a broom or stick, always step over it backward to prevent bad luck.

Don't let a black cat cross your trail going to the left. You will have bad luck. But if he goes to the right, you will have good luck.

If your right eye jumps, it is a sign of bad luck. If your left eye jumps, it is a sign of money.

If furniture falls off the load while you are moving, expect sickness or loss.

Don't sit on a trunk if you are going some place. You will be disappointed.

Never sleep with your shoes under the bed.

Never let a woman come to your house on Monday morning.

Never look at a cross-eyed person.

If you look at an undressed woman you will lose your money.

Never sweep dust out of your house after sundown because you are sweeping someone out of your family.

Never wash on New Year's Day, or someone in your family will die.

LOUISIANA

Rain

When the rain is coming the bullfrogs sing, or, as the Cajun says it: " 'La plie tombe' ouaouaron chante."

Three frosts will be followed by rain.

If you kill a cat or reptile, it will rain.

293

PART V. *Superstitions*

Death, Ill Health

If, when you are walking along the street or sitting quietly in the house, you hear a voice calling, don't answer, because that is a sign of death calling.

The transplanting of a weeping willow will bring about violent death.

If you plant a cedar tree, you will die when the shadow cast by the tree at high noon becomes large enough to cover your grave.

If you are hurt by falling out of a fig tree, you will never get well.

A death in a family is often preceded by a "little white dog" who suddenly appears in the house and then disappears. He will just "pass into the wall."—Mrs. HENRY PRUDHOMME, Natchitoches.

Kill de lizard on de grave, dey ain't no charm yo' life can save.

When "Chouette" (screech owl) or "Gimme Bird" sings around a house, it means there will be a death in the house.

A swallow in the bedroom is a sign of death.

A baby whose cradle is rocked while it is empty will die without fail.

To see a shooting star is usually said to indicate a death.

Weddings

Rain or tears at a wedding are bad luck.

Plants That Bring Bad Luck

It is bad luck to have Spanish daggers growing near the house.

Spanish moss brings bad luck.

Flowers out of season bring bad luck.

Don't let love apples grow in your yard; this brings bad luck.

Arbor vitae brings bad luck.

Night-blooming cereus brings bad luck.

Good-Luck Plants

Sweet basil planted on either side of the doorstep brings good luck.

A pepper bush in the yard brings good luck.

Cat

If you move a cat, put an ear of corn in the sack to break the spell.

If a cat follows you home, or if you befriend a cat, it is good luck.

Eat the heart of a black cat and no bullet or knife can harm you.

Hands on or above Head

Sleeping with arms over head, the sleeper is calling trouble. Resting the head on the hands, the Devil is hanging on your back.

Pigeons

Gathering about the house they bring good luck.

Popular Beliefs and Superstitions

Hunting

If the trail is straight, the animal will return over the same trail.

A hunter who eats the brains of the animal he kills will be able to out-think the next one he chases.

Animal Noises

If the dog howls with his nose to the ground, there will be a fire; with his head raised, there will be a death.

If the rooster crows at the back door, it means death; at the front door, visitors; if he comes to the step and crows three times, he is saying, "4-11-44," and if you like to play lottery, play this gig and win.

If the animals of woods, swamps, and barnyard are unusually vocal, it is a sign of rain.

Money Luck

When passing a lavender bush, known to the Negroes as the "money tree," pluck a sprig of leaves, count the leaves, and repeat the Commandment of the number counted. This brings luck. Nine leaves on a sprig brings money.

To cook Creole cabbage on New Year's Day is lucky. You will have green money the entire year.

Salt

"Don't loan no salt on Monday 'cause it will take all de seasonin' outen your home for a week."—ROXANNA MOORE

New Year Luck

Eat cowpeas and hog jowl on New Year's Day and you will have plenty to eat the rest of the year.

Lottery

If you play lottery in August, you will lose, because "It was on the 1st of August dat God put de Devil out of heaven, and dat's why we has a hell, an' since dat happen, de Devil crosses everything we does in August."

Sneezing

According to II Kings 4:35, when Elisha raised the child from the dead, the child sneezed seven times. "Ever since dat day, when anybody sneeze seven times, it is a sign a ha'nt is riz up f'om de dead."

Spitting

If you spit at someone, you will die like a dog.

Never spit in the fire. It will draw your lungs up.

A hungry person's saliva looks like cotton.

PART V. *Superstitions*

Whistling

Is always bad luck to a woman.

Singing

Is usually bad luck. Don't sing before breakfast, on Friday or Saturday till past noon, nor while eating, nor in bed, nor when going to bed. "You mustn't never sing befo' breakus'. In ol' times, my Pa said, 'Look at de pore mockin' bird, he so happy when he opens his eyes that he jes' lets out an sings—befo' night he's killed—and de slave, if he sang, he wuz whipped.' "

Sleeping

If a little baby cries and jumps in his sleep, an evil spirit is bothering him.

You should never sleep with the moon in your face. It will draw your mouth over and make it crooked.

Cutting Fingernails

Cutting a child's nails under a fig tree (or a rosebush) will make him a singer.

Old darkies do not cut their nails, for they say their strength is in them.

Hair

A red-headed Negro is a witch or wizard.

If birds weave some of your hair into their nests, you will go crazy.

A widely prevailing superstition among some groups in the Delta country concerns the curl and nail paring in a bottle. An enemy will try to secure one or the other, or both. These he will place in a bottle and hide it near the one he wishes to harm. Sickness immediately follows. One woman in the country makes her living by going to the homes of the sick to "discover the bottle," while another healer, when called in, places a bottle of charmed wine and a loaf of bread under the bed of the sick. This is supposed to neutralize the effects of the evil charm.

Sweeping

It is bad luck to sweep after sundown. Don't sweep under a sick bed or the patient will die. Don't sweep under a girl's feet or she will never marry. Don't sweep under a chair. Don't sweep when someone else is sweeping. A broom can be moved into a new house if the spell is removed from it by passing it through the window of the new house.

Ashes

Never take up ashes at night. Never spill any ashes. Never take up ashes until thirty days after the birth of a child, for if you do either mother or child will die. Don't take ashes out of the room of anyone ill.

Popular Beliefs and Superstitions

Mirrors

If you should break a mirror, you can wash away the seven years' bad luck by throwing the pieces in running water.

Creole mirror superstition: When three men look into a mirror at once the youngest is to die; but if three girls look into a mirror at once, the eldest will marry within the year.

Cover the mirrors in the room occupied by a corpse or the image of the dead will remain, and, if seen, will cause the death of the beholder. Others say that the part of the corpse reflected in the mirror is a part of the Devil's body.

Broom Superstitions from Isle Breville

A young couple must not bring an old broom with them into the new house unless it is thrown in, handle first.

An old couple moving into a new house must bring an old broom. If they don't, one of them will have bad luck.

August is a bad month in which to buy a broom, and housecleaning should never be done in August.

Days of the Week

It is good luck for a buzzard to light on your house on Monday.

If a red-headed woman comes to your house on Monday, there will be confusion all week.

Never let a woman come into your house on Monday or Friday until a man has first crossed the threshold.

If a person dies on Saturday, the Blessed Virgin will have that person out of purgatory by the following Saturday.

Cajun Beliefs concerning Children

Playing with keys makes children hard-headed. Looking into a mirror makes children's teething difficult.

Teeth

If a pig gets the baby tooth, a tusk will grow in the child's mouth; if a dog gets it, the child will have a fang.

If the child desists from placing the tongue in the place of the missing tooth, he will get a gold one.

Bread

If the loaf is upside down on the table, it means the Devil is around.

Fuel

Never use any kind of fruit or nut tree, or one struck by lightning, for if you do, your house will burn down before the year is out.

Clocks

It is bad luck to have two clocks going in the house at the same time.

Weather

A period of good weather is ahead in the summer time when the weather clears off warm, never when it clears off cool.

In the early spring if a bull bat swoops down and says "broke," it is a sign that winter is over.

A whirlwind is a sign of dry weather.

Heavy dew is a sign of fair weather.

A red sunset in autumn is a sign of cold weather.

When sounds like muffled footsteps are heard in a wood fire, there will be snow. As the Negroes say, "The fire is stomping snow."

Planting

Vegetable and melon seeds should be planted by a growing child, as they will grow as the child grows.

Always plant four seeds if you expect one to come up: One for the blackbird, one for the crow, one for the cutworm, and one for to grow.

Plant corn when the dogwood is in full bloom.

Some Negroes place rice on the graves to keep the dead from catching their hoes or spoiling their rice crop.

Sometimes rice husks are put in a fish trap and hung high so that the rice may be tall.

When shelling butterbeans (limas) for planting, throw the hulls in the road. If they are burned, your crop will be poor; if fed to the cows, the stock will eat your vines; if thrown in the trash, not only will your crop be poor, but your stock will not reproduce and your wife will not bear children.

Fruit Trees

Don't put your hand on a young tree that is bearing its first fruit or the fruit will always fall off.

If a tree bears wormy fruit, chop a piece from the trunk and tie a bottle of water somewhere around the tree. Next year you will have solid fruit.

To make a tree bear, bore a hole in the trunk and drop some Epsom salts in it. This purges the tree.

Seeds

Mix ashes with turnip or mustard seeds before you plant and they will "make" better.

Planting a grain of corn with seeds or cuttings will make them grow.

Plant beans in the scorpion or twin days (by the almanac) and they will bear well. Never plant vegetables on bloom days or you will have nothing but bloom.—BILL HARRIS, Spring Creek

Plant potatoes on dark nights.

Never plant peas until you hear the whippoorwill. His call is the signal that the season is at hand.

Plant English peas during the "Old Twelve Days"—the . . . six days before and after Christmas—and the peas will have a better flavor.

Never plant a crop while a woman near-by is holding a flower in her hand.

Cajuns say that sweet potatoes should always be planted when the moon is full because if planted when the moon is in any other shape the potatoes will be like the moon.

Plant pepper when you are mad, or let a red-headed person plant it.

Never plant okra while standing. Always stoop and the plant will bear while still low.

Plowing

If you plow on Good Friday, lightning will strike your field and the ground will bleed.

Eggs and Chickens

To protect one's chickens from predatory hawks, keep a horseshoe in the fireplace and it will cause the hawk's claws to become so soft that they will be unable to do any damage.

To keep eggs from spoiling, place nails in the form of a cross in the nest. When it thunders the eggs won't spoil.

If you wish to have more pullets from a hatching of eggs, place the eggs into the nest with your left hand. Using your right will increase the number of roosters.

Chickens which are set to hatch in May will be crippled or crazy.

Fencing

Fence in the dark of the moon if you do not want your fence to settle.

Building

Never start building a house on Friday. If this is done inadvertently, build a piece of green bough into the peak of the house to avert the bad luck. Best days for shingling are from the thirteenth to the twenty-second of the month. Best days for painting are the sixth, seventh, eighth, sixteenth, and seventeenth.

Cattle

Brand and castrate on the decrease of the moon; slaughter on the increase.

If you stir milk with a fork, the cow will have sore tits; if it is stirred with a knife, the flow will be cut down.

Killing a "toad-frog" will make your cows dry up.

PART V. *Superstitions*

More Weather Signs

Three frosts or three fogs on successive nights bring rain.

There is always a storm after the death of an old woman.

There is a frog whose call is like a mallard duck. To hear his cry at night foretells a high river.

"If the oak is out before the ash, it will be a summer of wet and splash. If the ash is out before the oak, it will be a summer of fire and smoke."

Fishing

A silver hook used to be used during full moon, as it was thought that the fishes' mouths were then too tender to bite on any other kind.

Best time to start going fishing is when the dogwood blooms.

Eat onions before you go fishing and you will have good luck.

Fish bite well when the country road is full of fiddlers.

When there is little bait, the fish bite.

If you are having no luck, put a bit of asafoetida on the bait and the fish will come.

If there is no bait, beat the ground with a switch, and the worms will think it is raining and come up.

Hunting

When a northwester blows it brings in high tide. This is the time of good hunting.

Don't go hunting on Friday night. It is bad luck. The dogs will bark as if they had treed something, but "dey won't be nothin' there."

A trapper must never take a broom or a cat with him when he breaks camp.

If a stick breaks when you are passing through the woods, there are two ghosts arguing over you, saying they know you.

If you hunt on Friday, you will see no jaybirds, for on that day every jay carries a grain of sand to hell where it will be heated to make things hot for you when you get there.

If you get lost in the swamp, you can find north and south by feeling the bark of the trees. Smooth bark is on the south side, rough on the north. —JACK PENTON AND FAMILY.

Don't hunt on Sunday.

Thunder

Some say that when it thunders, Le Bon Dieu is rolling his stones. Others, that the Devil is driving his two black horses and chariot across the sky.

300

Don'ts

Prayers

Every year on Palm Sunday have magnolia leaves blessed and place them in your house to calm storms. During a storm hold a leaf in your hand to shift the wind.

If you are drowning and accidentally cross your hands, you will come to the surface and float. You are saved by the sign of the cross.

Make the sign of the cross over your bread so that you will always have some; over your fire so it will burn, etc.

Stabbing

Blood spilled will kill the grass, and every time it rains the blood of the slain will appear fresher.

Banana

Cutting a banana is the same as cutting the cross of Christ.

Sex Change

If a girl kisses her toe, she will become a boy.
Kiss your elbow and you will change your sex.

Curing

One who has never seen his mother will be able to cure.

([Don'ts

The following superstitions were found current in Tidewater, Virginia:

Don't leave the griddle on the fire after the bread is done; it will make bread scarce.

Don't wash the inside of a baby's hand; you will wash his luck away.

Don't sweep dirt out of the door after night; you will sweep yourself out of a home.

Don't step over anybody's leg; it will turn to a stick of wood.

Don't comb your hair at night; it will make you forgetful.

Don't be the first to drive a hearse, or you will be the next to die.

Don't make any new garment for the sick; it will make them die.

Don't shake the tablecloth out of doors after sunset, or you will never marry.

Don't sweep a person's feet; it will make him lazy. So will hitting them with a straw.

Don't whip the child who burns another. If you do, the burnt child will die.

Don't measure yourself; it will make you die.

Don't lend or borrow salt or pepper; it will break friendship. If you must borrow it, don't pay it back.

Don't kill a wren; it will cause your limbs to get broken.

Don't pass anything over a person's back; it will give him pains.

Don't pour out tea before putting sugar in the cup, or someone will be drowned. Some say it will drown the miller.

Don't kill cats, dogs, or frogs, or you will die in rags.

Don't move cats; if you do, you will die a beggar.

Don't meet a corpse, or you will get very sick before the year is out.

Don't point at or speak of a shooting star.

Don't count the teeth of a comb; they will all break out.

Don't lock your hands over your head.

(Signs

Blue jays aren't fit to eat. They go to torment nine times on Friday to carry sand.

The owl is old-time folks. You mustn't hurt him.

Hear an owl holler in the day, sign of death.

Turn your pockets wrong side out or put a horseshoe in the fire, and the death owl will go away.

Mustn't let a toad in the house; sure sign of death.

When bats come in the house, you are going to move out.

To mock a whippoorwill is a sure sign of a whipping.

The first dove you hear holler, whichever way he hollers that is the way you are going to get rain that year.

When the hog carries a branch in his mouth, it is a sure sign of rain.

On the tenth of May if you hear the flying horse in the air it means good crops.

Take the eggshells that the chickens have hatched out of, put them in a tin bucket, put the cover on, and hang it in the chimney to keep the hawks away. Or put a stone on the hearth.

If the moon is on its point it will rain a good deal, and if it is on its back it will rain very little.

Always shell your seed corn in the field if you would have a good crop. And whatever you do, don't burn the cobs—your crop will burn up.

The first time you see the new moon, show it something and the thing will be yours before another new moon comes.

If you tear a dress the first time you wear it, someone will tell a story on you before night.

If you kiss a boy before you marry you'll never care very much for him.

If you cross the road where a snake crossed it, unless you go backward you'll have a backache.

You mustn't step in anybody else's track. It will give you the backache.

If you have the backache, find a creeping child whose father is dead. Let the child walk on your back and it will not ache any more.

When you hear the first dove moan, get down and wallow and you won't have the backache that year.

You mustn't walk backward. It is cursing your father and mother.

Dreaming about dollars is a sure sign of a whipping.

When mice cut your clothes it is a sure sign you are going to move or die.

To patch the clothes yourself that the mice have torn is bad luck. You must get someone outside the family to do it.

Mustn't let a cow low in the night, or some bad luck will happen to the family.

Don't skip a row in planting, or a member of your family will die.

It brings bad luck to mark any part of a building.

If a rabbit crosses your path on the right side, if you put your hat on the left side of your head it will keep you from having bad luck. Or if he crosses your path and you make a cross in the dirt with your foot, it will keep you from having bad luck.

Bad luck to go into the house with anything on your head.

Put graveyard dirt in your shoes and the dogs can't track you (a slavery time superstition).

(Weather Lore

COLD WEATHER SIGNS

After the change of the moon, if it lies to the north it is a sign of cold weather.

If the pointer of the star points to the north, it indicates cold weather.

If the large end of the Milky Way tends northward—cold weather.

A circle around the moon containing more than five stars—cold weather sure to come.

If a red streak extends across the sky from east to west overhead at sunset it indicates cold, windy weather.

To hear a killdee crying in the morning or evening—cold weather.

If turkeys roost high in a tree, it's a sign of cold weather. You will hear the old folks say, "Look out, children. Hawkins is coming."

To see a hog running around with a straw in his mouth—cold weather.

To see cows playing—cold weather is sure to follow.

To hear fire popping slowly and continuously ("treading snow" as it is called) indicates cold weather.

To hear a small owl hooting is a sign of cold weather.

WARM WEATHER SIGNS

When the moon changes and it seems to lie in the south, it is a sign of warm weather.

If the pointer of the seven stars points to the south—warm weather.

If the large end of the Milky Way points to the south—warm weather.

A circle around the moon containing less than five stars—warm weather.

FAIR WEATHER SIGNS

If the sky is gray in the east, it is a sign of fair weather.

Red sky at sunset indicates fair weather.

Heavy dew in the morning, fair weather.

On a foggy morning, if fog comes down—fair weather.

To find a spider's web spread on the ground—fair weather.

When sea birds are seen flying early toward the sea, moderate winds and fair weather may be expected.

Rainbow in the evening indicates fair weather next day.

STORMY WEATHER SIGNS

A circle around the moon with three stars enclosed indicates rain in less than three days.

Red sky in the east at sunrise—stormy weather.

Sun dog in the sky foretells rain the next day.

Rainbow in the morning, storm is on its way.

If any iron vessel containing water has drops of water on the outside, it foretells rain.

Turkeys going to roost with their heads all turned in the same direction —stormy weather.

Buzzards soaring high—rain.

The moon hanging on the point is called a wet moon—rain.

(Superstitions About Animals

Children sing, when they find a snail in his shell,

> "Snail, snail, poke out your horn,
> Give you peck o'corn."

or

> "Snail, snail, poke out your horn,
> Ding a ding a darden dead and gone."

To the periwinkle, or sea snail, they sing,

> "Penny winkle, penny winkle, poke out your horn,
> Give you chew tobacco an' a barrelful of corn."

The doodlebug makes a cup-shaped hole near the chimney or under the house. When children wish to make him come out they scratch on the ground and call out,

> "Doodlebug, doodlebug, come out your hole,
> Your house is afire."

This call repeated two or three times will bring the bug out.

If you catch a grandfather-long-legs and hold him by one leg and say, "Granddaddy, granddaddy, where are the cows?" he will point in the direction in which the cows are to be found.

If you drink out of a spring at night, there is danger that you may drink the "spring-keeper," in which case the spring will dry up. The "spring-keeper" is described as very much like a crawfish or a water lizard.

Snakes form, among the colored people of the South as among all people everywhere, a most interesting and fertile source of folklore. How much of this is true and how much the product of imagination we leave to those better versed in natural history than ourselves to decide.

305

All snakes except black snakes can whistle; moccasins can blow. Cornfield adders can puff up and flatten out. In a fight a black snake can whip a moccasin.

Snake poison is credited with strange results. One story is told of a dog bitten by a snake. He recovered apparently from the bite, but after a while began to have fits and at last died. A post mortem examination revealed a number of snakes inside him.

For snake bite, if possible catch the snake that bit, split it open, and tie it on the wound.

One story was told of a woman who had a snake inside her. It used to put its head out of her mouth to drink milk. It was thought that the woman must have swallowed the snake when it was small, in drinking water.

A man found a nest of eggs which he ate. They turned out to be snake eggs. After awhile he became ill with a tumor. The doctors opened it and found it contained two snakes.

It is said that a turtle contains all sorts of meats, beef, chicken, and pork.

You may fry an eel thoroughly, but if you allow the meat to get cold, it will become raw again. If cooked at night and left until morning, the blood will come back again.

If a fisherman has fished all day he ought not to eat any fish; they will make him sick.

In slavery times, when people held a meeting, if they heard a kildee holler they knew the "patteroller" was near.

The snake doctor, or mosquito hawk, is thought to be able to bring a dead snake to life again. In some places the presence of a snake doctor shows that there is a snake near by.

⦅ Folk Beliefs from Florida

Negroes, like all other ethnic groups, have their mythological cities and places. Those mentioned here are well known in Florida as well as other states where the folk Negro lives.

Diddy-Wah-Diddy is the largest and best known of the Negro mythological places. Geographically it is "way off somewhere." It is reached by a road that curves so much that a mule pulling a wagon-load of fodder can eat off the back of the wagon as he goes. It is a place of no work and no worry for man and beast—a very restful place where even the curbstones are good "setting chairs." The food is even already cooked. If a traveler gets hungry, all he needs to do is to sit down on the curbstone and wait and soon he will hear something hollering, "Eat me! Eat me!" and a big baked chicken will come along with a knife and fork stuck in its sides. He can eat all he wants and let the chicken go, and it will go on to the next one who needs something to eat. By that time a big, deep sweet potato pie is pushing and shoving to get in front of the traveler, with a knife all stuck up in the middle of it, so he just cuts a piece off of that and so on until he finishes his snack. Nobody can ever eat it all up. No matter how much you eat it gets just that much bigger. It is said that "everybody would live in Diddy-Wah-Diddy if it wasn't so hard to find and so hard to get to, after you even know the way."

Everything is on a large scale there. Even the dogs can stand flat-footed and lick crumbs off heaven's table. The biggest man there is known as "Moon Regulator" because he reaches up and stops the moon at his convenience. That is why there are some dark nights when the moon does not shine at all. Those nights he did not feel like putting it on.

Another place is Zar, which is way on the other side of Far. This is the farthest point of the imagination. Little is known about Zar because only one or two people have ever found their way back from there.

West Hell is some miles west of regular hell, in the hottest and the toughest part of that warm territory. The most desperate malefactors are the only ones condemned to West Hell. Their souls are changed to rubber coffins so that they go bouncing through regular hell and on to their destination without having to be carried by attendants, as the devil does not like to send his imps into West Hell oftener than is absolutely necessary.

⟨ Beliefs from Georgia

In death . . . a rigid observance of customs was prevalent. For example, one Negro's body had been shipped back from New York City, in order that it might be buried in Sandfly. Otherwise . . . the spirit of the deceased would have found no rest, but instead would have roamed the countryside. Here, too, was observed the practice of placing on the grave broken bits of pottery and possessions last used by the dead person, for the purpose of supplying the needs of the spirit.

"The spirit don't stay in the grave. When the funeral procession starts tuh leave, the spirit leaves the body an' follows the people frum the grave- yard. It nevuh stays with the body. . . . Fuh the spirit tuh rest in the grave, folks have to be buried frum home. They nevuh feel right ef they buried away frum home. The spirit just wanduh aroun'.

"Theah ain't supposed tuh be no sech thing as nachul death heah in Sandfly. Wen a pusson die someone have fix him sho'."

THE LADY IN BLACK

We questioned Collier again about his personal experiences with super- natural beings, and he related the following story: "Wen I wuz jist a young boy muh family use tuh live in Currytown. Me an' muh brothuh use tuh go an' see muh aunt, who lived in Yamacraw. Tuh git from our house tuh wheah she lived we had tuh go past a cemetery which wuz in back of the Union Station.

"One time we had ben tuh see muh aunt an' it got tuh be late. We stahted fuh home. It wuz beginnin' of night. Muh brothuh he had rheumatism an' he wuz hobblin' along on a stick. We stahted along by a fence tuh git tuh West Broad Street an', wen we had gone about a hundred yards we saw a lady comin' towards us. She was very feah, very feah, an' she wuz all dressed in black an' had on a long black veil. Her dress wuz black silk an' rustled as she walked.

"Muh brothuh an' I, we were suhprised tuh see the lady all of a sudden, fuh we hadn't noticed her befo'. She come up to us an' she say, 'Are yuh goin' round the fence?' We tell her we wuz an' she say, 'Yuh not afraid?' an' we say, 'No, we not afraid.'

"The lady wanted tuh walk with us an' we all staht walkin' along. We had gone a short ways wen all of a sudden we look in the cemetery an' we see a little white thing risin' up out of the groun'. It wuz kinda hazy an' shadowy an' it spring up from the groun' an' strak out tuh meet us on the path ahead. It looked like a li'l' animal.

"The lady, wen she see the li'l' white sumpin' a-comin', she daht out like lightnin' an' she go right tuh meet it. W'en she git tuh it she disappeah right intuh de eah, disappeah right befo' our eyes. Muh brothuh forget he was crippled; he drop his stick an' staht runnin', an' I run too. An' we nevuh stop runnin'. Kept right on goin' till we got home tuh Curry- town." . . .

A WITCH STORY

"Deah was a ole woman in Savannah dat dey say wuz a witch. One night a ole man wake up an' foun' dis witch ridin' 'im. He say it look lak a bug. He ketch it an' break off duh leg at de joint. Duh nex mawnin' he go an' see duh ole woman, an' sho nuff she have 'er han' all tie up wid a bandage.

Dey tell me 'bout uh, an' I go see uh. Uh finger wuz right off at de joint." . . .

FLYING PEOPLE

"Ain' yuh hea'd 'bout um? Well, at dat time Mr. Blue he wau duh obuh-seeuh an' Mr. Blue put um in duh fiel', but he couldn' do nuthin' wid um. Dey gabble, gabble, gabble, an' nobody couldn't unduhstan' um an' dey didn' know how tuh wuk right. Mr. Blue he go down one mawnin' wid a long whip fuh tuh whip um good."

"Mr. Blue was a hard overseer?"

"No, ma'am, he ain' hahd, he jis caahn' make um unduhstan'. Dey's foolish actin'. He got tuh whip um, Mr. Blue; he ain' hab no choice. Any-ways, he whip um good an' dey gits tuhgedder an' stick duh hoe in duh fiel' an' den say 'Quack, quack, quack,' an' dey riz in duh sky an' tun desef intuh buzzards an' fly right back tuh Africa. . . .

"No, ma'am, I ain' seen um, . . . but I know'd plenty wut did see um, planty wut was right deah in duh fiel' wid um an see de hoe wut dey lef' stickin' up attuh dey done fly away."

PART VI

❧

Proverbs

The most comprehensive group of proverbs to be published to date made up one section of a folklore volume written by J. A. Macon back in 1883, titled Uncle Gabe Tucker; or Reflections, Song, and Sentiment in the Quarters. *Joel Chandler Harris included a few "Plantation Proverbs" in his first and most famous book,* Uncle Remus: His Songs and His Sayings. *Almost half a century later a limited number of slave proverbs that I had collected appeared in the 1933 yearbook of the Texas Folklore Society. Other proverbs, occasionally as few as five, have been printed in various and sundry books of folklore.*

The scarcity of the proverb in the oral tradition of the Negro in the United States is due to the fact that the African slaves who were brought to this area of the New World had few if any proverbs in their culture. This is in direct contrast to those slaves who were brought from Africa to Jamaica with a cultural background that included thousands of proverbs.

(Plantation Proverbs

Big 'possum clime little tree.

Dem w'at eats kin say grace.

Ole man Know-All died las' year.

Better de gravy dan no grease 'tall.

Lazy fokes' stummucks don't git tired.

Rheumatiz don't he'p at de log-rollin'.

Mole don't see w'at his naber doin'.

Save de pacin' mar' fer Sunday.

Don't rain eve'y time de pig squeal.

Crow en corn can't grow in de same fiel'.

Tattlin' 'oman can't make de bread rise.

Rails split 'fo' bre'kfus' 'll season de dinner.

Dem w'at knows too much sleeps under de hopper.

Pigs dunno w'at a pen's fer.

Possum's tail good as a paw.

Dogs don't bite at de front gate.
Colt in de barley-patch kick high.
Jay-bird don't rob his own nes'.
Pullet can't roost too high for de owl.
Meat fried 'fo' day won't las' twel night.
Stump water won't kyo de gripes.
De howlin' dog know w'at he sees.
Bline hoss don't fall w'en he follers de bit.
Hongry nigger won't w'ar his maul out.
Don't fling away de empty wallet.
Black-snake know de way ter de hen nes'.
Looks won't do ter split rails wid.
Settin' hens don't hanker arter fresh aigs.
Tater-vine growin' w'ile you sleep.
Hit take two birds fer to make a nes'.
Ef you bleedzd ter eat dirt, eat clean dirt.
Tarrypin walk fast 'nuff fer to go visitin'.
Empty smoke-house makes de pullet holler.
W'en coon take water he fixin' fer ter fight.
Corn makes mo' at de mill dan it does in de crib.
Good luck say: "Op'n yo' mouf en shet yo' eyes."
Nigger dat gets hurt wukkin' oughter show de skyars.
Fiddlin' nigger say hit's long ways ter de dance.
Rooster makes mo' racket dan de hen w'at lay de aig.
Meller mush-million hollers at you fum over de fence.
Nigger wid a pocket-han'kcher better be looked atter.
Rain-crow don't sing no chune, but youk'n 'pen' on 'im.
One-eyed mule can't be handled on de bline side.
Moon may shine, but a lightered knot's mighty handy.
Licker talks mighty loud w'en it git loose fum de jug.
De proudness un a man don't count w'en his head's cold.
Hongry rooster don't cackle w'en he fine a wum.
Some niggers mighty smart, but dey can't drive de pidgins ter roos'.
All de buzzards in de settlement 'll come to de gray mule's funer'l.
Youk'n hide de fier, but w'at you gwine do wid de smoke?
Termorrow may be de carridge-driver's day for ploughin'.
Hit's a mighty deaf nigger dat don't year de dinner-ho'n.

314

Aphorisms from the Quarters

Hit takes a bee fer ter git de sweetness out'n de hoar-houn' blossom.
De pig dat runs off wid de year er corn gits little mo' dan de cob.
Sleepin' in de fence-cornder don't fetch Chrismus in de kitchen.
De spring-house may freeze, but de niggers 'll keep de shuck-pen warm.
'Twix' de bug en de bee-martin 'tain't hard ter tell w'ich gwineter git kotch.
Don't 'sput wid de squinch-owl. Jam de shovel in de fier.
You'd see mo' er de mink ef he know'd whar de yard dog sleeps.
Troubles is seasonin'. 'Simmons ain't good twel dey 'er fros'-bit.
Watch out w'en you'er gittin' all you want. Fattenin' hogs ain't in luck.

Aphorisms from the Quarters

De bes' sort o' pigs was born 'ear befo' las'.
A smart redbird don't have much to say.
Yistiddy kin take keer ob itse'f.
De dry-lan' tar'p'n kin make de trip ef you gib him little time.
Some folks must 'a' been born on de wrong quarter ob de moon.
Diggin' taters is gen'ully de bes' put-up job on de plantation.
De neighborhood oughtn't to brag on de physic trade.
Rats don't lub to 'sociate wid po' farmers.
A gra'-vine makes de bes' collar for some dogs.
Guardin' a watermilion-patch is a mighty sof' job.
Some folks' 'ligion nebber got a good stan' at fus'.
A nes' o' yaller-jackets kin crowd de roomatiz right sharp.
Fo'th o' July mus' 'a' been started by de blackberries gettin' ripe.
When de fros' sen' you wud by de norf wind, you better git in de punkins.
De new-groun's is de bes' yardstick to medjer a strange nigger by.
You can't tell much 'bout a chicken-pie tell you git froo de crus'.
Old Satun's watch is 'mos' always too slow.
It takes a soon nigger to argerfy wid a bran new mule.

You better not shake hands wid a crawfish.

Sharp ax better'n big muscle.

Old rabbit walks in de paf when de snow done fell.

De morkin'-bird nebber gits out o' chune.

Fiel'-mouse lay still when de sparrer-hawk sail.

De sun trabbles slow 'cross de new-groun's.

De mousetrap don't go to sleep.

De peach trees dat go to dressin' up too 'arly in de spring won't be pestered wid much cump'ny in de summer.

De ash-cake is close kin to de low-groun's.

De groun'-wums ain't anxious for de fish to bite.

De muskeeter says grace too loud for his own good while he gittin' ready to eat.

Dar mus' be sumfin' scan'alous 'bout chills; you ain't gwine to find no neighborhood dat 'ill own up to habin' 'em.

When a nigger git too sick to guard de watermilion-patch, you better sen' for de doctor.

Old Satun lubs a big crowd.

De sof' groun' tells heap o' tales.

Dark clouds ain't a sho' sign o' trade.

A mule kin be tame at one en' an' wild at t'udder.

Don't lay it on de cow when de milk gits sour.

De honeybees think sumfin's de matter wid de law books.

De old steer gits s'picious when dey feed him too high.

'Tis dangersome to let some folks fool wid a gun—ef de gun's any 'count.

Folks ain't ap' to fall out wid de morkin'-bird jes' 'cause he steals his songs.

Loadin' a waggin wid hay ain't de quickes' way for seekin' 'ligion.

Don't trade orf a coon-skin 'fo' you ketch de coon.

De paf to de tunnup-patch don't need no signboa'd.

Roomatiz an' happiness bofe grow bigger ef you keep tellin' folks 'bout 'em.

De pig's got 'nough 'rifmetic to take de shortes' cut froo de thicket.

'Tain't no use o' sp'ilin' de Sat'day night by countin' de time to Monday mornin'.

Some smart young folks need toppin' 'bout much as de 'backer-plants.

De old rabbit thinks 'speriunce cost too much when you git it fum a mash-trap.

Aphorisms from the Quarters

A 'possum-dog don't lose nuffin' by takin' de backtrack ob a polecat.

When de trees start to bud you kin tell de dead limbs mighty quick.

A cornstalk dat's dressed up in mornin'-glories ain't got much to brag on.

Heap o' strange cattle at de salt lick.

Old Satun lubs to dodge 'roun' 'mongst de crowd at de night meetin'.

Nebber take too big a chip on a saplin'.

De mornin'-glories wa'n't made for lazy folks.

A mule kin stan' curryin' wid a corncob ef you let him manerfacter de currycomb.

Old Satun mus' be a silent pardner in de ownership o' some folks.

De good farmer keeps 'quainted wid de daybreak.

A crooked cornstalk kin hab a straight ear.

Chickens kin hold on bes' to a good high roos'.

Ef you nebber got your clo'es wet in de jew, don't brag on it.

Nebber trus' a man too fur dat stays mad froo de Chris'mus week.

Don't take too big a start to jump a ditch.

Don't fling all your power onto a small job.

What you kin l'arn by boxin' wid a lef'-handed nigger cos' mo' 'an it come to.

De wheat-crap can't fool you when it comes to de th'ashin'.

Blood biles would fit better on somebody else.

De wus' road to de cote-'ouse runs froo de horgpen.

You'll loss your grip ef you stop too much to spit on your hands.

It takes a liar to git drunk on 'simmon beer.

'Possum graby keeps de skillet clean.

Mule don't pull so well wid a morgidge on his back.

Crab-grass line de paf to de po'-house.

Norf wind know all de cracks in de house.

Sick dorg 'mos' gone when de fleas leabe him.

Old otter would hab' mo' peace ef his clo'es wa'n't so fine.

Whipperwill singin' at de sun-down is 'mos' sweet as de morkin'-bird singin' at de sun-up.

Blind pig know de way home.

Rank wheat pesters de harves' song.

Convertin' some sinners is sort o' like beltin' a black-gum.

Pot bile ober when de squinch-owl holler.

317

Ef torment was a big icehouse, heap o' bad niggers would jine de chu'ch.

Groun' sparrers see de snowstorm 'way orf yander.

Books don't tell who tied de hag-knot in de horse mane.

Hole in your breeches lets in heap o' oneasiness.

Peelin' yams make a nigger smile all ober.

Nigger kiver up his head ef his toes freeze orf.

Hornit nes' in de chinkypen thicket is mighty ap' to raise a row.

Grubbin' roots softens de straw bed.

It don't he'p to rake up de fam'ly secrets ob eb'ry sassage you eat.

Distance to de nex' mile-pos' 'pen's on de mud in de road.

Sick nigger gĭt better when de sukkus come 'roun'.

Mule dat chaw up his own collar is fixin' for a so' shoulder.

Oberseer use to reggerlate de daybreak.

New mule some kin to de black-gum tree.

Partridge dat make nes' in de wheat-fiel' ain't ap' to be pestered wid her chillun.

Rabbit know a fox track same as a houn'.

Old Satun ain't so skeered o' long sermons.

Mule don't brag on de new plow-p'int.

Mole ain't 'fraid o' de moonshine.

De 'tater-patch don't go on looks.

Blackberry ain't gwine to tas'e good jes' 'cause it shine bright.

Cotton-wum spiles de Chris'mus.

'Possum-dorg jes' wuk for his boa'd an' furnish his own fleas.

Cotton-patch sorry when de fish start to bite.

Folks on de rich bottoms stop braggin' when de ribber rise.

Mushmilion vine ain't 'shame' to grow 'longside o' de mornin'-glory.

Little 'possum wonder how de old dorg kin see tracks in de dark.

Smart shotes do deir night rootin' by de full moon.

Hungry nigger ain't 'fraid o' de 'tater-peelin's.

When it take half a hoecake to ketch a catfish, you better let him 'lone.

No use o' signboa'd to tell de way to de watermilion-patch.

Tunnup-tops don't tell you de size o' de tunnups.

Spring-branch good 'nŏugh gourd for thirsty nigger.

Old Satun 'spec' to moobe out de neighborhood jes' soon as de bee-martin an' de chicken-hawk make frien's.

Aphorisms from the Quarters

Old sow know 'nough 'bout figgers to count her pigs.

A man dat 'ill steal a goat mus' be a rogue jes' for de fun o' de thing.

Nigger don't sing much plowin' de hillside.

Tin plate don't mind drappin' on de flo'.

Deep snow tell heap o' tales on de rabbit.

Pine tree laugh at de fros'.

Old ram keep quiet arter sheep-shearin' time.

Stan'in'-collar prize nigger's head up too high.

Fillin' de icehouse don't suit black folks' nater.

Old goose sort o' s'picious 'bout de feather-bed.

Roomatiz better cl'ar de track when de fiddler gits a drink.

Sleepy fisherman totes a light load home.

Turkey buzzard tends to his bizniss same as de morkin'-bird.

You can't tell what a nigger got in him by thumpin' him.

Better keep de rockin'-cheer in de cabin-lof' tell Sunday.

Ugly nigger don't fool wid de lookin'-glass.

De full moon tells heap o' secrets.

Old breeches lubs a long coattail.

A crow is a fus'-rate hand to thin corn.

A sunflower ain't so mighty putty in de dark.

Nebber clam a oak tree arter chinkypens.

Perliteness floats 'round loose on 'lection day.

Ripe mushmilions trabble mos'ly by night.

A pig kin beat de old sow gittin' froo a crack.

Don't holler 'fo' you strike de rank wheat.

De stars is jes' as bright as dey was 'fo' de war.

Blackbirds lub to help at de corn-plantin'.

Dar's some things dat will do to swop orf in de dark.

You can't pick your fish 'fo' you ketch 'em.

A dorg wid a block on don't brag on his sitivation.

Old Satun loads his cannons wid big watermilions.

De debbul ain't got no partick'ler objection to Chris'mus.

De punkin-vine ain't gwine to ax your 'vice 'bout what road to trabble.

De bullfrog nebber makes a mis-lick when he starts out singin'.

A nigger dat laughs at his own biles wa'n't made for dis wul'.

De feller dat sw'ars orf tell Chris'mus is jes' nussin' hisse'f for a big drunk.

319

De fat'nin' horgs ain't got no big 'vantage ober de lean shotes in de woods.

De rabbit dat sleeps in de groun'hog's hole needn't 'spec' to hab nice dreams.

Some sto'keepers is mighty ap' to find deir sins medjered wid deir own yardsticks.

Don't 'sociate too much wid de midnight ef you want to keep up a good repertation.

Gittin' de frien'ship o' some folks is sort o' like buyin' a rainbow an' payin' de cash for it.

Nebber trus' a man dat kin eat green 'simmons an' look happy while he's chawin' 'em.

Tryin' to unnerstan' some folks is mighty like guessin' at de 'rection ob a rat-hole in de groun'.

De smoke-'ouse is safes' in de blackberry season.

One good turn deserbs anudder; ef a man len' you trace-chain, go an' borrer his single-tree.

Some niggers' honesty is reggerlated mos'ly by de spunk ob de yard-dorg.

Grubbin' a stump is a good way to whet up your 'ligion.

Heap o' people rickerlec' favors by markin' 'em down in de snow.

Always drink pure water: many a man gits drunk fum breakin' dis rule.

A smart man ain't gwine to buck 'gin a mud-hole; he walks 'roun' it eb'ry time.

De sparrer-hawk would like to git a persition to 'tend to de chicken-yard an' keep orf de minks.

Rain-drops can't tell broadcloth fum jeans.

De black gum laughs at de red oak when de woodcutter comes 'roun'.

Waitin' on de table is a pow'ful way to git up a appetite.

De hen dat hatches out ducks is gwine to lose her chillun mighty quick.

Dar's nuffin' 'bout thinnin' corn in de spellin'-book.

De black snake keeps up wid de fam'ly secrets ob de settin' hens.

Smart folks don't feel de teef ob a live squ'el.

De fox wants to know how de rabbit's gittin' on.

'Tain't much diffunce 'twist a hornit an' a yaller-jacket when dey bofe git under your clo'es.

Some niggers got so much 'ligion dey want to hab Sunday eb'ry day.

It don't make much diffunce 'bout what sort o' plow you use, ef you jes' hab de right sort o' mule in front an' de right sort o' nigger behin'.

320

Aphorisms from the Quarters

It puts you in a good humor to git hold ob a fat pig—'specially right arter it's been bobbykewed.

De cotton-patch don't keer which way you vote.

You can't hurry up good times by waitin' for 'em.

It don't take no prophet to rickerlec' bad luck.

Dey don't hab no loafers in de martin-box.

De wire-grass lubs a lazy nigger.

Dar's right smart 'ligion in a plow-handle.

Twelve erclock nebber is in a hurry.

Nebber 'pend too much on de blackberry blossoms.

Don't bet on a 'tater-hill befo' de grubbn' time.

Heap o' good cotton-stalks gits chopped up fum 'sociatin' wid de weeds.

Many a nice corn-silk winds up wid a nubbin' in de fall.

A chicken-roos' is de debbul's steel-trap, an' a grassy corn-row is his flower-garden.

De mornin'-glories ain't pertickler lubly to a man wid de backache.

A sore-back mule is a poor hand to guess de weight ob a bag o' meal.

To-morrer's ash-cake is better'n las' Sunday's puddin'.

'Tain't easy to find a man dat kin git mo' 'tention arter he's dead dan de Chris-mus 'possum.

Countin' de stars don't he'p de meal-box.

De man dat always takes de shortes' road to a dollar, gen'ully takes de longes' road fum it.

All de jestice in de wul' ain't fastened up in de cote-'ouse.

A blind mule ain't 'fraid o' darkness.

De dinner-bell's always in chune.

De wood-pile don't grow much on frosty nights.

A man dat pets a libe catfish ain't crowded wid brains.

De pen'tench'ry's got some folks dat knowed how to call horgs too well.

You can't spile a ripe punkin by 'busin' it.

De bullfrog knows mo' 'bout de rain dan de olmanick.

De little backer-wum is de bes' fixed for hidin'.

De cheapes' way to he'p a man 'long in de wul' is to pile up flowers on his tombstone.

Heap o' folks is like crawfishes; dey lub to back water, but dey won't stan' no crowdin' for all dat.

Dar's right sharp good schoolin' in de tail ob a 'possum: nebber let go a thing long as dar's a chance lef'.

'Simmons gwine to take deir own time 'bout gettin' ripe.

Some corn-stalks is like lots o' folks—dey fling all deir power into de blades an' tassels.

You can't medjer a nigger's wuk by de 'mount o' singin' he does at de shuckin'.

A good 'possum-dorg may tell a lie by accident, but you can't proobe it on him ef de tree's holler.

De farmer dat nebber smells de daybreak kin git 'long wid a mighty little gin-'ouse.

A fat mule an' a straight furrer.

De coon puts up de bes' fight; but de 'possum is heap de smartes' an' is got de bes' edication.

De waggin'-wheels ain't 'fraid to tell you whar dey been.

De squ'el kin beat de rabbit clammin' a tree; but den, de squ'el makes de bes' stew, an dat sort o' ekalizes de thing.

Don't was'e no time coaxin' a sick 'tater-slip; stick a fresh one in de hill.

'Tain't no countin' on de notions ob a gra'-vine nor de chune ob a morkin'-bird.

It don't make much diffunce whar de rain comes fum, jes' so it hits de groun' in de right place.

De crab-grass b'lebes in polertics.

A short crap an' a long face.

De old sheeps wonder whar de yarn socks come fum.

A feather-bed ain't much service to de young corn.

Palin's wa'n't fixed for clammin' ober.

Some smart folks can't tell a rotten rail widout sittin' on it.

De people dat stirs up de mos' rackit in de meetin'-house ain't always de bes' Kwis'chuns.

'Arly peach-blossoms got to run de risk o' de fros'.

De fat beef ain't got much conferdince in de butcher.

Sometimes de runt pig beats de whole litter growin'.

Ef you ain't got nuffin' smaller'n a dime when de hat comes 'round in chu'ch, drap it in; you'll git de change some o' dese days.

Don't trus' a mad bull jes' 'cause he ain't got no horns; he kin do some right sharp pushin' anyhow.

You better not fool wid a watermilion dat puts orf gittin' ripe till horg-killin' time.

A meller apple dat drops on de groun' widout any shakin' is mos' too willin'.

Creole Proverbs

Folks dat go to sleep in de meetin'-house do heap o' late settin' up at home.

Muskeeters don't suit long pra'rs.

De people dat do de bigges' talkin' at home is ap' to do de mos' whettin' in de harves' fiel'.

Don't trus' a man dat nebber got tired in his life.

Satun habs de Scripter in his school-'ouse.

Better roll your breeches up high when you go to wade a muddy creek.

Mighty easy to git orf a wild mule.

Fat'nin' horgs don't hab much to brag on when de killin' time come.

Dead tree try to fool you by wroppin' itse'f up in de green pizen'-oak vines.

Fish-trap don't make no noise, but it do good wuk.

It takes a soon man to guess which way de rat-hole run.

De water-toter in de harves'-fiel' git heap o' 'tention.

Better not laugh too quick at de runt pig.

You can't buy corn wid de bag o' gold at de en' o' de rainbow.

Tired cutter in de wheat-fiel' git sassy at de en' o' de row.

De rabbit sw'ar he too hones' to steal grapes, an' de fox sw'ar he too hones' to steal cabbage.

Briers close to de ripe blackberries.

De cat mighty po' judge o' mustard.

Young colt ain't so ga'ly in de drought.

De honey-bee pay a pow'ful big rent for his house.

When de mushmilion in bad health, you better not fool wid it.

De dry-lan' tar'p'n lub to hide his face; but de snail ain't got no bizniss tellin' him 'bout it.

Creole Proverbs

Great to speak, little to do.

One goes everywhere with fine clothes.

Ox who comes first always drinks clear water.

That is not the baptism of a doll. (No laughing matter.)

When the tree falls the goat climbs it.

The best swimmer is often drowned.

When one is very hungry one does not peel the sweet potato.

His tongue knows no Sunday.

I keep nothing hidden in the sideboard. (I keep nothing back.)

Set your type before you go and then read it. (Have on your tongue what you are going to say.)

❨ Some Georgia Proverbs

Anybody wuh gwine back on eh prommus, an try fuh harm de pusson wuh done um a faber, sho ter meet wid big trouble.

Bad plan fur stranger fuh meddle long tarruh people bidness.

Mine you chillun well wei dem leetle; an soon dem big nough fuh work, mek um work.

Wen you want somebody fuh do you sarbis, call pon you fren, but don't trus you enemy fuh done um.

Nebber fuh trus nobody wuh call ehself fren, an wuh gwine run luk er coward soon es trouble come.

Et tek a smart somebody fuh head Buh Rabbit.

❨ A Few More Old-Time Negro Proverbs

Yuh kin sow in mah fiel' ef yuh wants to, but when hit comes up, hit'll be in your'n an' yuh won't know how it got dere.

Ol' massa take keer o' himself, but de niggah got to go ter God.

Yuh mought as well die wid de chills ez wid de fever.

Don' say no mo' wid yo' mouf dan yo' back kin stan'.

A Few More Old-time Negro Proverbs

Evah bell you heah ain't uh dinnah bell.

Whut you don' hab in yo' haid, yuh got ter hab in yo' feet.

Two niggahs 'll draw fo' niggahs an' fo' niggahs 'll draw eight.

Dey's jes' ez good uh fish in de creek ez evah been caught. Dey's jes' ez good uh timber in de woods ez evah been bought.

PART VII

Rhymes

The first standard work in the field of Negro rhyme was a healthy collection of folk rhymes assembled by Thomas W. Talley and published in 1922. Rhymes have been included in various other folklore volumes, but no work limiting itself to the folk rhyme has been published since Talley's. Despite this hiatus, the fact remains that the Negro is a prolific weaver of rhymes. This is evident by, among other things, the great number of street cries used by Negro peddlers in Charleston, South Carolina, and in New Orleans, to describe the wares they have for sale.

Negro children are very adept in coining what are known as Autograph Album rhymes—rhymes written at the close of the school year in one another's autograph books. All the rhymes carry some sort of advice or warning. Negro children also invent many jeering and taunting rhymes, designed to make fun of their comrades.

The Negro adult is especially good at creating rhymes called "The Dozens," in which one speaker attempts to heap a greater insult upon some female member of his companion's family than the companion can heap upon his kin. The adult also uses jeering and taunting rhymes to criticize his preacher. Even Negro soldiers use rhyming to complain about the daily routine of army life and imagined happenings with their families back home.

(Antebellum Marriage Proposal

He: De ocean, it's wide; de sea, it's deep.
Yes, in yo' arms I begs to sleep,
Not fer one time, not fer three;
But long as we'uns can agree.

She: Please gimme time, Suh, to "reponder";
Please gimme time to "gargalize";
Den 'haps I'll tu'n to "cattlegog,"
An' answer up 'greeable fer a s'prise.

329

(**Slave Marriage Ceremony Supplement**

Dark an' stormy may come de wedder;
I jines dis he-male an' dis she-male togedder.
Let none, but Him dat makes de thunder,
Put dis he-male and dis she-male asunder.
I darefor 'nounce you bofe de same.
Be good, go 'long, an' keep up yo' name.
De broomstick's jumped, de world not wide.
She's now yo' own. Salute yo' bride!

(**Raise a Rucus Tonight**

Two liddle Niggers all dressed in white (*Raise a rucus tonight*),
Want to go to Heaben on de tail of a kite. (*Raise a rucus tonight.*)

De kite string broke; dem Niggers fell (*Raise a rucus tonight*).
Whar dem Niggers go, I hain't gwineter tell. (*Raise a rucus tonight.*)

A Nigger an' a w'ite man playin' seben-up (*Raise a rucus tonight*),
De Nigger beat de white man, but 'e's skeered to pick it up.
        (*Raise a rucus tonight.*)
Dat Nigger grabbed de money, an' de w'ite man fell. (*Raise a rucus tonight.*)
How de Nigger run, I'se not gwineter tell. (*Raise a rucus tonight.*)

Look here, Nigger! Let me tell you a naked fac': (*Raise a rucus tonight.*)
You mought a been cullud widout bein' dat black. (*Raise a rucus tonight.*)
Dem 'ar feet look lak youse sho' walkin' back. (*Raise a rucus tonight.*)
An' yo' ha'r, it look lak a chyarpet tack. (*Raise a rucus tonight.*)

Oh come 'long, chilluns, come 'long,
W'ile dat moon are shinin' bright.
Let's get on board an' float down de river,
An' raise dat rucus tonight.

([

A Day's Happiness

Fust: I went out to milk an' I didn't know how,
I milked dat goat instid o' cow;
While a Nigger a-settin' wid a gapin' jaw,
Kept winkin' his eye at a tucky in de straw.

Den: I went out de gate an' I went down de road,
An' I met Miss 'Possum, an' I met Mistah Toad;
An' ev'y time Miss 'Possum 'ould sing,
Mistah Toad 'ould cut dat Pigeon's Wing.

But: I went in a whoop, as I went down de road;
I had a bawky team an' a heavy load.
I cracked my whip, an' ole Beck sprung,
An' she busted out my wagin tongue.

Well: Dat night dere 'us a-gittin' up, shores you're born.
De louse go to supper, an' de flea blow de horn.
Dat raccoon paced, an' dat 'possum trot;
Dat goose laid, an' de gander sot.

([

Cotton-Eyed Joe

Hol' my fiddle an' hol' my bow,
Whilst I knocks ole Cotton-Eyed Joe.

I'd a been dead some seben years ago,
If I hadn' a danced dat Cotton-Eyed Joe.

Oh, it makes dem ladies love me so,
W'en I comes 'roun' pickin' ole Cotton-Eyed Joe!

Yes, I'd a been married some forty year ago,
If I hadn' stay'd 'roun' wid Cotton-Eyed Joe.

I hain't seed ole Joe, since way las' Fall;
Dey say he's been sol' down to Guinea Gall.

(Four Runaway Negroes—Whence They Came

Once fo' runaway Niggers,
Dey met in de road.
An' dey ax one nudder:
Whar dey come from.
Den one up an' say:
    "I'se jes come down from Chapel Hill,
    Whar de Niggers hain't wuked an' never will."

Den anudder up an' say:
    "I'se jes here from Guinea Gall,
    Whar dey eats de cow up, skin an' all."

Den de nex' Nigger say
Whar he done come from:
    "Dey wuked you night an' day as dey could;
    Dey never had stopped an' dey never would."

De las' Nigger say
Whar he come from:
"De Niggers all went out to de Ball;
    De thick, de thin, de short, de tall."

(Bullfrog Put On the Soldier Clothes

Bullfrog put on de soldier clo's.
He went down yonder fer to shoot at de crows;
Wid a knife an' a fo'k between 'is toes,
An' a white hankcher fer to wipe 'is nose.

Bullfrog put on de soldier clo's.
He's a "dead shore shot," gwineter kill dem crows.
He takes "pot" an' "skillet" from de Fiddler's Ball;
Dey're to dance a liddle jig while Jim Crow fall.

Bullfrog put on de soldier clo's.
He went down de river fer to shoot at de crows.
De powder flash, an' de crows fly 'way;
An' de Bullfrog shoot at 'em all nex' day.

([

Wanted: Cornbread and Coon

I'se gwine now a-huntin' to ketch a big fat coon.
Gwineter bring him home, an' bake him, an' eat him wid a spoon.
Gwineter baste him up wid gravy, an' add some onions too.
I'se gwineter shet de Niggers out, an' stuff myse'f clean through.

I wants a piece o' hoecake, I wants a piece o' bread,
An' I wants a piece o' Johnnycake as big as my ole head.
I wants a piece o' ash cake, I wants dat big fat coon,
An' I sho' won't git hongry 'fore de middle o' nex' June.

([

Destitute Former Slave Owners

Missus an' Mosser a'walkin' de street,
Deir han's in deir pockets an' nothin' to eat.
She'd better be home a-washin' up de dishes,
An' a-cleanin' up de ole man's raggitty britches.
He'd better run 'long an' git out de hoes
An' clear out his own crooked weedy corn rows;
De Kingdom is come, de Niggers is free.
Hain't no Nigger slaves in de Year Jubilee.

333

The Cow Needs a Tail in Fly-Time

Dat ole black sow, she can root in de mud,
She can tumble an' roll in de slime;
But dat big red cow, she git all mired up,
So dat cow need a tail in fly-time.

Dat ole gray hoss, wid 'is ole bob tail,
You mought buy all 'is ribs fer a dime;
But dat ole gray hoss can git a kiver on,
Whilst de cow need a tail in fly-time.

Dat Nigger Overseer, dat's a-ridin' on a mule,
Cain't make hisse'f white lak a lime;
Mosser mought take 'im down fer a notch or two
Den de cow'd need a tail in fly-time.

Bedbug

De June-bug's got de golden wing,
De Lightning-bug's de flame;
De Bedbug's got no wing at all,
But he gits dar jes de same.

De Punkin-bug's got a punkin smell,
De Squash-bug smells de wust;
But de puffume of dat ole Bedbug,
It's enough to make you bust.

W'en dat Bedbug come down to my house,
I wants my walkin' cane.
Go git a pot an' scald 'im hot!
Good-by, Miss Liza Jane!

A Few Negroes by States

Alabammer Nigger say he love mush.
Tennessee Nigger say, "Good Lawd, hush!"

Fifteen cents in de panel of de fence,
South Ca'lina Nigger hain't got no sense.

Dat Kentucky Nigger jes' think he's fine,
'Cause he drink dat gooseberry wine.

I'se done heared some twenty year ago
Dat Mississippi Nigger hafter sleep on de flo'.

Lousanner Nigger fall out'n de bed,
An' break his head on a pone o' co'n bread.

Hoecake

If you wants to bake a hoecake,
To bake it good an' done;
Jes' slap it an a Nigger's heel,
An' hol' it to de sun.

Dat snake, he bake a hoecake,
An' sot de toad to mind it;
Dat toad he up an' go to sleep,
An' a lizard slip an' find it!

My mammy baked a hoecake,
As big as Alabamer.
She throwed it 'g'inst a Nigger's
      head,
An' it ring jes' lak a hammer.

De way you bakes a hoecake,
In de ole Virginy 'tire;
You wrops it 'round a Nigger's
      heel,
An' hol's it to de fire.

335

Religious Rhymes

Our Fadder, wich art in heaben
White man owe me leben an' pay me seben;
Dy Kingdom Come—Dy will be done;
Ef I hadn't tuck dat, I wouldn't git none.

Hit's eighteen hundred forty and ten;
Christ is de mourner's onlies' frien;
An' I don't wanna stay here no longer.
Hit's eighteen hundred forty and leben;
Christ'll be at de do' when we all git to heaben.
An' I don' wanna stay here no longer.

Rabbit in de springtime, rabbit in de fall,
Some o' dese Ole Folks can't shout a-tall.

Jes' tryin' to live lowly and humble;
Take what dey puts on me an' nevuh grumble.

Methodists, Methodists, you is dead,
'Cause you po' water on de baby's head.
Baptists, Baptists, you is right,
'Cause you puts dem candidates way out of sight.

Adam and Eve went out to play,
When Eve saw the apple, then she gave way.

I'se got religion way up de street;
I'se even got religion in my feet.

Fisherman Peter was on the sea;
Christ came down from Galilee
He say drap yo' net and follow me.

Snuff and tobacco you'll have to quit;
'Cause when you git to Heaben there'll be no place to spit.

Went to de river to be baptized;
Stepped on a root and got capsized.
De river was deep and de preacher was weak.
So de nigger went to Heaben from the bottom of the creek.

Preacher in de pulpit preachin' mighty well;
But when he gits the money yo' kin go to hell.

World War II Rhymes

Down in the valley; down on my knees;
I prayed so hard till I heard God sneeze.

The Lord has come from Heaben above
To bless us po' little scholars;
He hired a fool to teach our school,
An' paid her forty dollars.

❨ World War II Rhymes

I don't know, but I've been told,
A boot ain't nothin' till he's nine weeks old.

Ain't no need of looking down;
Ain't no discharge on the ground;
Raise the flags, and raise them high.
Squadron F is passing by.

The WACS and WAVES will win the war, Parlez-vous.
The WACS and WAVES will win the war, Parlez-vous.
The WACS and WAVES will win the war, so what in the hell are we
  fighting for?

Hit the floor, and don't get back in bed no more.
You slept all night and the night before,
And now you want to sleep some more.

There you are in your dungarees;
Jodie's wearing your B.V.D.'s.

I don't know, but I believe,
One of these days I'm gonna get a leave.
Left, right, hup. A hup, a hup,
A hup, a hup, a left-right hup.

Two more days and an hour or two
Nine day's leave, and O.G.U.
Hey left, right up (three times).
Hey left, right up (three times).

What's the use of going home?
Jodie's got your gal and gone.

Left, right, left. Left, right, left.
Left, right, left. Left, right, left.
When you stand retreat, Jodie's getting your meat.
When you dressed all up in brown, Jodie's with your wife, going to town.

Jodie's got your gal and gone,
One, two, three, four.
Ain't no use in feeling blue, Jodie's got your mama too,
One, two, three, four.

I don't know, but I've been told,
Jodie's wearing my one-button roll.

No more reveille, no more retreat.
No more formation in duh company street.

Off of yo' cot, and on yo' feet.
Fall out in duh company street.

("Dirty Dozens" Rhymes

*Examples of "ceremonial insults" heaped on one male Negro's family by
another male Negro.*

When yo' mama was young an' sweet, she called me sweet, sweet papa;
Now since she ol' and lost her teeth, she call me weet, weet, wopper.

De box cars rollin', de baby's a cryin',
I played yo' mama in the slavery time.

Yo' mama like me, and she like me pretty bad;
An I c'd git what she got if it wasn't for yo' dad.

I don't play de Dozens, and I never do try;
I just want yo' mama when yo' papa die:
She's a dirty mistreater, robber an' a cheater.

I saw yo' papa comin' 'cross the field;
Slippin' and slidin' like an automobile.

Yo' mama's in de kitchen; yo' papa's in jail;
Yo' sister's round de corner, hollerin' "Hot stuff for sale."

338

Yo' sister died wid de whoopin' cough;
Yo' mama died wid de measles;
Yo' granma died wid me in her arms,
An' now she's gone home to Jesus.

When yo' papa go to work roun' about ten,
Yo' mama's at home ready to sin;
She call me over the telephone
An' tell me dey ain't nobody at home.

Six times six is thirty-six;
De way dey talk 'bout yo' mama
She's in a hell of a fix.

I like the way she sling it from side to side;
And I'm halfway tempted to ask her to let me ride.
I know she'd like to do it, and so would I,
But I guess I'll have to wait until yo' papa die.

(Street Cries

I sell to the rich,
I sell to the po';
I'm gonna sell the lady
Standin' in that do'.

Watermelon, Lady!
Come and git your nice red watermelon, Lady!
Red to the rind, Lady!
Come on, Lady, and get 'em!
Gotta make the picnic fo' two o'clock,
No flat tires today.
Come on, Lady!

I got water with the melon, red to the rind!
If you don't believe it just pull down your blind.
You eat the watermelon and preeee—serve the rind!

Nice little snapbeans,
Pretty little corn,
Butter beans, carrots,

Apples for the ladies!
Jui-ceee lemons!

Blackber—reees! Fresh and fine.
I got blackber—reeeees, Lady!
Fresh from th' vine!
I got blackberries, Lady!
Three glass fo' a dime.
I got blackberries!
I got blackberries!
BLACK—BERRIEEEEEEEEES!

I got strawberries, Lady!
Strawberries, Lady!
Fifteen cents a basket—
Two baskets for a quarter.

Oyster Man! Oyster Man!
Get your fresh oysters from the Oyster Man!
Bring out your pitcher, bring out your can,
Get your nice fresh oysters from the Oyster Man!

We sell it to the rich, we sell it to the poor,
We give it to the sweet brownskin, peepin' out the door.
Tout chaud, Madame, tout chaud!
Git 'em while they're hot. Hot *calas!*

One cup of coffee, fifteen cents *calas,*
Make you smile the livelong day.
Calas, tout chauds, Madame, Tout chauds!
Git 'em while they're hot! Hot *calas!*

The little Jamaica boy he say,
More you eatta, more you wanta eatta.
Get 'em while they're hotta. Hot *calas!*
Tout chauds, Madame, tout chauds.

The Waffle Man is a fine old man.
He washes his face in a frying-pan,
He makes his waffles with his hand,
Everybody loves the waffle man.

Char-coal! Char-coal!
My horse is white, my face is black.
I sell my charcoal, two-bits a sack—
Char-coal! Char-coal!

Street Cries

Here's yo' chimney sweeps,
We goes up to the roofs,
Sweep the smokestacks down right now,
Don't care for soot, anyhow.
Rami—neau! Rami—neau! Rami—neau!

Sweep 'em clean! Sweep 'em clean!
Save the firemen lots of work,
We hate soot, we never shirk,
Sweep 'em clean! Sweep 'em clean!

Old Rag Man! Get your rags ready!
For the Old Rag Man!
Money to be made!
Get your rags ready for the old Rag Man!

Now's your time to git snap beans,
Okra, tomatoes, an' 'taters gwine by;
Don't be foolish virgins;
Hab de dinner ready
When de master he comes home;
Snap beans gwine by.

Oh! Hannah boil dat cabbage down,
Hannah boil 'em down,
An' turn dem buckwheats 'round and 'round,
Hannah boil 'em down.
It's almost time to blow de horn,
Hannah boil 'em down.
To call de boys dat hoe de corn,
Hannah, boil 'em down.

I live four miles out of town,
　　I am gwine to glory.
My strawberries are sweet an' sound,
　　I am gwine to glory.
My chile is sick, an' husban' dead,
　　I am gwine to glory.
Now's de time to get 'em cheap,
　　I am gwine to glory.
Eat 'em wid your bread an' meat,
　　I am gwine to glory.
Come sinner, get down on your knees,
　　I am gwine to glory.
Eat dese strawberries when you please,
　　I am gwine to glory.

Raw! Raw! Raw Swimp!
An a Daw-try Daw!
An a Swimpy Raw!
An a Daw-try, Daw-try, Daw-try, Swimp!

Old Joe Cole—Good Old Soul
Porgy in the Summer-time
An' a Whiting in the Spring,
Eight upon a string.
Don't be late, I'm waiting at de gate.
Don't be mad—Here's your Shad
Old Joe Cole—Good Old Soul.

Red Rose to-may-toes,
Green peas—Sugar peas,
    Strawberry!
An 'e fresh an 'e fine,
An e'r just off the vine;
    Strawberry!

Porgy walk; Porgy talk,
Porgy eat wid a knife an' fork;
Porgy-e-e-e-!

Vanilla, chocolate, peach cream
Dat surely freezed by de stream.
It was made in de shade, an' is sold in de sun.
If you ain't got a nickel, you can't get none.

I got yellow cat and the white cat,
Got everything but the tom cat,
And he's on the inside.
If you believe I'm lying
Buy one an' try him.
Take him home
An' then you fry him.

Here comes yo' fish man,
Go git yo' dish pan,
Peep out de winder, step back to de dinin' room,
Tell de Mrs. I got fish-o-o.

Any rags, any bones, any bottles today?
The same old rag man comin' this a-way.

Swimp man, swimp man, raw, raw, raw.
Fifteen cents a plate, two for a quarter.
Raw, raw, raw.

Jeering and Taunting Rhymes

Get 'em fore 'e too late, put 'em in de wash tub,
Raw, raw, raw.
Swimp man, swimp man. Raw, raw, raw, raw, raw, raw.
Ef you wanna see sum'pm fine,
Jes look in dis cart of mine,
Raw, raw, raw, raw, raw, raw.

Dry load, dry load of pine. . . .
Dry load, dry load going by.
Make up your mind before dis mule cry;
Make up your mind before I pass by.
I'll sell it to the rich, I'll sell it to the poor;
I'll sell it to the yellow gal,
Standing in the door.

Jeering and Taunting Rhymes

Nigger, Nigger, shiny eye.
Nigger, Nigger, never die.

A bushel o' wheat, a bushel o' san',
Ah'd rather be a nigger than a po' white man.

I had a baby and its eyes are blue.
It can't be mine, Cap'n; it must be you.

My name's Ran, I wuks in de san',
But I'd ruther be a nigger dan a po' white man.

Two times one is two.
Won't you jes' keep still till I gits through?
Three times three is nine.
Yo' tend to yo' business, and I'll tend to mine.

You bowlegged, lazy,
An almos' half crazy.

Needun be walkin' roun' heah wid yo' nose all snotty.
If you don't know better, ast somebody.

Copy cat, copy cat, sittin' on duh fence,
Tryin' tuh make a dollar out o' fifteen cents.

You ain't mah color, an' you ain't mah kind.
You a pretty liddle nigger, but yo' shoes ain't shined.

If youse white, youse right;
If youse yellow, youse mellow;
If youse brown, stick around;
But if youse black, git back.

Po' crawfish don' stan' no show;
Blue-bellied Cajuns catch 'im, make gumbo.
So all aroun' duh Cajuns' beds
Don' see nothin' but crawfish heads.

I don't like liver, an' I don't like hash,
An' I don't care nothin' 'bout po' white trash.

Rabbit in duh springtime—rabbit in duh fall;
Some of dese old folks can't shout at all.

Look at dat man dressed in green;
He got duh biggest feet Ah ever done seen.

Lawd, if you wanna show yo' powah
Please sen' a rain—don't sen' no showah.

Tuberculosis is a bad thing;
It'll git you down.
Not down on Beale Street,
But down in duh groun'.

Some folks say a nigger won't steal.
I caught two in my corn fiel'—
One with a shovel and the other with a hoe,
Digging up my 'taters, row by row.

Some folks say a nigger won't steal.
But I caught three in my corn fiel'.
One had a bushel and one had a peck,
And one had a sack tied round his neck.

Yaller gal's your'n, black gal's mine;
You never can tell when yaller gal's lyin'.

Early in de spring I plowed that lan';
I ain't nothin' but wages man;
Nex' down row with guano horn,
Never wuk so hard since I been born.
Little bit later, I swing that hoe.
An' I'm a nigger can lead a row.

Brother Johnson's Toast

Kill a mule, buy another.
Kill a nigger, hire another.

If I had my weight in lime,
I'd whip my Captain till I went stone blind.

Oh, Lawd! Jes' two cards in the deck I love.
Lawd, the jack o' diamonds, an' the ace of clubs.

Baby's in Memphis lyin' round,
Waitin' fer dollah I done found.

Good God-a-mighty, tain't bad as I said,
Three square meals an' a bunk fer a bed.

Well, it makes no difference how yo' make out yo' time,
White man sho' bring nigger out behin'.

Yellow gal, yo' train is here;
Brown skin gal, yo' train is near;
Black gal, yo' train is gone;
What in de hell you waitin' on?

Dey ast me why de nigger move;
I'm gonna tell you de reason why:
De grasshopper eatin' up evuhthing,
So it's nigger move, or die.

He punched my hog; he died in May;
My mule he died in June;
My cow, she's got de hollow tail;
I guess she'll die putty soon.

He eat up my britches, an' he slit up my shirt;
An' his appetite's growin' mo' bigger;
So I'm gonna leave here right now, folks!
Before he starts in on de nigger.

(Brother Johnson's Toast

This toast, from the private folklore collection of Dr. A. P. Hudson, University of North Carolina, is reprinted by his permission, with the following note: "One of my friends at Chapel Hill was the late Norman

Cordon, ex-grand opera singer, who sang all the great baritone roles at the Metropolitan. Norman told me about Brother Johnson Merritt, janitor at the Deke house in Chapel Hill during the 1920's. That was prohibition time, and the moonshine and bootleg whiskey were uncertain. So the boys used Brother Johnson as a taster. When they got a jug of untried liquor they would call for Brother Johnson. He would hold a huge tumbler in his hand; a boy would pour. 'Say when, Brother Johnson.' Brother Johnson would say, 'Right dauh, Marster,' as the tumbler was about to run over. Then he was supposed to drink the whole down without taking his lips away. If he didn't fall down dead, the liquor was okay. But Brother Johnson would, as a toast, first recite this riddle":

> Some folks claims hit's a sin,
>   But I claim that ain't true,
> 'Cause it have been practiced
>   Since God made the fust two.
>
> Ef hit wa'nt lawful, lawyers
>   Dey would not do hit.
> Ef hit wa'n't holy, preachers
>   Dey would rue hit.
>
> Ef hit was not modest, then
>   Maidens would regret hit.
> Ef hit was not plentiful,
>   Po' folks wouldn't get hit.

PART VIII

Riddles

The longest list of Negro riddles appears in Elsie Clews Parsons' book, Folklore from the Sea-Islands, South Carolina (1923). *Smaller collections occur here and there in various folklore publications.*

No complete volume of Negro riddles has been published, yet the telling of riddles was one of the favorite pastimes of the Negro slave. Next to the telling of animal tales, it was the most popular diversion for evenings and occasions. This practice survived into the Reconstruction era, as evidenced in numerous folklore publications during this period. Virtually every memoir published by the American Folklore Society that deals with the Negro has a section of riddles.

> A duck behin' a duck,
> A duck befo' a duck,
> A duck between two duck.
> How much dat a duck?
> —T'ree duck.

Somet'in' foller you ev'ywhey you go.—Dat's yer shadow.

I was goin' along de road. I met a man. He tipped his hat an' drew his feet. What was his name?—His name was Andrew.

What goes an' never comes back?—It's yer breat'.

Why is de President wife nightgown like de United State flag?—'Cause dey bof go off at his command.

Ef one drawp of rain come to a pailful, what would a shower come to? —To de groun'.

A stove cost ten dollars, a pipe cost five. What will the wood come to? —Wood come to ashes.

Constantinople is a wery long word. Can you spell it in two letters? —I-t.

Something turn and you can't see when it turn. What is that?—Milk (or milk turns to clabber).

Why a chimney smokin'?—Because he kyan't chew.

What is it that fly high and fly low, but haven't got any wings?—Dust.

I went to a house. I knock at the door. A little boy open it name George. I went upstairs. I saw a woman was washing. I went another room. I saw a ton of coal.—George Washington.

Why lazy people go to school?—Just because the school can't come to them.

Whitey sent Whitey to run Whitey out er Whitey. What's dat?— White man sent a white boy to run a white cow outer cotton field.

> Run up Willy Whelly Whackam
> Met Tom Takam,
> Tell Broom Shakam
> To run Tom Takam
> Up to Willy Whelly Whackam.
> > —Lady tell the boy to take
> > the dawg an' run the cows to
> > the cotton fiel'.

A house full, a yard full, a chimney full,
No one can get a spoonful.—Smoke.

> The whole house full,
> And can't catch a mouthful.
> Guess what it is.—Air.

Somet'in' holler all day an' holler all night, an' never stop holler.—Tree holler.

The black man sit on a red man head.—Pot sit on a fire.

Dere's somet'in' dead in de middle, an' live at de two en's.—Plough in de middle, man on one side, horse on de oder.

> Feather it have, an' cannot fly;
> Feet it have, an' cannot walk.
> > —Dat's a baid.

Something has a ear and can't hear. What is that?—A ear of corn.

Was a house. In de house was a table. On de table was a plate. In de plate was a saucer. In de saucer was a cup. In de cup was a spoon. In dat spoon was a drop o' somet'in' you kyan't do widout.—Drop o' blood.

Variant: There is a ship, and in this ship is a window. In this window is a table. On this table is a cup; and in this cup is something you neither drink it nor eat it, but you must have it.—Your ear-wax.

350

Riddles

Something goes all around your house and never comes in. Guess what it is.—A fence.

Somet'in' ran 'round de house an' didn' make but one track.—Wheelbarrow.

Dere's somet'in' goin' t'rough de wood an' don' touch a limb.—Dat's your voice.

Ol' lady an' ol' man was under de tree. An' de ol' man shook it, an' de ol' lady take up her dress an' took it.—Apple.

Something has one eye and one foot.—A needle.

Back in de road I met an ol' man. De mo' I shake his han', de mo' he bleed.—Dat was a pump.

> Once I was going to London,
> I met somebody standin',
> Cut his throat an' suck his blood,
> An' leave his body standin'.
> > —Jug o' whiskey.

There is something that run all time and never stop.—That's the river.

Go day an' night an' never get tired.—Wind.

Black water in t'ree lette's.—I-n-k.

Spell hard water in three letter.—I-c-e.

There was t'ree ships. One was rig, one was half rig, an' one was unrig. Which one would you like to go on?—The one dat is unrig. De one dat is rig is a married man, the one half rig is fixin' to be married, the one unrig is a single.

> Crooked as a rainbow,
> Smooth as a slate,
> Twenty-five George horses
> Can't pull it straight.
> > —Riber.

> A riddle, a riddle, as I suppose,
> A hundred eyes and never a nose.
> > —It is a sifter.

Two sisters set in an upstairs winder. Dey kyan't see each oder.—Eyes.

Was twelve pear hangin' high,
An' twelve pear hangin' low;
An' twelve king came ridin' by,
An' each 'e took a pear,
An' how many leave hangin' dere?

—Dat was twenty-fo'. De
man dat took de pear was
a man name Each, an' he
leave twenty-t'ree hangin'
dere.

PART IX

❧❦

Names

Although names are an interesting part of Negro folklore, very few of them have been compiled. The distinguished folklore scholar Arthur Palmer Hudson, who also collected and interpreted ballads, gathered a unique array of names in Mississippi in 1935 and published them in the Southern Folklore Quarterly. *A few of these were included in a master's thesis by Alice C. Reid at Fisk University in the same year, titled "Gee's Bend: A Negro Community in Transition."*

Hopefully, more attention will be paid in the future to collecting Negro names, for in every Negro community strange names abound. From my own native Travis County, Texas, I can still recall names like Red Horse, Cup Grease, and Grey Ghost. Some odd Negro names are used as titles for stories. And there are folk tales about such peculiar names of Negro children as Prescription, Furlough, and Diploma.

⟨ Some Curious Negro Names

The better we understand both the history of our own white man's culture and that of the Southern Negro, the more intelligently can we sympathize with his fumbling, upward struggle, the more tolerantly can we view his shortcomings, the more humanely and the less condescendingly can we enjoy his ignorances. An amusing, and perhaps enlightening, illustration of this truth may be found in the study of Negro proper names, especially Christian names.

Names sum up and may recall a great deal of folklore, linguistics, history, and poetry. The Negro has always been and still is less disposed to remain stodgily conventional, traditional, and unimaginative in his choice of names.

Recently a gentleman from Bennettsville, South Carolina, told me that in his city dwells a Negro named Monk Boofort. The Monk part, he judged, was a sobriquet which became a Christian name, for the man had no other; the Boofort part was derived from the name of the city from which he came to Bennettsville—Beaufort, S. C. (pronounced "Bewfort" by white South Carolinians, "Boofort" by Negroes). . . .

355

PART IX. *Names*

But it is in the Christian-naming of their babies and the re-christening by sobriquet that Negroes do the oddest, gaudiest, most humorous, most poetic, most picturesque, and sometimes most unaccountable things. Far more than the whites they illustrate the truth of Charlotte Yonge's observation, made over fifty years ago: "There (in America) our (British) habits are exaggerated. There is much less of the hereditary, much more of the Puritan and literary vein. Scripture names are commonplace. Virtues of all kinds flourish, and coinages are sometimes to be found, even such as 'Happen to Be' because the parents happened to be in Canada at the time of birth." . . .

Scriptural Christian names among Southern Negroes fall under several categories. Biblical characters are commemorated by King Solomon, Virgin Mary, Sonora Queen Esther, Matthew, Angel Ann, Image of Christ Lord God, Charity, Salvation, etc. . . .

Institutions and Societies

League of Nations, Methodist Conference South, Eastern Star, Scottish Rite

Geographical

America, Toledo, Ohio, California, Missouri, India

Circumstances of Birth

Valentine, June May, Tiny New Year, Fourth of July, Sunday May Ninth

Classical and Literary

Quo Vadis, Baby Venus

Famous and Infamous People

Admiral Dewey, Jesse James Outlaw, Queen Isabella, Ambishion Lincoln, George Washington

Pet or Basket Names

Cutie, Doodle Bug, Sugar, Sugar Pie, Rose Bud

Odd Combinations

Filthy McNasty, Pleasant Smiley, Ivory Keyes, Truly White

Long Names

Mary Jane Lethadorie Pardemar Lee Bethania Virginia Arkansas Tennessee Mims. . . . Ruth Matilda Love Divine Seymour Catherine Belle Caroline Thompson. . . . Rose Belle Locust Hill North Carolina Beauty Spot Evans.

356

Twins

Max and Climax, Kate and Duplicate, Pete and Repeat, Maters and Taters, Stink and Stunk, General Lee and General Grant

(# Mail Boat

You hear 'bout Lizzie Russell? She the one marry Uncle Tom Wright's boy, Esau. You never heard that story?

It happen 'for' her first child come. . . . She wantin' to go to Georgetown to see her aunt, so she take her clothes in one them handle baskets and footed it to Watchesaw landing and got on the boat. She stayed out half her visit, and her aunt saw she just had to be gettin' on home. Said she left word for Esau to meet her on every mail boat, 'cause she not knowing fer sure which day goin' to make it back.

And when Esau meet Lizzie that day, and she come off that mail boat she totes that first chile off the boat in that basket. . . .

She named the first child Mail Boat. I uster wonder how come people give him such a name, and I was grown up 'fore I hear Grandma and Mama talkin' one day 'bout that thing.

(## Some Folk Names from Gee's Bend, Alabama

MALE	FEMALE
Apple Jerry	Adella
Arlee	Afastine
Atlas	Angel Dove
Binam	Bama
Bizelle	Berries
Busbee	Birsey Bell
Censie Boy	Bonnie Kate
Clarin	Candy
Doctor Barnum	Ceatrice
Elijah	Chinese
Flane	Clevanna

PART IX. *Names*

Goleon
Ishmael
Job
Levi
Lindbergh
Master Lee
Mo Elrea
Mo Fatten
Mo Knighten
Needem
Nelius
N.R.A.
Quill
Rowden
Vanderville
Venican
Verpo
Wince
Yarbaugh

Clymdice
Delma
Dina Dell
Doxie Mae
Elkie
Fancy
Fellie
Floody
Gazelles
Glendette
Glennie Mae
Ideal
Idell
Inell
Leanna
Lemon
Linder
Lubell
Luberta
Luzanna
Mandale
Mandella
Matria
Mauree
Mazelle
Para-Z
Penanic
Zeolla

—Alice C. Reid, "Gee's Bend: A Negro Community in Transition," master's thesis, Fisk University, 1941

358

PART X

Children's Rhymes and Pastimes

Old-Time Rhymes

Mamma's Darling

Wid flowers on my shoulders,
An' wid slippers on my feet;
I'se my mammy's darlin',
Don't you think I'se sweet?

I wish I had a fourpence,
Den I mought use a dime.
I wish I had a Sweetheart,
To kiss me all de time.

I has apples on de table,
An' I has peaches on de shelf;
But I wish I had a husband—
I'se so tired stayin' to myself.

⟨[

Little Sleeping Negroes

One liddle Nigger a-lyin' in de bed;
His eyes shet an' still, lak he been dead.

Two liddle Niggers a-lyin' in de bed;
A-snorin' an' a-dreamin' of a table spread.

Three liddle Niggers a-lyin' in de bed;
Deir heels cracked open lak shorten' bread.

Four liddle Niggers a-lyin' in de bed;
Dey'd better hop out, if dey wants to git fed!

⟨[

Stealing a Ride

Two liddle Nigger boys as black as tar,
Tryin' to go to Heaben on a railroad cyar.
Off fall Nigger boys on a cross-tie!
Dey's gwineter git to Heaben shore bye-an'-bye.

⟨[

Two Sick Negro Boys

Two liddle Niggers sick in bed;
One jumped up an' bumped his head.
W'en de Doctah come he simpully said:
"Jes' feed dat boy on shorten' bread."

T'other liddle Nigger sick in bed,
W'en he hear tell o' shorten' bread,
Popped up all well. He dance an' sing!
He almos' cut dat Pigeon's Wing!

The Little Rooster

I had a liddle rooster;
He crowed befo' day.
'Long come a big owl,
'An toted him away.

But de rooster fight hard,
An' de owl let him go.
Now all de pretty hens
Wants dat rooster fer deir beau.

Training the Boy

W'en I was a liddle boy,
Jes' thirteen inches high
I uster climb de table legs,
An' steal off cake an' pie.

Altho' I was a liddle boy,
An' tho' I wusn't high,
My mammy took dat keen switch down,
An' whupped me till I cry.

The End of Ten Little Negroes

Ten liddle Niggers, a-eatin', fat and fine;
One choke hisse'f to death, an' dat lef' nine.
Nine liddle Niggers, dey sot up too late;
One sleep hisse'f to death, an' dat lef' eight.
Eight liddle Niggers want to go to Heaben;
One sing hisse'f to death, an' dat lef' seben.
Seben liddle Niggers, a-pickin' up sticks;
One wuk hisse'f to death, an' dat lef' six.
Six liddle Niggers went out fer a drive;
Mule run away wid one, an' dat lef' five.
Five liddle Niggers in a cold rain pour;
One coughed hisse'f to death, an' dat lef' four.
Four liddle Niggers, climb a apple tree;
One fell down an' out, an' dat lef' three.
Three liddle Niggers a-wantin' sumpin' new,
One, he quit de udders, an' dat lef' two.
Two liddle Niggers went out fer to run;
One fell down de bluff, an' dat lef' one.
One liddle Nigger, a-foolin' wid a gun;
Gun go off "Bang!" an' dat lef' none.

Little Boy Who Couldn't Count Seven

Once der wus a liddle boy dat couldn' count one.
Dey pitched him in a fedder bed; 'e thought it great big fun.

Once der wus a liddle boy dat couldn' count two.
Dey pitched him in a fedder bed; 'e thought 'e 'us gwine through.

Once der wus a liddle boy dat couldn' count three.
Dey pitched him in a fedder bed; 'e thought de Niggers 'us free.

Once der wus a liddle boy dat couldn' count fo'.
Dey pitched him in a fedder bed; 'e jumped out on de flo'.

Once der wus a liddle boy dat couldn' count five.
Dey pitched him in a fedder bed; 'e thought 'e dead alive.

Once der wus a liddle boy dat couldn' count six.
Dey pitched him in a fedder bed, 'e never did git fix!

Once der wus a liddle boy dat couldn' count seben.
Dey pitched him in a fedder bed; 'e thought he's gwine to Heaben.

Mother Says I Am Six Years Old

My mammy says dat I'se too young
To go to Church an' pray;
But she don't know how bad I is
W'en she's been gone away.

My mammy says I'se six years old,
My daddy says I'se seben.
Dat's all right how old I is,
Jes' since I'se a-gwine to Heaben.

When I Was a Little Boy

W'en I wus a liddle boy
I cleaned up mammy's dishes;
Now I is a great big boy.
I wear my daddy's britches.
I can knock dat Mobile Buck
An' smoke dat corncob pipe.
I can kiss dem pretty gals,
An' set up ev'ry night.

Pretty Little Girl

Who's been here since I'se been gone?
A pretty liddle gal wid a blue dress on.

Who'll stay here when I goes 'way?
A pretty liddle gal, all dressed in gray.

Who'll wait on Mistress day an' night?
A pretty liddle gal, all dressed in white.

Who'll be here when I'se been dead?
A pretty liddle gal, all dressed in red.

Washing Mamma's Dishes

When I wus a liddle boy
A-washin' my mammy's dishes,
I run my finger down my th'oat
An' pulled out two big fishes!

When I wus a liddle boy
A-washin' my mammy's dishes,
I sticked my finger in my eye
An' I sho' seed liddle fishes.

De big fish swallowed dem all up!
It put me jes' a-thinkin'.
All dem things looks awful cu'ous!
I wonder wus I drinkin'?

Autograph Album Rhymes

An apple is an apple an' cheese is cheese;
These 1968 women is sho' hard to please.

If you feelin' lonesome, if you feelin' blue,
Step to de telephone and call 8–o–2.

Le's go across the ocean, le's go across the sea,
Le's lock our hearts together and throw away the key.

I went down to the river an' I started to drown,
But I thought about my baby an' I couldn't go down.

I'm a cute little girl with a cute little figure,
But step back, stay 'way, boys, till I git a little bigger.

The river is risin', the boats are floatin',
Le's git married and stop our courtin'.

You can kiss beneath the grapevine, you can kiss beneath the rose,
But the best place I know of is to kiss beneath the nose.

You can fall from the highest mountain into the deep blue sea,
But you've never had a fall until you fall in love with me.

Apples on the table, peaches on the shelf,
If you don't love nobody, keep it to yourself.

Up the hickory, an' down the pine;
Good-looking boys is hard to find.

When you git married an' livin' upstairs,
Don't fall down puttin' on airs.

Sugar is sweet, an' coffee is strong;
Write me a letter, and don't be long.

When you're married and your old man gits cross,
Pick up a broomstick an' show him who's boss.

You can wish for a nickel, you can wish for a dime,
You can wish for a sweetheart—but I got mine.

I'm a cute little girl, with very sweet kisses,
But it won't change my name from Miss to Mrs.

It takes a rocking chair to rock,
A rubber ball to roll,
A tall, skinny papa
To satisfy my soul.

You can tell a tree by de fruit hit bears,
But you can't tell a boy by de gym shoes he wears.

Roses are red and grass is green;
I was kissed befo' I was sixteen.

If you don't like my apples, don't shake my tree.
Ah ain't after yo' beau—he's after me.

Orange is a city, Lemon is a state;
I wrote you a letter, but I forgot de date.

When you marry and have twins,
Don't come to me for two safety pins.

Autograph Album Rhymes

My papa is a butcher,
My mama cuts de meat.
Ah'm de little weiner-wish
Dat runs around de street.

When you marry and live up on the hill,
Send me kisses by the whippoorwill.

It's you I love, and will forever.
You might change, but I will never.
Death might come, and we might part,
But that will never change my heart.

When you marry don't marry a fool,
Marry a boy from Blackshear School.

A little today and a little tomorrow,
Come back again, but do not borrow.

If the ocean was milk, and the bottom was cream,
I'd dive for you like a submarine.

Cream cheese, cream cheese floatin' in the air,
That bald-headed man ain't got no hair.

Ring-Game Songs

Played like "Drop the handkerchief":
    Lost my glove yesterday,
      Found it to-day,
    All full of mud,
      Tossed it away.

Games usually accompanied by hand clapping and swinging of the body:
    Come home, Lily, sometime, sometime,
    Mammy needs you, sometime, sometime,
    To wash dishes, sometime, sometime,
    To wash them clean, sometime, sometime,
    To milk the cow, sometime, sometime,
    To milk her dry, sometime, sometime,
    To wind a ball, sometime, sometime,
    To wind it tight, sometime, sometime.

    O walk down in Lousiana,
    My home stays in Lousiana,
    Grind your cane in Lousiana,
    You walk like you broke down,
    Cut your step in Lousiana,
    Git 'em in a hurry in Lousiana.

Ring-Game Songs

Other ring game songs:
>   Draw a bucket of water
>   For my lady's daughter,
>   One berry bush, two berry bush, three berry bush,
>   And pretty little girl creeps under.

>   Chicken, chicken, my cranie crow,
>   I went to the well to wash my toe.
>   When I got there, my chickens were dead.
>   What time, old witch?

>   Plant my cotton in the middle of May,
>   If I don't make cotton, I sure make hay.
>   Ever since my dog been dead,
>   Hog been a-rootin' in my tater bed.
>   I give my cow rotten ear corn,
>   Give my cow hollow horn.

>> Way down yonder,
>> Soup to soup!
>> Where dem white folks,
>> Soup to soup!
>> Tryin' to make man,
>> Soup to soup!
>> Biscuits hot,
>> Soup to soup!
>> Cornbread cold,
>> Soup to soup!
>> Thank God Almighty,
>> Soup to soup!
>> Just give me a little mo'
>> Soup to soup!

Leader: Did you go to the hen house?
Chorus: Yes, mam!
>   Did you get any eggs?
>   Yes, mam!
>   Did you put 'em in the bread?
>   Yes, mam!
>   Did you bake it brown?
>   Yes, mam!
>   Did you hand it over?
>   Yes, mam!

Good old egg bread,
   Shake 'em, shake 'em!
Good old egg bread,
   Shake 'em, shake 'em!
Did you go to the lynchin'?
   Yes, mam!
Did they lynch that man?
   Yes, mam!
Did that man cry?
   Yes, man!
How did he cry?
   Baa, baa!
How did he cry?
   Baa, baa!

My old mistress promised me
Before she died she would set me free.
Take your lover in the ring,
   I don't care,
Take your lover in the ring,
   I don't care.
Now she's dead and gone to hell,
I hope that devil will burn her well.
Take your lover in the ring,
   I don't care,
It's a golden ring,
   I don't care,
It's a silver ring,
   I don't care.

Two children join hands, and two others join hands across those of the first two. They sway back and forth, singing:

Drawin' a bucket of water
For my oldest daughter.
Give me the racket and
   the silver spoon
And let my pillar come over,
   come over.

At this point the first two put their right arms over the heads of the other two, letting the arms slide along until they reach the waistline. Then they shout,

Ring-Game Songs

Bunch o' rags!
Bunch o' rags!
Bunch o' rags!
Bunch o' rags!

Inny ke nicky nacky noe
Rivaly divaly dommy noe
Ex a blow, soffa, low, tissue.

Ooka dooka soda cracker,
Does your father chew tobacco?
Yes, my father chews tobacco.
Ooka dooka soda cracker.

Tall Tales

⟨ The Tallest Man

Question. What de tallest man you ever see?
Answer. De tallest man Ah ever seen was gittin' a haircut in heaven an' a shoeshine in hell.

⟨ The Blackest Man

Question. What de blackest man you done see?
Answer. De blackest man Ah ever done saw, de chickens go in de chicken house, think hit sundown.

The Stingiest Man

Question. What de stingiest man you done ever saw?
Answer. De stingiest man Ah ever done see go in de darkest room to chew his tobacco, so his shadow won't beg him fer none.

The Darkest Night

Question. What de darkest night you ever done see?
Answer. De darkest night Ah ever done see, a raindrop knock to my doorstep an' ast fer a light to see how to hit de groun'.

The Runningest Car

Question. What is de runningest car you ever see?
Answer. The runningest car Ah ever see was my uncle's ole car—it run over Monday, kill Tuesday, sen' Wednesday to de hospital, cripple Thursday, an' tol' Friday to tell Saddy to be at de fun'al Sunday at 4 o'clock P.M.

The Fattest Woman

Question. What de fattest woman you done see?
Answer. De fattest woman Ah done see—her husban' have to hug her on de installment plan.

⟮ # The Coldest Day

Question. What is the coldest day you ever see?
Answer. The coldest day Ah ever did see—de sun rose wid a overcoat on, an' went down wid a bunch o' kindlin' wood to make a fire.

⟮ # The Longest Dog

Question. What de longest dog you done seen?
Answer. De longest dog Ah ever done seen—his head was in New Jersey, an' his tail was in Orangeburg. When his head was dead dey had to telephone his tail that his head was dead.

⟮ # The Poorest Horse

Question. What de poorest horse you saw?
Answer. Ah saw a ole horse so po' till he have to put on rubber boots to tip pas' de buzzards.

⟮ # The Lowest Person

Question. What de lowest person you ever saw?
Answer. De lowest person Ah done ever saw kin sit on a dime wid his feet hangin' down.

376

The Greediest Man

Question. What de greediest man you ever see?
Answer. De greediest man Ah ever saw—he ate up evuhthing on earth, ate all de angels out o' heaven, and snapped at God.

The Tallest Stalk of Corn

Question. What de tallest stalk o' corn you done ever seen?
Answer. Ah seen a stalk o' corn so tall till the angels in heaven was pickin' roastin' ears off o' it.

The Strongest Mule

Question. What de strongest mule you ever saw?
Answer. Well, Ah saw a ol' mule so strong till you hitched him to midnight, an' he break daylight.

The Fastest Running Man

Question. What de fastes' you done seen a man run?
Answer. The fastes' Ah seen a man run, he run down lightnin' an' hobble thunder.

⟪ # The Biggest Fool

Question. What de biggest fool you ever did see?
Answer. De biggest fool Ah ever did see
Run all de way from Tennessee.
His eyes was red an' his lips was blue.
God A'mighty shook 'im till his shirt tail flew.

⟪ # The Bowleggedest Man

Question. What de bowleggedest man you ever done see?
Answer. A man so bowlegged that he was goin' across de railroad an' he step so wide until one of his foot went in his back pocket.

⟪ # The Hottest Day

Question. How hot you ever done seen it?
Answer. Ah seen it so hot till two pieces of ice was walkin' up de street fannin'.

⟪ # The Poorest Land

Question. What de poorest lan' you ever done see?
Answer. De lan' in de graveyard whar my uncle buried. De lan' so po' till dey hafter put bakin' powder in de coffin so he kin rise in de Jedgment Day.

The Crosseyedest Man

Question. What de crosseyedest man you done ever saw?

Answer. De crosseyedest man Ah ever seen, he took one eye an' look at Canada an' de other eye in South America.

INDEX

Index

A NOTE ON THE AUTHOR

J. Mason Brewer was born in Goliad, Texas, in 1896. He received a Bachelor's degree from Wiley College and a Master's from Indiana University, where he studied under the renowned folklorist Stith Thompson. Author of seven previous books, including *Dog Ghosts*, *The Word on the Brazos*, and *Worser Days and Better Times*, Dr. Brewer is now Distinguished Visiting Professor at East Texas State University. He has lectured at Yale University, Duke University, and the Universities of Toronto, California, Colorado, Arizona, and Texas. He was the first Negro ever to be elected an officer of the American Folklore Society and is now a member of the Advisory Council of the National Folk Festival, Washington, D.C.

DATE DUE

MAR 3	NOV 0 4		
NOV 2			
a '83			
NOV 8 83			
41			
MAR 2 3			
APR 1 7			
MAY 8			
FAC			
JUN 4			
Moore			
CONWAY			
SHIRLEY			
12-17-01			